Supporting Adoption
Reframing the approach

Supporting Adoption
Reframing the approach

Nigel Lowe and
Mervyn Murch
Margaret Borkowski
Anna Weaver
Verna Beckford
with
Caroline Thomas

British
Agencies
for **A**doption
and **F**ostering

Published by
British Agencies for Adoption & Fostering
(BAAF)
Skyline House
200 Union Street
London SE1 0LX

Charity registration 275689

British Library Cataloguing in Publication Data
A catalogue record for this book is available
from the British Library

ISBN 1 873868 73 1

Project management by Shaila Shah,
Head of Communications, BAAF
Designed by Andrew Haig & Associates
Cover illustration by Andrew Haig
Typeset by Avon Dataset Ltd, Bidford on Avon
Printed by Russell Press Ltd. (TU),
Nottingham

Notes about the authors

Nigel Lowe is a Professor of Law at Cardiff Law School. A former Chair of BAAF's Legal Group (1984 – 1990), he has a long standing interest in adoption and, together with Professor Murch, has directed a number of empirical studies into its law and practice. He has published extensively and is the co-author of *The Children Act in Practice* (2nd edn) with Richard White and Paul Carr, and of *Bromley's Family Law* (9th edn) with Gillian Douglas. He is an editor of *Clarke Hall and Morrison On Children* and of *Family Law Reports*.

Mervyn Murch has taught Law and applied Social Studies and is a Professor of Law at Cardiff Law School. His 30 year research career has focused on the interdisciplinary work of the family justice system and has contributed to policy and practice development and law reform in divorce, adoption and child protection. He is currently studying the ways by which the voice of the child can be heard in divorce proceedings. His books include *Justice and Welfare in Divorce*, *The Family Justice System* with Douglas Hooper and *Grounds for Divorce* with G Davis.

Margaret Borkowski is a Senior Research Associate at Cardiff Law School. She has been involved in adoption research since 1987 and was co-author of *Pathways to Adoption* and was involved in *Freeing for Adoption Provisions* and *Court Observation of Adoption Proceedings*. She is currently involved with Our Place in Bristol, a centre for foster and adoptive families.

Anna Weaver is a Research Associate. She designed and administered the two surveys, assisted with interviews and analysed data in this project. She has researched qualitative methodologies in social research and is currently working on a computer package for training social work students.

Verna Beckford is a social worker with Bath and North East Somerset Council. She has worked as a Research Associate at the Bristol University's Norah Fry Research Centre and at Cardiff Law School. She is also co-author of *Consolidation or change? A second survey of family based respite care services in the United Kingdom* with C Robinson.

Caroline Thomas is a Research Fellow at Cardiff University. She took the lead role in the parallel study of older children's views and experiences of the adoption process, *Adopted Children Speaking*. She is currently on secondment to the Scottish Office managing a programme of research on the Children (Scotland) Act 1995.

Contents

Acknowledgements

Our first debt is to the adopters and their children who agreed to help with this research and without whom this book and the other publications arising from the research could not have been attempted. We have taken care to preserve confidences and ensure anonymity by changing names and disguising salient details in information they gave us which we have used in publication.

The research was funded by the Department of Health and supported by a specially constituted Advisory Committee chaired by Dr Carolyn Davies of the Department's Research and Development Division. Other members were Mike Brennan and Julia Ridgway of the Department of Health; Joan Fratter, Senior Practitioner, Barnardo's; Pennie Pennie, Assistant Director, Children and Families, London Borough of Lambeth; Jim Richards, Director, The Catholic Children's Society (Westminster); Alan Rushton, Senior Lecturer in Social Work, Institute of Psychiatry, Maudsley Hospital; Phillida Sawbridge OBE; Professor June Thoburn, School of Social Work, University of East Anglia. They have been an unfailing source of helpful advice and positive criticism. We would also like to thank Donal Giltinan, Dr Alexina McWhinnie, Professors Roger Bullock, Roy Parker and Spencer Millham and colleagues at the Dartington Research Unit, and Professor Gerald Caplan, for their expert help with our preliminary consultations.

The research could not have been undertaken without the generous assistance of most statutory and voluntary adoption agencies in England and Wales. Under the usual conditions to safeguard the privacy of confidential material these agencies were prepared to go to great lengths to let the research team enquire about their particular policies and practices concerning the provision of support services for families of older children adopted out of care. The team was given privileged access to policy documents and practice guidelines, and most agencies completed detailed questionnaires designed to clarify their approach to particular issues. In addition, a number agreed to staff being interviewed and made special arrangements to put the researchers in contact with a sample of parents who had recent experience of adopting older children.

The research itself, although a team effort, was largely conducted by Verna Beckford, Margaret Borkowski and Anna Weaver. In addition we received much support and help from Caroline Thomas, who undertook the lead research role in the parallel study of older children's experience of adoption. She was an integral part of the team. The formidable clerical and administrative load was undertaken by

Elizabeth Caddy, supported on occasions by Sandra Anstiss and Sharron Alldred. We must also thank our colleagues in the Cardiff Law School, particularly Professors John Wylie and Bob Lee, respectively Heads of Department, for their unfailing support throughout the project.

Whatever errors and deficiencies the report may contain are our responsibility as Co-Directors of the project and should not be held against any of our colleagues and advisors.

Mervyn Murch
Professor of Law
Cardiff Law School
Cardiff University

Nigel Lowe
Professor of Law
Cardiff Law School
Cardiff University

The Vernal Equinox, 1999

Part I

CONCEPTS

1 Introduction

1 The objective and aims of the research

This report is based on research funded by the Department of Health (DoH) and conducted at Cardiff Law School, University of Wales, between January 1994 and May 1998.[1] The study is intended to throw light on hitherto little-studied aspects of policy and practice concerning the support available to older children and their families as they make the transition from being looked after by the local authority into a new life with adoptive parents.

1.1 Key parameters

Initially, the research team intended to focus on the support needs of the children and their adoptive parents as they make the critical transition out of care into life within the adoptive home, particularly from the moment of placement to the making of the adoption order. However, we subsequently agreed to extend our enquiry into the period up to 12 months immediately following the making of the adoption order. Nevertheless it is important to stress at the outset that our research is not about post-adoption support *per se* but rather of support during the adoption process itself which, for our purposes, was defined as being from the time the adoption was proposed until one year after the adoption order had been made.

The project is concerned with *older* children, i.e. over five years old, to distinguish them from babies and infants, who had previously been "looked after" by local authorities, i.e. those who had been accommodated and/or the subject of care orders. "Support services" were conceived broadly to include formal services provided by adoption agencies (both statutory and voluntary) and by social, health, educational and psychological services of local authorities and health services. They were also taken to include informal support networks such as those provided by the families, friends, relatives, self-help groups and previous carers of the adopted child.

---

[1] The project is part of a larger programme of adoption research commissioned by the Department of Health. Other studies in this programme (many of them as yet unpublished) include work on permanent placement for children of minority ethnic families (Thoburn, Norford, and Rashid); a longitudinal study of adopted Romanian children (Rutter *et al*); a study of single parent adoptions (Owen, 1999); a study of social work practice (Rushton *et al*) and an ESRC funded project on step-parent adoption (Malos and Milsom).

1.2   The aims of the study

The **aims** of the study were to:

- gather empirical evidence about the use and organisation of adoption support services and plans for their development;
- sample parents who had recently adopted an "older" child out of care and to record their evaluation of support in terms of their expectations and experience;
- consider especially the perspectives of the placing agencies;[2] and
- explore the application of certain theoretical constructs (see below) such as the concept of status change and critical transition and the gift/donation and contract/service models of adoption (with a view to teasing out possibly different associated role expectations concerning the provision of support) in order to illuminate our understanding of the realities of support provision during the adoption process.

In addition, we recognised the importance of issues of "race" and ethnicity within the adoption process, particularly in the light of more than two decades of concern about the number of black children in care and the debate on transracial versus "same race" placements. Accordingly, we were concerned to consider the relevance of our research to minority ethnic children and parents and agencies working with them. To this end we developed our research methods to draw out such issues. However, in reporting these findings we have chosen not to write a separate chapter on the support services to minority ethnic children and parents, preferring instead to refer to these findings as they arose to avoid misinterpretation and to maintain the context of the data.

The primary purpose of the study was to inform the deliberations of the Government's Adoption Law Review and hence the formulation of new adoption legislation. Yet the scope of the research goes wider than that. There are many messages here for those concerned with more general aspects of adoption policy and practice in England and Wales – not only the social workers largely responsible for the workings of the adoption system, but other professionals in the medical, educational, legal and social welfare fields, all of whom from time to time are involved at key points in the lives of adopted children and their families.

---

[2] We had hoped to investigate why adoption was the preferred child care option in the case of a sample of older children. However, constraints of time prevented us from doing so and this information was not otherwise available in the cases studied.

2   Why the project was needed

2.1   The need for greater understanding of the challenges associated with the adoption of older children out of care

The challenge of adoption for the child

Being placed for adoption, after being "looked after" by a local authority following separation from birth parents, is likely to tax the emotional resources of any child, however sensitively the process is managed. Not only is the child expected to attach to the new adoptive parents and adapt to their way of life, but he or she may still have to come to terms with the separation and sense of loss of the birth family and any foster family with whom he or she might have become attached. The so-called pathway to adoption is known to be fraught with uncertainty for children not only in relation to the eventual outcome but because often the process is protracted.[3] If the child came into care because of neglect or abuse, and if there have been intervening periods "home on trial" which have not worked (often the precipitating reason for the local authority's decision to seek a permanent placement), the child's whole life might have been overshadowed by uncertainty for months, even years. Consequently, older children may well have experienced several changes of school, loss of friends and familiar activities. Little wonder then that the attainment of children whose lives have been so disrupted is often poor and their self-esteem low.

One of the paradoxes of child care experience in England and Wales is that the more time and care the professionals take to decide the future of children, the longer the uncertainty the children have to cope with; the more major life changes they have to absorb and the greater the risk that their resilience will be sapped. Nevertheless one needs to be wary of generalising.[4] Some cope much better than others.[5]

There are many potentially conflicting interests to be taken into account when considering the support needs of older adopted children and their families. Some children may have been victims of physical and sexual abuse which may have emotional or behavioural repercussions in their later childhood and adult life.

---

[3] We know from other researches both before and after the Children Act 1989 came into force (Murch and Mills, 1987; Thomas, Murch and Hunt, 1993; Lowe and Milsom, 1993) that children involved in care proceedings often have had to wait a long time before the final care order, in the meantime being subject to a number of interim care orders, sometimes involving several changes of foster homes.

[4] See the studies of children's psychological adjustment to separation e.g. Robertson, 1952; Rutter, 1985; Wadsworth 1984 and 1991; Fincham and Grych, 1990 and 1991.

[5] Rutter's important review of studies, which explores the link between children's personalities and their resistance to adverse life events, has teased out a number of key interacting variables such as age, temperamental characteristics, social support, prior experiences and patterns for parent–child interaction, which clearly have a major influence on their emotional resilience and capacity to develop successfully (Rutter, 1985).

Others may have physical disabilities or learning difficulties of varying severity. Some will have birth relatives who wish to maintain contact with them both during and after the adoption process even though the child and/or the adoptive parents may be ambivalent about it. Moreover, if members of the birth family have disputed previous care proceedings, freeing for adoption proceedings or the adoption itself, it may be particularly difficult for them to accept support from the adoption agency concerning the way the future contact issues are managed even if this is on offer. Accordingly, the degree and nature of contact with the child which they might seek, can cause difficult problems for the adoptive family and the agency. If foster carers have bonded with the child they, too, may have difficulties giving up the child to the care of prospective adoptive parents – difficulties which may be expressed covertly in the way introductions and possible continuing contact are handled. These children therefore, by any standards, have extremely complex networks of family relationships to manage.

The challenge of adoption for the adoptive parents

The challenges facing adoptive parents of older children are no less complex. Although some will have fostered and a number will have brought up children of their own, others will be childless looking to create a family by adoption. Their decision to do so may be prompted by the discovery that they are infertile and sometimes follows acute disappointment of unsuccessful treatment for infertility. Once an individual or a couple decide to seek approval as adoptive parents, they embark on a life journey which in certain respects matches many of the uncertainties faced by children on their pathway to adoption. Many of those who decide to adopt older children do so only after discovering that they would not be able to adopt a baby.

But even then the selection process can be tortuous: they usually have to undergo a lengthy assessment by professionals who sometimes, according to some adoptive parents, fail to keep them in the picture. Many have difficulties trying to divine the "rules of the game" in order to be selected as potential adopters. Moreover, relatives, friends, neighbours and employers may have little understanding of what can be involved in taking on the permanent care of an older child. In some instances this ignorance turns to suspicion of motives; while mystification and lack of sympathy can lead potential adopters to feel rejected as the shock waves of their decision to adopt an older child resound across their social network. Matters are not helped because there are so few cultural signposts and rituals to guide them.

At such times, even the most robust can experience periods of acute doubt and anxiety. Going through the selection process and anticipating the arrival of an unknown child can be testing in itself. Meeting the child (or children, if siblings are to be adopted) and then embarking on the critical process of getting to know the child and hopefully to begin the process of mutual confidence-building is an extraordinarily adventurous and sometimes hazardous personal enterprise: these parents will be taking on "for better or worse" a child whose capacity to trust adults may have been weakened by a history of unreliable or broken attachments. They have to learn very rapidly how to parent such a child, often discovering within themselves quite new parenting skills. The child may suffer private periods of grief and have to cope with difficult conflicts of loyalty to their birth family and even previous foster carers, which may make him or her all the more difficult to "reach" emotionally. In addition, the older child brings into the adoptive home a whole cultural world relevant to age, generation, ethnicity and class which initially may be quite different from and baffling to the adoptive parents. Moreover, the child may be struggling to figure out what the "imperatives" of the adoption situation are (i.e. what is expected, etc.). On the other hand, when it works out, the rewards for adoptive parent and child alike can undoubtedly be hugely enriching.

The challenges of adoption for agency staff

Those involved in the adoption "brokering business"[6] also face a range of formidable challenges which can test their professional knowledge and competencies to the full. All such work involves risk and uncertainty for the child, the adoptive parents and for those who professionally have to stage-manage the adoption enterprise. The selection and match-making which lie at the heart of this agency function – "playing God" as some would describe it – is fraught with anxiety, however much procedures, guidelines for good practice and limits imposed by a carefully thought-out legislative framework serve to limit risk and provide the community with reassurance. In this respect one of the more profound questions is whether this framework – in addition to its intrinsic merits – should also be understood in terms of an institutional defence mechanism, against anxieties that would derive from an otherwise freer exercise of professional discretion (Menzies Lythe, 1985 and 1989).[7]

2.2   The increasing scale of the practice

Adoption of older children previously looked after by local authorities is a significant aspect of current adoption practice. In contrast to the traditional model of baby adoption, which has markedly declined from 8,833 in 1970, amounting to 39 per cent of all adoptions,[8] to 253 in 1996 which amounted to 4 per cent of the total

---

[6] Some might think the use of the term "brokering business" (as used, for example, by Coombs and Hundleby, 1997) is impersonal and has commercial overtones. On the other hand, there is evidence that some social workers even use terms such as "horse-trading" to describe the bargaining which can go on in the adoption process, for example, over contact agreements (Social Services Inspectorate, 1995b, p. 26).

[7] Such thinking raises questions whether professional denial of anxiety is suppressed or held at bay by these organisational processes and systems, and whether this can unwittingly lead to its projection onto the children and their adoptive parents. If so, this means that they will "carry", as it were, a double dose of anxiety as they navigate the critical transitions of adoption.

[8] This figure is based on the returns cited by the Houghton Committee at Appendix B.

number,[9] the proportion of older children being adopted from care in accordance with childcare policies based on so-called "permanency planning" has steadily increased. Yet in 1990 in England and Wales, 2,605 children were adopted out of care representing 8.3 per cent of all discharges and 4.1 per cent of all children in care – more than double the respective proportions in 1980.[10] Until this study was undertaken, there had been no major research focusing specifically on support needs of these children and their adoptive families or on the way these were met by community services.

2.3   Concern over high disruption rates – could more be prevented?

Despite the growing practice to place older children for adoption, evidence began to emerge which showed that the risks of these placements disrupting were relatively high. Fratter, Rowe, Sapsford and Thoburn (1991), for example, found that, while on average about 20 per cent of adoptive placements disrupt, there is a significant rise in rates to almost 40 per cent for those children who are aged between 9 and 11 years at placement. These disruptions were associated with factors such as the child having a serious history of deprivation or abuse, becoming institutionalised and/or having major behavioural or emotional problems (Fratter *et al*, 1991, p. 54). Others have suggested that, while many such adoptive placements survive and work well, those that do break down most frequently do so two or three years after the making of the order (see Thoburn, Murdoch and O'Brien, 1986). It seems that most adoptive parents of older children are willing to put up with challenging and testing behaviour for a year or so, but if it persists tolerance eventually gets exhausted.[11] This finding raises the question whether more can be done at the beginning of the placement to facilitate attachments and help the child and adopters through any difficulties that arise before disenchantment sets in and the adoptive relationship is ruptured.

---

[9] Marriage, Divorce and Adoption Statistics 1996 ONS, Series SM2, No. 22, Table 6.2. According to *Adoption: The Future*, para 3.3, in 1991 there were under 900 baby adoptions amounting to 12 per cent of all adoptions. See also the analysis by Lowe 'The changing face of adoption – the gift/donation model versus the contract/services model' (1997), Vol 9, *Child and Family Law* Quarterly 371 at 372.

[10] Corresponding rates for 1980 were 4.1 per cent of all discharges from care and 2 per cent of children in care – sources R A Parker, Dartington Social Research Unit. In the year ending 31 March 1996, 1,700 children were either adopted out of care or placed for adoption amounting to 5 per cent of all discharges from care (DoH, 1997, A/F 96/12 p. 15).

[11] Macaskill (1986) suggests that during the first two years of placement adoptive families have the greatest energy and commitment to cope with behavioural difficulties but if the problems persist parents tend to become disillusioned. She writes 'as the formality of the adoption process receded into past history leaving the same accumulated problems, hope began to wane and problems took on a different perspective'.

2.4 The need to study changing patterns of adoption service

Other reasons why a study of support needs of families adopting older children out of care was required are as follows: first, since the last major substantive reform in the 1970s,[12] there have been significant changes in the pattern of service on offer to families involved in the adoption process. Because fewer babies were placed for adoption many voluntary adoption agencies ceased operation and, with their demise, valuable specialist experience was also lost (McWhinnie and Smith, 1994, p. 18). On the other hand, statutory adoption agencies – local authority social service departments – faced many competing childcare priorities, particularly in relation to the large scale and high media profile of child protection work. Murch, Lowe, Borkowski, Copner and Griew (1993) found that this tended to divert attention and resources away from the proportionally smaller and more specialist adoption work. Moreover, statutory adoption work suffered from inconsistent and unco-ordinated policy and practice both within and between agencies, and from problems arising from a lack of specialist training and understanding – particularly in those agencies where the scale of adoption work had decreased proportionately to other more frontline child care tasks. At the end of the 1980s, social services departments were having to absorb the implications of the *Children Act 1989*; the new community care legislation; and the more "commercial approach" associated with internal markets which was being encouraged by government. In addition, following local government reorganisation, a number of large social services departments broke up with a loss of some specialist adoption services. Accordingly, there was a need to investigate the potential impact of these changes.

Despite this organisational turbulence (which many considered beset and restricted local authority childcare provision) there was evidence, for example, from the investigations of the Social Services Inspectorate, that many authorities were maintaining and even trying to develop their adoption services, adapting them to the changing patterns of adoption including the placement of older children. The advocacy work of specialist voluntary organisations such as BAAF, NFCA, PPIAS, NORCAP and the Post Adoption Centre (London), served not only to alert the social work profession to changing needs but to prompt them to initiate a number of special services – particularly concerning post-adoption support. Many of these have been provided by voluntary organisations and self-help groups, sometimes working in partnership with local authorities. The Adoption Law Review Consultation Document (1992, para 32.4) urged local authorities to be more active

> ... in communicating with, and promoting co-operation between, their services and those of approved societies and other voluntary services and to plan for service provision which will meet local needs.

---

[12] Viz *The Children Act 1975* – consolidated by the *Adoption Act 1976* – which eventually came into force in 1988.

This entreaty raised the questions of which local authorities actively pursued this objective, how they did it and to what effect.

June Thoburn's (1990) review of research for *The Adoption Law Review* also raised a number of research questions concerning the provision and organisation of adoption services. For example, what are the most effective ways of providing pre-placement and post-adoption services and support to children with special needs, adopters and their families; and how should the so-called "comprehensive" adoption services be organised to meet the long-term needs of biological parents, adopters and children. Thoburn concluded that, with regard to the agency's duty to provide a "comprehensive service",

> *There is an urgent need to know to what extent the local authorities have moved into all aspects of adoption and to review the adequacy of services to all members of the "adoption triangle".*

Although adoption is seen by some as *the* solution to a child care problem, there is a growing realisation that, at least with regard to older children, there can be no question of the authorities washing their hands of the matter once the adoption order is made. Although adoption may well greatly improve the life chances of the children concerned, perhaps providing greater opportunities than other childcare options, the children's problems do not vanish overnight once they are placed for adoption or once the order is made. At best a committed, loving, supportive adoptive home performing the childcare task in a broader supportive network of significant people, backed up by good quality education and medical resources, gives an older child a reliable supported pathway into adolescence and on to adult life. Looked at this way, adoption and its associated support networks *should* give parents and children the resources they need to work on and through whatever problems arise. But for this to happen much will depend on how the key adoption services appreciate these problems and organise and implement appropriate helping strategies. This research was intended to find out whether – and if so, how – this matter was being addressed in the mid 1990s by the adoption services.

2.5 How do the adopters of older children experience the adoption services and how well do they think they meet their needs?

Because adoption of older children out of care is a comparatively recent form of childcare provision in England and Wales (i.e. dating from the 1970s), there was a particular need to investigate the experiences and perceptions of adoptive parents to see what lessons could be drawn from those on the receiving end. By the early 1990s, there was emerging evidence to suggest that it was harder for parents of these children to find appropriate sources of support compared with their counterparts who had adopted babies. For example, exploratory research (conducted by the authors) funded by the Economic and Social Research Council (ESRC) suggested that whereas parents of babies generally avail themselves of the many formal and informal support mechanisms culturally associated with the arrival of a baby, it is more difficult to identify *any* cultural supports concerning the arrival of an older child whether fostered or adopted.[13] There is no state provision for maternity/paternity leave for parents adopting older children,[14] even though many feel obliged to give up paid employment when the child is placed with them and accordingly take a drop in income just when the revenue might be needed. Also, apart from the court proceedings resulting in the adoption order itself, there are no obvious rites of passage to mark the arrival of such a child. Yet strong rituals might well be needed to underscore and reinforce attachment and bonding. Furthermore, adoptive parents usually have few role models against which to evaluate their own response to this situation.[15] Some adoptive parents feel that once the adoption order has been made they are expected "just to get on with it", and that to seek further support from the agency would be seen as a sign of inadequacy on their part and might prejudice any further applications they might make to adopt another child.

These matters called for research about what parents of older children adopted out of care had been led to expect of the adoption services, both during and after the formal adoption process.

2.6 The need to explore emergent adoption placement practice issues concerning older children

The provision of information

A particularly important aspect of support for adopted parents is the provision of accurate information about the child's background.[16] At the time the research was being planned, several cases had attracted media attention in which adoptive parents whose child had become disruptive, claimed not to have been given vital information in advance which could have forewarned them or indeed might have led them to decide against taking on this particular child. There was a need to investigate the extent of such possible problems.

---

[13] Similar unfamiliarities faced many British families who provided homes for evacuated children during the 1939–1945 World War.

[14] Provision by parental leave (unpaid) is included in the Employment Relations Bill 1999. This provision implements Council Directive 96/34/EC of 3 June 1996 on Parental Leave issued as part of the Social Chapter which the UK has opted into (see Roberts, 1997). We understand that parental leave is offered by some adoption agencies.

[15] Having friends who have adopted and meeting people in similar situations through adoptive parents' support groups can help here (See Chapter 9, *Preparation and Training*, at para 3.2).

[16] See also Utting (1997) at para 6.6.

It is now generally accepted[17] that adopters and their children should be given information about the child's birth origins and about the circumstances which led to the child's adoption – a practice sometimes known as "adoption with no secrets". Yet even when this happens there are still some particularly thorny practice questions, such as how much information should be passed on as the child's need for knowledge about origins expands and as their sense of personal identity, self-awareness and security develops (Brodzinsky, 1984). Because most of the extensive literature on this topic relates to baby adoptions (see McWhinnie, 1967; Triseliotis, 1972 and 1973; Rowe, 1970), there was a need to investigate the matter more closely in relation to the adoption of older children, particularly since some practitioners report that the task of the adoptive parents sharing background information with their child becomes even more problematic in such cases.

In our previous ESRC study, we met many adoptive parents who were worried about the child's background and said that they had not been told enough about it by the agency when the placement was made. Some had been taken unawares when the child had revealed disturbing information about, for example, earlier sexual abuse which the adoptive parent had not been told about by the placing agency. Of course, the agencies themselves might not always know all the facts; yet, on the other hand, there may be pressures on some staff to play down or even withhold certain information from the potential adopters for fear of discouraging them from taking on the child. There may also be particular difficulties about committing especially sensitive information to paper. At any rate the Social Services Inspectorate report (SSI, 1991) on three London local authority agencies suggested that there was little appropriate written information being given to adopters.

Another issue is the need for adopters to give information to the child. The Adoption Law Review Consultation document (Department of Health, 1992, para 27.4) recommended that:

> ... the legislative framework should underline the adopted child's right to know that he or she is adopted and contain measures to preclude the likelihood of any adopted child being deprived of this information.

It further recommended that agencies and guardians *ad litem* should stress to the adoptive parents the importance of "telling" and that agencies should

> ... have a duty to make available to adoptive parents services which may help them impart information to the child.

---

[17] The provision of information about the child has now been strengthened by the new reg. 13A of the Adoption Agencies Regulations 1983 which was introduced in 1997 by the Adoption Agencies and Children (Arrangements for Placement and Reviews) (Miscellaneous Amendments) Regulations 1997 (SI 1997/649).

Agencies or guardians *ad litem* have a duty[18] to compile a package of relevant information including details of the medical history of the child's family[19] (and social background and circumstances of the adoption and the reasons for it) which can be given to the adoptive parents so that it can be passed on to the child when he or she reaches a suitable age. There is, however, no obligation to pass this information on.

In the light of these concerns, we considered that the study should explore whether, and if so how, official rhetoric was being translated into practice and how adoptive parents experienced it.

Contact issues

Another major practice issue concerned contact. Although we were aware of the arguments that this issue has become clouded by dogma both on the part of those who argue for open adoption and those who argue against it (see Mullender, 1991), our concern was to explore how both the practitioners and the adoptive parents approach the matter of contact in the case of older children adoptions. Many children would have active memories and sometimes established links with members of the birth family (not necessarily with parents but with siblings or birth grand-parents) and even with foster carers, who might have long-standing, emotional significance for the child.

2.7 Some specific policy issues requiring evaluation

In addition to the broad issues outlined above, there were two specific policy matters which the DoH asked the research team to explore. The first of these was formulated in the following terms:

> *If the premise is that costs to the local authority are less if a child is adopted out of care, than if he or she remains in care or has to be re-admitted into care, it is important to discover what kinds of services can make the differ-ence in enabling the adoption to be sustained successfully.*

Accordingly, it was agreed that one major objective of the study would be to explore whether it is possible to develop the hypothesis that the application of well targeted and informed support during the adoption process will serve to strengthen the adoption itself and enable it to be more successfully sustained thereafter. Conversely, we needed to investigate what, if any, features of the policies and

---

[18] i.e. Under the Adoption Agencies Regulations 1983 (SI 1983/1964) as amended by the 1997 Regula-tions referred to in note 17 above.

[19] Details of acquiring satisfactory family medical history from both parents (particularly father) has long been recognised yet many social workers are not trained for this task. Moreover, birth family medical history may well come to light well into placement after adoption agency records are closed (see Turnpenny, 1994).

practices of the placing agencies might inadvertently hinder or undermine the chances of a successful adoption. It was consequently agreed that the study should consider the possible adverse effects of discontinuities in the pattern of support provided by local authority and agency staff, as well as those provided by educational and medical services.

Second, the DoH suggested we might investigate possible variations in adoption agency practice regarding charges and allowances. With respect to charges, The Adoption Law Review consultation document (1992, para. 32.5) had recommended that individual agencies should be free to decide which services to charge for and whether to waive charges in particular cases. It was agreed therefore that we should explore:

> whether, and if so under what conditions, charges are being made by particular support services; whether agency policies concerning such charges were likely to alter; whether adoptive parents are expected to pay for particular services; whether they chose to forgo such services because of the prospect (real or imagined) of such charges.

As far as adoption allowances were concerned, it was agreed that these could be seen as an important form of support for many families and that it would be important to examine the discretionary provision in accordance with the *Adoption Allowance Regulations* 1991,[20] both from the agencies' and the adoptive parents' viewpoints.

2.8   The need for some conceptual exploration and development

Apart from policy and practice considerations, there were also a number of more conceptual or theoretical reasons for the study. One of these concerned the interacting ways that adopters, their children and practitioners *defined* the adoption process. Foster carers, birth parents, children and practitioners hold a variety of rather different images of adoption. For example, as with fostering, there appear to be both inclusive and exclusive notions of adoption (see Holman, 1980). Some of these influence what parents expect from the adoption services and how they define their roles in relation to each other. In this context we are interested in what appear to be two contrasting models of adoption – the gift/donation and the contract/service – which complement notions of exclusivity and inclusiveness. While the gift/donation model broadly fits the traditional notion of adoption (the legal extinguishing of the birth relationship, etc.), that of contract/service suggests a complex, albeit as yet informal, pattern of reciprocal and socially defined obligations, for example, over issues of contact and the provision of information.[21]

---

[20] SI 1991/2030.
[21] See also Lowe (1997), at p 383 et seq.

While the regulated gift/donation model of adoption might have been applicable to the adoption of babies and younger children (yet even here there is surely a need for continuing support, particularly later on when the true origins of the child need to be discussed with that child), the contract/service model may be a particularly useful way of understanding the adoption of older children, where adoptive parents may have greater expectations of post-placement support and of being given more comprehensive information about a child's background. Moreover, birth families and some of the children themselves may have greater expectations of a degree of openness which will be permitted or agreed between the parties and the authorities, agency and court under certain circumstances.

3   The basic nature of the research

To meet its aims and objectives the research study comprised three distinct parts, namely, the agency study, the family study and, more recently, the children's study.[22] The details of the methodology used are set out in Appendix 1. Here we merely outline the approach.

3.1   The agency study

Preceded by an initial reconnaissance request for written data and by enquiry to see whether they would co-operate with the main study, the agency study comprised a national postal audit of all statutory and voluntary agencies in England and Wales (the questionnaire was slightly different for statutory and voluntary agencies). This was sent during autumn 1994. Despite being lengthy we had an excellent response rate of about 72 per cent, receiving completed questionnaires from 115 of the 160 agencies that currently operated. Topics covered in the questionnaire were: agency adoption statistics; agency organisation; agency policy and practice; support for older children; support for birth families; support for temporary foster families; support for adoptive families; and evaluation of and comments on support services.

This survey was followed by a more intensive study comprising a series of interviews designed to amplify some of the points raised in the questionnaire and to elicit information about support services peculiar to individual agencies, with a representative sample of the agencies responding to our questionnaires. Our sampling frame for this part of the study aimed both to ensure that we would have a broad and widely spread geographical view of support service provision in England and Wales and that we would interview a wide variety of agencies in terms of type, size of case-load, whether there was a purchaser/provider split, and of the level of support offered. This information was gleaned from that gathered in the recon-

---

[22] *Adopted Children Speaking*, Thomas *et al* (1999).

naissance and postal survey phase. On this basis a total of 48 agencies were selected for the sub-sample, 32 statutory and 16 voluntary. Adoption officers in all these agencies in the sub-sample were interviewed, save three (which, despite reminders, had not responded before our cut off date). Accordingly, we completed interviews with staff of 30 statutory and 15 voluntary agencies – 45 altogether.

3.2   The family study

As with the agency study, the family study comprised the sending of a questionnaire followed by interviews with a representative sample of the responding adoptive parents. We sent our questionnaire via 41 agencies (comprising 28 statutory and 13 voluntary) who had agreed to help us. They were asked to be sent in all cases where, between 1 January 1992 and 31 December 1994,

- a looked after child had been placed for adoption with an adoptive family approved by them, including where they formally sanctioned adoption to existing foster carers, and
- the child was five or more when the adoption was sanctioned by the agency.

Agencies were advised that these criteria should be applied regardless of whether or not the adoption order had yet been made and whether or not the placement had been disrupted. However, we now know that not all agencies followed these criteria. For example, six agencies explained that they had excluded a total of 13 cases between them where the placement had disrupted. Other agencies may have excluded cases without telling us. The questionnaires were sent over a period in the latter half of 1995. Not surprisingly the response rate was low compared with our agency return. Even so we received 226 completed questionnaires from an estimated 515 families – a creditable overall response rate for a postal questionnaire of 44 per cent – comprising a 40 per cent response rate from families approved by statutory agencies and 59 per cent from those approved by voluntary agencies.[23] Subsequently, we conducted interviews with 48 out of the 128 families responding to our questionnaire who had indicated a willingness to be interviewed. This interview sample had a south-western bias because of the constraints of time and costs. However, to ensure an overall balance in terms of other variables, we also interviewed families from all other parts of the country.

The sample frame was devised to ensure that a broad sample was obtained in terms of the following variables: the stage of the adoption process; whether there was any contact and what type; whether the adoption was contested or not; the ethnicity of parents; whether it was a sibling placement or not; current age of child; age of child at placement; sex of child; ethnicity of child; inter-agency and same-agency placements; whether there were other children in the adoptive family;

---

[23] For further discussion of this response rate, see Appendix B.

whether the child had special needs and what type; number of adoptive parents; level of support received; the type of agency which approved the family (statutory or voluntary) and its BAAF region (as they were defined at the time).

Families were automatically included in the sample if the adopted child or one or more adoptive parent had minority ethnic origins (7 cases,[24] all interviewed), or if the adoption had disrupted (6 cases, all of whom were interviewed except one which we were unable to arrange).

3.3   The children study

The final part of our project is the children study which was added to our brief at a much later date (it began in May 1996) and was designed to tease out the children's perspective. This study comprises a series of interviews with children aged eight or over, selected in the first instance from the families interviewed in our family study who had indicated a willingness for their adopted children to be interviewed. In fact, it was not possible to meet our interview target of 40 children from this cohort. Accordingly, some children were selected from some of the 226 families in the family study who had indicated a willingness to be interviewed but who were not in fact interviewed.

In all, 41 children were interviewed. This part of the study is published separately but references to its key findings are considered here as well.

4   Limitations of the research

4.1   Scheduling and resources

The project was initially programmed for three years. The main research team funded by the project comprised one full-time and two part-time researchers supported by a part-time secretary, assisted periodically by another secretary.[25]

The design of the project, involving as it did a number of different sub-studies, inevitably meant that the administrative task was complex. Moreover, the team was not always able fully to control the pace of the field work since we were dependent upon the co-operation of agency staff and the families themselves. Even so, most of the field work kept to schedule although there were occasions when we had to set strict time limits on the operation, for example, deciding the point to end the receipt

---

[24] Of these, four were "same race" placements in that one or both parents were of the same ethnic background as the child placed or where one parent reflected part of the background of a black child of mixed parentage. The three others were transracial placements where the parents were white and the children were of mixed parentage.

[25] The Co-Directors, Professors Lowe and Murch, supported and supervised the project but were not paid out of the DoH grant.

of replies to the postal surveys so that data processing and preparations for the next phase of data collection could begin, and determining the location and number of agency and family interviews, etc.

The very nature of the research meant that there was a great deal of qualitative material gathered from a range of sources making data processing and analysis complex and time-consuming. In this respect the team was fortunate to have as its full-time researcher, Anna Weaver, who is a specialist in the handling of qualitative data and who was able to train other members of the team in the use of the software packages. Nevertheless, the team was to some extent on the "cutting edge" in their software use of this technology, particularly since rather than preparing a straight-forward stage by stage series of mini reports, we wanted to bring together and relate all the material concerning particular topics so that this report could be constructed thematically. For this purpose we developed a computer application named "The Adoption Information Base" to bring together the data from SPSS, NUDIST and a multitude of documents relating to the study.

Modern qualitative packages impose their own internal disciplines which have to be learnt. There are no short cuts. Great care has to be taken with the framing and the coding of the material most of which has first to be word processed before selections can take place. Inevitably only a small proportion of the qualitative material can be used in a report of this kind. In this task we have striven collectively to be true to the material and to present it in as balanced a way as possible using as an initial guide the quantitative material which has been processed using SPSS for Windows.

4.2   Representativeness

The study was designed as a *national survey* (i.e. covering England and Wales) and for this reason we began both the agency-based studies and family studies with postal surveys which had the advantage of wide geographical coverage. But the inherent disadvantages of postal surveys were: first, the question of non-response although we think we have done well in obtaining a 72 per cent response to our agency questionnaire and a 44 per cent to our family questionnaire.[26] We have to acknowledge that our findings cannot necessarily be said to represent *all* agencies' practice or views while to some extent our adoptive family sample was self-selective. Second, one cannot amplify particular responses. However carefully the questions were worded, some respondents misread them or did not follow the instructions for completing the questionnaire. Third, there is a limit to what one can do to control the flow rate of the response.

To compensate for some of these deficiencies, we designed selective follow-up interview programmes of agency staff and adoptive parents. Although, as we have

---

[26] For further discussion about the representativeness of our surveys, see Appendix B.

explained, we attempted to make them as representative as possible, inevitably they too are to some extent idiosyncratic because we were restricted to relatively small samples by the limitations of time available to our two part-time interviewers.

4.3   Omissions

Although it was never our intention to ignore birth parents' support needs (indeed we foresaw that there would be many opportunities in our investigation of agency perspectives to examine what provision is made for such parents), it was not deemed possible to include in this research a special study of the perspectives of birth parents themselves. In this respect two broad points need to be made. First, although the Government is seeking to develop a "comprehensive" adoption service, priorities have to be set and at the time the research was commissioned, the support needs of the children themselves[27] and their adoptive parents were considered to be of primary importance to the DoH. Second, we took the view that given the already broad scope of the project and the limitations of time and funds available, together with the relatively small size of the team, it would have risked serious research management over-stretch to have attempted to take on a specialist survey of birth parents (particularly as this would have involved first, devising a methodology for obtaining a representative sample and second, an inevitably lengthy process of actually obtaining a sample of responding birth parents).

In any case the team had had some recent experience of mounting such a study in connection with its ESRC *Consumer View of Adoption Proceedings* research. Those data have been collected and are being analysed with a view to publication. Moreover, an important research of birth parents who had placed children – mostly babies – for adoption by Janet Logan and Beverley Hughes had recently also been published (see Hughes and Logan, 1993; also Logan, 1996). The essential message of that study is that the grieving process of these mothers for their lost adopted children can go on for years – often in private even though many pick up the pieces and live otherwise well-ordered, successful lives. The Hughes and Logan study mostly involved mothers who had placed babies for adoption many years previously. But the theme of unresolved grief also emerges strongly from a recent study by Freeman and Hunt (1996) of parents whose children had been committed to care following court proceedings brought under the Children Act 1989, a number of whom will eventually be placed for adoption. Here it was observed:

> *It did not appear from our interviews that parents were necessarily receiving help with what is essentially a grieving process. Again this is a role which is very difficult for the social worker to fulfil as they will almost certainly be*

---

[27] *Adopted Children Speaking* (Thomas *et al*, 1999) was added to our research brief at a later date, viz. 1996, as explained previously.

> *identified as the agent of loss, which needs to be provided by someone with relevant skills.*[28]

Nevertheless, despite these points we recognise that there is a case for a more specialist study of birth parents of older adopted children which we did not feel able to take on in this research.

4.4   How evaluative could the project be?

Although it was recognised that the study would have to be largely exploratory and descriptive, the DoH requested that it contain an "evaluative element". Potentially this raised tricky issues about what might be regarded as appropriate criteria of success or failure of adoption placements, issues which had already been carefully studied by Thoburn (1990). Much depends on who is making the assessment of outcome, what criteria are to be used and at what time. Contemporaneous assessments might produce a very different picture from those taken with hindsight after adopted children had reached adulthood. As Hilda Lewis – a famous paediatrician and child psychiatrist – wrote in 1962,

> *The answers to many essential questions about adopted children cannot come until the children are grown up. It is quite unsafe to draw pessimistic conclusions about the ultimate outcome even if a child's conduct appears to be very disturbed.*[29]

Of course, studies such as Triseliotis' (1980) follow-up of 40 young people in their early 20s who had been born in 1956/57 and who had been fostered between 7 and 15 years, indicate the usefulness of matching and comparing the views about outcome from the perspectives of carers and the young persons themselves. But to attempt to organise such a task would have been beyond the scope of our investigation.

4.5   Selection of material

The project was designed as an *extensive* contemporary examination of support provision for families living in various parts of England and Wales who had adopted older children out of care. As such it was hoped the research would *illuminate the background* to a number of specific issues and questions. A great deal of material – both quantitative and qualitative – has been gathered from a variety of sources. Inevitably therefore we have had to be highly selective in the choice of data for inclusion in this report.[30] In making that selection we have sought to ply that

---

[28] Freeman and Hunt (1996, pp. 57–58).

[29] Lewis (1962).

[30] All the material is held on the data base at Cardiff and can be interrogated using SPSS for Windows and NUDIST.

difficult line between providing sufficient information to justify our findings and not to obscure the very messages of our research by providing too much evidence.

Thus we have striven to present a balanced picture amplifying quantitative data with appropriate qualitative material illustrated where necessary by direct quotations – suitably anonymised – from postal questionnaires or from interviews. A possible danger inherent in our approach is that too much use is made of qualitative material which has such emotional power that its idiosyncratic nature is obscured. As against this it has to be remembered that the samples were carefully chosen in the first place to be as representative as possible. Moreover, we remind readers that law often develops on the basis of exceptional rather than typical cases. In any event, regardless of their frequency, episodes of malpractice in service delivery cannot be ignored.

2 The Legal Background

1   The legal definition of adoption

1.1   Permanence and severance

An adoption order, uniquely under English law, effects a complete and irrevocable transfer of legal parentage. Under the Adoption Act 1976, s 12(1), an adoption order gives 'parental responsibility for a child to the adopters' and, by s 12(3), 'operates to extinguish the parental responsibility which any person has for the child immediately before the making of the order'. Section 39 states:

(1)   An adopted child shall be treated in law –
   a)   where the adopters are a married couple, as if he had been born as a child of the marriage (whether or not he was in fact born after the marriage was solemnized);
   b)   in any other case, as if he had been born to the adopter in wedlock (but not as a child of any actual marriage of the adopter).

(2)   An adopted child shall [save in the case of step-parents adoptions], be treated in law as if he were not the child of any person other than the adopters or adopter.

It is the very essence of adoption that the prior legal relationship between the adult(s) (usually the birth parent(s)) and the child is permanently extinguished and replaced by a new legal relationship between the adopters and the child. It is both the permanence and the totality of the transferred relationship that distinguishes adoption from fostering, residence orders under the Children Act 1989 and even guardianship. Adoption is the only child related order under English law[1] that lasts throughout adulthood (an adoption order is truly for life) and it is the only means by which parents can lose their automatic parental responsibility over their child whilst a minor. By vesting exclusive parental responsibility, an adoption order puts the adopters squarely in control of the child's upbringing and by making the order non variable or dischargeable[2]

---

[1] With the exception of parental orders made under s 30 of the Human Fertilisation and Embryology Act 1990, which only has limited application.

[2] In truly exceptional circumstances adoption can be set aside, see eg. *Re K (Adoption and Wardship)* [1997] 2 FLR 221, CA: *Re M (Minors) (Adoption)* [1991] 1 FLR 458 or, even more rarely an order can be held void as in *Re R A (Minors)* [1974] Fam Law 182. But this power to set aside cannot be exercised many years after the order: *Re B (Adoption: Jurisdiction to Set Aside)* [1995] Fam 239, CA.

it puts them, at any rate as against the birth parents, permanently in control.

1.2   Inroads into severance

Marriage, incest and contact

Notwithstanding the complete severance of the prior legal relationship with the birth parents, the adopted child remains for the purposes of marriage within the same prohibited degrees of his birth family.[3] Furthermore, an adoption order does not affect the law relating to incest.[4] More importantly, however, in the light of current practice towards so-called open adoptions, the courts came to accept that it was not fundamentally inconsistent to make an adoption order and at the same time to make a formal order preserving some continuing contact between the child and his or her birth family. This was first established in the early 1970s[5] and authoritatively confirmed by the House of Lords in *Re C (A Minor) (Adoption Orders: Conditions)*[6] in 1988.

Before the Children Act 1989, any regime of contact had to be made under the power conferred by s 12(6) of the Adoption Act 1976, to attach conditions to an adoption order. However, although this power still exists,[7] the more obvious and simpler method is to couple an adoption order with a contact order made under s 8 of the 1989 Act.[8] Notwithstanding this power under s 8, the courts are generally reluctant to impose a contact order on unwilling adopters[9] and, where they are agreed, it has been said that there is no need for an order.[10] On the other hand, it has also been said that adopters cannot agree to indirect contact and then resile from it without explanation.[11] Where no such explanation is given, the court might well be disposed to grant the former parents leave to apply for a s 8 contact order.[12]

---

[3] Adoption Act 1976, s 47(1).

[4] Sexual Offences Act 1956, ss 10 and 11 as applied by s 47(1) of the Adoption Act 1976.

[5] See *Re J (A Minor) (Adoption Order: Conditions)* [1973] Fam 106, per Rees J and affirmed by *Re S (A Minor) (Adoption Order: Access)* [1976] Fam 1, CA. Though note the criticism by Maidment: 'Access and Family Adoptions' (1977) 40 MLR 293.

[6] [1989] AC 1.

[7] Though the courts have made it clear that they do not expect the power to be exercised very often, see *Re S (A Minor) (Blood Transfusion: Adoption Order Condition)* [1994] 2 FLR 416, CA.

[8] In fact, as conditions can only be attached to adoption orders and not to freeing for adoption orders, it is only possible to make provision for contact under s 8 when making a freeing for adoption order. See eg. *Re A (A Minor) (Adoption: Contact Order)* [1993] 2 FLR 645, CA.

[9] See eg. *Re H (A Minor) (Freeing Orders)* [1993] 2 FLR 325, CA and *Re P (Minors) (Adoption: Freeing Order)* [1994] 2 FLR 1000.

[10] *Re T (Adoption: Contact)* [1995] 2 FLR 251, CA.

[11] *Re T (Adopted Children: Contact)* [1995] 2 FLR 792, CA.

[12] As it did in *Re T*, ibid. In that case the adopters failed to honour their promise to provide annual reports on the children. The Court of Appeal was satisfied in the circumstances of the case that the proposed application for contact would not disrupt the children's lives so that they would be harmed by it.

In reaching this decision Balcombe LJ commented:[13]

> *I am not saying that it should never be open to adopters to change their minds*
> *and resile from an informal agreement made at the time of the adoption. But*
> *if they do so they should . . . give their reasons clearly so that the other party*
> *to the arrangement, and if necessary the court, may have the opportunity to*
> *consider the adequacy of those reasons. Nor need adopters fear that their*
> *reasons, when given, will be subjected to critical legal analysis. The judges*
> *who hear family cases are well aware of the stresses and strains to which*
> *adopters . . . are subject and a simple explanation of their reasons in non-*
> *legal terms would usually be all that is necessary. In my judgment where*
> *adopters . . . simply refuse to provide an explanation for their change of*
> *heart, especially where, as here, the contact envisaged (the provision of a*
> *report) is of a nature which is most unlikely to be disruptive of the children's*
> *lives, it is not appropriate for the court to accept that position without more.*

In summary, although the courts are empowered to make provision for continuing contact between an adopted child and his or her birth family, the preferred option is for the families to work this out for themselves. On the other hand, where such informal arrangements are made, which as this research shows is commonly the case,[14] then the courts have made it clear that the adopters will not simply be allowed to resile from their promises without explanation.

Tracing parents

As Lowe and Douglas (1998, p. 616) observe:

> *Traditionally adoption had been a secretive process designed not simply to*
> *facilitate the irrevocable transfer of parentage but to protect unmarried*
> *mothers and the children from excessive stigma and to enable childless*
> *couples to avoid the oppressive taint of infertility. Hence, law and practice*
> *were designed so that the birth parents would have nothing to do with the*
> *process of selecting adopters: on the contrary they would generally have no*
> *knowledge of the adopters and of course they would have no further contact*
> *with their child. Similarly, adopters would not know of the birth parents'*
> *identity. One result of this secrecy was that adopters were generally reluctant*
> *to tell their children that they were adopted.*

---

[13] [1995] 2 FLR 792, 798. See also similar comments by Butler-Sloss LJ in *Re T (Adoption: Contact)* [1995] 2 FLR 251 at 256F.
[14] See Chapter 15, *Contact*.

However, following the important work of John Triseliotis (Triseliotis, 1973)[15] it came to be realised that some facility should be made available to those adopted children anxious to trace their origins. Triseliotis' work on the operation of the Scottish system (which permitted a child's access to birth records at the age of 17) persuaded the Houghton Committee (Houghton, 1972, para 303 and recommendation 77) to recommend that adopted children should be able to obtain their original birth certificate.[16] Accordingly, as from 12 November 1975,[17] adopted children, once they have attained their majority,[18] can obtain from the Registrar General a copy of their original birth certificate from which they may be able to trace their parents.[19]

By 1990, it was estimated[20] that some 33,000 adopted children had taken advantage of this provision while, according to Stafford, 3,500 people received birth records counselling in 1991.[21]

Although access to birth records enables some adopted persons to trace and make contact with their birth parents, until the creation of the Adoption Contact Register in 1991,[22] it was difficult to discover whether that contact would be welcome. The purpose of the Register is

> . . . to put adopted people and their birth parents or other relatives in touch with each other where this is what they both want. The Register provides a safe and confidential way for birth parents and other relatives to assure an adopted person that contact would be welcome and give a contact address.[23]

The Register comprises two parts:[24] Part I, upon which is maintained the name and address of any adopted person who is over 18 and has a copy of his or her birth

---

[15] See also Van Keppel (1991) 'Birth parents and negotiated adoption agreements', *Adoption & Fostering*, 15(4), 81–90.

[16] The Hurst Committee (Hurst, 1954, para 201) had made a similar recommendation but this was not acted upon.

[17] Controversially this provision was introduced with retrospective effect. However, those adopted before 12 November 1975 are required to see a counsellor before they can be given information: Adoption Act 1976, 51(7)(b) as amended by the Children Act 1989, Sch 10, para 20(2). Counselling is also available for other adopted persons on a voluntary basis.

[18] Any person under the age of 18 intending to marry in England and Wales may obtain information indicating whether or not the parties are likely to be related within the prohibited degrees: Adoption Act 1976, s 51(2).

[19] Adoption Act 1976, s 51. This, however, is not an absolute right, see *R v Registrar General, ex p Smith* [1991] 2 QB 393, CA (access denied because of the danger of birth mother being physically harmed by the applicant).

[20] Adoption Law Review, Discussion Paper No *1 (The Nature and Effect of Adoption)* (1990), note 140.

[21] Stafford (1993), 'Section 51 Counselling', *Adoption & Fostering*, 17(1), 4 at 5.

[22] Under the Adoption Act 1976, s 51A (added by the Children Act 1989, Sch 10, para 21) the Registrar General is required to maintain such a Register. In fact the Register is operated on behalf of the Registrar General by the Office of National Statistics, formerly the Office of Population Censuses and Surveys.

[23] Department of Health's *Guidance and Regulations*, Vol 9, para 3.3

[24] Adoption Act 1976, s 51A(2).

certificate and who wishes to contact a relative and Part II, upon which is entered, subject to certain prescribed conditions,[25] the current address and identifying details of a relative[26] who wishes to contact an adopted person. The proposed Adoption Bill contains in clause 65(2) the provision that the Contact Register be extended to allow birth parents and relatives to register their wish *not* to be contacted.

Exchanging other information

At the moment there is no facility for exchanging limited information, such as medical information. However, as Cretney and Masson (1997, p. 885) observe,[27] some agencies and authorities are prepared to disclose information they have about the adoption, though this depends upon 'its nature, the perceived ability of the adopted person to cope with it and their intentions.'

Under clause 48 of the proposed Adoption Bill, agencies would be required to provide specified, non-identifiable information to the adoptive parents when the adoption order is made.[28]

1.3   Adoption allowances

Consistent with the notion that adoption severs all previous legal relationships, including that with the local authority where the child was previously in care,[29] there was for a long time no provision for the payment of adoption allowances by an agency. The suggestion that some provision might be made was first floated in the Working Paper produced by the Houghton Committee (Houghton, 1970, paras 119–122) on the basis that more adoptive homes might be found for children in need. This suggestion was not well received,[30] the principal objection being that it would amount to discrimination against birth parents.[31] In any event it was argued that the subsidising of adoption went against the notion that the child should be put in precisely the same position as a child born to the adopters. Notwithstanding this

---

[25] Viz, upon payment of a prescribed fee, that the applicant is aged 18 or over, that the Registrar General has either a record of the applicant's birth or sufficient information to obtain a certified copy of the record of birth and that the applicant is a relative: s 51A(3)-(6).

[26] I.e. 'any person (other than an adoptive relative) who is related to the adopted person by blood (including half-blood) or marriage': s 51A(13)(a).

[27] In turn relying on Haimes and Timms, *Adoption, Identity and Social Policy* (1985).

[28] Under the Adoption Agencies Regulations 1983, reg 13A (added in July 1997), agencies must 'provide the adopters with such information about the child as they consider appropriate', after the order is made.

[29] See the Adoption Act 1976, s 12(3)(aa), added by the Children Act 1989, Sch 10, para 3(3).

[30] In fact as the Committee acknowledged in its final report (Houghton, 1972, para 94) most witnesses were opposed to the suggestion.

[31] As the British Association of Social Workers later put it: 'It would be an intolerable situation if financial resources were made available to subsidise adoption when an allocation of similar resources to the natural parents may have prevented the break up of the family in the first place.' *Analysis of the Children Bill*, at 22 – cited by Bevan and Parry: *The Children Act 1975*, para 121.

opposition, the Houghton Committee nevertheless recommended that 'the law should be amended to permit pilot schemes of payment of allowances to adopters under the general oversight of the Secretary of State' (Houghton, 1972, Recommendation 17).

The issue proved equally controversial in Parliament and indeed in Standing Committee it was only the Chairman's casting vote that saved the provision.[32] Nevertheless, a provision permitting an adoption agency to submit a scheme for the payment of adoption allowances for approval by the Secretary of State was enacted under s 32 of the Children Act 1975. It was brought into force on 15 February 1982. Later this provision was replaced by s 56(4)-(7) of the Adoption Act 1976.

At the time of implementation, the expectation was that there would be relatively few schemes but it rapidly became apparent that most agencies would seek to have a scheme.[33] In fact, by the 1990s, virtually all statutory agencies and many voluntary ones as well had successfully applied for a scheme.[34] Reflecting this overall position, the law was changed by the Children Act 1989[35] so as to empower all agencies to pay an adoption allowance provided such payments conform to the requirements set out by the Adoption Allowance Regulations 1991.[36] In other words, instead of a series of individual schemes there is now uniform provision covering all payments of adoption allowances.

We shall examine the current scheme in a little more detail in Chapter 15 when we discuss practical and financial support. Suffice to say here that under the present law, agencies have a discretion both as to whether to pay an allowance at all[37] and, if so, how much.[38] However, reflecting the original intention of the scheme, which was to target payments for a minority of children whose chances of being adopted needed special encouragement, the current guidance states: 'Adoption allowances continue to be the exception rather than the norm.' However, like the schemes they replace, the Regulations are intended to give agencies sufficient flexibility to respond to individual needs and circumstances within this overall objective.' (Department of Health, 1991, para 2.2).

Virtually nothing was said about adoption allowances in the *Adoption Law Review*

---

[32] Standing Committee A (Ninth Sitting), Cols 447–480.

[33] Within two years 58 applications had been made of which 24 had been approved, see Lambert, 'Adoption Allowances in England: an interim report' (1984), *Adoption and Fostering*, 8(3), 12.

[34] For details of the early practice see Lambert and Seglow: 'Adoption Allowances in England and Wales: The Early Years' (1988, HMSO).

[35] Substituting s 57A in place of s 56(4)-(7) of the Adoption Act 1976.

[36] SI 1991/2030.

[37] However, as the Department of Health's *Guidance and Regulations* Vol 9 *Adoption Issues* at 2.3 point out, voluntary agencies who do not hold themselves out as normally paying allowances, unlike statutory agencies, are not even under an obligation to decide whether or not to pay an allowance, though are not prevented from doing so in exceptional cases.

[38] In no event, however, can the allowance exceed the foster allowance that would have been payable: reg 3(4)(b) of the Adoption Allowance Regulations 1991.

– *Report to Ministers of an Interdepartmental Working Group* (hereafter referred to as the Adoption Law Review consultation document (1992)) other than it was a 'valuable service' which should continue (1992, para 27.11). However, in clause 13 of the proposed Adoption Bill, the power to pay adoption allowances would be extended to enable allowances to continue to be paid to someone with parental responsibility for the child should the adopters die[39] (*Adoption Bill: A Consultative Document*, 1996).

2   The obligation to provide services

2.1   Historical background

The early years 1926–1949

When adoption was first introduced into England and Wales under the Adoption of Children Act 1926 it was remarkably unregulated. The 1926 Act essentially provided, as one commentator has put it,[40] 'a process whereby, under minimal safeguards supervised by the court, a civil contract was registered and recognised'. There was no regulatory body to supervise placements and consequently no provision for the provision of an adoption service. However, in 1936, a Departmental Committee was set up to 'inquire into the methods pursued by adoption societies and other agencies engaged in the arranging for the adoption of children' (Horsburgh, 1937, p iv). That committee, which reported in 1937, commented (at para 10):

> *It appears to us beyond question that the first duty of the adoption society is to the child. The child's future is at stake, and the society should take every reasonable step to satisfy itself as to the suitability of the prospective adopters on all grounds before the child is handed over.*

In this regard the Committee considered it as essential that references be taken up, that a personal interview with the applicant be carried out and that a home visit undertaken. At the same time the Committee was concerned to protect the applicants from having an 'unsuitable'[41] child being placed with them and to this end considered that there should be a thorough medical examination of both the child's physical and mental condition. As they put it:

---

[39] This proposal is apparently based on the lesson learned from the operation of the 1991 Regulations. An example might be where following the death of the adopters an older sibling decides to take care of the adopted child and applies for a residence order, see the notes to clause 13 of the proposed Bill.

[40] Cretney, 'From Status to Contract?', in *Consensus Ad Idem* (ed F.P Rose), (1996, at 252) in turn relying on G Restoul MP in the Second Reading on the Adoption of Children Bill, Hansard HL Vol 192, col 930.

[41] Viz, a child 'which is congenitally defective or otherwise unsuitable for adoption' – see para 11 of the 1937 Report.

Some adopters may be prepared to take a child suffering from a minor defect but it is essential that they should be in possession of the full facts concerning its physical and mental health' (para 11).

The Committee recommended that inquiries be made into the social and medical history of the child's birth parents. They also recommended that staff of an adoption society or agency should be suitably qualified and that there should be a Case Committee of suitably qualified persons whose sanction should be required before final approval is given to any adoption.

Following the recommendations of the Horsburgh Committee, the Adoption of Children (Regulation) Act 1939 s 1 made it an offence for a body of persons other than a registered adoption society or a local authority to make any arrangements for the adoption of a child. Provision was made for the local registration of adoption societies by a district registration authority. Although the 1939 Act made no provision for an adoption service as such, the Secretary of State was empowered, under s 4, to make regulations

(a)   to ensure that parents wishing to place their child for adoption were given written explanation of their legal position;

(b)   to prescribe the inquiries to be made and reports to be obtained to ensure the suitability of the child and the adopter; and

(c)   to secure that no child would be delivered into the care and possession of the adopter by the society until the adopter had been interviewed by a case committee.

In short, the 1939 Act created the rudimentary foundations of what might now be called an adoption service although at that stage it was only concerned with the placement of children and only controlled the activities of registered adoption societies.

Although the subsequent 1949 Adoption of Children Act made other crucial changes,[42] it said little about the provision of services but it did seek to clarify, through s 7(2), that a local authority had power 'under any enactment relating to children to make and participate in arrangements for the adoption of children'.

The Hurst Committee's report

Just a few years after the reforms of the late 1940s, another Departmental Committee (the Hurst Committee) was set up to examine the law and practice of adoption societies and other agencies. That Committee reported in 1954 (Hurst, 1954). Although, like the Horsburgh Report, the 1954 Report made no reference to the provision of an adoption "service" it was nevertheless concerned with certain issues

---

[42] Not least the provision that parental consent could be given to adoption without knowing the applicant's identity, and treating the child as that of the adoptive parents for the purpose of inheritance.

that would now be regarded as part of such a service. The Committee, for example, was concerned about placement issues, observing (at para 20):

> *The interests of the child are not well served, nor are the natural parents safeguarded as they should be, unless great care is taken in placing the child. This is the crucial stage in the process of adoption since, once the child is placed, much harm and unhappiness may result if a change has to be made. Our investigations have shown us that, unfortunately, even the more recent provisions of adoption law . . . do not always afford a sufficient protection to those concerned . . .*

It was the Committee's view that 'adoptions arranged by persons of special experience and training' stand a much better chance of success. Nevertheless, although they received 'much evidence' of the desirability of adoptions only being arranged by skilled workers (para 52), they were not prepared to recommend prohibiting private or third party placements (para 47). They did, however, make recommendations about the necessity for the social workers employed by societies to be fully trained (para 54).

Another concern was the reluctance of some local authorities and adoption societies to place any other than healthy children. In the Committee's view (para 21), 'almost any child is adoptable or with care could become so'. However, they warned that it was imperative that the adoptive parents be given the fullest information, but added that:

> *Adopters who have voluntarily assumed the responsibilities of natural parents, must not expect to be able to give [the child] back again at will, any more than they could relieve themselves of their responsibilities if the child had been born to them.*

Another of the Committee's recommendations was that local authorities be specifically empowered to arrange for the adoption of any child without that child having to be in care.[43] As the Committee put it (at para 24), they had no wish to see local authorities usurp the function of voluntary adoption societies but they had been 'impressed by the fact that it is clearly impossible for the small number of societies (then numbering 60 to 70) . . . to cover the needs of the whole country'.[44]

Among other of the Committee's concerns was the lack of co-operation between various departments of local authorities involved in the child's welfare which they blamed in part on the secrecy of the adoption process (para 65). They were also concerned about the child's needs to be told of his or her origins and recommended that all applicants undertake to tell the child of his or her adoption (para 150). They

---

[43] At the time there was some doubt as to whether this was possible.

[44] For a discussion of agency viability, see Chapter 19, *The Organisation of Adoption Services,* and Chapter 20, *Policy and Practice Implications.*

also recommended that both adoptive applicants and the child undergo medical examinations.

Some, but not all of these recommendations, were incorporated in the subsequent controlling legislation, the Adoption Act 1958.

The Houghton Committee's recommendations

It can be seen from the foregoing that while much thought had been given to the regulation of voluntary adoption societies, rather less attention had been paid to the adoption work of local authorities. Similarly, while much thought had been given to the placement of "suitable" children with suitable parents, little official attention had been given to what else a comprehensive service might offer. It is in both these respects that the Houghton Committee, which reported in 1972, made such an important contribution.

What the Houghton Committee wanted to see was the establishment of a nationwide comprehensive adoption service. With regard to the geographical spread of such a service, the Committee noted that at the time of their report only 96 of the then 172 local authorities in England and Wales acted as an adoption agency and, even where they did, not all of them had integrated their adoption work with their other services for children and families. Further, the geographical spread of the then 63 existing voluntary societies was uneven and in any event they offered a range of child care and family services. In short, not all areas were served by an agency at all (Houghton, 1972, paras 32 and 33).

With regard to the issue of what a comprehensive service should cover, the Committee considered that (ibid at para 38):

> ... it should comprise a social work service to natural parents, whether married or unmarried, seeking placement for a child ... skills and facilities for the assessment of the parents' emotional resources, and their personal and social situation; ... short-term placement facilities for children pending adoption placement; assessment facilities; adoption placement services; aftercare for natural parents who need it; counselling for adoptive families. In addition, it should have access to a range of specialised services, such as medical services (including genetic, psychological assessment services, arrangements for the examination of children and adoptive applications, and a medical adviser) and legal advisory services.

The Committee was concerned to see that such a comprehensive service should be established on a nationwide basis so that it would be available to 'all those needing it in any part of the country'. They accordingly recommended that all local authorities should have a statutory duty to provide an adoption service as part of their general child care and family casework provision (paras 42 and 44 and Recommendation 2). Further, having acknowledged that voluntary adoption societies had been pioneers of adoption and that they had a valuable continuing role *inter alia* to provide a choice of service (para 41), the Committee recommended that local authorities have a statutory duty 'to ensure, in co-operation with voluntary societies, that a comprehensive adoption service is available throughout their area' (Recommendation 3). The Committee also recommended a change to the system of registration of voluntary societies so that instead of being local, the responsibility should rest with the Secretary of State. Registration was recommended to be renewable every three years.

Consistent with their belief that children's interests could only be best served by having a well regulated adoption service, and that society was failing in its duty to the child to ensure that only the most satisfactory adoptive placements should be made, while it was open to anyone to place a child for adoption, the Committee recommended it to be an offence for any person other than an adoption agency to place a child for adoption with a person who is not a relative (paras 88-92, Recommendation 13).

Although all these recommendations were accepted and subsequently enacted in the Children Act 1975, because of the costs, implementation was delayed. In fact, the section relating to the provision of a comprehensive adoption service was not brought into force until 1988 at which time it was incorporated into s 1 of the Adoption Act 1976.

In contrast the prohibition against private placements, which could well be said to have completed the process of the "professionalisation" of adoption, took effect in 1982.[45]

Before examining the current law it is worth observing that wide though the Houghton Committee envisaged a comprehensive adoption service to be, they made no mention of *post* adoption support at all. However, as will be seen, although based on the Houghton Committee's recommendations, the wording of s 1 of the 1976 Act is wide enough to impose a duty on local authorities to provide post-adoption support.

2.2   The current law

Under s 1(1) of the Adoption Act 1976

> *It is the duty of <u>every</u> local authority to establish and maintain within their area a service designed to meet the needs in relation to adoption of*
> a) *children who have been or may be adopted*
> b) *parents and guardians of such children and*
> c) *persons <u>who have adopted</u> or may adopt a child and for that purpose to provide the requisite facilities, or secure that they are provided by approved adoption societies.* [Emphasis added]

---

[45] When s 28 of the Children Act 1975 was brought into force.

It is thus under this provision that *all* statutory adoption agencies must either themselves provide an adoption service (as these services are called, pursuant to s 1(4)) or secure that such a service is provided by other approved (i.e. voluntary) agencies.

Although, as we have said, the Houghton Committee made no mention of post-adoption support, it is now[46] accepted that by referring to children who '*have been adopted*' as well as those who may be adopted and to persons '*who have adopted*' as well as to '*persons who may*' adopt, s 1(1) imposes an obligation to provide a post-adoption service – though that provision could profitably be made clearer.[47]

It should be noted that, reflecting the Houghton recommendations, the obligation to provide a service extends to meeting the needs of children, birth parents or guardians (though again s 1(1)(b) could be clearer) and the adopters (both those who have adopted or who may adopt).

Section 1(2) spells out in a little more detail what the *requisite facilities* of an adoption service must minimally provide, namely

a) *temporary board and lodging where needed by pregnant women, mothers or children;*

b) *arrangements for assessing children and prospective adopters, and placing children for adoption;*

c) *counselling for persons with problems relating to adoption.*

The key provisions are (b) and (c); (a) now seems antiquated (and is omitted in cl. 2(2) of the proposed Bill).[48]

Section 1 (3) makes it clear that such an adoption service must be provided:

> ... *in conjunction with the local authority's other social services and with approved adoption societies in their area, so that help may be given in a co-ordinated manner without duplication, omission or avoidable delay.*[49]
> [Emphasis added]

These somewhat general provisions are supplemented to a small extent by the Adoption Agencies Regulations 1983, regs 7 and 8 of which place a duty on *all* agencies (i.e. both statutory *and* voluntary) to provide a counselling service for the birth parents or guardians, the child, 'having regard to his age and understanding', and for the prospective adopters. In each case the regulations impose a duty upon

---

[46] One of the first to mention this were Bevan and Parry: *Children Act 1975* at p15. Post-adoption support is specifically mentioned but only for adult adopted people in the list of services that must be provided in Local Authority Circular LAC (87) 8 and Welsh Office Circular 35(8).

[47] See further below at para 2.3.

[48] See further below at para 2.3.

[49] Bevan and Parry, ibid, argue that this falls short of the Houghton Committee's recommendations that local authorities should themselves provide such a service.

the agency to explain and give written information[50] about 'the legal implications of and procedures in relation to adoption and freeing for adoption'.

Regulation 12 also provides that once a parent has been approved as a suitable adoptive parent for a particular child then *inter alia* it 'shall provide the prospective adopter with written information about the child, his personal history and background including his religious and cultural background, his health history and current state of health . . .'[51]

Further guidance as to what an adoption service should comprise is to be found in the Local Authority Circular, LAC (87) 8.

Notwithstanding the Regulations and Guidance, the fact remains that under the current law there is precious little detailed requirement or guidance as to what a *general* adoption service should comprise. There is, as the Adoption Law Review, Discussion Paper Number 3[52] pointed out, a lack of clarity about what post-adoption services adoption agencies are supposed to provide. This in turn has led to a variety of interpretations as to what is required and thus to a consequential patchy provision of services which are 'more often likely to be available from voluntary sources'.

2.3   The proposed law

The Adoption Law Review consultation document (1992) made a number of detailed proposals in relation to the provision of an adoption service.[53] In particular, it recommended that the legislative framework should underline an adopted child's right to know he or she is adopted and that the agency or guardian should provide a package of information to be given to the adoptive parents to make it available to the child about his or her background.[54] It recommended that agencies should have a duty to give birth parents the opportunity to have their own social worker so as to be able to participate in decisions about their child's future. It wanted a system whereby medical information may be passed to the child's doctor and to inform the adopter that this has been done. Finally, it recommended that any legislation should make it clear that any user of a local authority adoption service has access to the complaints procedure and that approved societies have a duty to operate a similar complaints procedure. It also recommended that inspection and approval of voluntary societies should revert to local authorities.

So far as post-adoption services were concerned, the Adoption Law Review

---

[50] Our research suggests that not all agencies seem to comply with the requirement to provide written information, see Chapter 9, *Preparation and Training*, at para 3.2.

[51] Again our research seems to show that not all agencies discharge this duty. See Chapter 9, *Preparation and Training*, para. 3.3.

[52] *Inter-Departmental Review of Adoption Law, Discussion Paper Number 3, The Adoption Process*, para 88.

[53] See generally Recommendations 24-33, discussed in Part VII.

[54] For further discussion, see Chapter 20, *Policy and Practice Implications,* para. 3.1.

consultation document (1992) recommended that there be a general counselling service for birth parents, adopters and adopted children.

Notwithstanding the aforementioned recommendations, the Government White Paper (*Adoption: The Future,* 1992) in fact said little about adoption services. However, at para 4.25 it said:

> *Adoptive parents have a right to as much information about their adopted child as is possible. Agencies will therefore be given a duty to prepare for the adopters a package of information including health and family history. The information will also be retained in court records to which the adopted child will have access as of right having reached the age of 18. Agencies will be encouraged to offer post adoption support to new families. This is particularly appreciated by adoptive parents of children with special needs.* [Emphasis added]

Whilst most welcomed the idea of requiring agencies to provide adopters with a package of information, alarm was expressed at the phrase that agencies will be '*encouraged*' to provide post-adoption support, which seemed to imply that unlike the current law, there would be no obligation to do so. In the event these fears seem unfounded since cl 2(1) of the proposed Adoption Bill provides, in similar terms to s 1(1) of the current law, that

> *Each local authority must continue to maintain within their area a service designed to meet the needs, in relation to adoption, of*
> *a) persons who have been or may be adopted*
> *b) parents or guardians of such persons and*
> *c) persons who have adopted or may adopt a child . . .*

Again the obligation to provide post-adoption support hangs on the phrases '*persons who have been adopted*' and '*persons who have adopted*'. It would surely be better if the obligation to provide post-adoption support was expressly provided for in the statute. It might be noted that to allay any doubts as to whether there is an obligation to provide an adoption service in relation to intercountry adoption, cl 2(5) expressly so provides. Perhaps a similar provision could be added to cover post-adoption support. It might also be noted that the reference in cl 2(1)(a) to '*persons*' who have been adopted, rather than to '*children*', as in the current s 1(1)(a), arguably extends the obligation to provide a support service into adulthood, though whether this is intended is unclear.[55]

Clause 2(2) spells out the minimum '*requisite facilities*' of any adoption service in slightly different terms to the current s 1(2) namely:

---

[55] See also our recommendation in Chapter 20, *Policy and Practice Implications*, para. 2.1.

a) *counselling, and giving advice and information to, persons in relation to adoption;*

b) *arrangements for assessing persons, and placing children for adoption.*

Essentially the key requirements remain the same as under the current law as does the requirement under cl 2(3) to provide the service in conjunction with social services and approved adoption societies to provide help '*in a co-ordinated manner without duplication, omission or avoidable delay.*' What is new, however, is the proposed requirement under cl 3, namely, that each local authority must prepare and publish a plan for the provision of the adoption service maintained by them. Such a plan will have to contain information as laid down by regulation. Regulations will also prescribe the publication and review of the plan. They will also specify persons who must be consulted when preparing the plan.

This last proposal is a crucial and welcome innovation since it will provide the opportunity to bring much needed co-ordination and guidance as to what an adoption service should comprise. It is in this respect that our research findings could assume importance.

3 The Social Construction of Adoption

1   Permanence

1.1   The concept of permanence in child care practice

The practice of placing older children out of care for adoption, with which our research is centrally concerned, springs from that child care policy which, in the mid 1970s, began in the United Kingdom to be termed permanency planning[1] – a term that is not always synonymous with adoption since in social work terms[2] it can include long-term fostering and residential care and, some would say, a return to members of the family of origin.[3]

Commenting on the susceptibility of child care policies to fashionable trends and theories, Thoburn *et al* (1986, p. 9) have observed that 'whilst the 1960s and 1970s may be described as a period of "prevention" and "rehabilitation", the period from the mid 1970s to the mid 1980s can be characterised as the decade of permanence'. All three "fashions" were in effect a reaction to the shortcomings and expense of institutional child care. In the United States, although the "permanence movement" was initially largely led through pioneering projects such as the Almeda project (Stein, Gambrill and Wiltse, 1978), and the Oregon project (Lahti, 1982) which included return to birth families as one of the main permanency options, there was a tendency for practitioners to view adoption as a primary route to permanence. Thoburn *et al* (1986, p. 11) comment that:

> . . . *although it is not clear why this was so it was probably due to the*

---

[1] The emphasis on the word 'planning' probably reflects the influential work of Professor Roy Parker of Bristol in the early 1970s (see Parker, 1971). In these lectures Parker makes a powerful plea for rational but sensitive planning for children in long-term care. He writes 'by planning for children, I mean having a reasonably clear, practical vision of the future we wish for them and more specifically taking a sequence of steps which is instrumentally relevant to that end'. In making this plea Parker was in advance of his time in emphasising the need to take note of the child's own preferences and of the views of the parents.

[2] But not legal terms since it is only by adoption that legal parentage can be totally transferred, see Chapter 2, *The Legal Background*, at para 1.1.

[3] But as Shaw (1988, p. 62) points out, 'the recognition that "permanency" could not really be achieved within the child care system just worsened pressure on adoption services to provide family life for children who for whatever reason could not be returned to their families of origin. Within a remarkably short space of time, adoption agencies . . . switched their aspirations from "the perfect baby for the perfect family" to "a family for every child, not a child for the childless family" '.

"excitement" of achieving what had previously been seen as foolhardy: successfully placing older and handicapped children for adoption; rehabilitative work was less novel in its techniques and less dramatic in its results.'

Maluccio and Fein (1983, p. 197) attempted to trace the origins of the so-called permanency movement and, having explored various uses of the term, offered the following definition:

Permanency planning is the systematic process of carrying out within a brief time limited period, a set of goal directed activities designed to help children live in families that offer continuity of relationships with nurturing parents or caretakers and the opportunity to establish lifetime relationships.

Underlying such a definition is the premise that rearing children in a family setting has particular value and that the continuity of relationships with "psychological" parent-figures best promotes a child's growth and development. In the view of Maluccio *et al* (1980, p. 519) the essence of the permanency planning concept is the

. . . idea of removing the child as soon as possible out of temporary substitute care and returning him or her to the family as the preferred alternative or to an adoptive home as the second priority, or if necessary to another permanent alternative such as a family with legal guardianship.

Both in the USA and the UK the concept of permanency planning has had the effect of shifting the "mental furniture" which people use to construct their notions of adoption (Caudrey and Frewin, 1986; Reich and Lewis, 1986; Macaskill, 1985). In the USA, Maluccio and Fein (1983, p. 200) conclude their review of research with something of a mission statement indicative of the revolution in child care thinking which they considered permanency planning offered. Thus they state 'the movement holds great promise for achieving the goal of permanent families for all children. It is the minimum that we should expect of the two million children in the child welfare system'. Similarly in this country, Tony Hall – then Director of BAAF writing in 1986 – put the matter in a nutshell when he wrote:

This revolution has opened up the possibility of a new permanent family for large numbers of children previously thought to be unadoptable. It has transformed professional attitudes about who might be suitable adopters so that the types of parents adopting children today are as varied as the children who are looking for new families. It has stimulated enormous changes in methods of family finding, recruitment, preparation, selection, placement and support. Some new specialist agencies have been created; some traditional agencies have been transformed beyond recognition and the process of change is continuing. (Hall, 1986, p. 7)

What had brought about this major shift in practice? What were the implications for the development of support services for children and their adoptive families in the 1990s and for the design of this particular research project? Amongst the factors which seem to us to be important was the impact of the powerful book, *Beyond the Best Interest of the Child* by Goldstein, Freud and Solnit (1973). This advanced the hypothesis (supported it must be said by scant empirical evidence) that young children were not 'capable of dealing with situations where they maintained contact with their natural parents and lived with a set of substitute parents'. Arguing against the importance of the blood tie – 'the physical realities of conception and birth are not the direct cause of emotional attachments' – they advanced the notion of 'psychological parents', suggesting bonding and attachment 'results from day to day attention to the child's needs for physical care, nourishment, comfort, affection and stimulation'. By this view, only a person who provides for these needs would become the psychological parent in whose care the child would feel valued and wanted while 'an absent biological parent will remain or tend to become a stranger' (1973, p. 17). Delineating what in their view characterises psychological parenting, they set out a whole raft of suggestions which challenged the then prevailing traditional, legal mode of thought that biological and legal parenthood should take precedence over psychological parenthood. In adoption they were amongst the first to emphasise the idea that children – particularly babies and infants – have a different concept of time from that of adults and accordingly cannot normally tolerate uncertainty and delay in the same way as adults. This line of thought led them to the proposition that 'the adoption decree (order) be made final the moment a child is actually placed with an adopting family'. Such proposals were all intended to reinforce the security of the adoptive, psychological parent/child relationship. Where the feelings of foster carers had become 'totally involved with the child in their care . . . the adults advance from the status of foster parent to that of becoming psychological parent . . . in fact what they may have become are parents by common law adoption' (1973, p. 26) which in their view deserved legal recognition.

Many of these, at the time, revolutionary notions subsequently came to be accepted by social work and legal practitioners working in child care and adoption, and although such ideas were later questioned and qualified, a powerful residue has permeated professional thinking ever since (Wall, 1997). Certainly they strengthened the view that children from neglectful, disrupted and severely disordered families might often do much better if placed permanently with loving, secure and more stable families.

In the UK, this line of thought became reinforced in the 1970s and 1980s as a series of child care studies (for example Rowe and Lambert, 1973; Milham *et al*, 1986) showed that children who are shuttled backwards and forwards in and out of care, the so-called 'Yo-Yo Children', and those 'who get lost in care' in a series of placements as a result of bureaucratic delay, drift and lack of resources (Packman *et al*, 1986), were often failing to have their psychological and educational needs met.

1.2   Evaluating permanency planning

From the late 1980s onwards, since substantial numbers of older children – both in the USA and UK – have been placed for adoption, it became feasible to mount research which attempted to evaluate the effectiveness of the permanency planning movement. Rushton and Mayes (1997, pp. 121–127), in a valuable review of recent research on childhood attachments, have observed that following the optimism for permanency planning of the 1970s and early 1980s, there has been something of a reaction to the policy:

> ... with a growing bank of stories from practitioners and new parents concerning a proportion of children who appeared to have enduring problems with relationships in their new homes. By the late 1980s, the term "Reactive Attachment Disorder" was being used to signify a gross disturbance in social relationships.

Rushton and Mayes' research review sought to evaluate researches which might suggest that weak attachment is associated with later disruption. For a start they pointed out that the term "Reactive Attachment Disorder" may only apply to a very small number of children who had probably experienced gross abuse, neglect and/ or multiple changes of carer. Rightly they caution that 'attachment theory language' may offer only one set of explanations for children who resist intimacy, physical closeness and who show a lack of reciprocity in affection since these behaviours could be the result of numerous other experiences and adversities apart from having 'negative working models of relationships with their adults'.

The Rushton and Mayes research review of ten studies of fresh attachments in middle childhood thus presents a rather conflicting picture. The American Barth and Berry (1988) study of 120 placements, 57 of which disrupted, identified certain attachment behaviours which were thought to be associated with disruption such as insatiable attention seeking, an inability to give spontaneous affection and a lack of care or preference for their parents. But the research review points out that this study has certain methodological weaknesses being heavily reliant on retrospective recall of events by adopters. David Howe's (1996) British study of adopters' relationships with their adopted children from adolescence suggests that, by the time the children have grown into their early 20s, nearly all of the adopters (93 per cent) were able to report positive parent/child relationships. Howe suggests that, the difference between those who had positive and negative relationships with their adopters depends on the quality of the young person's early primary relationships during infancy. Rushton's own most recent research with David Quinton and colleagues of 61 late placed children concluded that 73 per cent of the children 'had shown the ability to make a satisfactory relationship with at least one of their new parents by the end of the first year in placement'. Rushton and Mays conclude their review by saying that 'most late placed children do establish satisfying relationships with their new parents within the first year of placement, but that less is known about the reasons for instability later – particularly in adolescence'. They suggest that the part played 'by new parents' parenting behaviour in promoting attachment deserves further attention' and that:

> More knowledge on the relationship between the growth of attachment in the child and on the new parents' responses to the children's social impairment should help in targeting resources to those families who need them most and eventually in the development of techniques for promoting mutual attachment.

2 Adoption, kinship and notions of family support

As part of our enquiry into the nature of support services for older adopted children and their adoptive families, we have had to consider those informal support networks potentially provided by friends and relatives. In relation to the adopters' own family of origin we have asked ourselves the question: does adoption alter people's notion of kinship and, if so, how? In referring here to "kin" we include not only people who might fall within an adoptive parent's immediate family circle, such as siblings and possibly grandparents, but also more distant relatives like uncles and aunts, cousins and even relatives whose existence is acknowledged even though contact with them is not maintained. Does adoption confer on the adopted child lifelong membership of such familial kinship groups? How are family decisions taken about whether the adopted child "counts" as a member of the kinship group? Will the adopted child be treated differently from any birth children of the adoptive family?

In relation to the child's birth family there are a similar set of kinship questions. Do adopted children lose membership of their birth family kinship network on becoming adopted or do they acquire kinship in the adopted family whilst retaining it in certain respects with their birth family? How much reliance can adopters place on their kinship networks for support in caring for an adopted child? Is it the same as for their own birth children? Does it make any difference whether the child has been placed and adopted as an infant or as an older child? Can adopted children themselves expect to rely on some measure of birth family sibling kinship support throughout life as might be expected between birth siblings born into the same family? Alternatively can some kinship be possibly activated in later life? How are kinship networks affected if contact is retained after placement and the making of the order?

At the outset of this research it seemed to us that culturally it was not easy to determine the answers to such questions, possibly because legal adoption is of relatively recent origin, under English law, only since 1926. We suspected that the key actors in the adoption context, including the agency staff, might have some difficulty working out the rules of the kinship game. Our impression was that in these matters there is considerable ambiguity. Much might depend both on explicit and implicit "negotiations" within the respective kinship networks of both birth and adopted families. By "negotiation" we are referring to the social processes whereby people construct with others the social world around themselves, thereby developing a shared understanding of what a particular situation, in this case adoption, means to them. This process takes place within a broader social structure shaped by law, social convention and, in the context of adoption, by social policies and practices mostly mediated through the brokering function of the adoption agency and its staff.

Although later in the report[4] we refer to instances which illustrate certain aspects of these negotiations, we have to acknowledge that our material about kinship support is not as extensive as that concerning the negotiated support from formal agencies. There are several reasons for this. First, it seems likely that most adopters would regard discussion of their relatives' response both to their decision to adopt and to the adopted child as a more private matter than discussion of their experiences with social agencies. Moreover, the social value of loyalty associated with notions of privacy might have constrained what they were prepared to tell us. Second, many of these negotiations within kinship networks would be implicit rather than explicit involving what Finch has described as 'silent bargains' (Finch, 1989).[5] Family members themselves might not therefore have been fully aware of the existence of social family rules which might have differentiated the adopted child from other children in the family in terms of the degree of family membership, or the extent to which other kin could be expected to offer support to the adoption. But of course if some families felt excluded by some of their kin in seeking such support because the adopted child was not fully accorded kinship membership, this might well influence how they cope with any difficulty experienced in the adoption process and how they viewed alternative potential sources of support. Moreover, we suspect that many adoptive family kinship groups might find it easier to accord full kinship membership to an adopted baby than to an older child, particularly where contact of some sort is being maintained with the kin in the family of origin. This is, however, a hypothesis that we have not been able to test in our family sample. Likewise cultural and ethnic factors seem likely to have a significant influence on the way kinship related roles (with associated influence on support) are defined in the adoption context. But here too we have not yet been able to test any emergent hypotheses.

---

[4] See Chapter 11, *Post Placement Issues*, para 4.

[5] Janet Finch (1989) writes: 'The idea that family life is characterised by conscious and rational weighing up of choices and carefully planned actions is inappropriate. The concept of negotiation seems to me particularly valuable precisely because it does not imply these things. Negotiations may be implicit as well as explicit and need not necessarily be conducted at the level of conscious strategy.'

Although we have explored kinship questions as far as we can in this study,[6] they deserve closer attention than we have been able to give them. As we have a number of families willing to be seen again, we might be able to re-interview them at a later date both to find out whether the problem of support alters significantly in the post-adoption period and to explore further with them how they define kinship in the light of their adoption of an older child, particularly to see how it might influence expectations of intra family support in the years to come.

3   Attachment and bonding – some particular concerns in respect to older adopted children

3.1   Attachment and bonding – distinguished

The whole point of good support during the adoption process is to promote and strengthen the attachment between the child and the adoptive parents. The literature on the social psychology of attachment is extensive. Virtually all authorities stress the importance of the interacting attachment process for babies and infants with their primary carers, particularly the mother. Attachment has been defined as 'an affectionate bond between two individuals that endures through space and time and serves to join them emotionally' (Klaus and Kernel, 1976).

Some such as Jenkins (1981) have distinguished between attachment which depends on proximity, and bonding which is defined as a form of attachment which persists over time regardless of proximity;[7] an important point when considering the issue of contact between older adopted children and members of their birth family.

The early primary attachments of babies and infants provide the psychological foundations to which Erikson (1968) referred as a sense of basic trust – a fundamental pre-requisite of mental health, emotional security and vitality. "Trust" in this sense means an essential trustfulness of others as well as a sense of one's own trustworthiness.

In recent years writers such as Fahlberg (1994, p. 379) have sought to describe *attachment* as 'the close inter-personal connections that children form with others ... connections that are strong enough to last through time and space'. Bonding is a correspondingly reciprocal process referred to as 'the close inter-personal connections that adults, especially primary carers, form with children in their care'. In this report we use the terms "attachment" and "bonding" accordingly.

---

[6] See Chapter 11, *Post Placement Issues*, see table in para 3.1.

[7] Thus, Spencer Millham and his colleagues found in studies of children in preparatory schools that although they often saw their parents infrequently (for example, when they worked overseas), the children nevertheless indicated that they felt close to them (see Millham *et al*, 1986).

3.2   Attachment between adopters and older children

Although there has been much work done on attachment theory, it has so far been largely confined to infants and birth parents. The question of the development of fresh attachments formed by older children to unrelated adults has been less well addressed (see Rushton and Mayes, 1997, and the authorities there cited).

In our study there were a number of potentially complex issues relating to attachment between older children and adopters.

First, placement workers and adopters often do not know how well the child's primary attachments as a baby and as an infant have developed. Social workers and adopters frequently have to surmise from fragmentary evidence and from stories gathered much later how strong/weak or non-existent these initial attachments had been. Foster carers and adopters by the nature of things are seldom close enough to the child's early life to have any direct evidence of the initial attachment process. Very often they have to rely on what the "experts" have been able to surmise,[8] and pass on to them.

Second, there is the issue whether any "damage" to a child's capacity to make attachments occurred *after* the child was placed with substitute carers. There are several aspects to this.

The nature of these attachments will vary according to the length and purpose of the placement, the needs of the child and the capacity of the carer. Much may depend on whether the child care authorities and the foster carer can promote and reinforce the child's capacity to form a close attachment to the foster carer. Besides, unresolved grief following separation from the birth family may block the child's capacity to attach to the foster carers and subsequent adoptive family.[9] Children have only a limited capacity to make and break attachments. Yet often one of the most intractable weaknesses of the child care system and the slow-moving nature of court proceedings is that children on removal from their often dangerous or neglectful families are placed in a series of short-term foster homes before permanent homes can be found for them. Some who begin to make roots in one

---

[8] The essential problem here is one of evidence. As we see it, however skilled the experts may be, much of the child's pre-care experience can only be surmised. There is sometimes very little firm, reliable evidence about a child's early primary experience and strength of emotional attachments particularly if they are several years old when they first come to the notice of the child care authority. Sometimes the family circumstances of the children will have deteriorated only after firm, initial bonds have been established, for example, if the family runs into a major disruptive crisis and disintegrates or if a parent becomes mentally ill or addicted to drugs which permanently damages their capacity to relate to and care for the children.

[9] Vera Fahlberg (1994, p. 17) asserts 'Many children in care have never learned psychologically healthy ways to connect with others. Their past relationships may not have supported growth and development. Unfortunately few children in foster care receive adequate help in resolving the grief they experience when separated from their birth families. These unresolved separations interfere with their formation of new attachments'.

situation find that they are then moved on (see Hunt, 1997; Rowe and Lambert, 1973; and Thomas *et al*, 1993), sometimes several times before the authorities take the decision to find a permanent adoptive home. Of course, some children are more resilient than others but the danger is that their capacity to trust is weakened; that they might come to believe that something is wrong with them; that they are to blame in some way; that they are unlovable.

Although from a practitioner's perspective delay can be purposeful and that in any event great care has to be taken both to investigate the case and then to find suitable placements, what should never be overlooked is how the child reacts to delay and uncertainty (and also how it affects the adoptive placement). Here a child's sense of time is a crucial dimension. All the professional thoroughness and care in the world can be nullified if the child's emotional resources are over-taxed and the capacity to form healthy attachments is damaged. Moreover, it is the adopters (not forgetting any other children they may have) not the professionals who have taken the primary risks involved in looking after the child and facing what Macaskill (1986, p. 41) has referred to as 'the onslaught of behavioural difficulties before and after adoption'.

But potential "iatrogenic" damage to a child's capacity to form attachments to adoptive parents caused by delay and discontinuities in the system was not the only adverse consequence with which we were concerned when planning this research. Another was the potential damage to a child's educational career which can result from a series of moves from one school to another occasioned by changes in foster home while awaiting permanent placement. In this respect we recognised the potential danger of paying insufficient attention to the educational experience of older children being adopted out of care,[10] particularly since much of our field work would be based on an exploration of the adoption agency's perspective which for various reasons might have a psycho-social rather than educational bias. In preparing this report we have sought to be mindful of these potential biases and to remember that attachment issues in the adoptive home might well interact with the child's school and wider social world.[11]

---

[10] As Parker *et al* (1991, p. 89) observed: 'Children looked after by a local authority suffer from a number of interlocking educational disadvantages. Some are "external", such as the experience of frequently disrupted schooling and the lack of opportunities to acquire basic skills. Others are psychological, such as low self esteem. However, a crucial factor seems to be the minimal expectation of social workers and care-givers about what children in their care are capable of achieving and the low priority that educational matters are accorded. Such attitudes permeate the care system . . .' See also Jackson (1987, pp. 133–151).

[11] See Chapter 11, *Post Placement Issues*, para 3.1.

4   Separation, loss, attachment and bonding

Children placed for adoption, like those involved in proceedings following parental separation and divorce and other forms of family breakdown, have to adapt to separation and loss. The period when the arrangements for the adoption are being set up and confirmed by the making of the order is normally one of maximum change for the child and the adopters, unless of course the child is being adopted by foster carers with whom there is already an established relationship.

The adoption process can thus be viewed as a form of status passage, defined by Glaser and Strauss (1971) as occurring

> . . . *whenever there is movement on the part of the individual from a different part of the social structure involving a loss or gain or privilege or power and a changed identity or sense of self. The concept of status passage thus covers a wide variety of transitions from illness to promotion from marriage to dying.*

In adoption the concept of status passage applies both to the child's loss of birth family (actual or qualified), and to the acquisition of the child's new adoptive parents,[12] a new name and identity. The concept of status passage also applies both to the birth parents, who may suffer a loss of parental status, and to the adoptive parents who gain it, often for the first time in their lives.

Looked at this way, those who offer support services to parents and children involved in the adoption proceedings can be viewed as "passage agents" working with them to achieve a successful navigation of the passage from their previous social statuses to the new one of adopted child and adoptive parents. Glaser and Strauss also postulate that the clients are often especially dependent on the passage agents for successfully completing the status passage. Thus they write:

> *Doctors, lawyers, social workers, counsellors and others see sections of the passage as rough and conceive of themselves as experts who are alert to unknown contingencies with consequences that can be softened. Passage agents make a profession of managing transitions to get passagees through without any bruises.* (1971, p. 51)[13]

In this study we take the view that it is the statutory and voluntary adoption agency staff who assume the primary role of passage agent in the adoption context, but

---

[12] Frequently occupying a higher level in terms of income and standard of living in comparison to the birth families, see Murch *et al* (1993). The hope is that the adoption will also over time serve to raise a child's esteem as well as social status – a sentiment expressed to us by a number of birth parents in our ESRC *Consumer Study*.

[13] Note also that Sarrat and Felsteiner have recently produced an excellent observational study on the way American divorce lawyers and their clients negotiate and ascribe meaning to these sorts of transitions (Sarrat and Felsteiner, 1995).

complementary roles may well be played by others from the medical, legal and educational domains, a matter which is explored later in this report. The research team is particularly interested in the part played by practitioners in the Family Justice System[14] because family law is an important social mechanism which frames and structures these transitions, setting out the principles by which they should be managed[15] and the practices and procedures which should be followed. Moreover, court hearings and resulting orders serve to provide the rituals and rites of passage which help to mark the ends and the beginnings of certain relationships and statuses in the social structure (Van Gennep, 1960). The legal process can thus be understood from psychosocial perspectives as providing public confirmation that a critical transition has occurred which has resulted, on completion of the rite, in a newly accomplished set of family identities which will thereafter be legally protected.

Some status passages are so sudden and far-reaching in their consequence as to cause (at least temporary) acute stress. Consequently, we thought we should be on the look-out for any evidence of episodes when children of adoptive parents experience, during the adoptive process, degrees of critical stress which appeared to have overwhelmed their normal coping abilities.[16] Our thinking about this has been influenced by the "Caplanian" crisis model of mental health and the associated practice of crisis intervention, based on the seminal bereavement studies of Lindemann (1944), Robertson (1952), Hill (1958), Caplan (1964; 1974), and Parkes (1972). These could provide theoretical justification for short-term intensive support of adults and children experiencing acute stress during the critical transitions associated with the adoption process.[17]

Because people at periods of crisis have been found to have increased susceptibility to inter-personal influence, supportive intervention from both professionals and non-professional care-givers can be particularly helpful. For example, when adults and children are preoccupied with loss they benefit from the opportunity to express their grief. It has long been recognised as good adoption practice to support children who are grief-stricken by the breakdown of their birth

---

[14] See further, Chapter 13, *The Legal Process*.

[15] See Chapter 2, *The Legal Framework*.

[16] See Chapter 11, *Post Placement Issues*, para 2.4, and Chapter 12, *Disruptions*.

[17] In essence this approach is based on the idea first formulated by Gerald Caplan (1964) that, when normal psychosocial equilibrium or homeostasis, and coping mechanisms are temporarily overwhelmed by acute stress provoked by loss, threat of loss or sudden change, there is a clear pattern to most people's responses as they adjust to what has happened, that is, an initial phase of shock and disbelief followed by distress and preoccupation as the impact of the stressful event is absorbed; a depressive slump in morale accompanied by psychological and physical exhaustion; then a phase when defences are marshalled to ease the pain of grief; followed by a gradual recovery or learning period as adjustments are made, new defences and coping mechanisms are developed and tested and a new psychosocial balance is established. This whole adaptive process (or crisis), depending on the severity and nature of the precipitating event, can last from a few days to a number of months.

family relationships and to help them come to terms with it sufficiently well before they are ready to be "placed for adoption". This is a task which normally falls to the child's local authority social worker (Rushton *et al*, 1998).

We were mindful, when planning this project, of the possibility that the adoptive placement itself, at least in the early stages, might trigger off in the child a renewed phase of grief. Thus, Bowlby (1979, p. 44) has written on grieving children generally that, even when conditions are favourable,

> *Children barely 4 years old are found to yearn for a lost parent, to hope and at times believe that he (or she) may yet return and to feel sad and angry when it becomes clear that he will never do so. Many children insist on retaining an item of clothing or some other possession of the dead (or absent) parent and especially value photographs.*

It seemed to us that the problem of grieving, or perhaps worse of not grieving if there is a major denial of loss while forming new attachments, may well be one of the most critical dilemmas facing older children being adopted out of care.

We were also concerned to learn how any associated conflicts of loyalty are dealt with. Not all children can express their feelings through words as clearly as adults. Often adults find grief in children difficult to acknowledge and hard to handle. Periods of denial, withdrawal and anger can easily be misinterpreted, for example, at school or by adopters or adoption workers who may mistakenly see grief for a lost or broken attachment as a bad reflection on the adoption placement. We needed to consider whether and, if so, when and how older children grieve for lost attachments during the adoption process. How do adopters/foster carers and adoptive placement workers recognise and deal with the children's grief? Can it always be assumed that the child's grief work[18] has been undertaken before the adoption placement is made?

One of the reasons why we are attracted to the Caplanian model of crisis and crisis intervention is because it seems to offer an "ecological" way of viewing the process of adoption of older children out of care in the context of support networks. It also provides a conceptual framework against which to assess the contribution, actual or potential, of a range of relevant support systems. When Caplan began developing this approach in the 1950s and 60s he was at pains to point out that his notion of support systems, which in general terms we adopt,

> *. . . comprises an enduring pattern of continuous or intermittent ties that play a significant part in maintaining the psychological and pyschosocial integrity of the individual over time.* (Caplan, 1961, p. 140)

---

[18] An expression to denote the normal process of mourning. See also Chapter 9, *Preparation and Training*, at para 2.5.

Viewed this way the purpose of support is to *augment* the child's and the family strengths to facilitate the status change. Integral to the Caplanian model is the idea that a relatively small amount of helping effort will produce a much bigger effect if it focuses on people at critical times – in our context during the transition to adoption – than if applied when children and parents are in relatively stable equilibrium. In our study, therefore, we set out to discover under what circumstances and how support is channelled to them as they adapt to one another and in certain contexts to other members of the birth family.

From the adoptive parents' perspective we hoped to address such questions as what kinds of support they seek when in the throes of the adoption process and when facing crises within this period. Who do they turn to for such support? What forms of support are available and under what conditions? What support roles are played by the professional services including GPs and other medical services, school teachers, lawyers, social workers as well as those employed by adoption agencies? What supports are on offer from kin, neighbours, friends, etc.?

From the view of adoption agencies, the stage managers of the adoption process, we wanted to explore questions such as how they mobilise support during the adoption process from other professionals e.g. teachers, GPs, etc. Are there effective channels of communication between the family, child and the agency and other potential support systems? What steps have agencies taken to ensure that they are alert to early signs of difficulty or stress in placement? What practices, procedures and special services have they developed to articulate with and respond to any special needs that might be posed by the placement for adoption of older children out of care? Are these adoptive families seen as meriting the organisation of programmes of primary prevention?

4　The Older Child's Status Passages through Systems

1　A conceptual approach to the study of structural continuities and discontinuities of care

Most older children adopted out of care have experienced exceptionally problem-ridden childhoods with complex histories of broken family attachments, sometimes full of sudden unexpected change. Often their life stories exemplify the old adage that trouble seldom comes singly: an enforced change of home can involve a consequent change of school, a change of friends, a change of all the health professionals who have had responsibility for the child's medical care, and of course a change of social worker who may have been dealing with the child's day-to-day welfare concerns. One of the fundamental purposes of adoption for older children is to provide them with a sense of permanence and emotional stability, sometimes for the very first time in their lives. Adoption offers a break from the turbulence and discontinuities of the past. It holds out the promise of a more stable life in a "permanent" committed family home in which children can experience reliable and continuous nurture, care and support.

Given what we know about the mental health implications of critical transitions, status passages and psycho-social adjustment,[1] we considered it important to examine the institution of adoption and its associated procedures and support systems to see if we could identify what structural continuities and discontinuities of care were built into the system. Assuming that some discontinuities could be experienced by the child as a loss of support and of care and might severely tax the child's capacity to adjust and make new and lasting attachments, we thought such an approach might serve to identify where there was a need in the system for "transitional bridges". Although the adoption system itself – and the child's pathway through it[2] – were obviously of major importance in this respect, conceptually it was also vital to consider the transitional pathways through those other social systems that directly impinge upon the child's life. These include the child's birth and adoptive family and kinship systems; various informal social networks of friends

---

[1] Discussed in Chapter 3, *Social Construction of Adoption*

[2] Our previous Department of Health sponsored research, *Pathways to Adoption* (Murch *et al*, 1993), had attempted to identify procedural obstacles in the pathways through the adoption system. In this study we have sought to widen the conceptual approach to include other social systems.

and class mates from nursery or school; as well as the other more formal social institutions of health, education and the family justice system.

Although we use charts to illustrate our thinking about these matters (see charts 1–4 below) there are three introductory points that should be borne in mind in considering this approach:

1) When talking about structural continuities and discontinuities, the crucial aspect to consider is the impact on the individual child's emotional/mental health development. It is how the child experiences these changes which really matters. In this respect our agency and family studies only have limited value. We can make certain inferences from the theoretical models to which we have already referred.[3] We can look at what the adults – adopters and practitioners – tell us and be alert to any testimony which refers to the children's adjustment to particular sudden changes and events in their world. But such "adult thinking" will be conditioned by their own social construction of adoption. In any event they may well not have sufficient evidence of the child's before and after experience to appreciate either the nature of or the degree of change to which the child has been exposed. Neither will they necessarily appreciate how the child has interpreted and coped behaviourally with such changes and made the transition from one (or several) social world to the next. Only a person who is close enough to the child and who oversees the various transitions that may have to be made is in a position to make any sort of evidence-based evaluation. Here we immediately encounter a problem with our samples in that by the very nature of things adopters come new into the child's world. Furthermore, many of our practitioners come new too, either as a family placement worker (particularly those who work for voluntary adoption agencies), or as a local authority children's social worker if the child has been placed in a different local authority area. In short, because of the nature of adoption procedures and the way in which our research was organised we were not able to draw on information from anyone who could be said to have acted in a close bridging role while the child made the crucial transition out of care into adoption.[4]

2) In our consideration of these matters we will be talking about pathways through social systems. Yet as Ivan Illich (1995) has cautioned, the term "social system" has a peculiarly 20th century usage and connotation which, although it has great organising power, can easily have the effect of depersonalising and objectifying what are essentially acutely subjective individual experiences. In his view such usage leads into administrative "managerial" thinking which implicitly places group organisational values above those of the human subject – in this context children. Therefore we have to be on our guard against such thinking.

---

[3] See Chapter 3, *Social Construction of Adoption*, para 4.

[4] For the children's experience, see our related study, *Adopted Children Speaking*, Thomas *et al* (1999).

3) Related to the two previous cautionary points, we recognise that our charts (see charts 1–4 below) are inevitably grossly generalised and over-simplified. If we are to take the issue of potentially damaging discontinuities seriously in the adoption context we must devise effective tools to record, identify and monitor the key patterns of system support available to the individual child. In this respect we believe that consideration should be given to extending the application of an important child-care tool, *Looking After Children – Information Record*,[5] to children adopted out of care as it is to foster children. This useful monitoring device is already used by a number of local authorities. Its merit is that it alerts those immediately responsible for the child's welfare to the importance of a whole range of social, educational and medical provisions which should support and enrich the child's world according to need. But we think it could also be an important monitoring tool for those older children adopted out of care, at least until the placement appears secure and to be working well.

2 The use of pathways charts

In the early months of the project we began to construct several charts to help identify potential points of discontinuity in the patterns of child and family support provision. We reproduce below four such charts: one each for the child, the adoptive family, the foster family and the birth family. They are each predicated on the assumption that the adopters are strangers to the child. Some of the discontinuities would be eliminated in cases where the adopters were the foster carers. We hope that these will be largely self-explanatory. Each is constructed to cover four key transitional stages in the critical pathway from care to adoption, moving left to right horizontally in a temporal sequence. The contrasting shaded bands indicate the various social systems – formal and informal – which might play important roles in the child's or the families' lives – remembering, of course, that in the case of particular services these would sometimes be represented by a number of people. We cannot, of course, tell from such charts which person or practitioner or set of practitioners might have any emotional significance for the child in terms of attachment. But what the charts do show are *potential* points of discontinuity, particularly at the stages when the child is removed from or leaves the birth family or a foster home and when the adoption placement begins. These are obviously critical points of maximum change/transition when potentially key aspects of the social structures surrounding the child are in a state of flux.

---

[5] Dartington Social Research Unit and Department of Health (1995), and Parker *et al* (1991) at p. 89.

Chart 1

The child adopted out of care: continuities and discontinuities

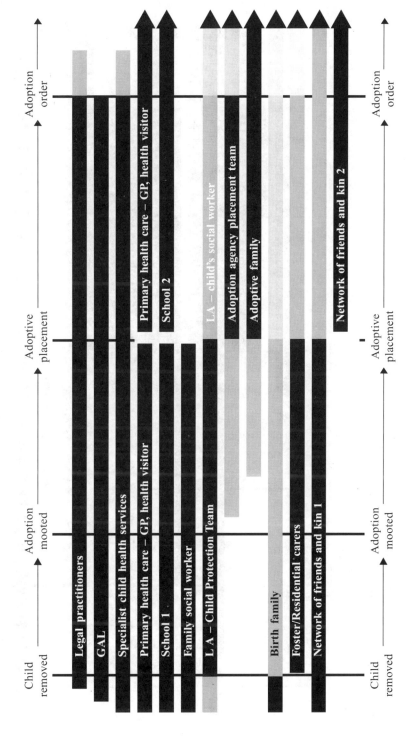

Chart 2
Adoptive families: continuities and discontinuities

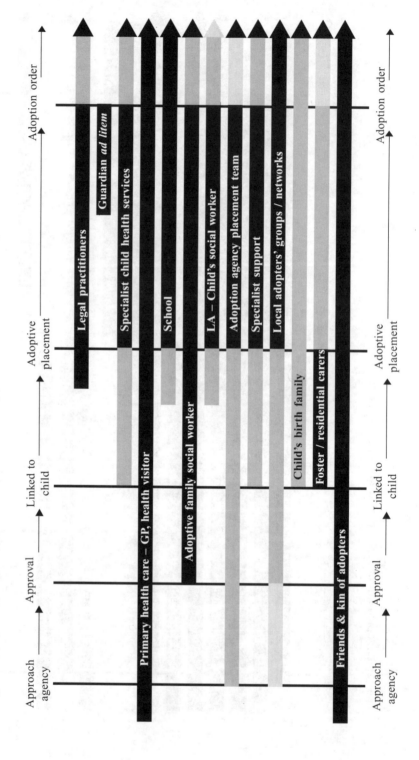

Chart 3
Temporary foster families: continuities and discontinuities

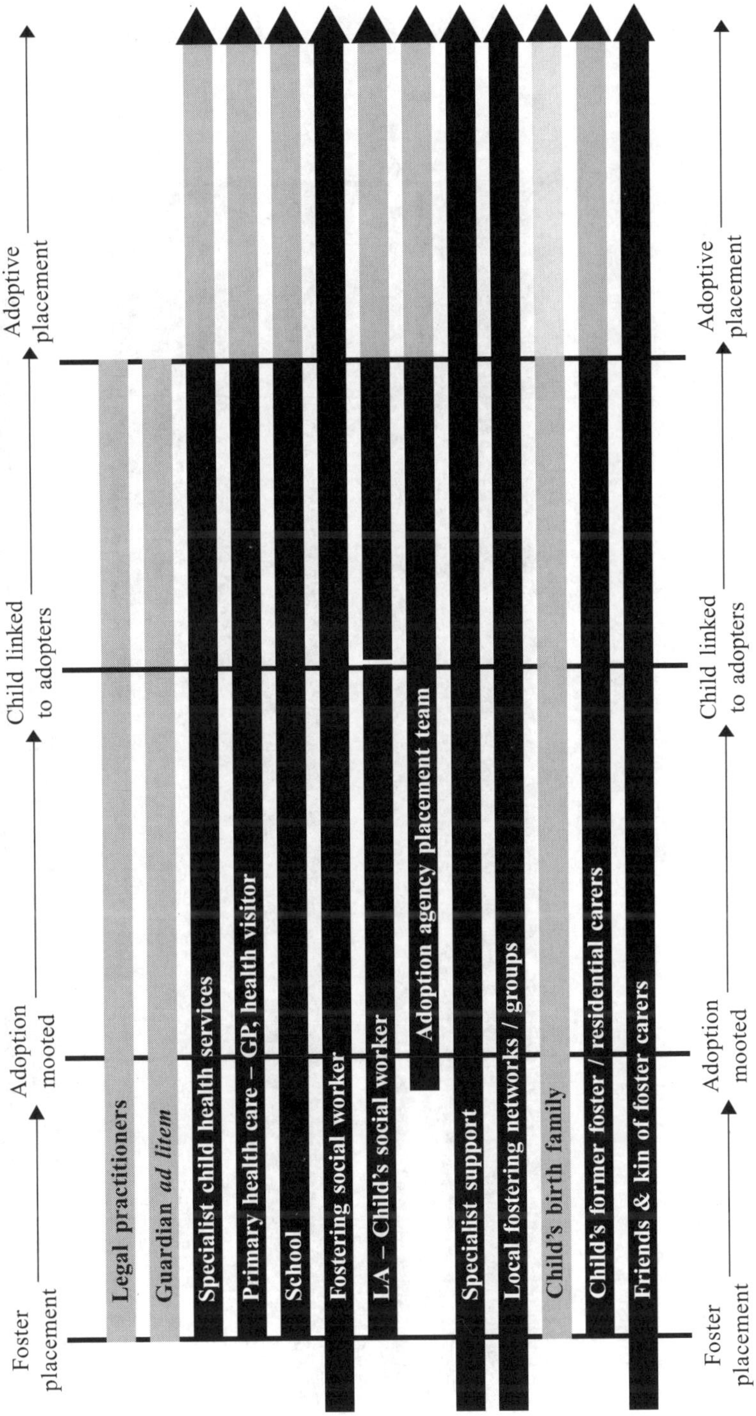

Foster placement — Adoption mooted — Child linked to adopters — Adoptive placement

Legal practitioners
Guardian *ad litem*
Specialist child health services
Primary health care – GP, health visitor
School
Fostering social worker
LA – Child's social worker
Adoption agency placement team
Specialist support
Local fostering networks / groups
Child's birth family
Child's former foster / residential carers
Friends & kin of foster carers

Chart 4
Birth families: continuities and discontinuities

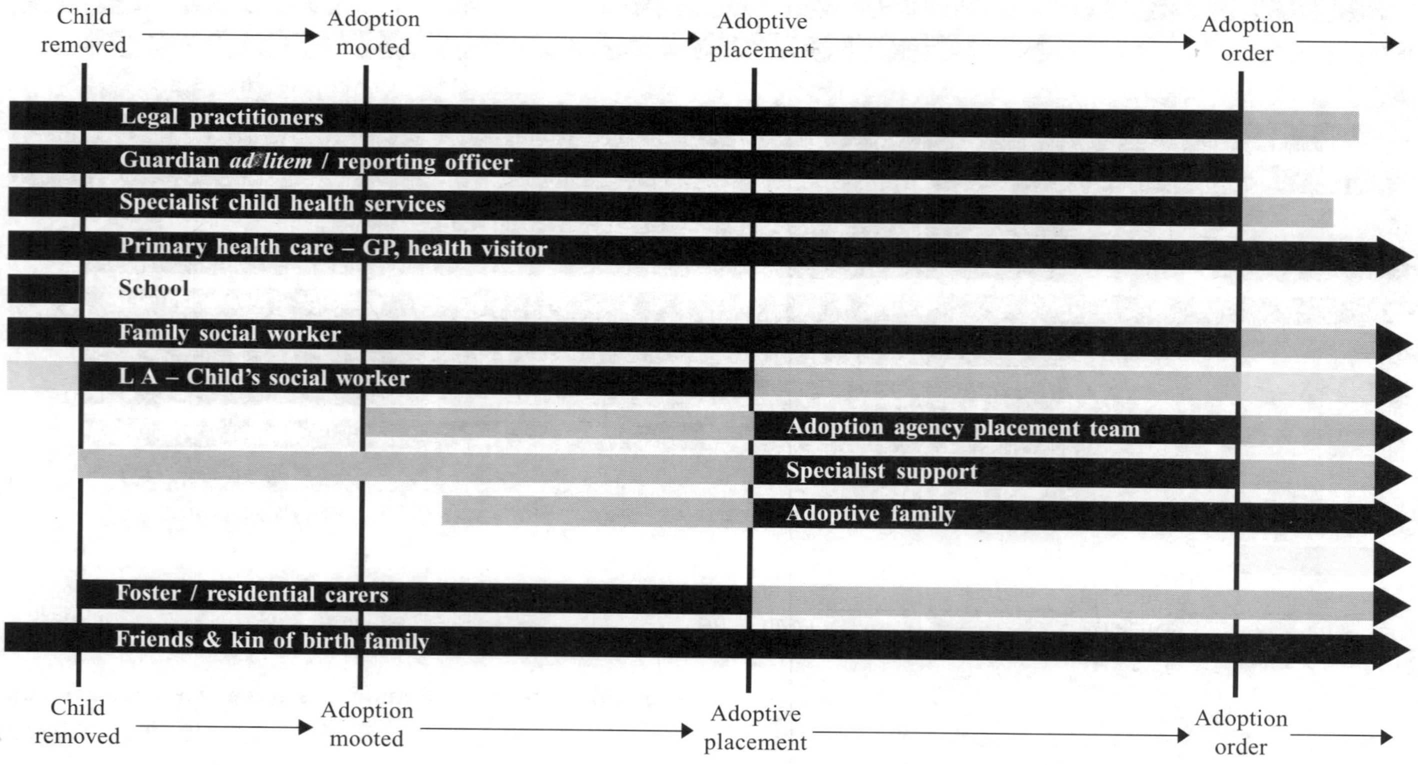

We would argue from a mental health point of view that these are the periods of maximum vulnerability where it is most likely to be necessary to have in place strong bridging mechanisms to support the child and the families. For these one looks particularly to supports provided by the statutory and voluntary adoption agencies and to the points where children and adopters may experience a change of social worker. In general the following arrangements are made:

2.1   Change of social workers

Until the time of linking, prospective adopters would see their own social worker. He or she will have assessed them and prepared the Form F and may have kept in touch with them from time to time during the waiting period post approval/pre linking. Once they are linked with a child, the prospective adoptive parents will also see the child's social worker. If the child is fostered they may also see the foster carers' link worker, particularly when they attend the matching meetings. During the introductions their own adoption social worker will offer them support, but they will also continue to see the child's social worker. After placement they may still see their own adoption social worker, though this will depend upon the degree of support the adoption agency is able to offer and on what the adopters themselves require. They will also continue to see the child's social worker who would be obliged to visit them to conduct reviews up to the time of the order. He or she may also continue any unfinished life story work post placement – another reason for visits from the child's social worker. If the adopters get on well with the child's social worker they may turn to him or her for help and support more than to their own social worker once the link has been made. If they do not, then they may be more reluctant to contact the child's social worker and would be more likely to ask their own for help. In this sense the child would then have to get used to yet another social worker.

There could be a change of social worker both for the adopters and the child at any time during this process. One reason would be that the social worker changes his or her place of employment or has leave or something of that nature; occurrences which, we will see, may leave the adoptive family feeling unsupported.

If the child is placed in a different locality from the one in which he or she is looked after, visits by the child's social worker may be few and far between from the time of placement up to the order. It could be that the local authority looking after the child will arrange for a social worker from the local authority in which the child now resides or from a voluntary adoption agency in that area, to visit the child and offer what help and support might be required in which case an inter-agency fee would be involved. After the order, support may be offered by the local authority in which the child now resides, or by the agency (either statutory or voluntary) which assessed the adopters, but this may well depend on whether or not there is a post-adoption service and on cost. The adopters' social worker may also offer help and support to the child.

We will give further consideration in our conclusion[6] 'to the significance, as we see it, of these structural changes in the provision of adoption services in the light of our research findings. Suffice here to say that we suspect they can represent in certain respects a worrying mismatch between administrative and organisational convenience on the one hand and appreciation of accepted tenets of good child care and mental health theory on the other.

---

[6] Chapter 20, *Policy and Practice Implications*, para 3.3

5 Support Systems

1 The concept of support

1.1 Introduction

The core goal of adoption has to be the promotion of secure attachments for the children. Kramer (1996) put the matter in a nutshell:

> *For humans, the important thing about good care-giving is that it is done by somebody who not only protects you from harm, but keeps you in mind and thinks about you quite a lot of the time, even when you are not there [. . .] A secure attachment is like an invisible elastic which can stretch and contract depending on your need for protection. So when you are ill or in pain, tired or afraid you move towards the person with whom you feel secure and when all is well you can move away to explore the world around you [. . .] The psychological health that results from such security means, amongst other things, being more competent in your own point of view and more curious about the world around you, including other people's point of view. (p. 14)*

The point about elastic is that it is fairly difficult to break. The great merit of adoption for older children who have been in care is that adopters are able to offer a degree of sustained individualised long-term care and protection which other forms of care (residential care and short-term fostering, etc.) generally cannot. Almost by definition the alternatives to adoption have discontinuities of care built into them.

1.2 Supporting the child

Security is not an easily achievable state for older children being adopted out of care. At least in the early stages of adoption most are likely to be what are sometimes termed "anxiously attached" – clinging to the care-giver in case he or she withdraws, gets ill or even disappears as possibly previous care-givers will have done. The danger here is that in Kramer's terms the elastic becomes very tight so that development becomes inhibited. Alternatively, if the parent is rejecting and no bond is established or if the bond, as Kramer puts it, 'loses its elasticity altogether', the child might well 'float freely apparently without needs, street-wise and self-reliant but actually desperate to be looked after'.

So when we use the notion of "support" in the context of older adopted children it is vital to be clear what we are thinking about. First and foremost it is about the capacity of the adopters (fathers as well as mothers) to give long-term support to sustain the child long-term through the development of a secure relationship which provides attentive but not over-protective care: a relationship which develops the right degree of elasticity.

1.3   Supporting the child's supporters

Since it is such a challenging task to embark on an adoptive relationship with an older child who may well have experienced a long and difficult time through the care and family justice systems following the breakdown of the birth family's capacity to provide secure nurturing, the adopters will, unless they are unusually secure and confident in their parenting skills, need encouragement and reliable support themselves. So the second sense in which we use the notion of support is in terms of support for the primary supporters for the child – the adopters.

This concept of "support for the supporters" is not dependent on notions derived from attachment theory, though in our view it also involves a quality of sustained service upon which adopters should be able to rely – just as the child should be able to rely confidently on the support of the adopters.[1]

2   The notion of an adoption support system

Potentially, adopters should be able to draw support and encouragement from a range of sources to help them deal successfully with the challenges and strains implicit in the adoption of older children. A range of high stress crises studies (Caplan, 1974; Caplan and Caplan, 1988 and 1993) have demonstrated the crucial importance of the stress-buffering effect of reliable, informal support networks such as provided "naturally" by friends, family and neighbours, etc.[2]

But notions about family support are easily romanticised. Janet Finch's seminal study, *Family Obligations and Social Change* (1989) points out the many conceptual pitfalls in any attempt to understand support between kin. For example, in a particular instance of support it can be difficult to determine whether it depends on "duty", "responsibility" or "obligation", themselves notions that can be subtly different. She writes:

> *I have been implying that duty, responsibility and obligation are "things" which may account for support between kin. But what kind of things are they?*

---

[1] See Chapter 20, *Policy and Practice Implications.*

[2] Although as far as we are aware none of Caplan's *Families in Crisis* studies refer specifically to adoptive families, this should not negate the general applicability of his work to this field.

Are they feelings or emotions like anger or happiness? Are they intellectual ideas which any of us are free to accept or reject? Or are they based on moral obligations which run counter to feelings and emotions? In public they tend to be treated as a mixture of moral values and "natural feelings" sometimes implying that they are based on biological impulse.

Finch alerts us to the importance of the social construction of the notions of social support and obligation. The sense of obligation does not develop in a vacuum. Culture, tradition, the role of the state and government social policies all play their part in shaping people's definitions of family responsibility. Thus in thinking about the promotion of support services in adoption one cannot be morally or politically neutral. Social policies aimed at supporting the adoptive family in effect mean that this particular type of household and mode of child care are being encouraged by the State. So when we come to consider the question whether practices and policies should be developed which "support the supporters" we are, in effect, making a value-laden statement that has a political dimension. This can be seen for example in the way the Department of Health wanted us to evaluate the hypothesis that:

> . . . *if the costs to the local authority are less if a child is adopted out of care than if he or she remains in care or has to be re-admitted to care it is important to discover what kinds of services make a difference in enabling the adoption to be successfully sustained.*

As the recent ADSS/NCH Report, *Children Still in Need* (1996), put it:

> *It seems clear, given resource constraints, that arguments in favour of family support (i.e. from State funds) will need to be supported by robust evidence of effectiveness if new investment is to be justified.* (p. 15)

Part II

RESEARCH FINDINGS – PROCESS

6 Introduction to Research Findings: Agency and Family Profiles

1 Introduction

By way of introduction to our overall findings we present a short profile of the agencies and families that responded to our questionnaire.

2 The agency profile

This section will describe some broad characteristics of the agencies responding to the agency postal survey. The figure below shows the regional makeup of the questionnaire response sample.

Figure 1

The region of agencies returning a questionnaire

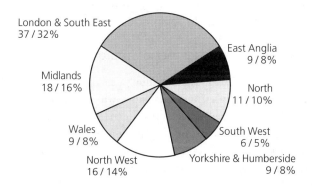

London & South East
37 / 32%

East Anglia
9 / 8%

Midlands
18 / 16%

North
11 / 10%

Wales
9 / 8%

South West
6 / 5%

North West
16 / 14%

Yorkshire & Humberside
9 / 8%

Source: Agency postal survey

2.1 Adoption statistics

It will be recalled[1] that of the 160 agencies that operated when we sent out our questionnaire in the autumn of 1994, we received replies from 115, comprising 85 statutory agencies and 30 voluntary agencies.

---

[1] See Chapter 1, *Introduction*, at para 3.1.

Agencies were asked whether they compiled statistics for their adoption work. Although all the responding voluntary agencies said that they did, only 92 per cent (77 out of 84) of the statutory agencies could positively say that they did. In addition, 4 per cent said they did not while the rest either said that they did not collect them on a systematic basis or did not do so regularly or that the departmental statistics were not specific to adoption;[2] 3 per cent did not compile adoption statistics at all.

The 111 agencies which kept statistics of some kind were asked what was the most recent year for which they were available and how they defined "year" for this purpose. Overall just over half (53 per cent) said 1994 was their most recent year but 43 per cent said 1993 and 3 per cent, 1992.

The majority (71 per cent) defined "year" for these purposes as the financial year but 25 per cent defined it as the calendar year with 5 per cent defining it in some other way.[3]

The absence (surely a depressing finding in itself) and variation of the statistics kept of course prevents us from making definitive statements about the general pattern of agency adoption work and indeed we have to caution the reader that the following overall profile is based on *each* responding agency's last "year" of statistics. Nevertheless, with all its imperfections, the ensuing profile provides an insight into the adoption work of agencies on a national basis and at the same time provides a useful comparator for our family profile. It should also be said that the following profile is of *all* adoption agency work, that is, it is not confined to children aged five or more, as is the focus of our research project.

2.2   Agency workload: the number of approved adopters[4]

In terms of approved families it was apparent that the scale of operation among agencies varied tremendously. Three agencies (two statutory and one voluntary) said that they had not approved any family in the last full year of their records while, at the other end of the scale, one statutory agency approved 67 families in a single year. The mean average was 20 in the case of statutory agencies and 14 in the case of voluntary agencies. A more detailed breakdown of the figures is given in Table 1 below.

---

[2] These calculations are based on responses from 84 of the 85 statutory agencies – one agency did not answer the question.

[3] E.g. six months or for even shorter periods – one statutory agency did not answer this question.

[4] For a more detailed analysis see Chapter 17, *Agency Workloads*, para 4.

Table 1

Number of adoptive families approved by each adoption agency

	Statutory agencies		*Voluntary agencies*		*Total agencies*	
0–9	20	26%	12	43%	32	30%
10–19	24	31%	10	36%	34	32%
20–29	14	18%	4	14%	18	17%
30–39	11	14%	1	4%	12	11%
40–49	5	6%	0	0%	5	5%
50–59	2	3%	0	0%	2	2%
60–69	1	1%	1	4%	2	2%
(N agencies providing data)	77		28		105	

Source: Agency postal survey

2.3   Profile of the approved adopters

In total, the agencies replying to us approved 1,932 families (comprising 1,539 by statutory agencies and 393 by voluntary agencies). Out of this overall sample (which, as we have cautioned, is based on each agency's latest year of statistics) less than 10 per cent (180 families) were black, Asian or of mixed heritage. Although 120 of such families were approved by statutory agencies as opposed to 60 by voluntary agencies, *proportionally* the latter approve more minority ethnic families than the former, 15 per cent as opposed to 8 per cent.[5]

Thirty-six agencies (just under one third of those replying) comprising 26 statutory and 10 voluntary agencies said that they had not approved a minority ethnic family in the last year. At the other extreme one agency (a voluntary agency in the Midlands) approved 10 such families. More commonly agencies approved one or two. Put another way about two-thirds of adoption agencies approved at least one minority ethnic family.

Among those approved for adoption were 96 single parents (that is, those living without a partner or spouse) which amounted to 5 per cent of the total.[6] Although this figure seemed surprisingly high, in fact, as we shall see, 9 per cent of our family sample comprised a single adult. Forty-four agencies (30 statutory and 14 voluntary) did not approve any single adult but that still left a majority (71 agencies – 62 per cent) that had.

A total of three gay/lesbian adopters were approved, all by statutory agencies.

---

[5] These calculations are based on responses from 99 agencies (72 statutory and 27 voluntary).

[6] These percentages are based on data provided by 99 agencies (73 statutory and 26 voluntary).

2.4   Agency workload: The number of children "approved" for adoption[7]

As with approved families, there were wide variations among the agencies in the number of children "approved"[8] for adoption by adoption panels. Only one agency (a voluntary one) said that their panel had not approved a single child for adoption in the last full year of their records. At the other end of the scale, one agency (a statutory agency) "approved" 91 children. In fact 10 statutory agencies "approved" 50 or more children. All voluntary agencies placed less than 30 children for adoption, except one which placed 40. The mean average was 26 in the case of statutory agencies and 13 in the case of voluntary agencies. A more detailed breakdown of the figures is given in Table 2 below.

Table 2

Number of children approved for adoption by statutory and voluntary agencies

	Statutory agencies		Voluntary agencies		Total agencies	
0–9 children	16	20%	12	43%	28	26%
10–19 children	20	25%	11	39%	31	29%
20–29 children	17	22%	4	14%	21	19%
30–39 children	14	18%	0	0%	15	14%
40 or more children	12	15%	1	4%	12	11%
(N agencies providing data) 79			28		107	

Source: Agency postal survey

2.5   Profile of the "approved" children[9]

In total, the agencies replying to us approved 2,396 children (comprising 2,036 by statutory agencies and 360 by voluntary agencies). Of those children approved by statutory agencies, 75 per cent had previously been the subject of care orders, while 25 per cent had previously been accommodated by the local authority.[10] The comparable proportion for voluntary agencies was 84 per cent of children who had previously been in statutory care and 16 per cent in accommodation. A breakdown

---

[7] For further analysis see Chapter 17, *Agency Workloads*, para 3.

[8] In the case of statutory agencies "approved" means approved for adoption by an adoption panel in their agency. In the case of voluntary agencies "approved" refers to children who were placed for adoption or who were found adoptive placements.

[9] For further analysis see Chapter 17, *Agency Workloads*, para 3.

[10] These percentages are based on a total of 1,424 children (1,071 in care and 353 in accommodation) since agencies failed to provide the legal status of 703 (612 by statutories and 91 by voluntaries).

of the statistics relating to children approved for adoption by statutory agencies by type of agency (viz. shire county, London borough and district borough) is shown in Figure 2 below.

Figure 2

Number of children approved for adoption by statutory agencies: comparing types of statutory agencies

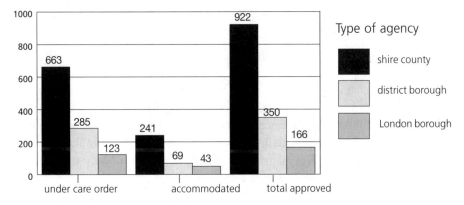

Source: Agency postal survey

2.6   Profile of children placed for adoption[11]

In addition to statistics on children *approved* for adoption in their most recent year for which statistics were available, we also asked agencies to provide information about the looked after children they *placed* for adoption. Of the 1,557 children who were placed, we received information about the ages of 1,525. Of this number, 41 per cent of children placed by statutory agencies were aged five or more; 11 per cent of the total number of children placed were aged 10 or above. In the case of voluntary agencies, half (50 per cent) were aged five or more, and 9 per cent of all children placed were aged 10 or above.

The overwhelming majority of the children placed for adoption were white (1,330) which constituted 87 per cent of those placed by statutory agencies, 79 per cent in the case of voluntary agencies. For children aged five or above the respective percentages of white children were 85 per cent in the case of statutory agencies and 92 per cent for voluntary agencies. Most of the 227 minority ethnic children were children of mixed heritage (60 per cent). This figure was 57 per cent for statutory agencies and 64 per cent for voluntaries; 21 per cent of the minority ethnic children placed by statutories and 11 per cent of those placed by voluntaries were black; 13

---

[11] For further analysis see Chapter 17, *Agency Workloads*, para 5.

per cent of minority ethnic children placed by statutories and 23 per cent placed by voluntaries were Asian. The remaining 16 children were children of other ethnic origins (e.g. Chinese).

Most of the children placed for adoption (63 per cent) were placed individually, 65 per cent in the case of statutory agencies, 57 per cent in the case of voluntaries.[12] However, 24 per cent were placed in sibling groups of two in the case of statutory agencies, 29 per cent in the case of voluntaries, while 12 per cent were placed in sibling groups of three or more in the case of statutory agencies, 14 per cent in the case of voluntary agencies.

2.7   Disruptions[13]

Although it is not possible to give a reliable overall "disruption rate" as by no means all agencies responded to our questionnaire enquires on this subject, nor in any event did the disrupted placements solely relate to adoption placements in the latest year, nevertheless some useful information can be gained by our returns. First, the returns do provide evidence that disruptions are less likely to occur in placements by voluntary agencies than with statutory agencies.[14]

Of the 138 disrupted cases reported to us (each of which occurred in each responding agency's last year of statistics) we can say that, in the case of statutory placements, half (50 per cent) occurred in the 5–9 age group, 24 per cent in the 10+ age group and 26 per cent in 0–4 age group. In the case of voluntary agencies, 45 per cent of the disruptions occurred in the 5–9 age group, 55 per cent in the 10+ age group and none in the 0–4 age group.[15]

So far as disruption by ethnicity is concerned, in the case of statutory agencies, 8 per cent of the 138 disruptions involved children of mixed heritage, 7 per cent black children and 5 per cent Asian children. However, given the small numbers of minority ethnic children placed for adoption these figures mask a higher "disruption rate" than for white children.[16]

So far as the *stage* at which disruption occurs is concerned, the overwhelming

---

[12] These figures are based on data provided for 1,353 of the 1,557 children placed for adoption (1,127 placed by statutory agencies and 226 placed by voluntaries).

[13] For further analysis see Chapter 12, *Disruptions*.

[14] Based on returns by 29 of the 30 responding voluntary agencies, there were only 11 disruptions notified compared with 127 recorded by 77 out of the 85 responding statutory agencies. Assuming all these disruptions related to the same year as the placement, a very crude overall "disruption rate" might be calculated to be 10 per cent in the case of statutory agencies, compared with 4 per cent in the case of voluntary agencies. In the case of children aged 5–9, the "disruption rate" is 17 per cent (statutory), and 5 per cent (voluntary), and for children aged 10 or over, the respective "rates" are 22 per cent (statutory) and 25 per cent (voluntary).

[15] The age of the child when the placement disrupted (when they were removed from the family).

[16] Of the 138 disrupted cases, 20 per cent involved minority ethnic children, whereas only 13 per cent (statutory) and 21 per cent (voluntary) of our overall agency sample of adoptive placements involved minority ethnic children.

majority, 94 per cent in the case of statutory agencies and 80 per cent in the case of voluntaries, occur during placement (i.e. before the order), with a further 3 per cent in the case of statutories and 7 per cent in the case of voluntaries in the year following the order and a further 3 per cent (statutories) and 13 per cent (voluntaries) more than one year after the order.[17]

3   The family profile

·This section will describe some broad characteristics of the families responding to the family postal survey.

3.1   About the sample

Two hundred and twenty-six families completed our questionnaire – 71 per cent (160 families) had children placed with them by statutory agencies, 29 per cent (66 families) by voluntary agencies. The regional breakdown of the sample is shown in Figure 3 below.

Figure 3
Regional makeup of the adoptive family study sample: those who responded to the postal survey

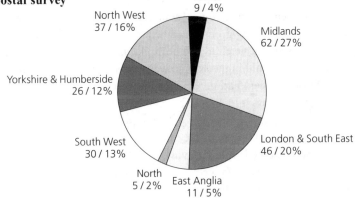

Source: Family postal survey

At the time of completing the questionnaire, in about two-thirds of the sample (67 per cent – 148 families) the adoption order had already been made. In a further

---

[17] We only know the *stage* of disruption for 130 of the 138 reported disruptions. The percentages are based on the former figure. It should be noted that this figure relates to all disrupted cases in our sample, *regardless* of age.

16 per cent (35 families) an application to adopt had been made but the hearing was still pending; 8 per cent (16 families) had not yet made the application. In 6 per cent of the sample (13 families) the child was no longer living with the family, that is, the placement had disrupted, and in a further 1 per cent (three families) it had been decided not to proceed with the adoption but to foster instead.[18] One family was "unsure" about their current position in the adoption process.

Interestingly, in those cases where the adoption order had already been made, in 47 per cent of the sample[19] the birth parent had not agreed to the adoption, though in only 21 per cent of cases[20] had the birth parent actively contested the adoption application.

3.2   About the adopters

Commonly, in fact in 91 per cent of the sample, the adoptive family comprised two (married) adults but in 9 per cent (19 families) the adopter was single.[21] They were overwhelming white with only 9 families (4 per cent) where one or both of the parents were of black or minority ethnic origins.

Two hundred and twenty-one families provided data about the number of adoptive children in the family. Nearly half (48 per cent) had just the one adopted child but a third (33 per cent) had adopted two children; 12 per cent, three children, with a further 6 per cent having adopted more than three children. Two families had adopted six children. Of course, many of these families were "serial adopters" adopting unrelated children at various times, sometimes through different agencies. However, many represented sibling group placements. In 75 (34 per cent) of the 218 families providing data, the sample child had been placed with one or more siblings (see Table 3). In one case, a child in the sample was placed in a sibling group of six. Fifty-two per cent (144 families) had no children of their own but 16 per cent (35 families) had one birth or step-child and 22 per cent (48 families) had two or more such children. One family had five of their own children.[22]

It would, however, be misleading to deduce from these figures that most families only had the one or more adopted children living with them. In fact, quite strikingly, nearly half (48 per cent) also had one or more foster children living with them. In this regard it was more common for families approved by statutory agencies to have foster children living with them – 55 per cent of such cases – than with those whose

---

[18] We had this information for 222 of the 226 families. Percentages are based on the lower base figure.

[19] Based on 142 replies.

[20] Based on 124 replies. This lower rate of actively contested court hearings is in line with our findings in *Freeing for Adoption Provisions* (Lowe *et al*, 1993, para 3.2.4).

[21] Parents were asked: 'Do you consider your current family situation to be a) a one parent family or b) a two parent family?' 221 families answered this question.

[22] Based on the data provided by 221 families.

child had been placed by a voluntary agency – 30 per cent of such cases.

Overall, just over half (54 per cent – 119 families) had non-adopted children living with them and a distinct minority, 18 per cent of the sample (40 families), only had one adopted child and no other children living with them.[23]

Table 3

Whether the adoptive child in the sample was placed individually or with siblings

	Statutory families		*Voluntary families*		*Total families*	
Child placed individually	111	73%	32	49%	143	66%
Child placed in sib group of 2	36	24%	21	32%	57	26%
Child placed in sib group of 3	4	3%	10	15%	14	6%
Child placed in sib group of 4	2	1%	0	0%	2	1%
Child placed in sib group of 5	0	0%	1	2%	1	0%
Child placed in sib group of 6	0	0%	1	2%	1	0%
(N families providing data)	153		65		218	

Source: Family postal survey

3.3   About the children

Families were asked to provide information about the child who was placed with them for adoption between 1992 and 1994 (in the sample of sibling groups, the sample child was the oldest sibling).

Two hundred and nineteen families provided data about the sex of their case child. Just over half the children (58 per cent) placed for adoption were male and 42 per cent female. The overwhelming majority (94 per cent) of the children were white (that figure was the same for those children placed by statutory and voluntary agencies), 4 per cent were of mixed heritage, 2 per cent black and there was one Asian child. Some of these children were placed transracially: two black children and four of mixed heritage were placed with a white couple. Two white children

---

[23] Though there were some who had a sibling group of children placed with them for adoption and who had no other children living in the household. Whereas 100 (70 per cent) families who had individual children placed with them had other children in the family, only 34 (45 per cent) families who were adopting sibling groups had other children. Of course, "other children" could include children in the family who were also adopted, or who were fostered, or birth/step children to the adopters. Fewer adoptive families of sibling groups had children in all of these categories, but especially in relation to birth and step-children. Whereas 61 per cent of people adopting an individual child had at least one birth/step child, the figure was only 40 per cent for families adopting a sibling group.

were placed in a household comprising one white and one black adult, while another white child was placed in a household comprising one white adult and one of mixed parentage. Two children of mixed parentage were placed in a household comprising one white adult and one of mixed parentage.[24]

Two hundred and nine families indicated their child's date of birth. From this information, we can say that 12 per cent (79 children) were aged 6–9 years, 50 per cent (105 children) were aged 10–14, and 38 per cent (25 children) were aged 15 or over by the time the postal survey was complete.[25]

Forty-three per cent of the sample children being adopted were reported to have "special needs". In the questionnaire, families were asked to indicate which, if any, special needs the case child had. The results of this question are shown in Table 4 below.

Table 4

'Case children' who were reported to have special needs

	Statutory families		*Voluntary families*		*Total families*		*Valid cases*
Physical special needs	7	5%	2	3%	9	4%	220
Health special needs[26]	12	8%	1	2%	13	6%	220
Learning special needs	45	29%	21	32%	66	30%	220
Behavioural special needs	43	28%	12	18%	55	25%	221
Emotional special needs	42	27%	16	24%	58	26%	221
Other special needs	1	1%	1	1%	2	1%	219

Source: Family postal survey

Nearly one-third of children in the sample (30 per cent) had learning difficulties of some kind, and a quarter had emotional special needs and behavioural problems. Some children had a combination of several types of special need.

4   Profile of the families in the interview sample

This section describes some broad characteristics of the families in the interview sample.[27]

---

[24] Figures about the ethnicity of children are based on data provided by 207 families on their case child.

[25] The closing date for the questionnaire – December 1995

[26] E.g. chronic illness or medical condition

[27] Although these data are largely based on the questionnaire that the family completed, it was possible to obtain further information, for example, about the adopters' current and former marital status, though this was less systematically recorded.

4.1   The sample

A total of 48 families were interviewed, 38 (79 per cent) were approved by statutory agencies and 10 (21 per cent) by voluntary agencies. Of these, 31 (65 per cent) were same agency placements and 13 (35 per cent) were inter-agency placements[28] (10 of which were placements by voluntary agencies and three by statutory agencies).

The interview sample did not attempt to be geographically representative but, on the basis of cost and convenience, had a South and West focus. However, to include a sample of minority ethnic families and of disruptions, families had to be selected from further afield. Figure 4 shows the resulting geographical profile of the family interview sample.

Figure 4

Regional makeup of family interview study sample: Number of interviews completed in each region

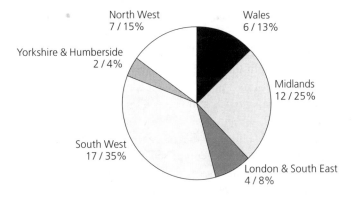

Source: Family interviews

The interview sample comprised 33 families (69 per cent) in which the adoption order had already been made, five families (10 per cent) where an application to adopt had been made, three families (6 per cent) where no such application had been made and a further three families (6 per cent) where the placement had disrupted.[29] In addition in one case the family had decided not to adopt but to foster the child instead.[30]

---

[28] This information was not available for four families, all of whom were statutory placements.

[29] In the questionnaire sample of 226 families, there were 13 disruptions (see para 3.1 above) but of these only six were willing to be interviewed. We subsequently learned that a further two placements had disrupted by the time the interview had taken place, making a total of five disrupted cases in the interview sample.

[30] Three other families ticked "other", "unsure" or left the question blank.

Of the 33 "post adoption order" families, agreement was said to have been refused in 15 cases (31 per cent of the sample) and in seven cases (15 per cent of the sample) the birth parent(s) had actively opposed the adoption in court. Of the 15 "pre order" families, parental agreement was said to have been refused in 6 cases (13 per cent of the overall sample). In total, therefore, parental agreement to the adoption was said to have been withheld in 21 (44 per cent) of our interview sample families.

Of the 48 families interviewed, seven were minority ethnic families (that is, where either the child or an adoptive parent had minority ethnic origins). Of these, four were "same race" placements in that one or both adopters were of the same ethnic background as the child. The remaining three families were transracial placements where the parents were white and the children were of mixed heritage.

4.2   About the adopters

Of the 48 families interviewed, the overwhelming majority of adopters (92 per cent, 44 families) were white. Although in their questionnaire return five of the 48 (10 per cent) families classified themselves as "single parent families" it was apparent from the interviews that the parents' status was rather more complicated than this bare statistic might suggest. We discovered that 79 per cent (38 families) were married applicants with a further 8 per cent (four families) being *cohabitants*.[31] Of the remaining 13 per cent (six families), five comprised a single adult, all of whom were divorcees and one who was still married but was applying for adoption as the sole applicant.

It is also of interest to note that of the 38 married couples, an appreciable proportion, 29 per cent (11 couples), comprised at least one partner who had previously been married to someone else.[32]

According to their questionnaire returns, 20 families (43 per cent)[33] had only one adopted child living with them, 15 (32 per cent) had two and 12 (26 per cent) had three or more adopted children. From our interviews we found that 13 families had adopted children previously. A number of placements were of sibling groups: in 11 families (24 per cent)[34] the child had been placed in a sibling group of two while in two families the placement was of sibling groups of three, and in a further two, the placement was of a sibling group of four.

---

[31] Under English law only married applicants can apply for a joint adoption, Adoption Act 1976, s14, so that in the case of cohabitants only one of them can apply to adopt, though it is possible for a joint residence order to be made as well, see *Re AB* (*Adoption: Joint Residence*) [1996] 1 FLR 27.

[32] As we discuss in Chapter 8, *Starting the Adoption Process*, at 2.1, the inability to have children in the second marriage is not infrequently a reason for seeking adoption.

[33] This proportion is based on a sample of 47 as one family did not complete personal data.

[34] This proportion is based on a sample of 46 as the data from two families were missing from the questionnaire returns.

According to their questionnaire returns, 21 families (45 per cent) said that they had no birth or step-children but from our interviews it appeared that 26 families (54 per cent) had had no children of their own. It was also clear from the interviews that not all birth or stepchildren were still living at home. In some cases the children had grown up and left home while in others they were living with a previous partner.

Although 43 families (90 per cent) said in their questionnaire that they had no foster children living with them, it was apparent from the interviews that rather more had had some experience of fostering. In fact 11 families (23 per cent) in the sample had either current or past experience of fostering.[35] All of these families had been approved by statutory agencies representing 29 per cent of that sample.

For 16 families (33 per cent) of the sample, the adopted child or children was their first experience of bringing up children[36] but when analysed according to whether they were approved by statutory or voluntary agencies, we found that in the former, only 25 per cent had had no previous experience compared with 62 per cent in the latter.[37]

4.3 About the children

Of the 48 sample children, 29 (60 per cent) were male and 19 (40 per cent) were female. The vast majority, 41 (85 per cent), were white.[38] Of the seven minority ethnic children, three (each of mixed heritage) had been placed transracially with white adopters. The remaining four children were in "same race" placements in that at least one of the adopters was of the same ethnic background.

Nine children (19 per cent) of our sample were aged 13 or above when placed for adoption, 17 (35 per cent) were aged 9–12 when placed, and 16 (33 per cent) were aged 5–8 when placed. The remaining six (13 per cent) sample children were aged 0–4 when placed with their current family (initially on a fostering basis) but were aged five or over when the placement became one for adoption.

Nearly half the sample, 23 children (48 per cent), had at least one type of special need: 17 (35 per cent) had special educational needs or learning difficulties; similarly, 17 (35 per cent) had special emotional needs; 16 (33 per cent) had behavioural needs, while five (10 per cent) had special health needs and two (4 per cent) had special physical needs.

---

[35] This was rather less than in the family sample as a whole, see ante at para 3.2.

[36] This was rather more than in the family sample, see ante at para 3.2

[37] This is explored further in Chapter 8, *Starting the Adoption Process*, at para 3 .

[38] It will be recalled, see para 4.1 above, that the sample was specially chosen to include minority ethnic families.

5   Summary

5.1   Agency profile

Approved adopters

- Not all agencies keep statistics.
- Statutory agencies on average approved 20 families per year; voluntary agencies 14.
- Overall, agencies replying approved 1,932 families (1,539 by statutories; 393 by voluntaries).
- Less than 10 per cent (180 families) were of minority ethnic origin.
- 5 per cent (96 families) were single.

Approved children

- Overall, agencies approved 2,396 (2,036 by statutories; 360 by voluntaries) children (of all ages).
- On average statutory agencies approved 26 children per year; voluntaries 13.
- Most "approved" children had previously been in care (1,296 as opposed to 397 being accommodated).

Placed children

- 41 per cent of children placed by statutories were aged 5+ and 11 per cent were 10+. For voluntaries it was 50 per cent and 9 per cent.
- Overall 87 per cent (statutories) and 79 per cent (voluntaries) of placed children were white.
- In the case of those aged 5+, the respective figures were 85 per cent and 92 per cent.
- 65 per cent of children placed by statutory agencies were placed individually, 57 per cent in the case of voluntaries.

5.2   Family profile

Some characteristics of adoptive families

- 67 per cent adoption order made.
- 16 per cent adoption pending.
- 8 per cent no application made yet.
- 6 per cent had disrupted by the time the family received the questionnaire (more had disrupted by the time families were interviewed).
- 37 per cent of families were approved by agencies other than the LA looking after the case child they were adopting (inter-agency placements).

About the adults

- 91 per cent were two-parent families, and 9 per cent were single-parent families.
- 48 per cent had adopted just one child.
- 33 per cent had adopted two children.
- 52 per cent had no children of their own but 48 per cent had one or more foster children.
- Only 19 per cent had no other children but the one sample adopted child living with them.
- 96 per cent of the adopters were white.

About the children

- 58 per cent of the children were male, 42 per cent female.
- 94 per cent of the children were white.
- 12 per cent of the children were aged 5–9, 50 per cent aged 10–14, and 38 per cent aged 14 or over.
- 30 per cent of the children were thought to have special learning needs, 26 per cent emotional special needs.

7   Changing Attitudes to Adoption

1   Introduction

Development of adoption support services is closely bound up with the way people view the institution of adoption, how they define it, and how they explain it. Accordingly, in our interviews we were keen to record and describe both the adoptive parents' and practitioners' views about adoption and to see whether there appeared to be major differences between them. As it was important to avoid imposing our own definitions, it was vital that we did not ask leading questions which might suggest a desired or expected type of answer and this was one of the reasons why our interviews were based on relatively open checklists of questions designed to allow respondents considerable freedom to explain their thinking in their own way. This is not, therefore, a chapter where we are able to present quantifiable data. Rather, we have used our judgment to select qualitative data to illustrate the main emerging themes.[1]

As previously explained,[2] there appear to us to be broadly two fundamental and related paradigms of adoption. First, the gift/donation versus the contract for service model and second, the exclusive/inclusive model of adoption.[3] We thought it likely that the gift/donation model would be used more in respect of traditional "closed" or exclusive baby adoption while the contract for service view would apply mostly to the adoption of older children particularly in respect of "open" or "inclusive" adoptions where there would probably be important issues of contact, the provision of information, and the arrangement of various kinds of support provision. In general terms this has proved to be the case although we have to say, rather against ourselves, that relatively few adoptive parents or practitioners in this study actually use imagery that relate to what we have termed the "gift" model.

One reason for this is that practitioners believe that their agency policies and practices are increasingly based on the open/inclusive paradigm which is seen as being the one which is normally in the best interests of the child. Indeed, we have some practitioner evidence which suggests that unless prospective adopters accept

---

[1] Because the interviews were tape-recorded and fully transcribed, we have been able to analyse the transcripts carefully and to frame and code them in order to do this.

[2] See Chapter 3, *Social Construction of Adoption*, at para 3.2.

[3] See also Lowe (1997).

the notion of open adoption they will not now be selected – and this is not just in relation to the adoption of older children out of care. For these reasons, those adoptive parents whose attitudes to or mindset about adoption are still largely based on a traditional/exclusive/closed view of the adoptive relationship are likely to be under-represented in our sample.

2   Parental attitudes

2.1   Exclusive adoption

Notwithstanding our foregoing observations, there were some adopters who seemed opposed to open adoption in any form, even if they qualified their attitude as being determined by the particular circumstances of the child's experience with the birth parents. For example, the adoptive mother of a boy aged six, whose birth father had killed his birth mother, resented the agency's suggestion that he should have contact with his birth father. She told us:

> I don't feel that it is in his interest to see his father four times a year. He's a child. I'm trying to get him on a so-called normal track and to bring him up to be a normal, healthy human being. And given the interference of his father four times a year it would be impossible to achieve this. John didn't want it. John didn't need it so I said 'no' to it. John's father, as he is now, is out of prison. Supposing he marries a very saintly, wonderful woman. I don't have the confidence in social services not to return John to him because they kept reminding me at the time that the current laws have changed and that birth parents now have more rights to see their children regardless of what they do. I wanted John adopted for his security.

Likewise, the adoptive father of a girl aged eight (who had been ill-treated both by her birth parents and again, subsequently, by her foster carer while in care) took the view that the birth parent should not have contact. He told us:

> To me those parents have no rights whatsoever. You can't treat a child like she was treated from a very young age and then think that when they get older these things are forgiven and forgotten, that anyone can say, 'There, there, shall we bring this child round to see you next Sunday to tea?' You know to me, the two things [i.e. contact and adoption] are mutually exclusive. Maybe I'm old-fashioned but that is how I see it.

Fear that birth parents would in some way threaten the security of the adoptive parent–child relationship seems, as one would expect, to be a most powerful factor contributing to an exclusive view of adoption. As one adoptive father put it:

> *If you take on an adoptive role, I see no reason why one should go through a lot of difficulties to absorb [contact]. As a member of the family, and that's what they are after all, to have someone to step in when they are 16 and disruptive to say, 'Thank you very much for doing a good job which I didn't do and now I'll see if I can persuade this child to come back to me.' I would resent that.*

Indeed he and his wife questioned the whole rationale for contact and whether it really is helpful to a child's development especially as the child has to hold in mind and understand so many relationships. They thought this was burdensome to children. But this father also told us that when he had expressed these views to adoption agency staff at the preparation stage, he was told that his views were "old fashioned" and unacceptable in the light of the agency's policy on open adoption and supporting contact. He had therefore, in his words, to "soft pedal" and keep his mouth shut. In fact this adoptive family does accept letter box contact with a great aunt in her 80s and with their adoptive daughter's half brother.

2.2   Inclusive adoption

Most of our adoptive parent material relating to the inclusive view of adoption concerns various forms of contact with members of the birth family and will be considered separately in Chapter 15. Here it is sufficient to illustrate attitudes of mind which these parents typically hold, remembering that they have been specifically selected to adopt an older child out of care where the agency assumption would almost certainly be that the adoptive parents have to accept the idea of open adoption and a degree of contact in some form. One adoptive mother of African-Caribbean origin, divorced with two older children and who was adopting a nine-year-old boy of mixed parentage who had three half brothers living with adoptive parents elsewhere, acknowledged her initial feelings of wanting an exclusive relationship. She told us:

> *There was part of me that just wanted to have nothing to do with anybody in his family . . . but I was aware that that's quite selfish. It was selfish and you have to come to terms with it. You can't do that. I had no right to do that to him. He's got other people in his life. It's like me cutting him off from anybody else. That would be wrong. So you have to come to terms with it. I actually like his father who we are meeting again tomorrow. So we just get on with it.*

Another couple who had had no children before adopting two girls aged seven and five seemed well able to accept the idea of their younger adoptive daughter wanting to maintain some contact with her birth mother. This adoptive mother took the view that:

If I was a child I would want to have control. I would want to have contact (with birth parents) even if I didn't want to live with them. I'd still want to know about them; to have information about them. I can't think of any reason why my kids shouldn't have it. I never feel bad if they want to talk about their mother. I never feel as though they are getting at me.

Another adoptive mother of a nine-year-old girl thought that as she and her husband had two children of their own (now aged 17 and 16) they could 'afford emotionally to be less possessive' than they might otherwise have been. But from what she told us she was not a possessive type in any case, remarking:

I've never felt we own our own children. We don't, do we? They are people. They want to get up and go and you want them to have the internal resources to do so.

This mother had encouraged the girl to make contact with her birth mother before the adoption took place because, although she was reported as having abused the child, her daughter (unlike her siblings) had not rejected her. Moreover, the adoptive mother herself thought it had been helpful to have had contact with the birth mother, since she consequently felt able to talk openly with her adoptive daughter about the birth family.

The continuing influence of birth family attitudes

There are also the attitudes of birth parents and their relatives to consider. We have received a number of indications from the evidence of agency social workers[4] that birth family attitudes can be a potent influence on the way the adoption of older children is defined, shaped and managed – particularly where there is a degree of ongoing contact. One voluntary agency social worker told us:

Birth family members generally, of course, are dealt with through the local authority social worker and in the early days they can be fraught. In the vast majority of cases it appears to be fraught. The longer we have experience of this (reference to "open" adoption) the more we recognise that some birth families are not able to accept what adoption is. So although they say they understand and agree with adoption and with contact on a couple of times a year or whatever it is – in fact they cannot change their views about the status of the child in their family. They want to treat the child as though they are still members of their birth families – which, of course, to a degree they are – but they do not understand the degree. So there is a tremendous conflict of interest here where the birth family is saying to the children, 'Oh you must

---

[4] As we explained in Chapter 1, *Introduction*, para 4, constraints of time and resources prevented us from acquiring first hand evidence of birth parents' attitudes.

> *come to Aunt so and so's wedding, would you like to be a bridesmaid'? And the adopters are sitting there thinking 'this cannot happen' and that sort of thing causes enormous difficulties.*

2.3 Implications for support

Although the inclusive/open and exclusive/closed models of adoption appear to form a conceptual continuum with people taking up attitudes at various points along it, these appear to be the two dominant models. Importantly, given the subject of our research, they seem to influence how people view the issue of adoption support. The nub of the matter was well put to us by a practitioner who said:

> *I think the difficulty we've got with post-adoption support is that a lot of what we think about it depends on where you are in the spectrum about open or closed adoption. If you believe in closed adoption you actually think that we support people to go off out on their own, sort themselves out and don't come back to us (in the agency) and that's it. If, on the other hand, you believe that children have continuing needs in relation to their birth parents, even if you might have very strict rules about letting them contact them and have information about them, if that's best for the child . . . then there's going to be more need for social work support because it's very difficult for most adoptive parents to take responsibility for all that on their own.*

It is clear from our practitioner interviews that virtually all agencies now favour a degree of open/inclusive adoption with respect to birth families in most if not all cases although, as the above comment indicates, individual practitioners may vary according to how much importance or emphasis they put on it when dealing with adoptive parents. For some, images of traditional adoption, still symbolised by some court and legal practice, now run counter to what they see as the modern "psychological" approach to open/inclusive adoption and set up mixed messages in people's minds. As one put it, 'On the one hand, we are saying to people, "as a result of this court order you are this child's parents as if these children had been born to you". On the other hand, we are saying, "but we are expecting you to do so and so about contact".' This practitioner thought that prevailing thinking does not sufficiently acknowledge the potential contradictions in the two positions.

3 Changing professional attitudes

Many of the more experienced practitioners told us how much they thought professional attitudes, policies and practices had changed in recent years towards the inclusive/open model. Here are a few typical comments:

The numbers of placements that involve contact now are a very high proportion – other than babies, and even then most baby placements involve letter box contact. But with older children, a lot of them have contact with somebody, whether a former carer or a sibling or a birth parent. It's a minority that continue face-to-face contact with birth parents but that figure too is probably growing. Whereas five years ago it wouldn't have been.

I can remember in my earlier days in adoption thinking this contact thing was a huge issue that had to be got across somehow. That's changed . . . Adopters are much more aware now that adoption . . . can have contact going along with it. It isn't the sort of closed thing that it once was. Even five years ago adopters would come wanting babies and wanting no contact. I think we just don't get these people any more because obviously people know that it doesn't happen.

The whole issue of contact, letter boxes, post-adoption work and that sort of thing has just come into our practice. It is now a standard feature of our assessment. There is a line in our agreement with prospective adopters which says, 'Mr and Mrs Smith would be very happy for you to exchange information' [reference to letter box contact scheme]. That's just par for the course now. In fact, if Mr and Mrs Smith weren't happy with that then we would wonder whether we should be approving them as adopters. It just shows how things are growing and developing.

This last point was echoed by another comment:

Our agency has a policy of only recruiting prospective adopters who under-stand what openness means and are prepared to actively work within it.

4   Other people's attitudes to adoption

Within the family it isn't just the adoptive parents' attitudes about adoption that matter. The child's views and understanding are, of course, crucial and we shall report on these in our *Adopted Children Speaking* report (Thomas *et al*, 1999). But it has also been made clear to us that the attitudes of other relatives can impact on the adoptive household – both positively and negatively – and affect the degree of kinship support available to the adoptive family. For example, one adoptive mother told us how upset she had been when her mother turned to the nine-year-old adoptive son:

. . . and said, 'I'm not your Granny'. Well John [son] doesn't need that. It wouldn't have hurt her to have accepted him. She has a great many grand-children, I know, but that is not the point. As far as I am concerned , he is my

> *son and her grandson whether she likes it or not. I found that very hard and*
> *I still do.*

The grandmother's attitude also affected this adoptive mother's relationship with her sister.

> *I used to be quite close to my sister who lived not far away and John used to*
> *play quite a lot with her son. Well, I've stopped that because John would go*
> *up there and it would be, 'Look what Granny's given me and Granny's taken*
> *me out, and Granny's done this'. Well, I'm not having John treated like that*
> *by anybody – whether it's my sister, my nephews or my Mother. I don't care*
> *who it is. He's not second best. He's as good as anybody else. So I don't let*
> *John go up there any more.*

Some adopters who thought their extended family generally supportive nevertheless told us that the knowledge that they were adopting an older child rather than a baby was sometimes met with incomprehension. Because the idea was so unfamiliar to the relatives, they felt that somehow their own relationship with them had been altered, even distanced. For example, one mother who had adopted two half-sisters aged eight and ten described the relative's reaction as being:

> *At first when we told them they said, 'Adoption's great, wonderful, little*
> *babies!' And you say 'No, two older ones' . . . and they go, 'You can't possibly*
> *know what you're doing.' And there was more that wasn't said. I think a lot of*
> *it is that they can't possibly consider it themselves . . . And then when you've*
> *done it they treat you like some super parent, like you've done something*
> *marvellous and wonderful. And, of course, to us it doesn't feel like that at all*
> *– it's just very normal to us. So it's weird, very odd with them now.*

Confirmation that the adoption of older children is often difficult for relatives and friends to understand or accept came from some of the practitioner interviews. One told us how, in her experience, this often emerges when the adoptive parents turn to their relatives for support when difficulties with the child are first encountered. This social worker ran a support group for adoptive parents and said:

> *It's very common to find the attitude, 'you went out and did this and now you*
> *can't cope with it'. It's like 'you've made your bed and now you must lie on it'*
> *sort of attitude. In the group a lot of them with older children are not*
> *supported by their families. They'd be supported with a baby but with an older*
> *child the attitude is 'you must be mad'.*

Another social worker told us how an adoptive mother of an older child had recently told him:

> *You lose some friends – rather you find who your friends really are when you*
> *take on these children. Lots of people don't want to know you. They don't want*

the child in the house. But you build up a new network of friends, you make
contact with people who have had similar experiences.

4.1   The 'blood tie' – a problem with relatives and others

As one would expect, a number of adopters had relatives with strong, some would
say primitive and irrational, views about the importance of the so-called blood tie.
Sometimes we were told they thought that a child had only been accepted by
grandparents because there were no other grandchildren or because, as in one
instance, the adoptive father's mother had remarried and there were no children of
that relationship. One adopter said of her husband's relatives:

> *It worked out very well because [my husband] has got a step-father and my*
> *in-laws haven't got any children of their own because they married each other*
> *later in life. They feel more that [our adopted son] is their grandchild because*
> *he is not a blood relative of her son's. They feel that he is a grandchild of both*
> *of them rather than his or hers.*

In contrast some adoptive parents came to accept that in the child's eyes they may
be seen as "second best" because they are not "blood" birth parents. An adoptive
mother of the boy whose father had murdered his mother told us:

> *He has this love/hate relationship with me and I think he always will, to be*
> *honest. I'll always be second best to him. If you are an adoptive parent you*
> *have to accept that. But it was hard because he needed so much and came to*
> *me for so much comfort and we would go through these horrific times with*
> *his screaming, 'Why, why did Dad do it?' [reference to birth father murdering*
> *birth mother].*

Unhelpful attitudes about the "blood tie" are also encountered by adoptive parents
in relation to potentially supportive services such as medical practitioners and
school teachers. One mother who had three birth children and who had adopted four
siblings told us how the school doctor had told the adopted children how "lucky"
they were to have been "taken in" and how the doctor had asked her, 'Which ones
are really yours?' She added, 'Nothing puts you off people more, I feel, than when
they make that sort of remark'.

4.2   Teasing at school

Some adopters told us how sometimes their children were teased by other children
at school about being adopted.[5] For example, one said of her ten-year-old son:

---

[5] In fact, according to our related *Adopted Children Speaking* study, over a third described themselves as
being bullied at school – see Thomas *et al* (1999), and Chapter 11, *Post Placement Issues*, para 3.2.

He used to get teased at school. He still does. People say to him, 'You haven't got a proper Mum and Dad'. I say to him, 'I'm not your first Mum, you were not born to me, you know that'. But what does a proper Mum and Dad give that we don't give him?

In the case of Mitch aged eight, who was hyperactive, the adopters told us that at the time of his placement, there were no other adopted or foster children in the small rural primary school and it seems he did experience some teasing before the adoption order because he did not share his new parents' surname. Following the intervention of the social worker, the school teachers were reported as having talked to the other children about adoption and how 'Mitch was coming to live with a new mummy and daddy'. The adoptive mother told us:

We said when he went to school, 'What do you want to be called? Do you want to be called Mitch E or Mitch T'? At first he said, 'Mitch E' and I said, 'You might like to think about that because a lot of the other children have the same last name as their Mums and Dads'. Later he thought about that and said, 'I want to be Mitch T' and he's called himself that ever since.

5   The implications for support service provision

It is clear from the selection of comments referred to in this chapter, that both the adopters and their children can find themselves grappling with powerful, confusing and sometimes conflicting attitudes to adoption both within themselves and within their social networks. Some of these views have to do with the processes by which an adopted child does or does not achieve acceptance by or membership of the adopters' wider family. Non acceptance by the adopters' own parents or their siblings can be emotionally painful and have profound and possibly long-term implications for the family support which they might otherwise have expected to receive.

All this points to a need for practitioners to explore these issues when placements and matching are being considered – not just with the adopters but arguably with other key relatives as well in the wider family network.

It is also clear that negative, unsupportive attitudes which adopted children can encounter when going to new schools need to be considered. It may not always be good practice to leave the management of entry to school simply to the adoptive parents.[6] In particular, there are occasions when teachers need to be alert to the possibility of teasing by other children (a matter to which we will return in more detail in Chapter 11 and in *Adopted Children Speaking* (Thomas *et al*, 1999). Maybe from an educational policy point of view more attention needs to be given to

---

[6] See also Chapter 11, *Post Placement Issues,* para 3. Also, Chapter 20, *Policy and Practice Implcations,* para 3.5.

the way all school children are able to understand and accept the wide diversity of family forms and organisation of which adoption and fostering are a small but not insignificant part.

We would suggest that our material points to the importance of considering those crucial processes of social definition which occur most acutely at critical points of transition such as placement, entry to school, the making of the order, etc. These are the periods when both child and adopters need to form and have reinforced positive new identities and social roles. They are the periods when their self-image can be acutely vulnerable to negative stigmatising – particularly from relatives and friends but also from other key persons in this wider social network such as doctors, school teachers, and, of course, those most closely associated with the adoption process itself, not least the previous foster carers.

8 Starting the Adoption Process

1   Introduction

In this chapter we are concerned with the beginning of the adoption process and the implications for support at the critical point of entry into the system. Drawing mainly on our agency and family interview data we explore such issues as: what makes people want to adopt older children; what experience do would-be adopters already have of bringing up children; how do individuals go about seeking agency approval and how, on the other hand, do agencies generally recruit would-be adopters. We also discuss the issue of rejected applicants as potential adopters and enquire into, for example, the frequency and reasons for agencies' withholding of approval and asking what support, if any, is given to those so rejected.

As will be seen, none of these issues are straightforward and indeed some are confusing but matters are undoubtedly complicated by the twin dichotomies of those (principally foster carers) who are seeking to adopt children they already know as opposed to those seeking to adopt a child that they do not know, and between those who are already experienced parents and those who have no such experience at all.

2   Motivation to adopt older children

Quite what makes people want to adopt older children seems a relatively unresearched question[1] and we did not initially set out to discover the reasons.[2] Nevertheless, this issue was touched upon in our 48 interviews with adopters from which sample it is apparent that the motivation to adopt can be quite varied and certainly not confined to the stereotypical image of a childless couple wanting to satisfy their urge/need to have children. In fact, in nearly half (46 per cent) of our interview sample, one or both of the adopters had children of their own and in just

---

[1] Cf Brebner *et al* (1985) and Houghton and Houghton (1984).
[2] We did not, for example, ask about this in our family questionnaire.

over a quarter (27 per cent) of our sample families those children were still living with the adopters.[3]

In this section we discuss first, why our sample of adopters sought to adopt at all and then, why they sought the adoption of older children.

2.1   Why adopt at all?

Although no doubt the motivation to adopt is ultimately quite complex and not always confined to a single reason nor indeed shared by each partner,[4] we found that in our sample those seeking to adopt could broadly be classified into those who did so because of infertility; those who did so for other reasons, as for example, professionals who had worked with children; and those who came to adopt via fostering or who were adopting for a second time (though this of course begs the question of why the adopter fostered or previously adopted in the first place). Another complication is that the immediate trigger point for applying to adopt, such as encouragement from other family members and friends, may have nothing to do with the underlying reason for applying. Furthermore, we found some evidence that some adopters came from a family with a history of adoption or fostering – in other words where looking after other people's children was something they were already used to.

Whatever the reason, it should also be said that in some cases the desire to adopt can be extraordinarily strong. For example, one adoptive mother, who had already had children of her own, told us:

> *It was always in the back of my mind as something I had to do and [husband] was putting up with this. I don't think he's felt the same compulsion that I've felt, but I've felt a compulsion to do this. And it was one that had been important to me. I did not want to be on my death bed not having done this.*

Another mother (who also had children of her own) explained:

> *I used to know a girl at school and she was adopted and I'll never forget the day she told me on the way home from school that her mother said, 'Would you like to know who your parents are? And would you like to meet them?' I was just so fascinated by that. It always stuck in my mind.*

Infertility

It was not an intention of this research to study infertility. However, with an estimated rate of one in six heterosexual couples experiencing reproduction problems,[5] in our

---

[3] Cf the family postal questionnaire sample in which 48 per cent of families said that they had natural children living with them, see Chapter 6, *Agency and Family Profile*, at para 3.2. For further analysis of adopters' experience of bringing up children see para 3 below.

[4] As one adoptive mother told us: 'I do it for selfish reasons. My husband does it for social reasons.'

[5] Clubb and Knight (1997).

attempt to establish the motivation of parents to adopt we inevitably came across those (both black/minority ethnic and white respondents) who had fertility problems, and who pursued adoption as a means to overcome childlessness.

The medical definition of infertility refers to an inability to conceive after a period of trying of up to a year or more (Woollett, 1991; Clubb and Knight, 1997). Both men and women can experience reproductive problems.

We did interview couples (including one cohabiting couple) who conformed to the stereotypical image of those seeking to adopt after unsuccessfully trying to have children of their own (including, for example, two cases where the couple had unsuccessfully undergone IVF treatment[6]). In one case, we interviewed a woman whose inability to have children contributed to her divorce but who then turned to adoption as a single person. However, we also found that quite a common reason for seeking adoption was the inability to have *further* children, rather than to have *any* children. For example, one couple had had one child but they then sought to adopt because the mother could not have more. More common were couples (five in all, representing 10 per cent of the interview sample) who, having remarried, then found themselves too old to have children together and so sought to adopt.[7]

For some of our interviewees, and this was true of both sexes, the experience of having reproductive problems was a key factor in their initial exploration of adoption. As one mother told us:

> *When we first moved here we saw something on the 'telly' – 'Find a Family'. We could never have children, we tried and tried (and it was me – not my husband). We decided, right, we'll try them and see. So we phoned them up and (to cut a long story short) Social Services got in touch with us.*

Yet, as two parents described, adoption was a consideration early in their marriages and was thought of as a way to start a family before any attempt at conception and the discovery of reproductive problems.

Whether it relates to male or female infertility, reproductive problems are wide-ranging. In our study it was not always clear why adoptive parents could not have children. However, we learned from a few that they had endometriosis,[8] or a low sperm count, or recurrent miscarriage.

It might be added that it should not be assumed that a childless couple seeking to adopt cannot have their own children. One couple we interviewed had positively decided that they did not want children of their own, and indeed were initially turned down as potential adopters on this very ground.

---

[6] In one case the couple had made 17 unsuccessful attempts, see below.

[7] In one of these cases both the husband and wife had had children in their previous marriage.

[8] Endometriosis is defined as 'Growth of endometrial tissue in areas other than the uterus, for example, the fallopian tubes or the ovaries', which may cause fertility problems (Clubb and Knight, 1997 p. 180).

Some psychological effects of infertility

Whatever the age a person is when he or she learns that they have reproductive problems,[9] the experience of personal and relationship crises are common, as evidenced in symptoms of anxiety and self-deprecation including a sense of failure. Medical investigation and treatment of reproductive problems, where they are pursued, are intrusive both physically and emotionally, and can consume a person's whole life especially when repeated attempts to have children are made. One adoptive mother decided not to have treatment for her infertility while another couple mentioned having up to 17 attempts at IVF before giving up. One couple, having been advised by the agency that they could not continue with IVF treatment and the adoption application,[10] found themselves in a difficult dilemma. As they explained, with medical advancement there is always hope that any attempt might bring success and to give up trying in order to adopt a child was an enormous decision to make (the agency having made it clear that they could not consider the couple for adoption while they continued IVF treatment). It involved eliminating an option and placing a great degree of hope in adoption which, with its rigorous assessment procedure, had no guarantee of success.

> We could understand their [agency] point of view to a certain extent but from our side of the fence it's a little bit like you can't have a light at both ends of the tunnel. You've got to shut one of them off before you go for the other one. There's going to come a point, if you carry on with the IVF, we'll be too old maybe to go for adoption. And if we go for the adoption and for whatever reason we don't get approved, then it might be too late to go back to IVF so that's the difficulty.

The assessment process

For many, going through the preparatory stages of adoption procedure can feel like an intrusion into their personal life. Some adopters mentioned that the questions asked were often deeply personal, as though no stone was left unturned in the agency's determination to find out about them. Those with infertility problems may experience more intrusive scrutiny of their personal life and motivation to adopt than most. For example, an adoptive mother of African origin with infertility problems found the early stages of her enquiry and preparation a difficult process to go through. The depth of the investigation into what she considered to be her personal life was upsetting and made her have second thoughts about going ahead with adoption. However, she continued because she grew to respect the open and

---

[9] In our sample we know of at least one child with future problems.

[10] Apparently, the reason for this condition was that if the mother became pregnant she would probably not pursue the adoption which, from the agency's point of view, would have wasted all their preparation and training given to that couple.

honest approach of the agency worker carrying out the assessment. She also said that by placing herself in the agency's and birth parents' position, she could understand both the aim of such thorough investigations and their necessity to place children in appropriate and stable family homes.

Dealing with other people's views

One adopter explained that when she was being assessed there was an inflexible text book application of the emotions and reactions (i.e. of grief and loss) involved in being infertile.

> *I kept getting all this stuff about 'Have you grieved?' I said, 'No, but it's not a problem for me'. In the end, I said, 'Yes, absolutely, because it must be a problem for me because you keep telling me'. This is such a big thing.*

Dragging up the past

Even after approval, adopters may face further scrutiny of their infertility. One mother, who had IVF treatment before exploring adoption, said that when she and her husband were considered for a sibling group of two children, their infertility problems were raised again, but this time by three social workers who were new to them. As she explained:

> *To have your past dragged up – not that there's a lot to drag up – but they kept going on about my IVF treatment and the five attempts that I'd had and everything else. That seemed more important than these two children that we were considering.*

The logic of repetition in this case and by more than one person is not clear and perhaps could have been avoided.

One adoptive couple, who also mentioned having to contend with the assessment of their personal life, talked about the difficulty of having to go through it all again when the longed-for placement of two sibling boys disrupted and was investigated.[11] They went through a re-awakening of emotions and a sense of failure. As the father said, 'It's quite painful to think that we're going to achieve nothing'.

2.2 Support issues

Prospective adopters with infertility problems might feel, during the assessment phase, that their personal lives are under great scrutiny. Agencies could possibly alleviate or reduce parents' anxiety by explaining the reasons for the depth of their enquiry. When investigation of sensitive areas is repeated, then information about

---

[11] See Chapter 12, *Disruptions*.

why this is necessary and why more than one person may be involved may prove helpful to maintain the morale and confidence of prospective adopters.

We are not aware of research to indicate the chances of placement disruption in cases where an infertile individual or couple adopts a child. However, it may be safe to accept that issues about infertility might be triggered in the post-placement period especially when parents face challenges in the task of parenting. Therefore, just as care goes into screening and assessing whether prospective adopters have come to terms with their infertility and are committed to adoption, there also may be a need to examine how to support parents after a match has been made, when issues of infertility may arise unexpectedly. The provision of support, perhaps in the form of counselling, might help to sustain the placement and keep it from disrupting.

Altruism and other reasons to adopt

There were a number of cases in our sample where the motivation to adopt can best be described as altruistic[12] though altruism can also be mixed with a degree of self-interest. For example, as one adopter[13] told us:

> I didn't realise how many children there are that need help and I need to be needed. That's the truth of it. I need it as much as they do. I'm not nursing now. I miss it dreadfully. I've got to be of some use otherwise I can't see the point of being here.

In some of these types of cases, the motivation and opportunity to adopt arose domestically as, for example, in the case of a couple who already had children of their own and had had a lot to do with a child who had been fostered by the adoptive mother's mother. Having learned that social services were actively looking for adopters, they sought to adopt her themselves. In another case, the couple sought the adoption of two children whom they had previously known because their birth mother (who together with her common law husband, who was not the father, had been killed in a car accident) was the adoptive mother's cousin. In other cases, the interest in adoption stemmed from a professional involvement with children. One, a single woman, was a child care worker and 'obviously interested in children'; another had been running a youth training scheme and was therefore involved in working with teenagers who had problems; another had previously worked in a children's home and felt she wanted to give a home to an older child who had had to leave their birth family, and yet another (a divorcee adopting as a single parent and who had had children of her own) had been a senior clinical nurse specialist on a paediatric ward. The most unusual example, however, was a case where the

---

[12] "Altruism" is used here as a shorthand expression to refer to that spontaneous concern which many people seem to have when they encounter children in need, in this case, the need for a home; what James Boswell (1988) in his classic history study of mediaeval child care, termed 'The Kindness of Strangers'.

[13] This was the mother whose husband and she did not want children of their own.

95

adoptive father was the deputy head at a special school where three of the four siblings attended. The father had to give evidence in care proceedings concerning the mother as a result of which they were removed from the birth family. The couple had said that if that were to happen they would take in the children themselves. This is what indeed did happen and, although they originally intended only to look after the children temporarily, they eventually adopted all four children.

Foster carers

A significant proportion of the statutory agency-approved adopters[14] in our interview sample were experienced foster carers (i.e. 12 families, representing 34 per cent of the statutory agency approved adopters) or else had initially fostered the child or children in question (a further three families fell into this category). In these instances the motivation to adopt varied from those where the child was the key influence, to those where the foster carers themselves decided upon adoption, to those where the agency actively encouraged the foster carers to adopt and placed the children for adoption with them in the first place.

With regard to the first type of case, we came across one instance where, having lived with her foster carers since she was six months old, a girl, then aged eight, suddenly asked to be adopted. This request apparently followed her viewing of a television soap programme in which one of the main characters was being adopted. In another case, the foster carers of a boy originally placed with them when he was 11 months old, left it to the boy to decide whether he wanted to be adopted, which he did when he was 10 years old. In another case, after being fostered for two years and learning that their social worker was looking for a permanent home for them, two brothers asked to be adopted by the foster carers. Similarly, two sisters asked to be adopted by their *former* foster carers following disruptions of two adoption placements with someone else. In two other cases, the child made it clear at the outset of what the authorities had intended to be a foster placement, that they wanted to stay permanently with the foster carers.

In two cases where the foster carers took the initiative to adopt children they had previously been fostering, it was because they felt that the children were well settled and they did not want them to have any further moves. In two other cases, the foster carers applied to adopt when they learned the local authority plans were for the child to be adopted. In one of these cases the application was initially turned down, but when attempts to find an adoptive placement failed, the local authority then asked the foster carers if they were still interested in adopting, which they were.

Rather less usual is where the agency itself encouraged the foster carers to adopt but we came across two such instances where this happened. In one, the agency

[14] Cf voluntary agency approved adopters in which none were experienced foster carers although one child had initially been placed with the applicants as a foster child.

wanted the foster carers to adopt two half siblings whom they had been caring for for four years, during which time the foster carers seemed almost to "drift" into adoption. In the other, the initiative came from an adoption officer at a course on abused children which the foster father was attending.

In addition to the above cases, we came across those who were experienced foster carers and indeed those who had previously adopted, and who sought to adopt a child that they had not been previously looking after. In one case the agency effectively "head hunted" a previous adoptive couple to adopt a child with particular emotional needs and learning difficulties.

2.3 Why adopt older children?

Having explored why our sample of adopters sought to adopt at all, we now consider why they were motivated, or at least came, to adopt older children. In the case of those who adopted children they had previously fostered or those who they had known, the reason is self-evident and requires no further discussion. However, the motives of those who sought to apply to have a child (who was a complete stranger to them) placed with them for adoption can be elaborated further. In this respect our sample seemed broadly to be divided between those who from the outset definitely sought to adopt older children and those who knew or were told that only older children were available for adoption and who nevertheless either pursued or were persuaded to continue with the process.

Among those who definitely wanted to adopt an older child at the outset were those who had already had children of their own and wanted an adopted child to fit in with the age profile of their other children. One mother told us that having had the chance of having her own baby she and her husband did not want to deprive childless couples of adopting a baby given, as she put it, 'There's not many babies around'. Of two childless couples who wanted to adopt older children, one mentioned being able 'to get away without late nights and dirty nappies' while the other mentioned that her husband was not that interested in babies. Another couple, having had experience of working with older children, wanted specifically to help older children, while yet another mother 'just thought about older children'. One mother simply told us, 'I knew I just wanted to have a child in some way or form. I didn't want a baby and I just came to the point in my life where I had to do something about it.' In short, there were a variety of reasons behind those definitely wanting to adopt older children.

In contrast to those who definitely set out to adopt older children were those who were more ambivalent. A number accepted that because they themselves were "old" they could only adopt older children. Others, who having made the decision to adopt and then discovered that they were only likely to be able to adopt older children, then thought about it and eventually came to wanting to adopt older children. Some, however, were evidently more reluctant than others. One mother told us:

> *We didn't really have an input. It was just a question of going down the route of adoption and 'this is what you're suitable for'.*

Another mother similarly commented:

> *We didn't ever go into adopting really wanting to adopt an older child. In a way it was forced upon us because we wanted to adopt and that was the only option available to us.*

She added had they been able to afford it they would have chosen to adopt a Romanian baby.

It might be added that several adopters told us that the agency placed slightly older children than they had initially indicated wanting.

2.4   The significance of motivation

The foregoing discussion bears testimony to both the variety and complexity of the motives of those adopting older children. The significance of motive (and more research on this is needed) is twofold. First, it might help agencies better target their recruitment and advertisement policies. Second, it has been suggested to us (although we have no direct evidence) that where adoptive applicants are only pursuing the adoption of older children as an action of last resort, there may be more risk of the placement failing. As one statutory agency worker put it:

> *I don't think it's a good idea to give people something that isn't what they want. For an adoption to be successful everybody's needs have to be met. You can't just meet the child's needs, if the adults are not having their needs met.*

3   Adopters' previous experience of bringing up children

As mentioned in Chapter 6[15] it was only in a minority of cases (19 per cent of the 221 families responding to our postal questionnaire on this issue) that the adoptive family only had the one adopted child and no other children living with them. In other words the majority already had some experience of bringing up children. We were able to analyse this experience in more detail in our interview sample.

Amongst those in our interview sample approved by statutory agencies, only a minority (24 per cent) had had no other previous experience of bringing up children. This compared with 62 per cent of those approved by voluntary agencies. So far as those approved by statutory agencies were concerned, just over half (54 per cent) had had their own children, many of whom were still living at home (32 per cent of the overall sample).[16] In some cases (14 per cent of the sample), however, the child

---

[15] At para 3.2.

[16] Others had since grown up and had left home.

lived with a former partner and not with the adopters. Over a third (37 per cent) had already adopted another child and nearly a third (32 per cent), most of whom were experienced foster carers, had previously fostered.

In relation to those approved by voluntary agencies, the profile was a little different with just under a third (31 per cent) having had their own children (in half of these cases the children were living with the adopters and the other half with a former partner) and in one case (8 per cent of the sample) the adopters had previously adopted a child.

In summary, adopters varied from those who had never looked after children to those who had done so only to a limited extent and to those who were vastly experienced in looking after children. This considerable range of previous parental experience (or lack of it) has obvious implications for initial vetting, training and preparation of the potential adopters and for the eventual matching of children with the would-be adopters which we explore further in Chapters 9 and 10.

4   Taking the first steps

It is obviously a momentous decision for individuals to decide upon adoption.[17] One problem, for those who have no pre-existing connections with an adoption agency, is knowing how to start and who to contact.[18] We know from our previous ESRC study that individuals get to know who to contact in a variety of ways, for example, from family or friends, or from professionals, or from telephone directories. In this study, too, some adopters mentioned that they had used a telephone directory. As one mother told us:

> *I was sitting here one day and I thought I'm going to start the ball rolling. So I got the Thompson's or Yellow Pages out and spoke to a lovely chap at BAAF.*

Another not infrequent method of initial communication is by letter. It was also evident that a number had seen children in agency advertising material, the *Be My Parent* newspaper published by BAAF being most frequently mentioned. One father told us that, having been rejected by one agency for a particular child, they had been advised to carry on with other agencies. Accordingly, he obtained magazines like *Be My Parent* and made over 200 phone calls! Such extensive enquiries, however, do not seem to be usual. Indeed one adopter commented:

> *With hindsight I would advise people to go to different agencies to look at them all. To be quite honest I didn't know about anything else . . . Well I'd*

---

[17] As one voluntary agency worker put it, 'It's quite a big step to pick up the phone, particularly if they are people that have been through infertility'.

[18] This is not a problem for foster carers wishing to adopt since they already have connections with the local authority.

heard of Dr Barnardo's, but I didn't think about those things. I only knew about social services.

A number of agency workers to whom we spoke also mentioned telephone calls and letters as being the first point of contact. The standard procedure after the initial telephone call or letter was to send the enquirers an information pack sometimes together with a family details questionnaire. Some then left the initiative to the enquirer, but other agencies seemed to be more proactive in arranging a subsequent meeting.[19]

Clearly, these initial contact points are important both from the individual and agency points of view. We have no evidence to suggest that the first communication between individuals and agencies is not sensitively handled (though, as we shall see, adopters seem to pick up very quickly key messages about agency recruitment policy).[20] However, agencies would do well to consider whether what they do is enough to publicise their existence. Do they have appropriate entries in telephone directories and no doubt, in due course, should they be on a web site on the Internet? Do they leave leaflets in appropriate public places, for example, doctors' surgeries, churches, local community centres, etc.? In this respect, careful thought needs to be given as to how best agencies should advertise their existence to minority ethnic communities.

Another strategy adopted by some agencies is to run active recruitment campaigns, "advertising" particular children. Although we had some evidence that some adopters were inspired to apply to adopt particular children as a result, we also came across some ambivalence on agencies' part as to their value.[21]

5   Some background information about general agency policy on adoption of older children out of care

We had hoped to explore what makes agencies decide on adoption for a particular child but our data only permit us to make some brief comments, by way of background, as to general agency policy on the role of adoption for children being looked after by local authorities.

5.1   Changing agencies' perspectives

Adoption is not a static concept, rather it is an evolving and developing one. As we saw in Chapter 2, although an adoption order has always effected a legal transplant

---

[19] See further below at para 6.2.

[20] See below at para 6.1.

[21] See further below at 6.2. For children's, sometimes very striking, views of advertisements about themselves, see *Adopted Children Speaking*, Thomas *et al* (1999).

of a child from one family to another, the precise legal effects have changed and developed. The overall result is that now more emphasis is placed on the permanent nature of the order and less on the ending of the birth relationships. Similarly, as we discussed in Chapter 7, the public attitudes to adoption have also changed, particularly with regard to the ongoing contact with the birth family. Perhaps, not surprisingly, given this background, agency policies and attitudes to adoption have also changed and developed. For example, as one statutory agency worker commented:

We've been through the same sort of evolutionary process as every other agency in terms of having a lot of children drift in care and then getting very keen on adoption, but thinking that continuing contact was not compatible with that [and focusing instead] on helping the child to cope with the fact that they couldn't have contact, rather than asking what are this child's needs for contact in adoption, post adoption.

Now the thinking is:

Either you don't place children for adoption or you arrange your adoptions in a different way, in a more open way. That's the route that we are taking.

5.2   Adoption versus rehabilitation

It was apparent from our interviews that individual worker and agency enthusiasm for adoption varies considerably and there is evident uncertainty as to how it ties in with the perceived policy of the Children Act 1989 of keeping families together wherever possible, especially where the child is to have continuing contact with his or her birth family and continuing support from the agency. For some, adoption is clearly not a priority as the following two comments illustrate:

Our basic approach is that we should always be looking to the needs of the child within his or her own family. With most children who are in the public care system, adoption should not be looked at as a solution. It needs to be placed within a whole continuum of choices . . . adoption is on the menu but it's not a primary objective.

The system isn't perfect. It won't work every time. It has got flaws. It isn't the only answer to these situations which is once again why we tend to think as an agency in terms of keeping children in families and I think research is beginning to show that children who are placed within [their own] families as foster carers . . . are more successful than adoption placements or foster placements which are outside the family.

Indeed one voluntary agency worker expressed alarm at the trends and wondered whether adoption is 'slipping off the agenda in local authorities in terms of planning for families'. But a further point, which should not be forgotten, is that over-optimistic repeated attempts to rehabilitate children with their birth families may be emotionally disturbing for the child and weaken the child's capacity to successfully attach to future adopters.

5.3 Other dilemmas about the place of adoption in local authority child care practice

It may well be inevitable that the longer a child stays in a placement, the greater the chance of them forming an attachment to their carer. When this occurs and where attachment between the child and foster carer is mutual, agencies face the major dilemma of whether to leave or uproot a settled child. One view may be that if a child is happy and thriving, why separate him or her from the current carer? Indeed in the opinion of a clinician, uprooting a settled child will have a psychologically damaging effect on them. As one worker told us:

> It was the consultant who wrote a very strong letter to the Department saying that he felt this child ought to stay there [with foster carers] and that we were committing child abuse if this child was moved on because the child had bonded. In this case, when the child was placed, as a young baby, the parents were in their early 50s, and were really pressurised by the consultant and felt it was their fault that they weren't fighting for this child.

But what is the rationale behind decisions to place children for adoption if they already have a strong attachment to the foster carer? One social worker told us that regardless of the attachment formed, it is not always in the child's long-term interest for them to remain in foster care.

Even in an agency that was more clearly in favour of adoption there were still dilemmas. For example, as one worker explained:

> Contact and planning officers are quite often saying, 'I've got a real dilemma on this because, yes, we need a permanent placement, but they are going to need a lot of contingency help, and I don't know whether to go for adoption when we haven't got a well organised, properly funded post-adoption service'.

Another dilemma is the relationship between fostering, particularly long-term fostering, and adoption. One agency worker told us that their agency made no distinction between fostering and adoption for training purposes and 'instead of saying that we're looking for adoption or foster homes, we're talking about permanence'. Another worker said that their agency no longer drew a rigid distinction between short-term and long-term homes because 'that used to cause enormous problems when you did get a real bonding between the child and his or her carers'. It was evident from our interviews with adopters, however, that other agencies did make such distinctions and were against foster carers adopting. Furthermore, some of these agencies operated a policy of not returning children to the same foster carers if a trial placement elsewhere broke down.[22] Another agency worker commented that, 'temporary fostering, short-term fostering, whatever you want to call it is in essence, an insecure situation for children'. But, this worker continued:

> The problem is that it is not simple to change the placement without at the same time both raising expectations and increasing insecurities with the result that older children can be in so-called temporary foster care for considerable periods.

However, in a scenario where a child is black and the foster carer is white, agencies with an inflexible approach may need to address their "same race" policy, where one is in place, when looking at permanency. As one worker told us:

> There's a same race policy in [this Borough], which is perhaps politely 'being examined lately' by a number of different people in the Council and Social Services. That does impose on the social workers a responsibility to seek as near as possible, a permanent foster carer or adopter of the same race, religion and so on. That often is quite difficult and I think that has been a particular problem in that one of the perceptions is that too often children have been left that little bit longer because the suitable carer hasn't been found.

> Some historical placements where a child has been placed in an emergency – say a black child with a white carer – you can get the situation where that particular carer has become attached and will then want to adopt or permanently look after the child. That causes difficulties for all the parties in many cases. There have been a few of those which have been, I wouldn't say a cause célèbre, but they have certainly been ones which made people question the kind of blind following of a particular precept shall we say.

Given this uncertainty and sometimes ambivalence towards adoption it is hardly surprising that the level and commitment to supporting an adoption service should vary so much throughout the country.

---

[22] Agency policy concerning foster carers being adopters is further discussed at para 6.2 below.

6 Agency recruitment policy and practice

6.1 The adopters' experience

Eligibility

As intimated in our discussion of why people sought to adopt older children,[23] potential adopters very quickly get the message that there is little chance of adopting babies. Several adopters, and indeed agency workers, told us how that point is made immediately clear to those enquiring about adoption. One couple who 'were too old by the time we got around to start our own family' were told by the agency that they probably would be eligible for a child in the 7–12 age group and, as the mother put it, 'we didn't really have an input into what that age group was going to be'. One father made the point that as he was excluded from adopting a baby because of his age, so was his wife even though had she been able to apply by herself she would have been eligible. The father commented that there 'doesn't seem to be any rhyme nor reason to it and it varies, I gather, from one region to another'. Another couple were told that they had to adopt a child who was younger than their own youngest birth child.

Apart from age, other criteria mentioned were: any adopted child had to be of the same ethnic background as the applicants; the mother would have to give up her job,[24] and the couple should not continue with IVF treatment and the adoption application.[25] Another couple were told that the agency 'frowned on foster carers going on to adopting' since that is a way of 'manipulating the system'.

Re-assessment

Apart from eligibility criteria the other issue mentioned by adopters, in particular by those who had previously been approved as adoptive parents, was the question whether, as they put it, they had to be 're-vetted'. This issue could arise in different ways. One couple, for example, having been approved by one statutory agency were shocked to discover that they would have to be re-assessed before being approved by another agency. Another couple who had previously adopted some time before and were currently approved foster carers, nevertheless also found themselves having to be re-interviewed and re-assessed in relation to their application to adopt a child being with them as a foster child.[26]

Whether a *complete* re-assessment is always necessary can surely be questioned, at any rate in the type of circumstance last mentioned.

---

[23] See above at para 2.2

[24] Cf, the adopter who explained, 'Social Services have been told quite categorically to look for people who can afford it'.

[25] Discussed above at para 2.1.

[26] See also Chapter 9, para 3.2.

6.2   Agency practice and procedure

Responding to initial enquiries

As previously mentioned,[27] the common practice among agencies following an initial enquiry about adoption is to send the enquirer an information pack. While the content of such packs varies, they usually explain what fostering and adoption mean and some will include a current status sheet, that is, whether the baby list is open or closed and the current position on the toddler list. Some agencies include both a leaflet about themselves and (where appropriate) ones about their consortium and even about other agencies. Commonly, agencies also send enquirers a family detail form or question-naire which they are asked to complete and return to the agency if they are interested in pursuing their enquiry. Additionally or alternatively, some agencies hold regular open meetings at which the nature of adoption and agency policy are explained, at the end of which those attending are asked to take away an application form and to return it when completed if they are still interested in applying to adopt. Commonly, at these initial stages the message seems to be conveyed that adoption of babies is either impossible or extremely unlikely. We spoke to some agencies which simply rejected those who were only interested in adopting babies.

Following the initial enquiry, though practice varies, the initiative is generally then left to the enquirer to take the next step either by completing the family detail form or by attending an interview in the agency's office, or by attending an open meeting and completing an application form. The clear sub-text of this practice is to test the enquirers' true resolve. As one voluntary worker told us:

> Lots of people ring up and don't ever come. We don't follow up because it's got to come from them and people may be frightened. They hear about older children and they know it's not for them.

If the enquirers do come back then a preliminary assessment is made. For example, in the case of a completed questionnaire, an assessment will be made whether to follow it up immediately or to place the enquirer on a waiting list. This latter course of action is normally taken where it is apparent that the enquirer is only interested in babies, assuming, that is, that adoption applications for babies are still being accepted by the agency (which by no means is always the case). Where applicants are considered worth following up, as they commonly will be if they have expressed interest in adopting older children, then a home visit, sometimes referred to as a "screening visit", is conducted. At this stage although the applicants are given more insight into adoption, the process begins to take on more of an assessment nature and if the applicants are obviously not suitable (for example, they have a criminal record or are clearly racist), then they are normally told so immediately and counselled to withdraw. But unless there are extreme circumstances, some agencies

---

[27] See above at para 4.

at least are reluctant to make judgments at this early stage. As one statutory agency worker commented, unless there is something really striking such as a 'massive police record or something',

> ... we don't sit in judgement over them and cancel them out right at the beginning. We ask them to come on the course and a lot of them cancel themselves out. I think it's a much more healthy exercise rather than somebody up on high after one meeting saying to you 'you're no good'!

After the initial screening stage, would-be adopters are commonly invited to attend workshops or preparation meetings but some agencies prefer to undertake the so-called "statutory check",[28] under which an investigation and report is made into the prospective adopters' general (eg. whether they have a criminal record) and medical background, before inviting applicants into expensive preparation and training sessions.

At each stage there is a considerable drop off of interest. As one statutory agency worker commented:

> Through the process of families inquiring, to inviting them to open meetings, to taking up statutory references, we're probably left with 25 per cent of the people who initially phoned us. So it's a self-selection kind of thing really.

Another worker commented:

> A lot do drop out and apologise for wasting our time which is silly because that is part of the process.

One clear advantage of this attritional process is that it is only the most determined applicants that make serious applications while at the same time agencies are relieved of having to make "painful" decisions to reject applications since many applicants reject themselves.

Proactive recruitment

Of course agency recruitment practice is not entirely passive. We spoke to a number that actively advertised in the press and on television. One particularly enterprising voluntary agency attended various local shows, took out features in football programmes and even inserted material into local government pay slips and milk bills! Sometimes campaigns can cause problems as experienced, for example, by one statutory agency when members of the public complained that they could not access the agency's service. As a result of that experience the agency has now installed a recruitment hotline. Of course, these campaigns cost money and not all

---

[28] Viz, those made pursuant to reg 8 and Schs VI and VII of the Adoption Agencies Regulations 1983 and which must be undertaken by agencies before the applicant can formally be approved as a potential adopter.

agencies can afford to do so and some questioned whether the "return" was worth the effort. As one voluntary agency worker told us: 'We used to go out to shopping centres; but staff have decided that's a lot of effort for no return'.

Two voluntary agencies told us about a different recruitment strategy, namely to recruit for particular children at an early stage. As a worker in one of the agencies explained, because far fewer people are interested in the types of children who are in the care system, they had to be more proactive. A worker in the other agency explained that the advantage of seeking adopters for specific children was that when recruiting they could have the child's specific needs in mind which meant that 'because you're not looking for a mythical idea of an adoptive family but instead will have a pretty good idea of what you're looking for, you can therefore look at more unusual families'. It also meant that instead of making a general assessment and asking whether they will make good adopters, it's 'will they be able to adopt and manage these children?'

Another issue of proactive recruitment is the recruiting of minority ethnic adopters. Although some agencies mentioned they had enquiries from minority ethnic applicants, many expressed concern about the difficulty of recruiting prospective adopters from all parts of the community. One statutory agency worker told us that, notwithstanding their agency's anti-discrimination policy, 'the fact remains that we've one family of black adopters, one black member on one of the panels, and we've got four panels . . . I can think of only one black social worker in the department'. A number of agencies said that they simply did not recruit sufficient numbers of black or Asian applicants and one voluntary agency worker told us that 'the black adopters we use are just snapped up'.

Several agencies, both statutory and voluntary, had mounted campaigns specifically to recruit minority ethnic adopters and one voluntary agency had begun developing links with black adopters in the local community. However, as the worker in this agency acknowledged, this process of nurturing was a slow one and would take 'at least five years'.

Although our survey on this issue is relatively narrow, the data that we have collected do suggest some cause for concern about the recruitment levels of prospective adopters from minority ethnic backgrounds. Although there are agencies which are actively engaged in trying to widen their community pool, there are others which need to think about the issue and to develop an appropriate strategy.

Agency policy towards foster carers as adopters

Although, as we have seen,[29] a significant proportion of our adoptive family sample adopted a child they were fostering, agency policy towards foster carers as adopters

---

[29] See above at para 3.

ranged from the hostile to the uncertain. Although no agency worker we spoke to actually said it was agency policy not to allow foster carers to adopt, we know from our family sample that some agencies at least do *prima facie* operate a strict policy against foster carers adopting. On the other hand, judging from our agency sample, other agencies are more encouraging, and one worker told us that if foster carers have been approved 'for permanency, then probably there is a possibility they could become adopters but they're not approved with that in mind'. Another worker told us that his agency was having a re-think on this issue, commenting:

> *Whether we should move a child on from a foster home when the foster carer is saying that they want to adopt and when the child is well settled, is another thing we are becoming less sure about. We used to say, very firmly, you are foster carers, you were assessed as foster carers, you do temporary placements.*

While we are far from suggesting a rigid policy in favour of foster carers, from what we have seen, there seems evident sense in supporting applications where foster placements have matured into *de facto* adoptions, particularly where it is the child's wish. As one statutory agency worker put it:

> *To foster with a view to adoption is not a good basis for an adoption, but to endorse a fostering which has developed naturally into a de facto adoption is a good basis for permanence.*

Moreover, as one statutory agency worker said, there is an inherent irony in being opposed to adoptions by foster carers and placing children with strangers, for:

> *In many ways in adoption we're placing the most damaged children with the least experienced people. Whereas our foster carers (and we've got a specialist teenage team) are well paid, well trained, well supported and prepared to cope with the incredible difficulties that they'll have.*

7   When applications for approval are rejected

As we have seen,[30] many agencies work on the principle that a number of would-be adopters turn themselves down while others, who are clearly going to be unsuitable,[31] are commonly counselled or persuaded to withdraw at an early stage. Consequently, the number of formal refusals by adoption panels are said to be relatively low.

---

[30] Above at para 6.2.

[31] As might be apparent following what is commonly referred to as the "statutory references", i.e. particulars about the prospective adopters' general and medical background which agencies are required to obtain pursuant to reg 8 of, and Schs VI and VII to the Adoption Agency Regulations 1983.

However, we found that in our interview sample, which after all comprised only those who were eventually approved as adopters, at least six families (13 per cent)[32] experienced rejection or deferment by an adoption panel, two had been advised to withdraw and three experienced outright rejection by an agency. In other words, even among a sample of families eventually approved for adoption, at least 23 per cent (11 families in our sample) had experienced at least one serious rebuff to their application for approval.

The reasons for rejection or deferment at the various stages varied: in one case a statutory agency refused to assess the applicants because they were too fat, while another statutory agency would not assess the applicant as she was an employee of that agency. Other reasons for not assessing the applicants included the brevity of the applicants' marriage and the brevity of the applicants' residence in the area. Two applicants were advised to withhold their application following the breakdown of their marriage. In one of these cases, after the applicant had remarried, she was told to wait for a further two years. Other reasons for panel rejections or deferrals included concern about the children's schooling; concern about the female applicant's upbringing (her mother had committed suicide and she had been brought up by an "unloving" grandmother); and concern that the applicants did not want children of their own. One couple (with one white and one black partner) thought they had been initially rejected because of 'blatant racial prejudice' on the part of the agency.

7.1 Some adopters' reactions to being rejected

Obviously those whose applications for approval were rejected were hurt by the experience. One couple said they were 'devastated'. The mother told us:

> The worst thing was, we had a lot of nieces and nephews who used to come and stay with us regularly, and we have godchildren that we were very close to. And when we were turned down, to be honest, I thought people will think that we're not suitable; that there's something wrong with us; that we're going to abuse the children. It broke my relationship with all the children that came to us because whereas I would normally pick them up and cuddle them and not think anything of it, I suddenly felt I ought to keep them at arm's length in case anybody wasn't comfortable with us anymore.

Others, too, mentioned being devastated or insulted. In every case, however, either upon their own resolve or with the encouragement of friends, the applicants all successfully re-applied for approval.

---

[32] All six were rejected or deferred by statutory agency panels, which amounted to 17 per cent of the statutory agency sample.

7.2   Attendance at adoption panels

According to our agency postal questionnaire response, it is relatively unusual to allow prospective adopters to attend panel meetings with only 5 per cent of statutory agencies and 15 per cent of voluntary agencies saying they could.[33] Some agencies, however, said they had a more flexible arrangement allowing prospective adopters to attend a subsequent panel if they were dissatisfied with the original decision and, in our sample, one couple whose initial application had been deferred because of the wife's upbringing, did attend a subsequent panel in person. The wife told us that they felt that this opportunity was a 'good thing'. Another adopter thought that applicants 'should have the opportunity to meet the panel, that were judging you because some people can put across answers on paper and some people can't'.

Notwithstanding this general inability to attend the panel we were not aware of any applicants who failed to discover why their application for approval was either rejected or deferred.

7.3   The agency view of rejections

It was clearly evident from our interviews with agency workers that they were well aware of the need to handle the rejection of potential adopters with care and understanding. One worker described it as a 'painful' decision. Some told us that they tried to identify problems at the earliest possible stage. As one statutory agency worker said:

> We, I believe, are very honest about them and say to them from the outset if we know it's going to cause an issue. If we can't resolve it we make the general suggestion that they withdraw. If they say they want to continue and have that decision left to the panel, then we will do it.

However, another statutory agency worker put it:

> We try to be as honest as possible but the other side of it is, we also say that the whole point of all of this is about meeting the needs of our children. So, if at any stage of the process something happens which could suggest that it's not going to meet the needs of the children, then we reserve the right to say so, and pull the plug.

As we have already mentioned, none of the applicants that we interviewed said that they could not find out why their application was rejected or deferred. One statutory agency worker explained that it was felt that as Chairman of the Panel he should speak to couples who have been rejected. While this practice might not be that common, we learned from our postal questionnaire that most agencies (84 per cent

---

[33] Five per cent of statutories and 4 per cent of voluntaries also said that they allowed the children to attend; 4 per cent of both statutories and voluntaries said that birth parents were allowed to attend.

of statutory agencies and 74 per cent of voluntary agencies) make arrangements for a meeting between the applicants and a social worker. Rather less (5 per cent of statutories and 7 per cent of voluntaries) said that they referred couples to support groups though a few more (8 per cent of statutories and 11 per cent of voluntaries) gave couples information about referrals to other agencies and still more (15 per cent of statutories and 22 per cent of voluntaries) discussed appeals and complaints procedures.

It should be added that, since our fieldwork was completed, new regulations, namely, the Adoption Agencies and Children (Arrangements for Placement and Reviews) (Miscellaneous Amendments) Regulations 1997[34] established, as from November 1997, a new procedure whereby prospective adopters whom the agency considers not to be suitable as adopters must be notified of the agency's reasons and given an opportunity to make representation before the agency reaches its final decision. While these new provisions represent a welcome tightening up, one may question whether they should go further and allow the applicants to make their representation in person before the Panel.

8 Concluding points

As will have become evident from the foregoing discussion, many of the issues that arise at what might loosely be termed the beginning of the adoption process are far from straightforward. For example, what makes people want to adopt is a complex issue and on reflection, because of its implications for recruitment, we now wish we could have enquired more deeply into it. Even at a relatively superficial level we found that the motives were varied and certainly not confined to issues of infertility. We suspect that had we delved deeper into motives we might have found that the desire to adopt at least stemmed in part from a need to have or to continue to have a "family" around the applicants. Certainly, the influence of other family members and earlier experience of adoption or fostering should not be overlooked. We had some evidence that those who were used to their families looking after other people's children, naturally themselves looked to adoption. Such a finding has obvious implications for recruitment policies.

A striking finding, at any rate in our interview sample of adoptive families, was just how many were already experienced parents. Of course, already being a parent does not necessarily fully prepare one to take on highly disturbed children but the difference in parenting experience does have important implications for their subsequent preparation and training to be adopters which we are not convinced has been properly taken on board by all agencies.[35]

---

[34] SI 1997/649.

[35] See further Chapter 9, *Preparation and Training*, para 3.2.

A further striking finding was the relatively high proportion (in our sample) of adoptions by foster carers. There is, as we have seen, active debate about the role of foster carers as prospective adopters but it does seem evident that they are an important resource which some agencies seem either to be ignoring, or even actively to be discouraging. We seriously question, for example, the wisdom of an agency policy that is rigidly opposed to the adoption by foster carers of children they have been looking after for some time, notwithstanding that the child is well settled and has an established secure relationship with the carers who want to adopt.

Foster carers were not the only people adopting children that they already knew. As we have seen, there were other cases in our interview sample, for example, the couple who adopted the children of parents that they knew, and cases of the adoption of children known to the applicants in their professional capacity. Indeed, notwithstanding what may be thought of as an elaborate machinery for arranging adoptions, we were surprised to find just how many adoptions seem to happen almost by chance. It is perhaps worth reflecting whether adequate attention is paid to this given that so much of the adoption system is still predicated on the assumption that adoption of children is by strangers.

It is evident that some agencies put a lot of thought and effort into recruitment strategies, notwithstanding the limitation of resources, but we have some evidence to suspect, nevertheless, that nationally insufficient thought is being put into the recruitment of minority ethnic families.

Once the process has started, agencies generally seem to handle applicants sensitively and with understanding. They take care to explain the process and generally seem to give reasons if applications are rejected. However, few agencies allow prospective adopters to appear personally before Adoption Panels and it may be that further thought should be given to the wisdom of such exclusion.

9 Preparation and Training: Learning to adapt to adoptive family life

1   Introduction

This chapter deals first with the preparation of the child and second the preparation of parents.

There are a number of different perspectives to take into account when considering the general issue of preparation and training of adopters and their children. One can look at it from the point of view of the children and adopters and consider how they prepare *themselves* for adoption i.e. viewing them as potentially the key central actors in the process. One can also look at it from the agency perspective, in order to explore how they go about preparing children and adopters for the placement and a new life at the adopted home. One might add that the perspectives of birth parents and foster carers also come into the reckoning, but they were not the main focus of this study.

Initially, when we planned the research, we saw preparation and training as part of our general remit to consider support services broadly defined. On reflection, we might have had a tendency to do so too much in orthodox social welfare terms. Certainly as the project developed, we came to the view that it is more appropriate to focus on the educative/learning elements in preparation and training since the fundamental issues are how children learn to live in an adoptive home and how adopters (and any other children they may have) learn the particular skills and understanding associated with the rather special kind of adoptive parenthood and family life – processes which we have termed "the learning of social competence". These include, on the one hand, the learning of competencies and coping strategies for handling the adoption situation and, on the other, the social support mechanisms which might facilitate such learning.[1,2]

---

[1] Gerald Caplan has referred to the learning of such skills and understanding as the learning of competence, which he views as 'an internal constitutional and acquired quality of individuals that enables them to withstand the harmful effects of hazardous circumstances' such as broken family attachments. Complementing the notion of competence is the all important matter of social support which Caplan views as external mechanisms that serve to protect individuals against the damage that might be caused by external stressors. In the adoption context these mechanisms potentially include a host of both informal (friends, relatives, etc.) and formal support on offer to the child and adopters. Amongst the formal support are the legal, educational, health and social welfare services associated with the adoption process which

We collected a large quantity of quantitative and qualitative material on this subject from our agency and family postal questionnaires supplemented by follow-up interviews with agency staff and adoptive parents. Our study, *Adopted Children Speaking* (Thomas *et al*, 1999) also touches on the child's perspective, although we found that many children have only a hazy memory of how they were prepared for the adoption placement.

2 Preparing the child

Here we consider the following key questions: Who is responsible for the preparation of the child? Who does it? What are the aims and how do they go about it? What are the main policy and practice problems in attempting this task?

2.1 Responsibility

Until the adoption order is made, case responsibility lies with the placing agency or the family finding agency. Responsibility for preparing the child usually falls to a local authority social worker while the preparation of the parents is the job of the family finding agency "Link" worker. In our agency postal survey we asked: Who normally holds case accountability for the child at each stage of the adoption process? We defined the relevant stages as far as preparation is concerned as: pre-placement for adoption, during introductions, and during the placement until the order was made. As one would expect the pattern of responses (see Table 5) differed somewhat between statutory and voluntary agencies.

Although in most cases – particularly in statutory agencies – case responsibility rests with the local authority, it is clear that it can be shared with another agency (statutory or voluntary). This has significance when it comes to the policy question whether responsibility for preparing the child should remain with local authority social workers who have dealt with the child when in care, or whether it should

---

will of course be pre-eminently the potential support offered by statutory and voluntary adoption agencies. Caplan suggests that the two key elements of competence and social support 'articulate and reverberate with each other rather in the manner of themes in a musical composition'. Although every family and every child will have their own complicated idiosyncratic elements and generalisations can lead to oversimplification, he suggests that it is nevertheless possible to observe general patterns about the way children and adults learn competence and utilise social supports of various kinds to help them cope with potentially stressful events. In his view, which we accept, 'social supports not only buffer reaction to current stress but also were probably a crucial element in determining whether a past risk factor . (such as a previous separation or child placement) led to a current unhealthy (one could say maladaptive) outcome, as well as being a central element of the mediated learning process whereby children acquire self-efficacy and problem-solving skills that form the core of competence' (Caplan, 1989, p.368).

[2] For further development of the importance of social learning theory and cognitive perceptions as applied to the task of learning to adjust to the demands of adoptive family life and related stresses, see Barth and Berry (1988).

usually be transferred to or shared with the family finding agency's link worker once the decision has been taken to place the child for adoption – an issue which we consider later in this chapter and in our conclusions. Suffice it to say here that evidence from our agency returns suggests that, in a small minority of cases (about 10 per cent), changes in case accountability in statutory agencies occur both pre-placement and during placement. However, in the majority (63 per cent) of cases, case accountability for the child changes from the local authority social worker to the family link worker only when or after the adoption order is made.

Table 5
Who holds case responsibility

	Statutory families		Voluntary families		Total families	
Before the match						
Usually child's LA	54	64%	4	15%	58	53%
Usually adoption agency	3	4%	0	0%	3	3%
Either	6	7%	4	15%	10	19%
Both/partnership	4	5%	3	12%	7	6%
Not specified	16	19%	10	38%	26	24%
Miscellaneous	1	1%	5	19%	6	5%
During introductions						
Usually child's LA	47	56%	1	4%	48	44%
Usually adoption agency	6	7%	5	19%	11	10%
Either	11	13%	7	27%	18	16%
Both/partnership	5	6%	2	8%	7	6%
Not specified	14	17%	6	23%	20	18%
Miscellaneous	1	1%	5	19%	6	5%

Source: Agency postal survey

2.2 What are the specific aims of preparation and how is it done?

Our agency postal questionnaires did not go into the specific detail about the way children were prepared for adoption. We decided to leave that subject to our follow-up interviews with agency adoption staff. Nevertheless, a number of written replies to the general question about what were thought of as the main needs of children adopted out of care included references to the need for good preparation as can be seen from the following typical responses from statutory agencies:

Children need first to understand their situation – truthful information and explanation about why they have been placed for adoption. We need to recognise and respect their feelings about their families of origin and help them to develop a confident sense of their identity, showing that they have permission and encouragement to make a new start while helping them cope with loss.

They need help to separate from their birth families (or reduce contact) while retaining understanding and links as appropriate; continuing life story work; help to bond with the adopters and to integrate into the new community.

Preparation for moving involving grief work, life story work, counselling and support, settling in and forming new attachments. They may need periodic news about their foster family, birth family and siblings if they are placed elsewhere.

Support in adjusting to the idea of living with a new family.

Coping with feelings of loss, of birth and a foster family.

Negotiating contact – they have to deal with feelings of guilt and conflict.

Developing a sense of trust.

Reassurance that the placement is permanent, i.e. having their own worker to whom they can talk.

Broadly similar responses were received from voluntary agencies except that overall they were rather less specific, reflecting no doubt the general practice that the local authority social worker has the main responsibility for preparing older children out of care. Thus a number of comments refer to the family link worker giving *indirect* support to the local authority social worker's attempt to work with the child in the initial stages of the placement, to ensure that the child was prepared, that life story work had been carried out, and to see that, where necessary, specialist psychological/ educational work with the child was undertaken.

More detailed illustrative comments derived from our interviews with statutory adoption agency staff cover a number of important points indicating a varied approach.

The practice of delegating the child preparation task to area social workers

A number of adoption officers from larger statutory agencies mentioned that their particular role was usually to support the area social worker, some of whom were experienced and well trained for the task of preparing a child for adoption, while others were less so. As one put it:

We have an important role as the support worker for the newly qualified, hard pressed or not very experienced in adoption social workers to work with the child and the foster carers . . . this is the ideal we try to achieve.

Others told us:

When a child actually gets to the stage of being identified for permanence, there's a link worker from my adoption team appointed to work with that child's social worker. It is a bit of a moveable feast in practice but it ought to be the child's social worker, with us advising and perhaps giving some direction as well about the kind of things that ought to be done . . . The level of preparation that's undertaken with each child, I would have to say, is variable because it depends on the individual child and individual social worker.

Much depends on whether the child's social worker has a well-established and important relationship with the child. Obviously, anybody who has to do direct work with the child, needs to have established a level of trust. Normally it would be the child's social worker but it may be that the adopter's link social worker is able to do that and might have the skills in that area that the other social worker doesn't. But it would be for the child's social worker to make sure that the preparatory work was done. It's really under the auspices of the child's own social worker. How much they actually do these days I think is very dependent on the individual worker. Beyond that, if the child is in residential care, then obviously there would be key workers who would do it or sometimes the foster carers. I would have to say that I think our work is patchy. Sometimes it is done very well and sometimes less well.

It's not a fixed person. It's either someone in the child care team or sometimes they get workers in from day centres to do it. The question of who does the preparation of the child is decided at the planning meeting. It's an area for negotiation – basically who is available to do the work, not always the one who is most appropriate.

A number of these statutory agency specialist adoption staff indicated that they were not entirely happy about the usual policy of delegating responsibility for preparing children for placement to area social workers, to foster carers, or even occasionally to residential workers. Although their designated role was that of adoption officer (or some such title) they did not usually have any direct control to ensure that the necessary preparatory work was done, although some mentioned sometimes that the Adoption Panel took a close enough interest to check with them what was being done with a particular child and who was doing it.

A number mentioned that direct work with children in their field is a specialist and highly skilled task. It might, for example, involve complex life story work, some play therapy and other specialist communication skills, particularly if children have behavioural or learning difficulties. Sometimes statutory agencies work closely with the child and family psychiatric services of the health authority or with an educational psychologist, but because extra cost can be involved, sanction from the Panel may first need to be sought.

Conflicts of interest

Some adoption officers suggested that the child's social worker can find it difficult to prepare a child for adoption if they have been previously working with a view to rehabilitating the child with the birth family. As one put it:

> Before the review (when the permanency decision is made) you are trying to keep the child as much a part of their own birth family as possible, keeping alive those relationships. But afterwards, although you may want to keep these relationships alive, you are also wanting the child to be prepared for the permanent separation that is going to occur.

If the change of focus and role is difficult for some of these social workers, how much more confusing and difficult might it be for the child? There are clearly important role boundaries here to distinguish and navigate if ambiguities are to be avoided.

Competing local authority priorities

Several statutory agency adoption officers told us that pressures of child protection work in local offices meant that often preparatory work with a child was either delayed or simply not done. For example, one said:

> I've had examples recently where the urgency of child protection assessments for the courts – that sort of thing – has just had to take priority . . . and so the preparation of the child for adoption, say a weekly session that was promised, all the life story book work that was to be done, hasn't in fact gone ahead. So it is about engineering staff availability as well as having the people with the necessary skills.

Another told us:

> One of the things that gets in the way of the child's social worker or area worker either doing it themselves or ensuring that it gets done, is that by the time you are at the stage in the process that the child is moving towards adoption, it becomes a low priority because of the never-ending pressure of crisis work in the area offices – the child protection work, etc. This is why I think that child preparation work needs to be sent somewhere else. I think we need to put it in the family placement work, so that we can offer a wider package of support to the child and the adopters together.

Are statutory agencies best suited to undertake the child preparation task?

Much of the material already considered raises the fundamental policy question whether it is any longer appropriate for the agency that carried out the initial child protection task to continue with the specialist child placement task as well. Would it be better for a few larger specialist voluntary agencies to take over these highly skilled responsibilities instead? We have plenty of material, not surprisingly, mostly from voluntary agencies, which suggests that this needs to be considered. Before examining the way voluntary agency staff severally made the argument for such a policy change, we should mention that some voluntary agencies already provide a specialist child preparation service for certain local authorities. One such, established for over 15 years, is known as "The Bridge". This provides a specialist fostering service for children in care who are deemed not ready for placement in an adoptive home, children who need special support but whose birth family or legal situations are such that the local authority is not ready to place them for adoption.

We spoke to a number of voluntary agency workers who suggested to us that their agency had the necessary specialist skills and understanding to provide, in their opinion, a consistently higher level of preparation for children than could be provided by many hard-pressed local authority social service departments. For example:

> We would like to have more involvement because we feel that basically many children are not sufficiently well prepared for adoption. Frequently they have not had the same social worker for any length of time. Sometimes, it seems they've been told they're going into one foster home and then they find they are moving to another family instead. Frequently children don't understand that. Some children think they are staying with their foster family and then find they are placed elsewhere for adoption. Some of the work we have to do afterwards is helping the child come to terms with the loss of the foster family.

In a similar vein another voluntary agency worker commented:

> We would actually prefer to do the direct work with the child ourselves and we offer to do that in the hope that the local authority will agree. However, we are finding that a lot of local authority social workers want to retain the responsibility . . . even though the way things are going in local authorities these days, there just doesn't seem to be the time for thorough preparation. Unfortunately, with some of the older children that have been placed with us, we've been told that preparatory work has been done, but we find that once the placement has been made it has not. We then really have to struggle when the child is initially in the placement to get over some of the issues that we feel would have helped the child enormously if they had been addressed before the placement . . . Where it hasn't been done properly the potential for breakdowns are much greater, and the children take much longer to settle. Attempting to prepare the child after the placement has begun is never the same. You can never make up for not doing that preparatory work beforehand.

Some voluntary agency workers told us that they no longer take for granted the local authority's assurance that adequate preparatory work has been done with the children. For example, one told us:

> *Some children are better prepared than others and in fact there are some who are not prepared at all and some who are very badly prepared. You build up a feel about it over the years with certain local authorities; we know roughly the sort of preparation and the level of input to expect from them. We now seek to find out as much as we can about the preparation that the child has had before we arranged the placement. We get as much written information as we can – copies of reviews, specialist reports from consultant psychiatrists, educational psychologists – and here usually what you read between the lines is more important than what you read on the lines. Then you would probably in 90 per cent of the cases want to meet the child and check out with them what they understand – certainly before the placement and sometimes before the matching although sometimes that's difficult to arrange.*

Another voluntary agency worker said:

> *The trouble is that these days we don't know what the quality of the preparation of the child has been. We don't know whether the local authority's placement decision or the suggestions being made by the social workers are really and truly in the child's interest. Other factors can come into play so there are sometimes difficult negotiations between our social workers and their social workers just to check out these things without treading too heavily on their toes . . . More and more what is happening here in this agency is that children are getting into our placements and then we are discovering the preparatory work has not been done. It's at that stage we have to go in and do it ourselves. Possibly you might have to re-work it – children may understand at one point in their lives and we often find there are great gaps that they don't really understand what's happening or why they are in this particular placement.*

Overall, it seems that a number of voluntary agencies feel that they have more experience, more time and more expertise to undertake child preparation and can perhaps offer a better all-round package to both children and adopters than a number of the larger, possibly less well-resourced statutory agencies. As one worker from a well-known voluntary children's charity said to us:

> *We've been in this business so long that some of the children we worked with 18 –20 years ago are still coming back to us – people who were adopted then and who are now telling us what was good and what was bad about their adoptions. That informs our preparation and training for adoption these days. We know we are good at recruitment, good at preparing adopters and good at supporting them. Why shouldn't we do the specialist prepara-*

> *tory work with the children too and let the local authorities worry about their child protection work? We'll do the rest. It happens to some extent already with our partnership with Blankshire. They know they are getting exceedingly good value for money from us, so why shouldn't it be more generally extended?*

Another specialist voluntary agency simply said:

> *You see we've got more time to really think about some direct work with children than many local authority social workers – and we do find the preparatory work with older children, particularly if they have been abused, is very, very time-consuming.*

2.3   Life story work

What has become known as "life story work" (i.e. the construction with the child and family of an ongoing record of a child's life history) is now generally regarded as a potentially important aid in the psychological development of an adopted child's sense of identity – a concept which encapsulates questions of both: "Who am I?" and "What sort of person was I, and might I become?" The significance of life story work was highlighted in the 1970s by John Triseliotis' seminal work, *In Search of Origins* (1973). We were interested in several aspects – not only whether agencies normally ensured that life story work had been undertaken but also who was involved in it and how it was recorded. We explored these questions initially in our agency postal survey.

Agency questionnaire data

It will come as no surprise that virtually all statutory agencies now claim normally to provide older children adopted out of care with a permanent life story record (98 per cent). Even so, as we have seen, some adoption officers acknowledge that this can sometimes not be done, and, as will be considered below, a number of adopters told us that they were not satisfied about this either. Nevertheless, as an aspiration of adoption practice it is clear that agencies regard it as a key component. Voluntary agencies reflect their statutory counterparts in this respect, although (20 per cent) qualified their answers by telling us that they only undertook life story work if it had not been done by the child's local authority.

Agencies were also asked to specify *inter alia* who participates in the process. As one would expect, the child's social worker topped the list of those mentioned most often (67 per cent), followed by birth parents (57 per cent) and foster carers (50 per cent). Others mentioned included the child (15 per cent), siblings and other birth relatives (17 per cent), family centres or residential units (11 per cent), the prospective adopters (10 per cent) and occasionally medical advisers, therapists, and child psychiatrists. Some agencies (19 per cent) replied that it varied too much to say and eight voluntary agencies (27 per cent of the sample) commented that they saw it primarily as the responsibility of the local authority agency, not themselves.

As to the means by which the record was compiled, a range of methods were mentioned, often in combination, the most common being books (53 per cent), videos/audio cassettes (27 per cent) and photo albums (23 per cent). Occasionally other devices were mentioned such as Barnardo's *Memory Box* (10 per cent) and also 'a later life story letter' to be opened when children were considered to be old enough (17 per cent).

Family questionnaire data

All families were asked: Does your adopted/prospective adoptive child have a permanent life story record containing information about his/her past (e.g. life story book, video or audio cassette, etc.?)' Of the 157 replies received to this question from parents approved by statutory agencies, 114 (73 per cent) answered affirmatively and 37 (24 per cent) in the negative. Corresponding figures from the 66 parents approved by voluntary agencies was 59 (89 per cent) affirmative and six (9 per cent) in the negative. Since, as we have seen, agencies said that they normally ensure that the child has a life story book, it was both surprising and worrying to learn that almost a quarter of the families approved by statutory agencies claimed their child had no such record, at least by the time they replied to our postal questionnaire.

In line with our finding generally about information, while just over half (52 per cent) thought that the life story was complete and up to date, a substantial proportion (38 per cent) said that it was not. Ten per cent were unsure.

We attempted to tease out from adopting families who, to the best of their knowledge, had helped to compile the life story. This drew a 76 per cent response rate but from this, we can say, as one would expect, that the child's social worker is commonly involved (81 per cent) followed by the child him/herself (64 per cent), previous foster carers (42 per cent) [underlying the importance of their involvement] and the adopters themselves (35 per cent). Much less common was the involvement of the child's birth parents (11 per cent), other members of the birth family (8 per cent), other members of the adoptive family (8 per cent) or even the adoption agency staff (16 per cent) or Family Centre (7 per cent).

2.4   Other ways in which children are prepared

Information about support

In addition to questions concerning life story work, agencies were asked: How are older children who are being adopted out of care made aware of support services that are available to them? Our intention here was to find out how agencies approached *children's* needs, both for information and for individual support. The most frequent answer was first, that information was given verbally to the child by the child's social worker – mentioned by 81 per cent of the voluntary agencies and 46 per cent of the statutory agencies and by their adoptive parents respectively 38 per cent and 42 per cent. A few agencies (three statutory and two voluntary) said that they had a standard written information pack for children. These included a list of useful names and addresses, an "information sheet" and one even mentioned a special booklet or handbook.

Encouraging support networks

Given that children learn understanding of their circumstances and social competence from each other, particularly from other children who have been in a similar situation to themselves, we asked agencies whether they actively encouraged or developed informal networks for older children who are being or have been adopted out of care, so that they can mix with or gain support from other children in a similar situation. Overall, 30 per cent of the 99 agencies responding to this question said that they did. On closer examination, however, we found that proportionately this broke down to 62 per cent of the 26 voluntary agencies responding, contrasting with only 20 per cent of the 73 statutory agencies, although several of these indicated that they were beginning to explore ways and means of doing so. We suspect that the size of an agency's adoption workload is crucial as to whether it is feasible to make such a specialist provision; a point which touches on the more general question of agency viability which we consider in Chapter 17.

2.5   Preparing the child – the adopters' perspective

It is an obvious point but if a child is poorly prepared for placement, the adopters will get the backwash and might have to try and remedy the deficiency themselves with or without the help of their family placement link worker. For example, if a child has become attached to foster carers and has not been helped to understand the temporary nature of the fostering arrangements, then the child may resist moving on to the adoptive placement and the adopters may find themselves with a distressed and grieving child. Although some adopters told us that they thought that their children had been poorly prepared, others said that they were pleased by the way the child seemed ready for the placement. In this section we give contrasting illustrations to highlight important points about the child preparation process in general.[3] We should, however, say at the outset, that overall a mixed picture emerges which, taken together with some of the comments from adoption agency staff already considered, suggests that a number of statutory agencies are not doing a good enough job in preparing children for adoption. We have chosen material from our

---

[3] More detailed data about information concerning the child's background which is an aspect of parental preparation will be found in the next chapter on matching.

adopters' interview sample to illustrate the range of adopters' impressions about the way their child has been prepared.

An example of inadequate preparation

We begin with a problematic example – a couple who adopted three sisters aged five, six and seven when placed. The adoptive father had been previously married and when the girls arrived, had a son aged eight, whom he saw regularly. The youngest and eldest girls had been fostered in one home. The middle one was with other foster carers to whom she was attached and who had also wanted to adopt her. Apparently the local authority adoption plan was that all three girls should be adopted together even though they had little experience of living together. In fact, because of the long delay between the decision to place the children for adoption and the authority actively seeking adopters, all three children had settled into the foster homes which the adopters told us led to difficulties in moving them. It was clear at the interview that the adopters had experienced quite a lot of challenging behaviour which, amongst other things, had strained the relationship with the adoptive father's son. We quote from the father:

> They hadn't had a lot of preparation. Social services had only talked to them in very general terms about notions of moving on. It was clear to us that they didn't really have very clear concepts about it and we struggled for a long time because of that. The children's social worker from social services had changed on a number of occasions. The person who contacted us at the point when we were being considered for them had only been working with the girls for a relatively short time. Several other people had worked with them before, so her role appears to have been limited to talking to them in her office about the concept of moving on.
>
> Now the foster carers have told us that they were glad at that time that the kids didn't understand the position. The social workers were saying, 'We have done this work. It has been explained to them,' but the foster carers were saying, 'No, they don't understand'. And it is clear to us now that in the light of our experience with the girls that they didn't understand, that the ground work hadn't been done properly... I mean basic stuff like a life story book hasn't been done. I mean [the child] was in care from six months to nearly five. She hadn't got a life story book. She didn't understand why she was in care. She didn't know the difference between having a birth family, having foster carers and then having a forever family as adopters... None of the girls had got hold of these concepts. Any preparation by the social worker seems to have been done in their offices outside of the foster homes, so that it couldn't be properly reinforced by the foster carers. They weren't around when social workers were talking to the children... And then, of course, the

girls had been with their last lot of foster carers continuously for three years and their foster carers had found it hard to let go of them. As far as social services are concerned it seems that the girls had been through several social workers. They had obviously drifted quite a lot after the decision to place them for adoption, and then eventually the department decided the priority was to get them moved quickly. That's what happened. But they moved without the benefit of proper preparation and support. And we think that led to a lot of the problems that we have had.

The adopters collected the children from the foster homes when the placements began, which, with hindsight, they felt was a mistake because the combination of the girls' inadequate preparation and their attachment to their foster carers meant that they were unwittingly cast in the role of "kidnappers" and subsequently the "baddies" when they tried to reduce the amount of contact between the girls and their foster carers. More positively, it should be said that a year after the children moved to live with the couple, the voluntary agency's family link worker had undertaken some life story work with the girls but the adopters felt strongly that this should have begun at least a year before they were placed for adoption.

Preparation by foster carers

Our next illustration is one of a number which exemplifies the potential importance, for good or ill, of foster carers preparing the children for the move to an adoptive placement. Indeed, our impression is that from the adopters' perspective, foster carers are as important as the agency social workers in this respect, if not more so. This is because they have the closest day-to-day experience of the children and, provided they are sensitive to the children's needs and do not feel possessive, can choose the most appropriate moments to work on the preparation issues with the child.

We encountered a number of instances where the adopters were appreciative of the foster carers in this respect – sometimes where the "wheening" process was quite complex. For example, S, an eight-year-old girl when placed, had not lived with her birth family since she was three-and-a-half and had had a number of short-lived foster placements and one failed adoptive placement. However, she had been in her last foster home for a year and for several months previously before the first adoptive placement disrupted. She had been described by social services to the adopters as 'frozen' and not able to attach, but in fact she was showing signs of attachment to her last foster carers and cried for the first time, when she had to leave. A family bereavement which necessitated the foster carer moving was the precipitating reason for the local authority placing S for adoption a second time. We quote from our interview with the adoptive mother:

The foster carers had talked to her about it (the move to the adoptive home). The other thing was that they were moving as well because J's (the foster mother) mum had died a little while ago and they were going to move to a new house. They had to explain to S that she couldn't come with them. J told me that when she told her that she clung on to her and said, 'I don't want to go. I don't want to go. I want to stay with you'. J had said, 'Well, you can't stay with us because we are moving too. You are moving to a new home and we are moving to a new home.' You see they used that as a way of saying, 'Well, people move on. Everybody moves on. It's not just you that keeps moving on. You have moved more often than many other people but we are moving on too, soon.' In fact they took her to see the new house that they were going to move to so that she knew that it was real. So that was really sad for S but they were able to talk about it.

She then describes S's gradual introduction to the adopter's home in which the foster mother played an important part:

We did it gradually and that helped. She and J came here and we visited there. So it was like J saying to S, 'Yes, I approve. You can go to these people. They are nice.' Everybody was working towards the same thing. S talked about it all too, of course, when she first came here with J. And when J went home she phoned her up. She'd phone her up two or three times a day. If she said she wanted to phone up then I would say, 'Yes, of course you can phone J and talk to her'. And then J would say something positive like, 'What are you doing?' and 'that's nice'. So you see, J did all these positive things.

Preparation and "telling" – an ongoing task

Helping children to understand why they were placed for adoption is often an ongoing process. Children growing up in an adoptive home have to learn what is special about it, for example, over the management of contact issues and/or as they get older, how they deal with the urge to trace lost relatives. So for the child, preparation and training for adoption is not just to be regarded as a one-off task to be undertaken by social workers and/or foster carers when the decision is made to place the child for adoption. Rather it is the beginning of a process, the particulars of which will be uniquely idiosyncratic for every child and in which all the main figures in the adoption can have key roles at particular stages. This was well understood, for example, by Mr B, a school teacher in a special school, and his wife who initially provided a temporary home for four children from an abusive and neglectful family. The brothers were adopted elsewhere and Mr and Mrs B ended up adopting the two sisters, after their placement elsewhere had broken down and the girls had been returned to them. In fact they found themselves playing a role in the preparation of all four children at various stages in the story. The adoptive mother described some of this ongoing process of preparing the children:

I think it was largely us that did that. First, we made it clear that they were not to call us Mum and Dad. We were always [adopters' first names]. In fact that was quite easy because they had very little concept of Mum and Dad and had very limited bonding with them and had just referred to them by their first names anyway. Then, as each stage in the story developed, we talked with them about it: First that they had just come to stay for a while and then eventually when social services decided they should be adopted we talked about that. The boys were initially freed but they were relatively easy to prepare. They were seven and six and by then they had the language skills to understand what we were talking about and some of the concepts that we were trying to get across as to why they couldn't go back to their original family and the reason why at the time we didn't want to keep them. In fact that was never an issue. They never questioned us keeping them and we never raised their expectations. The boys were able to go on and cope with all the concepts which we were putting over to them.

By the time the girls came back to us, of course, we had the boys (who by then had been adopted elsewhere but who had kept in touch with their sisters) as the model to show the girls the process we were all going through.

She then told us about the importance of the family video in compiling the girls' life story:

From day one we were fortunate in that we knew their natural parents and had filmed them. So we were able to prepare them in terms of where they had come from and all the life story book issues. Right from the beginning we had videoed almost everything they did. We videoed their parents' flat, their original nursery and other significant people in their life. We've retained some links with their previous family. So we've prepared them in a sort of historical process.

Yet working on these important life story issues with the girls had not been all plain sailing. As the mother said:

I think that the most difficult issue was why they couldn't go back to the birth family. It was difficult not to give them the message, 'Well, your parents were inadequate and incompetent and they didn't really love you in the true sense of the word'. At the time we have tried not to raise their expectations of what their parents were like so that in future, when they are older, they will not have a tremendous shock. We have talked about what their parents have been able to give them and about the difficulty of having four children in a high rise flat, about the physical restrictions and how some people don't understand how to look after children. We have talked in these terms rather than whether they loved them or not.

3   Preparing the adopters

In the following sections we explore the fundamental questions: how agencies see their role in respect of the preparation and training of adopters; how adopters acquire the understanding and skills of adoptive parenthood; and how in this respect they view the contribution of the agencies. How adopters prepare themselves and acquire the understanding and skills for adoptive parenthood is a major subject ideally deserving more than we can give in this report. Preparation for adoption of older children out of care in particular is not, as yet, well-covered in research literature. This may be because it is not easily grasped as a discrete subject since it overlaps with selection and matching issues. Further, concepts of support merge in people's minds with notions of training and education for adoptive parenthood. Also, as far as the agency's role is concerned, there is a certain ambiguity whether preparation still involves assessment and a degree of supervision.[4] As Donley (1978) observed, 'investigating' or 'vetting' applicants, the probing, inquisitive approach to placement, 'creates a climate of game-playing between family and worker and establishes inferior/superior roles which do not translate well into the kind of relationship necessary at placement', which in her view is essentially "educative" in nature. Likewise, Barth and Berry (1988, op cit at p. 153) comment that: 'post-placement services begin with good pre-placement services. If the home study helps the family to feel less defensive, they will consult more readily with the agency during the probationary period'. They conclude: 'The purpose of post-placement services should be to offer help as needed and desired by the family and child in both the development of the parent/child relationship and the resolution of problems inherent in adoption . . .' Elsewhere (at p. 153) they state: 'The adoption worker's role has become, in great part, that of an information resource. Adoptive families must be treated as consumers who need information in order to decide on a child to whom they might commit their resources. In order to be information brokers, adoption workers must learn all they can about the child.'

---

[4] See Goodacre (1966, pp. 83, 90–92). Although Goodacre's study mostly involved adoption of babies and infants and related to policy and practice over 30 years ago, it remains an important milestone in British adoption research since she influenced the structure of the system that operates today. Her interviews with adopters and local authority adoption practitioners revealed, amongst other things considerable ambiguity about the nature of the supervision of children placed for adoption. She reported that Children's Departments, as local authority agencies were then termed, 'saw the purpose of supervision as two-fold. First as a means of ensuring that the choice of home was in the best interests of the child; and second as an opportunity of helping adopters deal with the social and emotional implications of their new role'. On the other hand, she reported that the adopters, 'having said they appreciated the necessity for supervision made it clear that, as far as they were concerned, supervision has created much anxiety and sometimes even resentment. The necessity of having to prove their fitness as parents rankled, particularly as (at least in retrospect) the inspectorial role of supervision remained uppermost . . . Few adopters said that they could recall having received an explanation of the local authority's supervisory aims and duties. This appeared to aggravate mistrust or misunderstanding'.

We have attempted to identify a number of key elements in what we broadly consider to be an educative process for adoptive parenthood. These include:

1) the provision of information;
2) the creation of opportunities for parents to meet other adopters in order to learn from their experience;
3) access to other social networks in which adopters can test out and reflect on their developing parenting skills and understanding;
4) the provision of support that is more educational than supervisory or therapeutic in aim;
5) the existence of 'encouragers and facilitators' (often the link worker from the family finding agency) who can utilise their passage agent mentoring role to provide adopters with a reflective sounding board as they develop their special individual competences as adoptive parents.

These features are highlighted and illustrated in the remainder of this chapter.

3.1   The agency view

Agency questionnaire data

The general approach

Our questionnaire asked all agencies what they considered to be the main needs of adoptive families approved for older children in care during the adoptive process and for a year after the order. As one would expect, this question drew a varied response but nevertheless, overall we feel that the emergence of certain issues were such as to enable us to give a reasonable indication of how both voluntary and statutory agencies saw the matter. Some put the main emphasis on support, others on educative preparation, a few on supervision or even therapy and a number gave us composite replies. Also, it is worth noting that many replies were couched in aspirational terms, some qualifying them with comments such as 'in practice this agency often falls short of what is needed'.

The educative approach

It was noticeable that proportionately more voluntary than statutory agencies emphasised educational aspects. The following examples illustrate the range of topics that the educative approach covers:

> *Preparation and training in common behavioural problems; infertility and loss; helping children with identity and contact questions; general support and contact questions; general support once placement is made and the family is adjusting to the new addition; support and advice through the statutory and legal process of adoption; the provision of information about the child's needs.*

> *Helping them understand the impact that the child can have on their life. Increasing their awareness of the child's needs and its past; helping the family's confidence in managing difficult behaviour and learning new parenting strategies; maintaining tolerance and a sense of humour; being open with the agency staff so that joys and worries can be shared; listening to them about what they want.*

There were similar "educational" answers from some of the statutory agencies as well. One, for example, put the whole matter in a nutshell by saying, 'They need training and support to develop confidence in their parenting skill'. Many emphasised the need for quality information about the child, the process of adoption, and about how to handle potentially tricky issues like contact with members of the birth family. A typical answer was:

> *They need lots of emphasis on preparation and training in respect of children's behaviour, knowledge of birth family background, knowledge of the Adoption Contact Register, and about developing of the child's life story record.*

Another mentioned the need for 'knowledge about what post-order support and services are available, information about groups like PPIAS and information about specialist services e.g. child psychiatric services, etc.'.

Preparation and support

Although some replies clearly put the main emphasis on aspects of education for adoptive parenthood, there were many more – particularly from statutory agencies – which merge the educational role with that of support, supervision and sometimes psychotherapy. It was not always clear what the support element involved, as can be seen in the following replies.

> *Support from the child's social worker and the link worker during the adoptive process to help understand and manage behaviour; to help understand what is happening in the birth family; to manage and negotiate contact with birth siblings etc.; access to other professionals where appropriate (e.g. psychiatrists); access to post-adoption groups and counselling.*

> *Regular support from the link worker and the agency; preparation groups continue as support groups; access at all times to a worker they know if they need advice; a network of support to enable space to be given to parenting time, personal time and partner time; help when their fantasies are dispelled by experience!*

> *Constant supervision (i.e. support from parent groups and post adoption*

agencies) and regular training in respect of placement issues and the provision of any information resource.

They need individual casework support; specialist psychotherapeutic support in many cases; regular group work support three or four times a year and a Christmas event.

Specific provision

Two particular aspects of preparation for adoptive parenthood about which we sought quantifiable information in our questionnaire concerned the promotion of support learning networks, and the provision of information about support services.

In respect of *networks*, we asked all agencies whether they 'actively encourage and develop informal networks for families who are adopting or who have adopted older children out of care so that they can mix with other adoptive families'. Virtually all voluntary agencies replying to this question (27) indicated they did so, as did the majority (72 per cent) of the statutory agencies (58 out of the 83 statutory replies).

As for *information about support services* we asked agencies how parents were made aware of the services available to them. The most frequent answer was that they had been told by the child's or family link social worker (83 per cent). About a quarter (27 per cent) said that they had written information in the form of leaflets, information sheets, lists of useful names and addresses, etc. Other methods less frequently mentioned included special information through support groups, advertising events in the media or annual events such as a Christmas party for adopters, and via specialist organisations such as PPIAS, NFCA and BAAF's family-finding service, 'Be My Parent'.

Preparation for adoption: the agency approach

Although agencies vary in how they go about preparing prospective adopters and, once they are approved, training and supporting them, there is a general pattern to the broad educative provision. Many of the larger agencies, both statutory and voluntary, once they have recruited people with an interest in becoming adopters, invite them to preliminary preparatory sessions – often a weekly or fortnightly gathering of other potential adopters – sometimes for a weekend, led by experienced social workers. Some agencies link this with a form of preliminary assessment while others assess solely on an individual interview basis. Once prospective adopters are approved, further training and support can take the form of formal meetings with other adopters, or can proceed entirely on an individual basis. Nevertheless, most agencies attempt to make group provision of some sort, partly because it extends the range of educational input and partly because it is seen as an economical way to proceed. As practitioners and policy makers will be well aware of this, our purpose is to illustrate some of the more problematic issues associated with preparation and training of adopters of older children who have been in care from the practitioner's perspective and from the adopter's viewpoint.

Should initial preparation groups be optional or compulsory?

It was clear that in most agencies which ran preparation groups attendance was compulsory – at least for first-time adopters.[5]

> Even if they come from another local authority and have already done some preparation groups we still make it compulsory because we want to know what they know and we want them to know how we work. If they don't come to the group we don't proceed with them.

As we shall see,[6] some adopters would have preferred not to have attended groups – sometimes finding them an intrusive, pressurising experience. Most accepted it as part of the price they had to pay for adoptive parenthood. Of course some of our practitioners recognised this. As one said:

> We recognise some people feel comfortable in groups and others not. We don't regard it as necessarily a black mark if someone comes along and doesn't say very much but obviously if they don't want to hear about some of the issues then that concerns us.

The value of these initial preparation groups is that they give people a chance to explore the idea of adoption before they make a final commitment. Indeed some people select themselves out at this point, giving up the idea before formal assessment has begun.

Should preparation and assessment go hand in glove?

Perhaps the most difficult matter concerning preliminary preparation group meetings is the relationship between initial preparation and assessment before people are actually approved and before children are placed with them. Here there are differences of professional opinion and sometimes obvious ambiguity of purpose which can be resented by adopters.[7]

---

[5] In some of the smaller agencies or geographically dispersed authorities it was sometimes not possible to provide groups, in which case preparation and assessment would proceed on an individual basis.

[6] See para 3.2.

[7] See para 3.2.

Option 1: Separating the tasks

Some practitioners believe preparation and assessment should be approached as two distinct tasks. For example:

> We start with a six week introductory course for those who express an interest in adoption. After that if they're still interested a worker will be allocated to them and their assessment will start . . . When they are invited to the introductory course they are told it's preparation only, not an assessment course. The introduction is their first opportunity to see whether they really want to go through with it.

> We start them on the initial preparation groups. Then we move on to the individual assessment looking at who they are, what they've got to offer, their strengths and weaknesses and trying to home in on what sort of child, what sort of age groups and what range of acceptance they've got.

Although the above pattern seems to be quite common, there are agencies that do not like to approach initial preparation on a seminar basis.

> We found that preparation just doesn't happen in a group setting – we find it happens best on an individual basis with their own family placement worker.

Another statutory agency worker told us that they start their initial assessment on an individual home visit basis and only invite the "very probable" to preparation groups:

> Sometimes it may be three or four months before we start the group. By the time the couples come into it, there are no obvious barriers to their being accepted. Otherwise it's wasting our time and theirs. In that way we find we end up with contented and less defensive groups!

Option 2: To merge the tasks

More usually we found that most agencies – both statutory and voluntary – held preliminary information giving group sessions during which agency staff observe prospective adopters' reactions to particular issues. They then passed on their observations to the individual social worker doing the assessment, for example:

> They're not put forward as assessment groups. Nevertheless, the fact that they (prospective adopters) are in the group means we regard their response to it as part and parcel of the assessment and it is passed on to the assessment social worker. It would not be honest to say that we don't begin to form ideas about people by the way they perform in that initial group – so we really try to share that with the people who come. Very occasionally something happens

in the group which we think is sufficiently serious to tell people that we are not willing to proceed with them – for example, somebody who makes very racist remarks.

How it works here is that preparation and assessment are pretty much all one process. Most of it is done individually but part of the assessment has a group component . . . It tends to be very full what with the kind of information we want to impart and while trying to make an assessment of the people who are participating.

Playing down the value of group assessment

One or two agency practitioners told us that they doubted the value of using initial preparation sessions as a means of assessment. As one put it:

I have a problem with group assessments. What do we actually mean by it? I know there is a lot of professional investment in so-called assessments – but what actually are we doing when you sit down talking to people about the needs of teenagers or abused children and about sexuality? I don't know what you can judge from people's reactions in such a setting.

Another pointed to the difficulty of judging how people might react in a crisis with an older child from what they said in either a group or an individual assessment session:

During an assessment session you never see a family in crisis. You may ask them how they would cope but you never see them. All the assessment you make can go out of the window when they actually are in crisis.

Initial preparation groups for information giving only

A few agencies organised initial group meetings simply for the provision of information about adoption and related issues. One could term them seminars. The aim was to orientate people to the idea of adoption, sometimes specifically the adoption of older children out of care. One agency called such a group 'the adopters' information meeting'. Held at weekends they organised a varied menu of imaginative educational activity which sometimes included the involvement of children, talks from experienced adopters, more formal sessions on child development, the law, etc. Some of these seminars were spiced up with role playing including:

. . . a string sculpt with a child in the middle who's got all its strings going round birth parents, adoptive parents, brothers, sisters and other relatives which we use to talk about contact and how they might formulate a contact agreement.

3.2   General preparation for adoption – the adopters' view

All adopters of older children learn their special skills and understanding required for adoptive parenthood in their own idiosyncratic way. As with all parenting it is an ongoing and largely experiential learning experience, forged in their interactions with the child, other members of the families involved, and with their wider social support networks both informal and formal. It is worth remembering that the part played by the adoption services may be of relatively minor importance and is in any case often limited in time. Rightly or wrongly, the main input from these services is focused on the gateway to adoption, generally tailing off once the child is placed and the legal formalities leading to the court order have been completed. Nevertheless, because this study was primarily concerned with adoption support services during the adoption process, we now concentrate on what adopters told us they learnt from the system. How were they prepared for the idea of adoptive parenthood during the initial assessment and the placement stages of the process? From where did they get their key information? What did they think of the various methods of formal "preparatory training" and any ongoing periodic supportive learning facilities that they may have encountered? How valuable as learning sources were other adopters, foster carers, social workers and any child psychologists, paediatricians, and psychiatrists with whom they may have had dealings? We approached these *general* questions[8] in various ways – first in the context of our postal survey of adopters and then during the follow-up interviews with our sub-sample. We consider the postal survey data first.

Ways of learning about adoption

Two hundred and twenty-two families (156 from statutory agencies and 66 from voluntary agencies) responded to the question, 'In which of the following ways did you learn/prepare for adoption?'.

This was a closed question which listed 10 possible main sources of learning but which allowed for those who considered they learnt from other unspecified sources, or who were unsure, or who felt that they received no preparation at all. Table 6 below quantifies the responses listing the most popular affirmative replies in descending order.

---

[8] For more detailed data about parents' views of the adequacy of information about their particular child's background, see Chapter 10, *Issues in the Matching Process.*

Table 6
Parental sources of learning about adoption

		Statutory families		Voluntary families		Total families	
1.	Individual visits/interviews	105	67%	45	68%	150	68%
2.	Agency preparation/ training groups	82	53%	54	82%	136	61%
3.	Discussions with adoptive family	91	59%	31	47%	122	55%
4.	Reading/videos	65	40%	44	67%	109	49%
5.	Discussion with friends	71	46%	27	41%	98	44%
6.	Discussion with experienced adopters	49	31%	39	59%	88	40%
7.	Discussion with prospective adopters	50	32%	34	52%	84	38%
8.	Discussion with adopted children	22	14%	12	18%	34	15%
9.	Discussion with birth parents	12	8%	4	6%	16	7%
10.	Discussion with GP	11	7%	4	6%	15	7%
11.	Other preparation	29	19%	5	8%	34	15%
12.	Had no preparation	7	4%	2	3%	9	4%
13.	Unsure	1	1%	2	3%	3	1%

Source: Family postal survey

Not unexpectedly, as Table 6 shows, visits and interviews with agency staff together with attendance at agency preparation groups were mentioned most frequently. In this respect it is also noticeable that the great majority of families from voluntary agencies (82 per cent) mentioned preparation groups compared with only 53 per cent of the statutory agency group. When it came to discussion with families and friends there was very little difference between the statutory and voluntary agency adopters, but in respect of discussions with experienced adopters, with prospective adopters, and in their use of reading materials and videos, it is noticeable that a greater proportion of voluntary agency families mentioned these sources. Interestingly, a small but significant proportion of families (about 15 per cent overall) mentioned learning from adopted children. Astonishingly, 12 adopters (or about 5 per cent of the sample) told us that they had either had no preparation or were unsure about it.

Other sources of learning

The question seeking quantifiable information about sources of learning was followed by a supplementary open question: 'Did you/your family learn/prepare for the adoption process in *other* ways not mentioned in this section?'.

This produced a number of illuminating replies, the most usual being that the adopters had previously been foster carers and had consequently learnt a good deal about parenting in the process such as:

> We have been foster carers for ten years and have been involved in pre-adoption placements – so we have seen adoption from several perspectives.

> I had fostered 15 children and previously adopted a child over five so I was well prepared. I also have a brother who is adopted.

In addition to these kinds of replies, there were some more unusual and rather pointed even poignant ones such as:

> The process of preparation for most couples starts long before any approach is made to an agency, when people like us are coming to terms with their own childlessness

> We had to do a lot of the preparatory work ourselves through contacting various organisations like PPIAS.

> If I hadn't already been a foster carer, involved in training other carers, I don't think I would have had the information that I did. I had already adopted two children and I am very assertive and ask lots of questions and expect answers. Information wasn't usually offered. It needed to be asked for. I usually found that with the high sickness leave of the social worker it was easier to seek out information myself. The child was placed with us for fostering for three years prior to adoption.

> I went to our local library as I wanted books on the subject. Unfortunately there was very little aimed at the adoptive parent. Most are social work texts and written before the Children Act. There is a great need for good, informative books for prospective adoptive parents, especially ones for single parents like me!

> Being church attendees we also spoke to our minister and prayed and fasted.

Stage at which adopters learnt most

All the parents in the postal survey were asked, 'At what stage did you do most of your learning/preparation for adoption?' Overall, 50 per cent indicated that they learnt most before they were approved; 43 per cent both "before and after" approval, and only 6 per cent "after approval"; there being not a great deal of difference between the statutory and voluntary agency groups. However, it was noticeable that 52 per cent of the voluntary agency group compared with 39 per cent of the statutory group ticked the composite "before and after" box which might suggest that voluntary agencies provide longer term preparation and training. Indeed it would be a little surprising if they did not.

Legal information about adoption

All families were asked: 'Have you obtained verbal or written information about any legal aspects of adoption (e.g. types of court order, applications under the Children Act 1989, complaints procedure, etc.)?'. Table 7 below sets out the pattern of their response.

Table 7
Learning about legal aspects of adoption

	Statutory families		*Voluntary families*		*Total families*	
Verbal information only	52	33%	30	45%	82	37%
Written information only	7	4%	3	5%	10	4%
Both verbal and written information	81	52%	28	42%	109	49%
No information on legal aspects	12	8%	4	6%	16	7%
Unsure	5	3%	1	2%	6	3%

Source: Family postal survey

Again, only a few parents replied that they had *not* received legal information or were unsure about it, but also it is worth noting that only 50 per cent received written information about legal aspects to which they could refer later. This response contrasts with data obtained from agencies in which we were told that 79 per cent of statutory and 81 per cent of voluntary agencies provided written information about the law.

Those replying that they had received some legal information were then asked: 'Overall did you think it was a) clear b) helpful c) too little and d) too much?' The replies are summarised in Figure 5 below. Although the majority of adopters (about 70 per cent) considered legal information was clear and helpful it is noticeable that a sizeable minority (about 45 per cent) thought it was not enough. This suggests that agencies need to give more attention to this in their formal preparation of potential adopters.

Figure 5

Family reactions to the information (written or verbal) they received about legal aspects of adoption

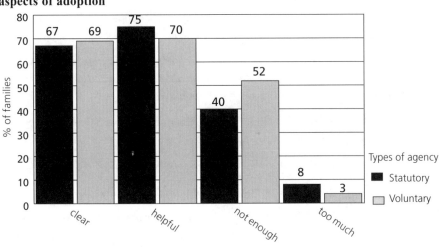

Source: Family postal survey

As far as general preparation for adoption was concerned, our postal questionnaire asked all parents to make an evaluation of the preparation that they thought they had received. The question asked: 'Reflecting on how you and your family learnt about or prepared for adoption, please comment on what you found a) helpful b) unhelpful?'

A large number of written replies were received. Here we only have space to give a few typical illustrative examples of both the 'helpful' and 'unhelpful' categories:

Helpful preparation

Amongst the many replies to this category there is a strong endorsement of the value of the adopters' agency social workers – testimony to their role as supportive passage agents encouraging the adopters and facilitating the process. Here is a small selection:

> *The social worker was particularly helpful and thorough in all the explanation of procedure, etc.*

> *Our social workers who gave us preparation classes were brilliant. They took us through every step very carefully. Though at times it was very stressful, the waiting for placement was worse, and the consent from the birth parents held the placement up. It took two and a half years and we nearly gave up. Now we can see why preparation must be carefully handled.*

> *The two field social workers assessing us were very professional and*

supportive. It was a distinct advantage that the child's social worker had known her [the child] for many years (five) and she had not had a multiplicity of social workers. The residential staff also worked very closely with us as we prepared ourselves – including a high degree of selflessness and use of their own personal time to support our placement.

The most helpful person when we were preparing for adoption was our social worker. She gave us support at every stage and told us exactly what to expect from adoption so we felt we were fully prepared.

A number of other replies indicated how a combination of services had been helpful in their preparation for adoption. For example:

The preparation days organised by the adoption agency.

Mixing with other people who are going through the same as you.

Having a social worker that you can fire questions at – whatever the hour and not being made to feel stupid for asking. Also they provided lots of leaflets and books which were always very useful to read.

Social services and the foster carers helped a great deal but our greatest help came from the children's school teacher and headmistress who fully supported our application, so much so that three teachers and the headmistress attended the adoption review meeting in the middle of their summer holidays.

Having a good 'vetting officer' who we found to be open and honest with us. Talking to friends. Having each other (husband and wife). Having a good solicitor. Support from the child's teacher and support from our adopted son's natural aunt.

Having a really good agency social worker who was clear about his role, who was task centred and professional.

Preparation and training groups were helpful because of the opportunity to meet other prospective adopters.

Constant support of family and friends – encouragement and faith in our ability to meet the challenge!

It was also noticeable from these written comments that certain voluntary services come in for special praise – particularly PPIAS:

We found a local PPIAS group and subscribed to their journal.

PPIAS, BAAF, adoption literature books and books on child development and the discussions we had during the training course for prospective adopters with those who had adopted or fostered.

PPIAS meetings and speakers from NCH, etc. These were the only real help to prepare us for difficult children.

Occasionally adopters told us of particular circumstances in which they had received special preparation and support such as:

Talking to other single women who had adopted.

Talking to and reading about other lesbians who had adopted.

The adoption agency training course – some parts more than others.

Individual sessions with my social worker.

Long discussions with my partner and close friends to pass on information gleaned in other settings, and to try and be clear about what was likely to be involved for us.

All our family have been supportive. Our child has had and has learning difficulties and behavioural problems which initially were extreme. We have received a lot of involvement and support from our family which has been beneficial. Everyone's viewpoint and anxiety needed discussions. We had good support from the social workers as well.

But again amongst the replies there were a smattering of barbed and double-edged comments hinting at difficulties experienced:

Support from each other in our decision to appeal against the panel's decision to place T with us at all (prior to adoption). Some people on the panel who rejected our application unanimously accepted us six months later once they got the right facts! We were delighted.

A deep determination to know their reasons – we had to be a nuisance to achieve this.

Going through the process twice somehow made us even more committed to our son even when the going was tough living with him.

Learning that you don't have to rely on social services to provide the information. HMSO publication books.

Books written humorously to introduce children to adopters.

Unhelpful preparation

Although there were many plaudits about agency preparation there were almost as many negative comments about what people had found unhelpful. Again, we have had to be representatively selective in our illustrations, but it is clear that when people experienced frustrating or hurtful responses from the adoption services they were not hesitant to say so; mentioning in particular problems of delay, being left in an "uninformed limbo" at various stages of the process; being made to feel that their own previous experience of looking after children was not being given due credit by the social workers in assessment; and feeling powerless in the face of mechanistic bureaucracy and official procrastination; all of which imply that they were not given sustained empathetic support in the preparatory phase of the adoption.[9] The focus of their resentment was often the agency but it could extend to the court-related services, to lack of support from relatives and friends and to unhelpful, discouraging things they came across through the media. First, we illustrate some composite replies before turning to comments which illustrate particular aspects:

Composite grumbles

Some people answering the question about what was unhelpful in preparation and training did so by referring to a number of factors they found frustrating. For example:

> The long delays in starting the process of our application. My husband works for the Social Services Department, therefore an outside agency had to be arranged.

> We were not allowed to see the report of the first social worker who recommended that we should not be approved.

> Serious inaccuracies in her report which we learned of much later and which caused more delay.

> The Panel refused to see us or hear what we had to say in our defence.

> No appeal system. In the end we had to write to the Director.

> The preparation/training group actual content was at times unhelpful i.e. patronising towards prospective adopters and over-amplifying the birth family's role/significance. We also had a very unhelpful consultant/specialist in infertility who suggested we travel overseas "to find a baby".

> The time span from first applying to being approved and then the wait for children – approximately three years which the agency considered was fast! The racist attitudes of some counties i.e. "whites" unable to adopt an older child with one Mediterranean parent or an Afro-Caribbean grandparent. The uncertainty of it all. Other parents with their own children saying to us, 'Oh, you can't have mine, ha, ha, ha'.

---

[9] For similar comments re: the adopters' experience of the legal process, see Chapter 13, *The Legal Process*.

Foster carers who had looked after a child for 15 years before applying to adopt wrote:

> We believed the agency was supposed to be acting in the best interest of the child. Had we known the time adoption would take, or the interrogation we would have to face time and time again, and the painful process this would be for our daughter, as well as the strain of her reactions to painful information about her past which imposed on our family life together, we would probably never have filled in the application form.

Delay and a sense of being unsupported

Anxieties caused by delay and the feeling of being left in limbo for periods were recurrent complaints:

> When you are approved as adopters you don't hear from anybody until a child is found. Then you are bombarded until the adoption goes through and then you never hear from anyone again. It's appalling!

> Initially the social workers were unhelpful and we had great difficulty in contacting them at times. Overall the council dragged its feet. The adoption took ten years.

> Being patronised during assessment and preparation

A number of those who had previously brought up children of their own, or who had fostered and adopted before, complained of not having their child-rearing experience valued. They felt patronised.

> I felt the in-depth interviews in such detail were unnecessary before the Panel approval, given our record as foster carers and our obvious ability to look after Jane with love and care over many years. Also, my two children from my first marriage were adopted by my husband and I over 22 years ago.

> The fact that much of the groundwork was covered again and again. We were already foster carers with 19 years' experience – 15 years of them looking after Maureen. Our knowledge of Maureen and her needs was far more than anyone else's including the independent doctor who had to do a detailed medical. It took six years to send us an application form and the adoption dragged on for another three years. It proved a strain all round.

Adoption by foster carers being discouraged by agency policy and practices

Several foster carers felt that they were being discouraged from adopting. For example:

> From being foster carers we had no more preparation from the local authority. In fact, we were discouraged from adopting John and got the impression that social services didn't want to lose us as foster carers. Instead, they seemed to want to disrupt his life further by placing him with adoptive parents who hadn't been foster carers. We were told the "two jobs" were totally different and their policy was generally not to encourage foster carers to become adoptive parents.

Feeling powerless in the face of the bureaucracy

There were a number of comments where people said they had felt alienated or diminished by the bureaucracy of the adoption process, such as:

> The balance of power lay very much with the approving authority. In this sense there was no partnership principle. There was also the feeling of not having any status as "prospective adopters". Rather one was part of a bureaucratic process. The questioning of us was rightly very thorough but little could be given by the approving body in terms of specific response to our queries. There was a feeling of powerlessness which, if we felt it – as articulate professionals working in a related field (teaching) – must be exacerbated in the case of children.

Complaints about the way in which information was provided by agencies

A number of points about this emerged – allegations that agencies withheld vital information or skewed it to suit their particular purpose. For example:

> We found nothing particularly helpful. It was almost like entering a secret society. We were only told things about the children that Social Services wanted us to know. Any information that was released to us was only advantageous to Social Services. Only after prolonged questioning by us did we get some of the information we needed.

> The local authority social workers were not completely honest about the circumstances of our adopted child and her birth mother.

> There was not enough information passed to us about our adoptive son. He had a poor track record and we found Social Services reluctant to pass the information on to us as if they were afraid of putting us off. If we had not known the child since he was born, this lack of information which we were aware of would have hindered the progress we have made with him.

Other complaints about specific aspects of preparation

Not enough preparation

> *If anything was unhelpful it was that the discussions were too few and too short – just two hour long sessions over ten weeks.*

Too problem focused

> *There was too much of 'what would you do if this happens'? 'How would you deal with this situation'? There are no set rules on how to deal with each problem and it is something you just have to face at the time. Their approach was too off-putting.*

Too child-focused

> *There was a lack of any real focus on how you prepare for what the placement/adoption will do to you. We weren't given any real practical strategies to care and survive. All the focus of the preparation by our agency was on the needs of the child, what their problems would be and the "right thing" to do. It didn't help us to know how to do the right thing, so it probably contributed to the feelings of inadequacy and guilt we felt later.*

Personally intrusive

> *At times I felt the detail and depth of the questions to us was too intrusive. I felt at times that we were expected to jump through hoops, specially during the introductory period, and when we questioned things our commitment was challenged.*

3.3   Preparing for the adoption of the child – the adopters' perspective[10]

We now move from the general to the particular and consider our postal survey data concerning the information which parents obtained about their adopted child's background, when it was provided, and how helpful it was.

Family questionnaire data

Sources of information about the child's background

All parents were asked to complete a form which focused on various aspects of the child's background, medical, educational, care history, ethnic background, etc. They were asked to tick one box for each aspect indicating what information they had or

---

[10] For further data concerning agency policy about the provision of information on the child to prospective adopters, see Chapter 10, *Issues in Matching*, at para 6.1.

had not obtained. They were also asked to specify any other background information they might have received. Table 8 below sets out the overall positive responses.

Table 8

Verbal and written information adopters obtained about the child's background

	Verbal only		Written only		Both verbal & written	
Child's medical background	48	22%	23	11%	124	57%
Child's educational background	57	28%	21	10%	113	55%
Child's emotional needs	83	39%	5	2%	103	49%
Child's care history	45	21%	28	13%	133	63%
Child's history in birth family	44	20%	30	14%	133	61%
Child's ethnic background	58	29%	31	16%	90	45%
Child's religious background	70	33%	26	12%	77	36%
Child's cultural background	65	32%	21	10%	84	42%
Impact of above on child's behaviour	79	38%	4	2%	85	40%
Other background information	3	1.5%	6	3%	8	4%

Source: Family postal survey

Two items call for comment in the data on Table 8. First, with respect to the *mode* in which they received the information, although most received both verbal *and* written information (i.e. that which they were able to keep) about the various aspects, quite a large number were only given information verbally. This raises practice questions about the best way to help parents obtain, absorb and understand information about a child's background. There may be a case to establish a minimum standard of practice. Second, as one would expect, information about the child's birth family and care "career" are the most commonly recorded items of information closely followed by information about the child's educational and medical background.

Figure 6 sets out the percentage of replies where parents could *not* remember receiving any information about the child's background, including areas in which they thought information was inadequate or deficient. Here perhaps the most notable finding is the relatively high proportion who could not remember receiving information on the possible impact of the child's behaviour.

As well as sources of the child's background information, parents were requested to tell us whether they received the information mainly before or after the child was placed with them. Figure 7 below indicates the pattern of replies. From this one can see that most information, both written and verbal, was obtained before the placement although a significant minority of parents only received information (particularly written information) after the placement began, which might well have been too late to be helpful.

Figure 6

Aspects of the child's background on which families received no information (either verbal or written)

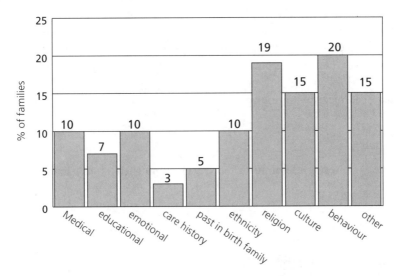

Source: Family postal survey

Figure 7

Stage at which background information about the child was provided

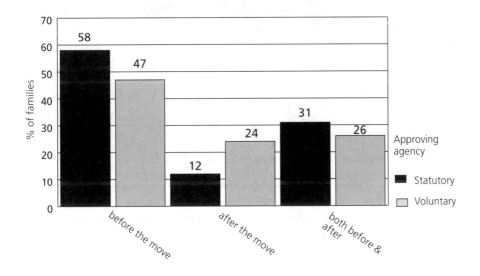

Source: Family postal survey

The clarity and helpfulness of the information

If parents had obtained information, they were then asked whether they thought that it was on the whole a) clear, b) helpful, c) up to date, and d) too little, or e) too much. Figure 8 below sets out the pattern of response. From this it can be seen that the majority of replies considered that the information they received was helpful and clear. However, only about half thought it was up to date.[11] Nevertheless, a sizeable portion of the sample from both statutory and voluntary agencies considered they had not received enough information about the child's background. Hardly any thought they had received too much.

Figure 8

Family reactions to the information they received on their child's background

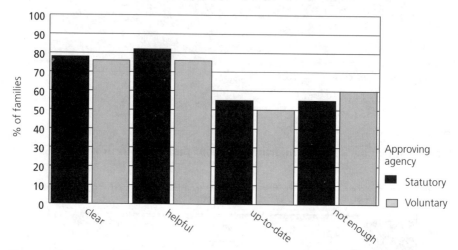

Source: Family postal survey

Parents having sight of the adoption agency file

All parents were asked whether they had seen the placing agency file on their adopted/prospective adopted child. Of the 221 parents answering this question (156 statutory agency families and 65 voluntary agency families), 33 per cent had and 58 per cent had not seen the file. The remainder (9 per cent) were unsure or

---

[11] See also similar complaints about information being out of date discussed in Chapter 10, *Issues in Matching*.

could not remember. A rather higher percentage of voluntary agency families (37 per cent) than statutory agency families (31 per cent) had seen the file. Of the 76 adopters who saw the file most (66 per cent) did so before the child was placed, and there were only two who only saw the file after the adoption order had been made.

The provision of information: what was helpful and unhelpful

All the adoptive parents receiving our postal questionnaire were asked what they had found helpful and unhelpful regarding the information they received about their prospective adopted child's background. Because of the way we framed these questions, and because of the diverse answers they gave, it has not been possible accurately to quantify the replies into a single helpful/unhelpful division although it may be worth mentioning that we have itemised 105 "unhelpful" answers from some 230 returned questionnaires.

A number of themes emerged. For example, almost everyone replying to the question about what they had found *helpful* stressed accurate, up-to-date information and the importance of information which helped them understand the child's background and any behavioural problems they were experiencing:

> *Every bit of information is always helpful, even very small things – it helps you to understand why they get upset sometimes.*

> *Details given on child from birth have enabled us to answer his questions.*

> *The information is very helpful. It will enable me to talk to my daughter about her family.*

> *Details of the many carers he has had, the reasons for all the moves and breakdown in relationships gave insight into the level of disturbance and his need for stability.*

> *I don't think you can have too much information. It may not be helpful at the time but can be useful later on as different situations and questions from the child arise. Medical, educational, family background, photos of his relatives and as a baby are all helpful.*

> *It was very detailed both in medical history and also in relation to moves within the care system and behaviour resulting from these many moves. We were in no doubt what we were taking on.*

The converse of these sorts of replies featured, often in greater detail, in the written responses to the questions of what had been found *unhelpful*. For example, several had complained about inaccurate, misleading or exaggerated information:

> *Vague hearsay stuff spouted by the foster carer, school and social workers.*

It was insufficient and her medical records were incomplete.

The foster mother's evaluation of the two brothers was misleading and inaccurate in assessment of their personalities. The life book was glossed over and in some instances she lied about events. How does this help a child if it is sanitised?

There was no knowledge of the problems he had experienced at school. If we had known he had behavioural difficulties, we would have prepared his school better and ensured appropriate support was available.

We were not told by social services of any reason why 13 placements broke down prior to the children coming to us. They were conservative in what they told us about their behaviour.

In some of these comments one could detect clear resentment that information had been deliberately withheld (a theme to which we return in Chapter 20).

Medical information about J's epilepsy was very difficult to trace. There seemed to be no proper records of this. Information on his behavioural problems emerged only very gradually after the placement commenced. I felt as if this had been deliberately withheld from us.

We had the feeling the agency was not being honest with us (a) about the needs of the children and (b) about the legal situation regarding birth parents. Our fears have turned out to be well founded.

Being misled by the child's own social worker. We were told quite wrongly as it turned out that there had been no history of physical abuse.

We should also point out that several parents complained particularly about the non availability of medical information – sometimes over simple things like whether or not the child had been inoculated against infectious diseases, occasionally on more complex matters such as whether there were serious risks of inherited disorders.[12]

Family interview data

We close this chapter by illustrating from our interview sample some positive and negative experiences of how parents learnt to be adoptive parents of older children. To begin with, we have chosen what might be regarded as a copybook case of careful assessment, selection and good preparation.

Mr and Mrs V had adopted a boy who, at the time of the interview, was aged 10, and his sister aged eight. Because of the adopters' age, they realised they were not

---

[12] See further Chapter 10, *Issues in Matching,* at para 6.1.

likely to be chosen for a very young child or baby, and indeed, at an introductory meeting with the voluntary agency which made the placement, it was made clear to them they would only be considered candidates to adopt older children. They attended a series of initial preparation seminars before panel approval which they found helpful and instructive and which they felt prepared them realistically for the adoption of their two older children. Preparation seminars were seen as distinct from the individual assessment which they went through at the same time. Both processes helped them reach a decision to take on the two siblings. After they had been approved, they attended a further series of preparation classes which they described as more "technical" – addressing behavioural and related issues such as resources and services to help adopters cope with any problems they might later face. At all the seminars and classes they were given abundant written information which they still have and find useful. All the other prospective adopters attending the post approval class were, like themselves, awaiting placements. This group met about once a month and has since developed a mutual social support dimension. Mr and Mrs V valued the second series particularly since they thought they could concentrate more on the content once their anxieties about being approved had been set aside. Overall, it was clear that they had built up a trusting relationship with the agency which they felt they could rely on for support and advice if they needed it as the placement proceeded and as their new-found family coalesced. As the adoptive father told us:

> I think the most crucial thing is the honesty and professionalism of our adoption agency . . . The early preparation was excellent because we came to the placement knowing pretty well what we were getting into. That's the biggest help I think. If we hadn't been very well prepared and briefed, I think it would have been very very hard. A lot of the things we would worry about we don't because we know from what we've been told that it's normal. That preparation was vital and we know the agency is there if we are worried. That security is priceless. I think we've had more preparation than a lot of parents get. I've got a box file upstairs of literature on different topics which they (the agency) have given us. It's all useful stuff. We know if we had a problem you'd have to start looking into it . . . We were pre-warned you might say.

There are many points here to emphasise – the confidence building of their trusting relationship with the placing agency; the keeping of the boundaries between the educative function of the preparation groups and the more personal individual assessment process; the provision of written information; and the access to a support network of fellow adopters who were at much the same stage in the process as themselves, and which allowed them to compare each other's experience of family-making and to learn from it in an ongoing context of professional support from the agency.

Defensive reactions in the preparatory process

We turn now to some problematic preparation and training issues as revealed through our parent interviews. As previously mentioned, it is not always easy to distinguish the learning or educative elements from matters concerning assessment and selection on the one hand, and support on the other. If agency staff are unclear what the primary task is (i.e. assessment, supervision, social casework or training for adoptive parenthood) then it is understandable if parents get confused too and the scope for misunderstanding is needlessly increased.

Above all, confusion of purpose can make parents defensive, strain the adopter–social worker relationship, impede learning and the adopters' willingness to seek help and support if they run into problems. For example, a mother who was in the process of adopting an eight-year-old girl told us about a preparatory interview with a social worker in which she had been asked whether she was prepared to take a disabled child. She explained how she had told the interviewing social worker:

> *I couldn't see myself having a dependent child all of their life or all my life. I was quite clear about that . . . but there was a sense that you were hoping to give them the right answers. Of course, rationally you know that there are no right answers. It's just that you have to be honest and say what you feel: that you've got to regard yourself as part of a team with them. But there is still that anxiety afterwards: How much did I tell them just what they wanted to hear?*

Some adopters had a chance to compare the approach of preparation and assessment of several agencies and several social workers. For example, one mother said of the first agency social worker she met:

> *Assessment was never a problem because of our first social worker. She was more of our age. She never made notes. She just chatted with us like chatting to a friend. It was a very nice relaxed talking situation. She told me so many things I wanted to know. Like talking to you now, I didn't feel under pressure in any way. Yes, you'll go home I expect and write it all down but you do feel under pressure when someone is writing notes all the time. That's what the second one did – made notes and that's off-putting because I used to think, 'What am I saying? I must be careful what I am saying because it's being written down.' I think her questioning was delving deeper all the time. I used to think, 'Is she trying to trap me here?'*

Mr and Mrs A, a couple adopting a seven-year-old girl, found some parts of the preparation helpful and other aspects unnecessarily intrusive. Mr A had been previously divorced and the couple had had extensive IVF treatment before deciding to start a family via adoption. Mr A told us:

We both found the assessment and preparation very daunting at times, even traumatic . . . There were times when we said to each other, 'Well, is it worth all this? Is it really worth it?' And then we sat down and decided that whatever we had to go through to get to the goal, we would go through it. But we did disagree with a lot of the questions, didn't we?

Mrs A:

I just thought that some of the questions were impertinent . . . They would delve into our family history . . . Now I understand the point of asking about family medical history but some of the things like whether my relatives had a criminal history – what the hell has that got to do with it? If my father was a bank robber, what's that got to do with having a child? I felt like saying the history of my family isn't any of your business. But I didn't say that. We were more than humble to these people. My attitude was, 'Whatever you want to know, I'll give you my soul if you'll give me a child'. We were so desperate you could ask me anything. I mean some of the questions – like we were courting for five years and then we were living together for two years and they wanted to know, 'Why didn't you get married before'? Well, what did they ask us that for? I mean when we applied we were married. I don't think that was any of their business. We just said that we never really got round to it. We were quite happy the way we were. Another question was, 'Do you have a healthy sex life'? Well that's a bit much isn't it? What do you call healthy? Is it once a week, once a month, once a year? What's healthy? I thought that was a bit below the belt but I said, 'Yes, sure, yes we do'. In the end we were so desperate you get to the point it doesn't matter if I tell you a pack of lies. I'll tell you anything you want to hear because we want this child so much.

4   Concluding points

Two major points emerge from our material concerning the way children and adopters are prepared. As far as *children* are concerned it is clear that despite the good intentions of the statutory agencies (whose job it normally is to prepare the child) many children are inadequately prepared, e.g. sometimes no life story work has been undertaken; some are moved without any proper preparation at all; others being prepared in such a way that they remain confused, etc. A great deal seems to depend on the skill and expertise of the child's social worker, on the opportunities for continuity of social work support for the child, and on whether the agency can so organise its child preparation work to permit it to proceed at an appropriate pace.

In this context, although published after our fieldwork was completed, attention needs to be drawn to the Social Services Inspectorate's (1996) Report, *For Children's Sake,* particularly to Appendix E which sets out the Inspectorate's standards and criteria for best practice. This states that work with children identified for adoption should be based on a clear assessment of their needs and should be supported by the development of adoption/care plans which need to be regularly reviewed with the children's welfare being the paramount consideration. The criteria supporting this principle include the requirements that:

> Direct work is undertaken with the child at a pace and in a manner appropriate to his/her age and understanding which helps explain the significance of adoption to his/her own situation;

> Specific work is done with children which helps secure for them both an understanding and a record about their circumstances and their origins;

> The nature of the child's post-placement contact with previous care figures is agreed, taking account of the child's wishes and feelings, and is recorded.

> The child is involved according to his/her understanding in deciding what information on his/her background will be given to prospective adopters.

Our research indicates that taken, overall, agency practice has to improve considerably in order to ensure that these criteria are complied with.

As with other aspects of the adoption process, the central problem appears to be that many statutory agencies face too many obstacles from competing priorities of work, lack of resources, etc. to ensure a high enough minimum standard of child preparation for adoptive placement. This means that subsequently often the adopters and their link worker have to struggle to make up the deficiency in the hope that the child's inadequate preparation will not precipitate a disruption. We argue in the Conclusion of this report that consideration should be given to restructuring adoption support services and improving a number of practices.[13] One approach might be to require all statutory agency adoption officers to ensure that child preparation and family link work is undertaken by the same social worker who we think should always have specialist child care training and proven expertise in direct work with children.[14]

As far as the preparation of *parents* is concerned, the main implication of our findings would seem to be the need for agencies to acknowledge that preparation is essentially an educative task. This may mean that some social workers have to modify what might appear to be a somewhat orthodox social work/psychotherapeutic mindset. We see their educative role as one of encouraging and facilitating the learning of the particular, and sometimes very demanding, social competencies

---

[13] See Chapter 20, *Conclusions*, paras 3, 4, 5.

[14] See likewise Barth and Berry (1988, p. 153). This American study found that, 'whether they had high risk placements that endured or disrupted, families reported that having more workers made placements more difficult. The change in workers between pre and post-placement services may undo careful planning and relationship building.'

associated with parenting older children who have usually lived disturbingly turbulent lives. Again this points to a rather specialist child care family support role. This might not be best suited to large general purpose and often highly pressurised local authority social service departments, especially those which have only a small adoption workload.

Another important aspect of parental preparation seems to be the need to distinguish preparation work from assessment and/or supervision. While one can understand the temptation to merge these tasks, our evidence suggests that to do so risks making prospective adopters defensive and hence negating the value of both preparation and assessment. The practice message is that *the role boundaries between preparation and assessment need to be firmly maintained.* Moreover, we believe that preparation needs to proceed on the basis of prospective partnership between the adopters and their agency in the ongoing learning process of parenting the child. Assessment, on the other hand, implies a degree of doubt about suitability, an element that is hard to combine with the notion of partnership. We do not think you can have successful partnership where one party is effectively on trial by the other. On the other hand, as there is a statutory requirement that agencies should supervise the placed child we do not see how the dilemma can be avoided.[15]

Preparation of prospective adopters of older children is a vitally important, if daunting, agency task. For it to succeed there has to be mutual trust between adopters and agency staff. Each has to be on the same wavelength. For that to happen adoption workers have to be honest, informative – both verbally and in writing – keep prospective adopters up to date with developments and, throughout the preparatory phase, they have to be appreciatively sensitive to the adopters' particular needs. All that may sound like a statement of the obvious but, as we have seen from the evidence of adopters, all of whom were eventually approved by the system, there are occasions when practice falls some way short of what is required.[16]

Finally, bearing in mind that, at least on the evidence of our interview sample, a significant proportion (76 per cent) of those approved as adopters by statutory authorities[17] had previous experience of bringing up children – over half had their own birth children – 32 per cent had previously fostered and 37 per cent had

---

[15] But see Chapter 20, *Conclusions*, para 4.

[16] The same appears to be true of American adoption practice in the 1980s. Barth and Berry (1988, pp. 119–120) write that 'amongst placements predicted to disrupt the strongest relationship was when little information was provided . . . Findings show that information is important to stability (of placement) whether or not that information is positive or negative. Families want accurate information and when workers and families agree that accurate information is provided, adoptive placements generally work out.'

[17] As was seen in Chapter 6, *Agency and Family Profiles,* the voluntary agency adopters had a different profile. Even so, nearly a third already had children of their own.

previously adopted children[18] – it is clearly important that agency preparation policies and practices give due recognition to such experience. The educative needs of those with no previous child-rearing experience may be very different and need to be catered for separately. These factors argue against too many fixed training and preparation policies. Rather, the need is for preparatory educative provision to be tailored to the requirements of particular groups of adopters. Obviously the economic viability of such provision has to be considered and here, agency location, workloads and resources are crucial considerations.[19] As we argue in the Conclusion (see Chapter 20) of this report, much of our evidence concerning preparation, as with other matters, suggests the issue of what is a viable agency is of fundamental importance and indicates that there is a strong *prima facie* case for radical structural reorganisation of the existing services.

---

[18] These figures reflect the parents' postal survey findings in which just over half the sample (53 per cent) had non-adopted children living with them and only 19 per cent had just one adopted child and no other children living with them.

[19] See particularly Chapter 19 at para 5.1.

10 Issues in Matching

1   Introduction

In this chapter, using data gathered from the agency and family postal questionnaires and interviews, we present in essence a descriptive portrait of the matching process.[1] We highlight the issues and problems which concerned agencies and families including background information, timing and support. The actual placing of the child is addressed in Chapter 11.

1.1   Some background issues

We use the term "matching" to refer to the process by which particular adults are selected to adopt a particular child – a process which inevitably involves an assessment of the suitability of the one for the other. Before considering issues concerning this process, it is necessary to outline the general context concerning the policy and practice of matching.

From a policy perspective, the matter is covered by the Adoption Agency Regulations 1983 reg 8 explained in paragraphs 53–64 of Local Authority Circular LAC84(3). These provisions require local authorities to have a policy and procedure which cover all aspects of the recruitment process. The Department of Health's 'Standards and Criteria' (see SSI Report (1996) *For Children's Sake: An SSI Inspection of Local Authority Adoption Services, Appendix E,* paras 6.8–6.9), require that prospective adopters

> . . . *are given detailed information on those children with whom they are proposed for matching.*

and that

> . . . *detailed decisions taken about matching are confirmed in writing, with reasons given.*

More generally, it should be noted that, since the mid 1970s, the range of children considered adoptable and adults whom agencies have been prepared to consider as

---

[1] Those who might wish to understand the social work principles of matching in child placement should refer to texts such as Thoburn (1994), Fahlberg (1994), and various publications from the Department of Health (e.g. 1985, 1988, and 1989).

adopters have widened. As far as potential adopters in England and Wales are concerned, the impetus for this development arose largely from the pioneering work of the voluntary agency, Parents for Children. This was established in 1976 with the support of PPIAS (Parent to Parent Information On Adoption Services).[2] Parents for Children was founded on the belief that "all children are adoptable" and that the agency would be prepared to accept referrals

> . . . irrespective of age, handicap or extent of disturbance provided that the child or sibling group was definitely available for adoption.

Moreover, as far as prospective parents were concerned, the agency was willing

> . . . to talk to anyone expressing an interest in a particular child and to be adventurous regarding the type of applicant it would consider. The rationale for this was that, in order to place more challenging children, it would be necessary to move away from the traditional concept of young, childless, middle-class couples being the most suitable applicants (Reich D and Lewis J, op cit pp. 30–31).

In the above study it was found that, although married couples formed the majority of those who were introduced to children (76 per cent), many of whom had children of their own, 17 per cent were single with no children and 5 per cent were lone mothers with children. About half were over 40 years of age.

Thus, in recent years, agencies in general have become much more flexible in their approach to the assessment of suitability of both children and prospective adopters. In this respect our aim was mainly to record what practitioners and adopters told us about the so-called "matching" process. Nevertheless, it should be noted that agencies still vary in the criteria they appear to use. However, concern in recent years to research "outcomes" in childcare generally, together with studies concerning disruptions,[3] mean that the early rhetoric that "all children are adoptable" needs to be tempered by real experience – both positive and negative. As Wedge (1986, p. 78) observed:

> The indicators from research suggest that this is an over-ambitious claim given our present state of knowledge and our present public attitudes . . . it could be that there will always be some children who for one reason or another are unadoptable . . .

One should also add that there are clearly always going to be people who would be quite unsuitable to adopt, even though the criteria for acceptability used in the matching process may continue to change over time.

---

[2] See (i) Reich and Lewis (1986, pp. 30-39) and (ii) Caudrey and Fruin (1986).
[3] See for example, Fratter et al (1991).

2   The process: waiting to be linked

Approval as prospective adopters is followed by a period of waiting before being linked, usually by the agency which approved them, with a child or children. If the agency and adopters then wish to proceed further, the match is agreed and a planning meeting is arranged at which the pace and length of introductions between the adopters and child/ren are decided. The progress of the introductions is monitored. Such meetings can be chaired by an independent person. A time is then agreed for the placement of the child/ren with the adoptive family.

Social workers and prospective adopters alike have told us how the process of adoption is like going through a series of "hoops" on an obstacle course. Each one presents its own challenges. Approval is a major "hoop" but, even if it is successfully negotiated, adopters then begin a waiting phase before the next obstacle, matching. Adopters have described their feelings of relief and joy when they are first "approved" but this euphoria can wear a bit thin if the waiting period for matching proves to be lengthy. Social workers cannot say how long it is likely to be before a possible match is made and warn adopters that a year or two may pass before a child or children become available. This uncertainty can prove difficult to live with for many prospective adopters. In practice that "year or two" becomes all too true for many. But for some others a real shock may be in store when social workers contact them within weeks of approval concerning a possible match.

Prospective adopters manage this waiting phase in a variety of ways. Some try to forget all about it and get on with their lives as vigorously as they can. Others fear making too many plans in case these get in the way of the call for which they are so desperately waiting. Changing jobs – even taking a job for the adoptive mother – is put on hold, as are house moves and holidays. Life is in limbo. If they have already joined a support group, it can be quite painful when some who are waiting are matched whilst others still wait. Self doubt and anxiety can creep in. Some who are waiting take positive steps themselves to hasten the matching process by scanning the newspapers for advertisements placed by agencies who want parents for a particular child. They may also subscribe to *Be My Parent* and make enquiries about the children who are featured in it.

Some adopters who took an active role likened the process to 'shopping'. One mother who had seen photographs of children displayed in a little shop window in her high street could see the point but felt it was 'very impersonal' and that a newsletter giving details of children might have been preferable. But another who had the opportunity to 'pick a child from the pictures' in a magazine found that difficult. A couple who did the same explained:

> *[Adoptive mother] We'd go off and we'd read them all separately and he'd be in one room and I'd be in another . . . Then he'd say, 'Read this one again – it sort of jumps out from all the others,' and he could never explain why it did.*

159

[Adoptive father] I don't know why it was. It's not like a lottery, but it's a bit like choosing something and these were just pieces of paper really . . . The reasons for actually picking out one and saying yes, can we find out more, or can we see this child . . . I don't really know.

It should be noted that the research has found that children, too, have important things to say about waiting to be adopted and being "advertised" for adoption. These findings will be reported separately.[4]

The role of agencies varies during this waiting time. Some social workers contact the prospective adopters minimally, perhaps once in every six months. Adopters can feel isolated and forgotten if this is the case, especially if the waiting becomes lengthy. Other social workers contact the adopters regularly, reassuring them that they are not forgotten and they are actively looking for a match. Some agencies continue their preparation courses after approval for adoption, sensing that this is a positive way of using the waiting time and a way of supporting the adopters at the same time. Some social workers and adopters told us that they feel more receptive to preparation once they have successfully negotiated the approval "hoop".

When a possible link is being considered, the child's social worker and adopters' social worker attend a Panel where the suitability of the match is considered. But when the Panel does not recommend that the match should be pursued agencies face a dilemma. As a local authority social worker explained:

Do we let families know if they have nearly been linked up? Because you can get that situation where you have a family out there where, for twelve months, from their point of view, nothing has happened. It might be that a couple of times along the way they've actually been to Panel as second choice, unbeknown to them.

Some take the view that if, they tell adopters, this will be encouraging in that something is happening, whilst others felt that it would be so disappointing that it would be better not to tell them.

Whatever happens, when it comes, matching is a complex operation requiring patience, thoroughness, skill and support. Many of the social workers whom we interviewed considered mishandled matching to be one of the reasons why a placement may subsequently disrupt. How the waiting phase is handled may contribute to this. Adopters who have waited a long time are vulnerable. They may be so relieved when a child is identified that, even if they have doubts about the match, their anxiety to adopt may override their concerns. Social workers, too, can be anxious to place a child who may have been waiting years for an adoptive placement after many temporary moves whilst being looked after. Foster carers who

---

[4] See *Adopted Children Speaking,* Thomas *et al* (1999) .

had taken on a child on a short-term basis only to have the child live with them over many months or years may also be keen for the child to move on. Others may be very resistant to the move.

3 The linking process

3.1 Factors which influence selection

Some agency considerations

Geography

Commonly, the local authority which looks after the child will look first to its own approved adopters for a match. However, those local authorities which cover a small geographical area may wish to place a child outside its boundaries because, even if face-to-face contact is envisaged, as one social worker said: 'The adoptive parents don't necessarily want to bump into them [birth parents] at the supermarket'. If the local authority does not think it expedient, therefore, to place a child locally, or there is no suitable match from within their pool of approved adopters, they then have to go outside to other local authority or voluntary agencies. To resist doing so could risk subsequent placement breakdown because, as one worker suggested, corners are cut, the needs of the child minimised, and the adopters' skills may not be appropriate.

Conflicting pressures

The need for efficiency and to avoid delay has to be weighed against the need for thorough assessment of suitability, a dilemma which obviously affects both statutory and voluntary adoption agencies. One voluntary agency worker told us:

> *Children are not baked beans. I get very upset with what I think is the sort of management view – the baked beans mentality: 'I'd like 15 placements by September please'. Well yes, fine, you can have 15 placements by September . . . there is this pressure, 'Quick, that looks good! Get them placed! That will be cheap! That will look as if you're doing your job.' Well, if you're moving baked beans around the supermarket, if the odd can falls off and gets damaged, it's not the end of the world. But I really feel it is so important to get the right placement for a child, to take your time, to do it properly.*

Inter-agency contracts

If the local authority looks to a voluntary agency for a match they set up an inter-agency contract. The voluntary agency then needs to ascertain the matching policies of the local authority. For instance, they may have a "same race" policy which will have to be borne in mind when looking for a match. One agency told us that they have a lengthy consultation once the local authority refers a child, discussing what has been done already and whether it would be a suitable referral. However, as the social worker explained, 'The more they tie us down, the less scope they're giving us for looking for families'.

This particular agency has a number of "excellent" approved single adopters. Whilst they might search for couples initially, if they have no success they might return to the local authority suggesting a single parent. Many local authorities approve single applicants,[5] but they can be kept waiting longer than couples and there is a risk that they will drop out if they have too long a wait – another hazard of the waiting period between approval and linking.

Many agencies, both statutory and voluntary, now belong to a consortium.[6,7] Approved adopters are placed in a "pool" from which the agencies can draw. This can be a great help to agencies which may be experiencing recruitment problems. It also increases the choice when a child is proving particularly difficult to place. It should also be noted that family finding services which link children and families such as *Be My Parent* and BAAF*Link* can also be very useful in this respect.

Children's needs

Several agencies emphasised the importance of children's needs and wishes. One worker told us that in her agency they have "needs" meetings at which they assess the child's needs in relation to placement in a family. Another said it was something of a balancing act, taking account of the multiplicity of the child's needs and acting in his/her best interests.

Many social workers made the point that it is the child who is matched to the adopters and not vice versa. This is a blunt message for adopters to take on board. A voluntary agency worker felt that matching works best when

> . . . you prepare the child first and get to know their needs and then go out and look because you have a pretty good idea of what you're looking for and therefore will look at more unusual families – you're not looking for a mythical idea of an adoptive family, you're looking for someone now that you've got this particular child in mind.

---

[5] See Chapter 6, *Agency and Family Profiles*, para 2.3 for the overall incidence of single adopters.

[6] See Chapter 17, *Agency Workloads*, para 5 and Appendix D.

[7] There are various models of consortia with different approaches. Some seem to have relatively senior local authority staff as members. But we have been informed that with others membership has been delegated to junior staff with the result that they become 'talking shops devoid of any ability to influence policy and budget holders'.

She felt that matching in that way lessened the risk of "bending the child" and his or her needs to fit the prospective adopters. It also enables the agency to match the child with a person or family whose life experiences give them the strength to cope with the particular needs of a child.

Adopters' needs

During assessment and preparation the matter of what kind of child the adopters may want is raised by the agency. They ask whether the adopters could cope with a child with learning difficulties, or one needing education outside a mainstream school, or a child with special needs. As one social worker explained, they get the adopters prepared so that if a child comes up 'we have a fair idea'.

The voluntary agency worker quoted above said that they ask couples to think about

> . . . the type of child and the behaviour that will get under your skin and the ways that you were brought up because they will affect your parenting and are there ways that you've got to change? Or what sort of child is going to fit best? Is there something that the child is going to trigger off in you because that child will find it if there is. They have to be aware of those things I think. We start them off with things to go away and think about. It will probably put a lot of people off! But it's no good in not telling the truth is it?

Involving birth parents

Local authority partnership with birth parents, which is one of the key tenets of practice under the Children Act 1989, has recently been reinforced by the Social Services Inspectorate's 1996 Report, *For Children's Sake.*[8] This sets out in its Standards and Criteria that the local authority should

> . . . provide or otherwise ensure the necessary services to work in partnership with birth parents to enable effective plans to be made and implemented on behalf of their children.[9]

Although our fieldwork pre-dated these guidelines, it is evident that the partnership principle was already working in practice in that many agencies involved birth parents in the selection of prospective adopters in some way. Birth parents may have an opportunity to say what type of placement they want for their child in general terms, for instance, whether in a family with some or no other children. They may request that their child be placed in a family where she/he can be brought up practising or belonging to a particular religion or denomination.

---

[8] Op cit, para : 1.1.
[9] See Adoption Agency Regulations 1983 reg 7. Also paras 31–52 of Local Authority Circular LAC 84(3).

Once social workers have identified likely adopters, birth parents may play some part in their selection to the extent of even having a part in the eventual choice of adopters. One worker said that she had learned a great deal from birth parents who had renewed their contact with the agency some years after their child's adoption. As a result she was involving birth parents more, giving them two or three couples from whom to choose. Another, who advocated birth parents' involvement even when they contest the adoption, says to them:

> *Have your fight, but let's talk about how you handle it yourself and how you can participate in this being good for your child. Because actually you can make it good for the child if you are able to do so. Even if you lose your fight with the Department, you have still been enabled and empowered to be good parents in your own eyes by helping choose your adopter, helping your child to see that you can work with this, putting together material for the child. In other words, making it a positive placement and that's much better in the adoption.*

Another way of involving birth parents is to encourage them to give more information about themselves, perhaps writing it down or producing a tape, which could be kept on the file for the child to access at an appropriate age. The social worker who mentioned this thought it was particularly important to do this if there was to be no future contact between the child and birth family, although with older children adoptions she thought that no contact would be unlikely.

Ethnicity, religion, "race", culture and language

Many agencies have a "same race" matching policy where the aim is to place children with parents of the same racial background. Under the Children Act 1989, s 22(5)(c) local authorities are required to '... give due consideration ... to the child's religious persuasion, racial origin and cultural and linguistic background' when making decisions in respect of a child they are looking after. But there is no such specific enjoinder in relation to adoption.

As will be readily appreciated, the issues of ethnicity, religion, "race" and culture have become particularly contentious in adoption work. In this section it is not "our" intention to enter into the merits or otherwise of a "same race" matching policy, but rather to report on the range of approaches that seem to be evident in practice.

In the agency questionnaire we asked: Does your agency place older children transculturally? The response is shown in Table 9.

Of those who responded to the question, statutory agencies appear more likely to place transculturally than voluntary agencies. The latter were more adamant than the former that they would not place transculturally. Of those in the "other" category, typical of most answers were: 'only as a last resort'; 'when in the best interests of the child'; 'only when long-standing foster placements become adoptive placements'.

Table 9
Agencies which place older children transculturally

	Statutory agencies		*Voluntary agencies*		*Total agencies*	
Yes	37	44%	8	30%	45	41%
No	20	24%	14	52%	34	31%
Unsure	5	6%	1	4%	6	5%
Other	22	26%	4	15%	26	23%
(N. agencies providing data)	84		27		111	

Source: Agency postal survey

Social workers in voluntary agencies placing looked after local authority children also made the point that they have to 'go along with' the authority's policy. A typical response[10] was that of one statutory agency worker who said:

> This authority doesn't have a written down same race, same culture policy, but we pursue it in practice.

Others agreed that this was the ideal but that in practice it was not always possible to achieve, so some flexibility was needed. As a voluntary agency worker put it:

> We have a policy of what the preferences are. So the first preference is same race placement with both partners. And the second preference is where one partner is from the same ethnic background as the child. And the third preference is where there's perhaps extended family or another sibling. Then to maybe where there's no possibility in the family, but there is in the nearby community. In practice we are not always able to place with our first preference.

Many said they would go to some lengths to achieve the ideal by going 'all over the country first' but 'if you've done a search and there is nothing there then you're into the next best option'. Another factor is the time it takes to achieve the ideal. The next best option would be sought if it was considered that the search was taking too long.

Matching with adopters where at least one is black or of mixed heritage was a solution for many. One worker spoke of a case where two sets of twins of mixed heritage whose mother was white had been placed with adopters one of whom was black, the other white. She said that whilst there was evidence to suggest that a black family best meets the needs of a black child in relation to identity and culture,

---

[10] A less typical response was one worker who reported that her local authority adoption panel only considered ethnicity to be an issue if the child was black. Otherwise it was not a factor.

those considerations have to be balanced with all the 'other needs' in the case.

Faced with a black birth mother's request that her child be placed with a white family, a typical response was that the agency would work very hard with her to understand why she was insisting on that and to help her appreciate the issues both for herself and her child and why the placement should reflect the child's ethnic heritage. One worker acknowledged that whilst the birth mother's wishes were important they were but part of a whole picture. Another worker explained that if she was not successful in helping the birth mother understand what would best meet the needs of her child then she would have to ignore the mother's wishes and feelings since the 'bottom line' was the agency's responsibility to the child.

A voluntary agency worker talked about a case involving a birth mother of mixed heritage (English and Caribbean) who had herself been adopted by white parents who wished to have her baby placed with white adopters. The birth mother felt that if her child was placed in a white family, she would be saying to her own adoptive parents that her placement had been good. The social worker felt she was also saying:

> '. . . there's a black part of me and a white part of me. Why is everyone picking on the black part of me as being important and not the white part?'

In the end the mother decided that a placement with a black and white mixed partnership couple would be acceptable.

In another agency, the social worker described a case in which white adopters had adopted a daughter of mixed heritage who was now pregnant. The family wanted the baby placed in a white family. Their local authority was not willing to agree to their request and the voluntary agency they then approached said they would take the same stance and would counsel the daughter about this. The parents were very angry.

It can be hard for some adopters and adoptees who are of a different ethnic origin from each other to come to terms with the shift in policy away from transracial to "same race" placements as the two cases cited above illustrate.

A statutory agency worker said that transracial placements had been made by her agency some years earlier when there had been 'less understanding of the issues'. Even so, she felt that it would be wrong to have a policy now which totally excluded placing a child of mixed heritage with a white family. Each case had to be looked at on its merits. She felt that it was particularly difficult to adhere to a "same race" policy when there were so many prospective adopters who say that they do not mind taking on a child of mixed heritage and claim to have an awareness of the issues involved. However, white prospective adopters who wished to adopt a black child were discouraged by another agency. The social worker said that it was important that the child had parents to whom he or she could relate. If the child lived in a predominantly white area he or she would 'suffer' later on because they would 'stand out'.

In some cases the child's ethnic heritage had become what one agency worker described as 'diluted', meaning that it was several generations removed. She questioned how far the match had to take account of the child's minority ethnic heritage.

A worker in one agency told us that she had encountered birth parents of Jewish origin who wanted their child placed with non-Jewish or non-practising Jewish families. She continued:

> . . . A Jewish person might be Jewish in Jewish law but not have been brought up within the Jewish community and may be anxious that we don't place her child perhaps with a strictly Orthodox family. But, of course, we [agency] represent the whole Jewish community from the most Orthodox to the least Orthodox so we can actually match that child with a family wherever a suitable family exists. If it's that sort of fear, then we want to explain to the birth parent how we do the matching . . . Likewise some local authority social workers don't understand the issues either. So we'll do some work with the local authority social worker first and then with the birth parent and usually both together.

Some adoptive family considerations

Children with special needs

A common anxiety was about coping with a child with special needs, particularly a physical or learning disability. One adopter explained that her reason for not taking on a child with special needs was because she was a teacher of children with special needs and did not think she could cope with such a child at home, given she also had other children of her own to consider.

Age of child

Some parents, particularly those who already had children of their own, were concerned about the age of the child to be placed with them. One couple thought it would have been 'disastrous' if the adopted children were older than their natural children. They felt that neither group would be able to cope. A mother was adamant that the child she adopted should be between her own two natural children in age so that they could retain their oldest and youngest status. She also felt that childless couples should be given the chance of any younger children available for adoption. Many wanted a child as young as possible but eventually had to up their age limits because they were unavailable. When a child of seven was suggested to one mother, her first reaction was that she was too old, but looking back she now says:

> I can't imagine having a younger one. I know it sounds ridiculous, but you've got rid of all the plastic years, the plastic dinky toys and the plastic cars

around the house, and the nappies, the teething, the screaming – we got rid of all that. We've passed those years and we've got a nice, healthy seven-year-old who was an extremely bored girl for her years. Academically she was way behind so we knew we had to do a lot of work with her.

Children's needs

It is difficult for prospective adopters to have a sense of the child's needs at the linking stage. Some had reflected on them once the child was in placement and expressed their view with the benefit of hindsight. However, some adopters in our sample had fostered the child or children before adopting them and learned from them what they felt their needs to be in relation to where they lived. For instance, in one case, sibling girls were twice removed to adoptive placements which broke down, returning after each to the foster carers who subsequently adopted them themselves. The girls had explained that they did not want another home, they wanted to remain with the foster carers. Eventually, after 10 years they had their wish.

Ethnicity, religion, "race", culture and language

Nine (4 per cent) of those adopters who completed the family questionnaire were of black or ethnic minority origin.[11] Out of 48 families interviewed, four were of black or minority ethnic origin. However, looking at the sample in terms of placements, three were transracial, the parents being white and the children of mixed heritage; four were "same race" in that one or both parents were of the same ethnicity as the child placed or one parent reflected part of the background of the child's mixed heritage. Comments by adopters about ethnicity as a matching issue are therefore limited.

Some adopters were puzzled by the way agency policy on matching children from minority ethnic backgrounds was put into practice. Others thought that a transracial placement could be better than no placement at all, one explaining:

Very often the choice is between no-one and someone of a different cultural/ racial background. I've worked with children in care. The immense amount of damage that does I think is far greater in proportion to the damage that would be done by looking physically like someone but having a slightly different blood group.

She considered that much depended on the child's age. A child taken into care aged 10 or 11 who had been brought up in a particular religion should ideally be placed within a family with knowledge of that faith. She had expressed interest in a child

---

[11] See Chapter 6, *Agency and Family Profiles*, at para 3.2.

who had one Asian parent but had been told that such a link would be inappropriate. She said:

> *To presuppose that an Asian child will feel more at home in a family that had Afro-Caribbean roots just seemed to me to be totally illogical, particularly in view of the physical appearance of our family. My husband is Italian and he's frequently been mistaken for Asian and our natural children are varying shades.*

By contrast, in another case white adopters were being considered by an agency for linking with a Moslem child of mixed heritage (Malay and Caribbean) who was living with African-Caribbean foster carers. The child's social worker was reported as having explained to the prospective adopters that the child would have to have 'input from a mosque, be taken to Malaysia and the black side of his culture'. The mother asked:

> *Do you think we are an appropriate family for him living here in a white area, with no religion, no contact with a mosque? I ended up having this real argument with the social worker who was basically calling me a racist . . . They just wanted rid of this child and it was awful.*

4   When a link is made

Generally the process is that the prospective adopters' social worker will contact them about a child or children. At this stage he or she will probably give just a brief description and if, on the strength of that, they are interested, the *child's* social worker will visit them, giving more information to help them decide whether to proceed to the next stage, a sighting of or meeting with the child. If they still wish to proceed, a plan for the introduction to the child/ren will be made. During this time the adopters will become more involved with the child's social worker and carers and may meet other professionals who are helping the child in some way. There are many variations on this basic process which will be influenced by a number of factors such as the needs and age of the child; more than one couple may be considered as adopters; the adopters may have doubts about proceeding.

In the selection process agencies will often have more than one set of adopters in mind. Where this is known to the potential adopters there is inevitably a feeling of competition. Those who are rejected will feel disappointment and their resolve to become adopters may be weakened. We report first on the experience of selection and rejection.

4.1   Selection and rejection

The adopters' perspective

Several parents interviewed told us that they had been one of two or three being considered for a particular child. One mother, who found it difficult to feel very involved knowing that others were being considered, described her feelings:

> There was a small sense of feeling on trial, but that was only to be expected. I didn't feel very strongly about it. I was aware all the time that it could go either way and the decision would be made for [the child's] sake and not for ours.

In another case, the adopters were told that they lived too near to the child's birth family to be selected but, about a month later, the social worker returned saying that they needed two couples to consider anyway. In the end they were selected.

One couple who had been waiting some time to be matched were informed about two siblings, both of whom were very young and, as the mother said, 'just what we wanted'. She said:

> I always remember the time when they rang me at work and they said, 'Sorry, you haven't been successful; we've given them to another couple'. It was terrible because I was in an open office . . .

Another mother who experienced rejection said that because she was a short-term foster carer she viewed children 'as a job of work' and did not get 'over-emotionally involved' as a result. This could have helped her to cope when she was turned down.

Other prospective adopters who do not have the experience of fostering may find rejection harder, especially if they have been waiting for what they feel to be a long time for a link. There are implications here, too, for the preparation phase when prospective adopters could be introduced to the idea of not necessarily being chosen for the first child for whom they are considered and for sensitive handling of rejection.

The agency perspective

One voluntary agency worker explained that when more than one family is considered for a child, interviews would be conducted with them by different members of staff. If there was still no couple who was more obvious than another, the team would go through what appeared to be the advantages and disadvantages of them all before choosing a 'front runner'. The family would then be assessed for the particular child.

A statutory agency worker explained that they did not send adopters to compete with one another at the panel. Rather, they chose the most suitable adopters on paper beforehand. They would then talk to the couple specifically about the child so they knew what they would be letting themselves in for before presenting the details to the matching panel.

Another worker felt it was important for adopters to understand why they had not been selected for a particular child. It was not because they had failed in any way but because the couple selected had attributes over and above theirs in this particular instance. She said they were also trying to do this for children so that in years to come when they had access to their file they would understand why the particular family had been chosen for them.

4.2   Models of practice

Background information

We have already considered in Chapter 9 adopters' views about the helpfulness or otherwise of the information or lack of it which they had received about the child placed with them. Suffice here to say that from what we have been told, agencies appear to vary in the amount of information they give prospective adopters at this stage and in the way in which they present it. Some were given brief details initially whilst others were given forms and reports to read. These might be left by the social worker for a day or two so that the adopters could take time to decide whether they wished to proceed further with the link. In contrast, other adopters had to rely on the social worker's verbal account amounting to no more than outline details.

Whether the information is superficial or detailed, it is nonetheless very powerful since it is the key to what adopters so long for – a child. They may be tempted to proceed with the link whatever the quality of the information they are given.

As we have already seen in Chapter 9, the issue of background information proved to be contentious, particularly for prospective adopters, and is addressed again more fully from the point of view of matching later in the chapter.[12]

Photographs and videos

Several adopters were rather uncertain about the value of photographs and videos, one parent expressing the view of many:

> We weren't shown any photographs until they had made a decision [about the match]. I know some authorities do show photographs and, of course, Be My Parent has photographs in. But it means you can't form that visual attachment, you don't have that fantasy figure in your mind for that sort of sweet little child. So I think that's a very good idea, because it does force you to look at what's written down, listen to what's said and be realistic about this child, not just look at a pretty picture.

Another mother who supported this view had been linked with a child and, having seen the photographs, was devastated when the match did not proceed. She thought

---

[12] See para 6.1.

it was all the harder because she had seen the photographs. When she was linked with two other children whom she subsequently adopted, she asked not to see photographs or videos until the match had been approved.

But a statutory agency worker took a different view by explaining the value of videos thus:

> Because sometimes people are worried, 'What if I take an instant dislike to this child?' But I think most of that is overcome by us using videos very extensively and quite imaginatively.

Blind sightings

"Blind sightings" of a child or children – when prospective adopters see the child with whom they are linked from a distance and unbeknown to the child – appeared to be another practice which varied from agency to agency, or perhaps simply from case to case, depending upon the circumstances. Sometimes the request comes from the adopters, sometimes the agency. Such sightings take place in a variety of places, perhaps seeing children at play in a sports centre or park, or out with their social worker, say, at a favourite fast food restaurant.

One mother spoke of the value of such sightings which helped them decide whether to proceed with the match:

> They became real and you could see what sort of personality they were to a very limited extent. You get all this information about what they've done right and what they've done wrong and what's happened to them. It's very difficult to convey who they are and I felt that I'd have known if they were wrong if I'd seen them, sort of like an instinct thing. And there were no negative feelings at all. After about five minutes we looked at each other and we said, 'They're all right, aren't they? Yes.'

A variation on the theme of "blind sightings" is that some prospective adopters visit the foster carers' home and are introduced to the child as friends of the foster carers, enabling them to see the child at close quarters. Some suggested that the child can see through such ploys. One mother said that her children had subsequently told her that they knew though 'nobody had explained it to them'.

One mother regretted not being given such an opportunity. She felt that once you were introduced to the child as his or her 'new mum and dad' that put pressure on everyone, making it very difficult for the prospective adopters to say that they did not want the child after all. She said that the adults could recover from that, but questioned whether the child would do so. Another parent agreed, saying that 'on the piece of paper this is make-believe, but once you've seen them you've made the commitment'.

A social worker agreed with this. She felt that introducing prospective adopters to a child as 'your new mum and dad' gave a feeling of a *fait accompli*. She said that adopters got very upset when things went wrong at this stage, but added:

> *I always think that's fine and that's what this is for. Better a broken engagement than a divorce.*

Seeking additional information

Once a link has been made, adopters are sometimes encouraged to seek additional information to learn more about the child's particular needs, enabling them to make a more informed decision about whether to continue with the match. If the child has a medical condition they might consult the doctor to learn first hand what the implications of such a condition are. The child may be having therapy so they may meet the therapist or psychologist. Parents sometimes visit the school the child is attending to talk to the teachers and head-teacher. Many reported finding this particularly helpful.[13] They may also be encouraged to explore the support that might be available to them. For instance, there may be a self-help support group in their area for children with a particular kind of condition or problem. Parents may also learn more by studying available literature. Current and previous carers can also shed more light on the child.

Saying 'no' to a link

The adopters' perspective

Several adopters told us about previous links with which they decided not to proceed. One couple explained that they could not cope with reading the past histories of some children with whom a link had been suggested. A mother explained that she had rejected a mixed heritage boy with 'severe special needs' because she was concerned about the effect it might have on her own son. She explained:

> *I did not want him to look back on the adoption as something that changed his life for the worse. He may not always agree with it but I didn't want it to be a negative experience in his life, so I had to be very careful and I kept that in mind whenever I looked at a child's paperwork...I was very aware that I was not going to have a child imposed on me and also she [social worker] understood that. She understood when I turned the children down without any reflection on myself. She understood my reasons and I didn't feel I was badgered.*

She emphasised the need to be realistic. She said that when she read *Be My Parent* she wanted to look after *all* the children, mentioning sibling groups particularly who, in other circumstances, she would like to have considered.

---

[13] See further Chapter 11, *Post Placement Issues*, para 3.1

Another mother was wracked by guilt when she rejected a link, describing it as the worst experience in her life.

The agency perspective

A statutory agency worker told us:

> In my experience it's very difficult for adopters who are anxious to adopt to be able to say, 'No. Something doesn't feel right. We don't feel capable here.' And I think that has to be a very skilful part in helping them look at it, so that they go ahead feeling a strong degree of confidence about this. So it's about the skill of being able to listen and hear them say they've got worries and concerns, and not judge them on that but to see that as a very positive thing.

A voluntary agency worker, who was of a similar view, described a case in which the foster mother told prospective adopters that she did not feel they were right for the child. As they drove away the social worker explained that they had the right to turn down the child, whatever his needs, saying, 'He doesn't need you if you don't feel right about him'. He acknowledged that this was particularly difficult for adopters, especially if they had been waiting two years or more for a match.

A period of adjustment before seeking another placement was suggested for adopters who had rejected a match. Contact with other adopters who had had a similar experience could help. One worker explained that the agency would back the adopters' decision and re-negotiate what they wanted to offer. Another said, 'the individual nurturing worker carries on supporting until a match is made'.

Another worker said that from her agency's perspective, saying 'no' was not a problem; adopters would be assured that it would continue trying to match them and that they would all learn from the experience.

The match does not proceed because the foster carers wish to adopt the child

The adopters' perspective

Some adopters told us about their experience of being matched with a child only to be told that the foster carers with whom the child lived now wished to apply for adoption. In one case the prospective adopters had been waiting over two years when they were linked with a boy, shown photographs and a video and, as they thought, the match was proceeding. About a week and a half later, they had a visit from the social worker who said that the foster carers had decided that they wanted to adopt him. He had been in their care for two years, but they had not felt able to say they would like to adopt him until it came to the "crunch". The prospective adoptive mother was heartbroken, likening the experience to the loss of her own babies. She wondered whether she could face going on:

I thought, I don't know whether I want to go through all this again, having this initial phone call. Because you get the phone call and you just can't believe it. It's so exciting and then to be suddenly dropped. I couldn't have coped with it again.

Her daughter was upset too, having announced to her school friends that she would have 'a new brother coming soon'.

Another couple had gone through the experience twice. On the first occasion they had been through the introductions when it 'fell apart'. The father said:

We were quite bruised by that experience and quite frustrated because a lot of the other people who we'd been through the home study preparation with had, by that time, got kids placed with them.

On the second occasion they were linked with two children whom they met, already knowing that one was visually impaired but discovering at the meeting that the baby also had a problem. Because of the long-term health implications they asked for time to consider whether to proceed. This was interpreted by the social worker as a lack of commitment on their part and they were withdrawn from the match.

In situations of this kind, the adopters need support from their social workers to help them cope with the loss as well as reassurance that the agency will continue its quest for a match.

The agency perspective

Agencies told us that when foster carers indicate their wish to adopt they are then re-assessed by a social worker who may well be independent of the child's case. They might receive counselling. Financial implications would be discussed since they might receive a reduction in income. They would not necessarily be entitled to an adoption allowance even though they currently had an allowance.[14] The adoption panel would examine the assessment according to what was in the best interests of the child. If it was decided that the foster carers were suitable, the agency would support their application. If not, they would be given extra support to help them come to terms with the decision.

One social worker suggested that most foster carers do not foster with the intention of adopting although she acknowledged that some did do so for that very reason. She described it as 'getting in the back door'. These foster carers would take on children and 'keep shunting them out' until, say, two nice little ones came along whom they would then 'claim'.

---

[14] See Chapter 14, *Financial and Practical Support.*

5   The introduction process

5.1   Foster carers and prospective adopters

The adopters' perspective

Many adopters had positive things to say about foster carers. Several built up such a good relationship that they were still seeing each other at the time of our interviews. They proved a valuable source of information and support for many adopters. One adopter explained that once she had met the foster carers she felt happy partly because they loved the children themselves but also because she was able to 'get a completely different slant on the children from the official documentary report'. Getting a feel for what the children were really like made a difference to her. In one case the prospective adopter lived several hundred miles from the foster carers' home. The foster carers moved out of their home for a week so that the adoptive mother and child could get to know each other in the child's 'comfortable environment'.

Yet for other adopters, meeting the foster carers proved a negative experience. Some were obstructive, particularly if they had wanted to adopt the child themselves or in some way disapproved of the adopters. The period of introductions became something of an endurance test for the adopters if the foster carers were unco-operative. Such situations cannot be easy for a child who may sense the friction unless the carers keep their feelings to themselves and concentrate on preparing the child for the move.

In a case involving four siblings, three sisters were in a different foster placement from their brother. At their first meeting with the girls' foster carers, the adopters were told that they were 'not right for this family' and that 'they were completely opposed to it'. The match proceeded but the introductions were very difficult because of the attitude of the girls' foster carers. The adoptive mother said:

> Jesus, I thought, what sort of messages is it giving them [girls] about us? And it got worse. Oh my God it got worse! The whole thing was a complete shambles towards the end.

The boy's foster carers were, on the other hand,

> . . . smashing people. They genuinely loved him and they wanted what was best for him. They believed that we were best for him, so that must have helped.

Some foster carers were always present when the adopters visited the child, making it difficult for them to interact. Many adopters saw foster carers as very powerful, one mother regarding a foster mother as 'the most powerful person in the whole scene'. Discussion with foster carers could prove difficult. Some adopters mentioned that the information they were given by them was not accurate, and felt that this was because the foster carers were anxious for the child to leave and did not want to risk the placement not proceeding. Indeed, given the difficulties some adopters experienced with foster carers, the period of introduction to the child was sometimes reduced.

The agency perspective

Several social workers mentioned the importance of the relationship between the foster carers and the adopters. As one explained:

> We involve the foster carer in very early meetings with the identified prospective adoptive family so that hopefully they can build up some sort of rapport or a relationship together so that the carers can feel secure about passing on the care of the child they've been looking after to somebody else.

But, as another explained, introductions which started with 'good intentions' could begin to go wrong a week to 10 days later with adopters experiencing obstructive behaviour by the foster carers. Some might change the times of visits at short notice or refuse to 'put the kettle on' for adopters who had driven 30 miles for the meeting, an attitude which social workers found upsetting.

The transferring of attachment from the foster carers to the adopters was another reason why a good relationship was 'critically important'. One saw the process as a building up of contact with the adopters and a building down by the foster carers which needed careful handling so that everyone would be comfortable. Another summed up the dilemma facing carers when she said:

> When it works well, it's wonderful. But it doesn't always work well, obviously, and I think when children have been with the foster carers a long time and then adopters come in, it's been made to be almost inevitable that at some point it's going to be like two families competing and it causes friction and tension. There are foster carers who handle it exceptionally well. I think when they have been very clear about their role in the child's life and they want the best for the child then they can almost stand aside and allow it to happen and help the child along with it. It works very well. But I think foster carers often get caught up in their own emotions and that can cause problems.

There are implications here for training and support for both foster carers and adopters. Foster carers need to be supported in their loss to which adopters should be sympathetic. One voluntary agency social worker said that during introductions she tried to contact adopters most evenings so that if they had any problems with the foster carers they could be sorted out.

5.2   Prospective adopters and birth parents

The adopters' perspective

Some adopters had been encouraged to meet birth parents, usually before the child was placed, some even before the adopters had met the child. Most described the meeting, usually with the birth mother, as a positive experience even if somewhat fraught emotionally, appreciating that it could be as traumatic for the birth parent as it was for them. Although the value of such meetings was not always apparent immediately afterwards, one mother spoke for many when she explained that it gave her a much better picture of what the birth mother looked like, for instance, how tall she was, which could not be judged from a photograph. She also thought it would be helpful in the future as the children asked more questions about their birth mother and contemplated meeting her. In another instance, where the birth mother was opposing the adoption, the meeting had the effect of clearing away 'all the misunderstandings and the hassle'. The birth mother subsequently agreed to the adoption.

Some viewed their meeting with the birth parent negatively. For instance, one adoptive mother described it as 'a horrible meeting' where she felt the birth mother 'picked up the ambiguity of my attitude to her'. Another described the meeting as 'so false it was farcical' claiming that every time she tried to say something her social worker would 'butt in'.

Some adopters refused to meet birth parents, one explaining that she was 'too frightened' to do so and found the prospect of standing in the same room as the woman who was giving her son away 'impossible'.

The agency perspective

In the postal questionnaires, agencies were asked if they normally encouraged meetings between birth parents and adopters. The overwhelming majority said they did so.[15] They also told us that the social worker for the child and the adopters was most likely to be present and that most meetings took place before placement of the child.

The benefits were described variously as helping birth parents who might have been negative about the adoption, helping the new family with life story work and, more generally, 'answering a lot of questions'. The adopters had a 'picture' of the birth parents which would benefit the child and help them understand the child in the future. Agreements for contact were sometimes signed at such meetings.[16]

---

[15] See Chapter 15, *Contact*, at para 3.3.
[16] See further Chapter 15, *Contact,* at para 4.

5.3   Introducing prospective adopters to children

The first meeting usually took place at the foster carers' home. Some adopters reported that this occurred immediately after the child had returned from school, putting the child under a lot of pressure. Sometimes there were a number of people present – about 20 in one instance which the adopter thought far from ideal. Foster carers were usually present and, as reported above, some proved supportive, others the opposite. This can be very difficult for the child who may feel a conflict of loyalties between the foster carers and their new parents.[17]

Many adopters were concerned that they were introduced at the outset as the child's future 'mum and dad'. Others were surprised when the child addressed them as such without any hesitation. One mother said:

> *The first time he met us – he'd been told that we were going to be at the foster parents' house after school – he came in the front door and he said to his foster mum, 'Are they here?'. She said, 'Yes,' and he came tearing in and hurled himself at us and said 'mummy and daddy' straightaway. No hesitation. He just threw himself at us. We were overwhelmed. We didn't expect that. We thought if anything he'd be very cautious.*

As introductions proceed, the adopters usually take the children out, first for a few hours, then graduating to a day, returning them to the foster carers each time. Then the child will begin visits to the adopters' home, eventually staying overnight and for weekends. Some would telephone each other between visits, many children wanting the reassurance that the adopters were still there for them.

We heard several harrowing accounts of the problems encountered when the adopters returned the children to their foster homes. One adoptive mother said:

> *The first time we brought them [brother and sister] here and then we had to have them back for a certain time. That was awful. We had to peel him [boy] out of the house. He was hysterical. We got him out of the front door and then we tried to get him into the car and he went to the fence and grabbed hold of the fence post crying, 'I want to stay, I want to stay'. I think he really felt that we weren't going to go back for him. This was because of this rejection [a disrupted placement]. We had to keep saying to him, 'We will. We promise we will come back for you'.*

Another described 'going backwards and forwards between the foster carers and us' as 'torture' for the children. The problems were exacerbated because the adopters lived 200 miles from the foster home. The social worker insisted that the children spend one last night with their foster carers which the adoptive mother described as

---

[17] For children's views on first meetings with adopters see *Adopted Children Speaking*, Thomas *et al* (1999).

'prolonging the leaving and that's hell for them' when they were already confused and hurt by a lengthy period of visits back and forth between the two households.

Because of problems encountered some introductions were cut short, leaving some adopters feeling that they had been too rushed with no time to reflect on what was happening.

6   Issues arising

6.1   Background information[18]

Some statistics

Our questionnaires asked agencies whether they provided a written social history of the child/birth family for the adopters: 93 per cent of statutory and 59 per cent of voluntary agencies said they did so. The lower percentage for voluntaries may be explained by the fact that such information usually comes from the local authority which looks after the child. We also asked when the information was provided: 48 per cent statutory and 35 per cent voluntary agencies said they did so before placement of the child. A further 41 per cent and 13 per cent of statutory and voluntary agencies respectively said they provided it at the time of placement or after. A further 43 per cent of voluntary agencies said they expected or encouraged the local authority to provide the information.

Agencies were also asked if they provided a written medical history of the child. Of those who replied, 85 per cent statutory and 59 per cent voluntary did so. Voluntary agencies were less likely to do so because again they saw that as the responsibility of the local authority. Some agencies provided a medical summary, or the medical report was part of another report: 44 per cent statutory and 50 per cent voluntary agencies provided the information before placement; a further 46 per cent statutory and 21 per cent voluntary doing so at placement or after; 25 per cent of voluntary agencies encouraged the local authority to do so.

In the family questionnaires, adopters were asked whether they received verbal and written information concerning specified aspects of the child's background. Most appeared to have received both. An analysis of 168 responses to the question whether the information obtained gave a clear/realistic picture revealed that only 36 per cent were wholly positive, 33 per cent wholly negative, the remainder being a mixture; 35 per cent said the information was not up to date and 55 per cent said there was too little information.

Adopters were also asked if they had seen the agency file concerning their child: 33 per cent had done so, but the majority, 58 per cent, had not; 66 per cent of those

---

[18] See also Chapter 9, *Preparation and Training*, at para 3.

who saw the file did so before the child was placed with them, 32 per cent after placement and 2 per cent after the adoption order.

Parents were asked if their child had a permanent life story record containing information about their past (e.g. life story book, video or audio cassette). Only 78 per cent replied positively, 19 per cent negatively. Asked if the information was complete and up to date, 52 per cent said that it was, 38 per cent that it was not.

Agency perspective

The ideal

A voluntary agency worker aspired to the ideal when she talked of obtaining as full a picture as possible of the child and his/her background so that the right adopters could be identified. She felt that some adopters were shocked by the depth of problems some children have, experiencing real problems in 'taking it on board', thinking that 'a bit of tender loving care' would put matters right.

Another worker said that a paucity of background information would result in adopters 'working blind'. The better the picture of the child's life, the more appropriately the adopters would be able to act and respond when problems arose. A statutory agency worker said:

> *We've certainly got a policy that says that there shouldn't be any information withheld from them [adopters]. If ever a situation arises in which a social worker felt that certain information had to be withheld, it could only be agreed at a fairly high level. So the message is, you tell them. But I still come across situations where a child's history of having been sexually abused is not communicated. That's not practice, but in some instances it's just ignorance on the part of the social worker thinking that it has no relevance whatsoever to the people that are caring for them. So that's quite worrying.*

Another local authority social worker said that adopters 'get whatever information we have all along really'. That information, together with discussions with social workers, foster carers and other professionals who may be involved, is given before going to the matching panel.

Why the information is sometimes less than ideal

Compiling a comprehensive history of the child can be a lengthy and complicated task, especially if the child has been in care for some years and has had several moves. This problem can be exacerbated by changes of social worker.[19] The child's social worker at the time of matching may have limited personal knowledge of the child which may account for why information the adopters receive is less than

---

[19] See further Chapter 11, *Post Placement Issues*, at 2.5.

comprehensive and up-to-date. Unless information is carefully recorded as the case proceeds, it risks being lost when the social worker moves on.

Pressure of other work, such as child protection, may be another reason why background information is not as thorough as it might be. For instance, one social worker told us that one of her colleagues, whilst admitting it was 'bad practice', did not have the time to 'do a social history'. She said that if the information was recorded properly then it should only be a question of drawing it all together. If the information is not gathered and recorded at the time when the agency is working with the family of origin, it will be much harder, if not impossible, to acquire when the link might have been lost. Indeed, one voluntary agency social worker spoke about gaps in reports about things that can be so important to a child. Such gaps will be important for the adopters too. One social worker spoke of

> . . . the wonderful little things that happen in families that a lot of children in care don't have. They don't have these lovely little myths and stories that are embroidered on. I think that's a very impoverishing experience and somehow they have to learn all of those things.

This must strengthen the argument for making available all the known facts to the adopters.

Child's medical history

Some comments were made about medical histories.[20] For instance, a statutory agency social worker said that they 'pay a great deal of attention to the child's medical needs and development'. It was particularly important to obtain medical information about the birth parents as well 'for obvious reasons for the child's future well-being'.

A voluntary agency worker explained how difficult it could be to obtain this information from local authorities because of competing priorities in their work. She mentioned a case where the child might be dyslexic, but the local authority social worker had not had time 'to quietly sit down and discuss it'.

The adopters' perspective

Sufficient information

Several parents told us that the background information they had received was excellent and accurate. It helped them to make an informed decision at the time of matching and also influenced the way they dealt with the child after placement whose behaviour they felt they could better understand because of the information they had been given.

---

[20] See further para 6.1 and also Chapter 9, *Preparation and Training*, at para 3.3

One couple had been able to look at the social worker's assessment forms – 'a big wodge of information' – which they felt was better than taking notes, whilst another reported the benefit of having a written account to which they could refer which saved them having to remember the details of a complex case history and enabled them to give truthful answers when their child asked any questions about his background. One mother said that she had been shown lots of photographs and a video so that 'we probably knew everything that we needed to know about her [child]'.

Some praised the child's social worker for sharing with them all that she knew about the birth family background. In one case, where siblings were being placed separately from each other, the social worker of the sibling who was placed elsewhere talked to the adopters. She was able to give a different perspective having known the birth family longer than their child's social worker had done.

Several who were satisfied with the information had previously fostered their child or knew the child in some other way. In one case the foster mother – as she then was – had met the birth parents and other birth family members over a period of years. By so doing, her knowledge of the child's history and background was considerable, helping her to understand him.

An adoptive father knew the siblings and their birth family in a professional capacity before the children went into care. When the children moved to his home, he felt this knowledge enabled him to understand at least some of their behaviour. A mother who had worked professionally with the child whom she subsequently adopted told us:

> We've had problems with a relatively known quantity. What it would have been like with an unknown quantity doesn't actually bear contemplating!

Insufficient information

One mother said:

> I think adoptive parents should be allowed to look through the files or have more information before they actually go to a panel. They give you the barest information and you can't really make a good decision before you go to the panel as to whether you are going to have this child or not, whether the child is suitable, or you would be able to cope with the problems.

In her case it was the description of the boy as 'outward going and lively' which appealed, but she felt she had been given insufficient information about why two previous adoptions had disrupted: 'it was very sort of sketchy'. The child had a relatively new social worker whose knowledge of him, she felt, was somewhat limited.

Perceived accuracy of information

One adopter who said that she felt she had been 'lied to' about her child's background, spoke for many others who shared this view, feeling that they had been told something short of the truth. She called for 'far more openness and the true history and the true problems'.

Several adopters mentioned that when they had first met their child's social worker, everything they were told about the child was negative. One mother was prompted to ask:

> *Has anyone got any nice words to say about this child? Has she got a sense of humour? They go, 'well, yes'. I think at the end of the day they are going to make you as aware as possible of what you're going to get or could be getting into. They always put forward the things that you could find that you don't like, rather than the nice things. You should be given every scrap of information whether they think it's relevant or not. Even if it's the worst thing on earth you can think of we need to know. Even if it meant that the decision was then I couldn't adopt her. You need to know beforehand and be given that choice. Not having that choice is the problem.*

Some then found that the children, once placed, were the opposite of what they had been told. For instance, children were variously described as 'difficult, with serious behaviour management problems' or 'having tantrums and throwing chairs and things like that' or 'the older child will be ideal and no trouble, but the younger one could be problematic'. The parents in these cases said that, once the children were placed, they experienced no such difficulties or found the opposite to be true. One father said:

> *The papers that were written at the time when they were matched to us . . . basically painted a picture of [child] as Atilla the Hun. She was the child from hell. She was absolutely appalling, awful and dreadful. But the others were fine, and the middle child in particular was a treasure.*

In fact, these particular adopters subsequently found all three children to be challenging, so much so that the father carries a bleeper so that his wife can call for his help when she needs it.

Dated information

Several parents reported being given out-of-date information.[21] One adopter told us that he had been given the Form E (profile of child and birth family) to read which had been written when the adoption plan had been agreed, but it had not been

---

[21] See also Chapter 9, *Preparation and Training*, para 3.3.

updated and was therefore at least two years out of date. Another stressed the importance of information being as up to date as possible. The report she had received from the placing agency stated that the child she adopted had badly burned feet which required regular treatment, but progress had been made since the report had been prepared and the foot problem had become less onerous. She thought some people could be put off by inaccurate, out-of-date information.

Timing of information

Several adopters could not understand why it took so long for them to be given information. Some received it after they had met the child but before placement. Others learned more as the placement progressed. Some had to wait until after the adoption order had been granted. Worryingly, all those in our family interview sample who experienced a disrupted placement – five families in total – told us they learned most about the child after the disruption occurred.[22]

One mother told us that she was given a report on the child's birth mother several weeks after the introductions had been initiated and just before the boy was to move in. She learned more about the birth family as the placement progressed because the child's social worker was still visiting his birth mother once a week to supervise the two siblings who lived with her. The child lied a great deal apparently in part because he had been brought up by his birth mother to do so. The adoptive mother felt that the social worker withheld detailed information because she wanted to place the child with them and did not want them to be put off at the matching stage. The placement disrupted after a year.

Role of social workers and foster carers

Some parents were critical of the role social workers and foster carers played. In one case, the foster carers (who subsequently became the adopters after an intervening adoption disrupted) were very much involved by the local authority in the matching process. They thought that prospective adopters should know

> ... *exactly what they were taking on, absolutely down to the finest detail... Some of the social workers were anxious that we didn't do that in case we put parents off. We were more concerned that we would rather put parents off than have parents think that they were taking two fairly easy children who would turn out not to be.*

All those to whom we spoke in the placements which disrupted[23] complained about the lack or quality of information. In one case the adopters had felt 'iffy' about the

---

[22] See Chapter 12, *Disruptions.*

[23] See Chapter 12, *Disruptions.*

match, but because it was a completely new experience admitted to being naïve. They placed great faith in their own link social worker who did not say that she thought the child would be unsuitable, but they did not think that she had been briefed properly by the child's social worker. The father said:

> At the end of the day if somebody tells you black is white and you've got nothing to disprove it, what are you going to do?'

Just like other prospective adopters, this couple were entirely dependent on the information the social worker chose to divulge – or not – in deciding whether to proceed with the match.

In another case, the adopters reported hearing 'quite a few colourful stories' about things that had happened in the child's past from the foster mother after the disruption.

Medical history

Information about the child's medical history[24] was singled out by many adopters as a great concern. Few who mentioned it were positive but one who was said:

> He (social worker) told me absolutely everything there was to know basically... He gave me all the answers, he gave me all the information. He had been to see the child's birth father so that we would know about sickle cell[25] ...

Another, whose adopted son had a few health problems, felt she had a very good picture of his medical background and future prospects which she found very useful. In another case, the adopters were grateful for sight of 'relevant bits' of a psychiatric report.

In sharp contrast, negative experiences abound. One adopter told us:

> When I asked about his medical background I was told, 'It's nothing to do with you, it's confidential' ... I feel it's the adopters' right to know these things because we were the kind of people who couldn't cope with certain illnesses ... You need to be able to say I don't think I can cope with this possibility so it's not wise for me to take this child on.

Another adopter discovered only after her child had been placed that she was eneuretic. She had been given no indication of the extent of the problem either by

---

[24] See also Chapter 9, *Preparation and Training*, para 3.3.

[25] Sickle cell disorders are severe inherited anaemias affecting mainly people of African, African-Caribbean, East Mediterranean, Middle Eastern and Asian Indian origins. The birth rate incidence amongst people of Nigerian origin is about 1 in 60 and amongst people of Jamaican origin about 1 in 300. For the first seven years of life there is a risk of sudden death from infection so that children need to be diagnosed early and started on regular penicillin as a prophylactic measure.

the social worker or previous carer. It was only when they set about trying to solve the problem that they learned how persistent it had been.

Just two weeks before the adoption order was due to be made, adopters in another case learned that their daughter had a gene which, if passed on to male children, could result in learning difficulties. The adoptive mother claimed that the local authority 'couldn't see the importance of the information'. Additionally she, like a number of others, had no information concerning inoculations the child may or may not have had.

One adoptive father showed us the medical record he had been given which was a photocopy. Half of it was missing. He said that the school doctor had tried 'desperately hard' to get the child's medical records but was told that they were lost. It was as if the child did not exist up until the time of his adoption medical. He continued:

> That is the first medical thing we can find on [the child] and be it the school medical or the GPs, they're all saying, oh well, it's been lost. She [school doctor] said, 'There's been a cover up – they don't want us to see those records'.

6.2   Timing

The adopters' perspective

Considering the match

Once adopters were given information about a child, some felt they were given time to decide whether or not they wished to proceed with the match whilst others thought they were rushed. One mother explained how the decision-making went at her pace:

> I never felt I was rushed. I could say I had doubts and she [social worker] would deal with them and we'd talk them through. It was never, 'go ahead and you'll be all right'. It was more, 'let's deal with these doubts, where are they coming from? Let's sort them out'. I found that useful. I never felt I was being pushed into anything.

This contrasted with a couple who were given the information about the child one day and asked to decide by the next. The agency was prepared to talk about it, but urged the adopters not to take too long.

The pace of introductions

Having made the decision to proceed, one mother said she wanted

> . . . to get on with it. When you've made a decision you can feel yourself committing emotionally. It is very emotional. I think that's the problem with it really. To have people respond quickly then is very, very good I think, rather than leave you dangling and wanting to get to the next decision.

However, some adopters experienced frustrating delays. In one case, the delay was caused by the foster carers' refusal to prepare the child for adoption until adopters were identified. In another case, two sisters living in the same foster home were to be placed in different adoptive placements, but had to be moved at the same time. The delay occurred whilst adopters were found for the other sister.

In contrast once introductions began, some adopters found the pace too rushed. For instance, one child was placed within three weeks of the initial meeting with the adopters. The agency said that, 'they didn't want him [the child] to start feeling insecure about whether he was coming or not'. The mother would have preferred some weekend visits. He stayed overnight just once. In another case, the introduction was even shorter because the foster carers wanted the child to move as soon as possible. The adopters felt they were given no chance to get to know the child. The placement disrupted after five days.

There were some instances where the introductions were cut short. In one involving two sets of foster carers, one was so obstructive that 'the situation was spinning out of control'. Because 'nobody seemed able to do anything about them' it was decided to place the children sooner than intended. In another, involving a brother and sister living in different foster homes, the boy was becoming more and more distressed each time he had to return to his foster carers from a visit to the adoptive family. Because of his anguish the children were placed after one week.

Agency perspective

Only a few comments were made by social workers. One said that the length of time adopters had been waiting to be matched was not a consideration in their selection. A voluntary agency worker said that the more the local authority tied them down to what they wanted in prospective adopters, the longer a match was likely to take.

7   Concluding points

In this final section we draw together what we consider to be the key emerging points.

1. Recruiting adopters

- Agencies should not be hidebound by rigid views about, for example, age or marital status, in terms of who they recruit as adopters which might preclude consideration of those who have much to offer.
- Agencies should be prepared to look outside their own pool of approved adopters for a match. This might help reduce the time the child languishes in care. It may also help when the child and carers have to separate because the longer the child

stays, the stronger may be the attachment and the harder will be the loss for both child and carers to cope with. It may also help reduce the waiting time between approval and linking for some adopters.

- Social workers and foster carers should listen to what the children are looking for in a permanent family. If they have become attached to their foster carers – especially if the placement has been a long one – they may wish to stay with them.
- Before looking for a match elsewhere, agencies should explore foster carers' views about the child moving on, ensuring that they are not interested in offering the child a long-term or permanent home themselves or, if they are, that they are not suitable.

2. Ethnicity

- Whilst "same race" placements might be the ideal, consideration of a transracial placement should not be ruled out, especially if the child has been waiting to be matched for a long time.
- The views expressed by some adopters and social workers about ethnicity in matching can be regarded as sensitive and controversial. Pejorative terms such as "problem" and "racist" were used. Some agency workers appear to be negative and defensive about this aspect of their work, their views and language reflecting the wider social context of racism and discrimination. This has implications for the recruitment and training of both adopters and social workers.

3. The role of foster carers

- Foster carers may have the power to make or break the transition. If they are supportive of the move, they are more likely to prepare the child well, support the child and ease the move for the child. Their support is also more likely to extend to the adopters, again making for a more positive transition.
- Foster carers need training to better enable them to prepare and support the child and to support the adopters

4. Respecting the adopters' position

- Agencies should respect what adopters consider to be their limitations regarding the child in terms of age, number, gender, special needs. They should resist the temptation to bend and extend what the adopters can manage in order to place a child.
- Adopters should be enabled to say no to a match by assuring them that to do so does not preclude them from further consideration. They should be supported when they do so.

5. Supporting adopters

- Adopters need support during the waiting time between approval and linking. Further training sessions during this time could be useful, helping to keep the issues and challenges in mind when they have to decide whether to proceed with a match.
- Informing adopters when they have been considered as a potential match for a child even when they were not selected is probably desirable. It should be explained why they were not selected and they should be reassured that there will be other chances.
- When rejected for a match in favour of others, adopters should be supported and encouraged in their resolve to continue.
- Adopters should be given all the available background information about the child. This will help them to make a more considered decision about the match and help them in their future care and understanding of the child if they proceed. Agencies expect prospective adopters to be open and honest when they are assessed. They should be likewise with the adopters.
- A medical history of the child should be available as of right.
- Adopters should be supported when they have to deal with obstructive foster carers. There is no guarantee that they will get on. They may take an instant dislike to each other. Their life-styles may be very different, making communication harder. Their ideas about bringing up children may differ. Whilst the agency will have taken care to match the child and adopters, foster carers and adopters are not matched. In the best case scenario, they will both have the future welfare of the child as a common aim, will be sensitive to each other's needs, and will help and support each other. In the worst case scenario, where the carers are opposed to the removal of the child, the skill and support of the professionals involved will be vital.

6. Introducing adopters to the child

- Careful thought should be given to how the child is introduced to prospective adopters. To be introduced as 'mum and dad' puts pressure on everyone, suggesting that there is no turning back for either child or adopters.
- Blind sightings should be a matter for individual choice.
- The plan and pace of introductions will depend on individual needs – of the child, foster carers and adopters. Their progress should be monitored so that problems can be aired and addressed. The plan and pace may need to be adjusted.
- Adoption leave – the equivalent of maternity leave – would help adopters to cope with introductions and placement.[26]

---

[26] But note under the Employment Relations Bill 1999 provision is made for parental leave (unpaid). See further Chapter 1, *Introduction*, note 14.

190

7. Supporting the birth parents

- Involving birth parents in the selection of adopters can have positive short and long-term benefits. It may help them come to terms with their loss; it may help adopters in their current and future care of the child; and it may help the child in later life, knowing that the birth parents were involved. A meeting between birth parents and adopters can be beneficial, helping the birth parents who may be reassured that the adopters will care for their child and helping the adopters in that they will be able to tell the child at the appropriate time about their birth parents.

8. Adopters' suggestions for future practice

When talking about matching, adopters made a number of suggestions for alleviating some of the difficulties they experienced. These were:

- Agencies should have clear definitions of what they are looking for in families.
- Adopters should be given details of more than one child to consider at the linking stage.
- Every scrap of background information should be made available.
- Guidelines should state what background information should be given to adopters who should sign a document saying they have been given the information.
- There should be access to agency files before the application is considered by the matching panel.
- There should be an opportunity to see the child in neutral surroundings before being formally introduced.

11 **Post Placement Issues**

1   Introduction

In this chapter, we examine qualitative material concerning critical stages in the adoption placement, particularly the children's move out of care to the adoptive home and adjustments that have to be made including entry to new schools.[1]

Several introductory comments need to be made: first, the case material is in some respects surprising. While we have a number of "copy-book" placements where transitions have been well prepared, anticipated and supported and where the children appeared to have settled well, there are others where despite all the careful preparation, matching and support, both children and parents have found the transitions hard to cope with. One of these placements has *subsequently* disrupted as we know from our related study, *Adopted Children Speaking* (Thomas *et al*, 1999). Yet also there are instances of what seems to have been poor preparation and inadequate support when placements were made; where the children's behaviour on placement was extraordinarily testing but where the adopters, despite being "taken by storm", appeared to have weathered the initial crises. By the time we interviewed them, things appeared to have calmed down and the children were apparently thriving. Nevertheless, there were also instances where what appeared to have been poor and inappropriate placements in the first instance, sometimes inadequately supported, were either on the verge of collapse when we interviewed the adopters or had actually resulted, after months of perseverance, in the child returning to care.

Superficially, therefore, one might be tempted to conclude that, because of such a mixed picture, it is not possible to draw any hard and fast conclusions from the adopters' experience about the way these key transitions should be handled. We disagree. First, the data indicate where it should have been possible to have shielded the child and adopters from needless stress or at the very least to have enabled them to feel better supported. Second, we suggest that closer examination of the material – as we hope to show – gives ample evidence to support what we know theoretically and from other child studies about psycho-social processes of attachment and loss and adaptation to critical transitions.

---

[1] Reference also needs to be made to Chapters 3, *Social Construction of Adoption,* and 4, *The Older Child's Status Passages,* in which we discuss attachment theory, critical transitions and status passage.

2   Post-placement case studies

2.1   Horrid beginnings, happy endings

The C family has been chosen as an example of where the placement began in the most unpromising circumstances but which survived the initial traumas and appeared to be progressing well.

The adopters already had three children of their own aged 12, 11 and nine and after being selected as prospective adopters by a statutory agency, agreed to provide a home for a sibling group comprising a boy aged eight, twin girls of six and a younger sister of five. The three sisters had lived in one foster home and their older brother in another. The adoptive mother, Mrs C, painted a picture of a placement which, at the time it commenced at the beginning of the summer holidays, appeared to have been poorly supported by the children's social workers. Also the girls' foster carers seemed reluctant to support the move in contrast to their brother's foster carers who were described as having prepared him very well. We quote from Mrs C's description of the initial weeks of the placement:

> *The first two weeks everything hit the fan. It was appalling. It really was. It was diabolical. All three social workers went on holiday – the whole lot of them together. It was just bad luck I suppose or bad communication, but it happened. Realistically I suppose there was nothing anyone could have done to help us in these first two weeks. The fact of the matter was that there were suddenly nine people in this house and we all had to get used to each other and live together. No outside agency could help with that.*

She describes in some detail a chaotic few days as the new arrivals effectively 'crashed' into their lives.

> *John (the nine-year-old boy) went ape. He'd pull things out – fingers into everything – smashing things up. Nobody could control him. He was flying off the walls. He'd fuse the lights. The girls were having the screaming hab dabs. One of them had made friends with my eldest daughter and the other one felt excluded. Every time John went into hyperspazz and every time someone's back was turned Lorna, his younger sister, would use it as a diversion to go and drag all the stuff out of the cupboards or go and make mud pies in the sink. The kids just seemed to hate each other's guts. They all hated all of the others.*

She described the impact of all this on her three birth children:

> *My son Peter was going to leave home. Geoffrey just largely stepped out of it and shut himself into his room and waited for it all to go away. John wanted to be friends with Peter but on the other hand he didn't want Peter putting any restrictions on what he could do. So they were at it hammer and tongs.*

> *My daughter Julia just couldn't handle the younger children blowing hot and cold. She's temperamental anyway so the younger children had hell with her.*

On top of all this one of the twins accused their brother John of sexually assaulting her. Mrs C told us that she thought the girls' foster carers 'had put it into the girls' heads' that they should not live with their older brother for fear of abuse. At all events this episode in the first week was the trigger for Mrs C to seek help from the social services department. She said:

> *So I phoned Social Services and found out all our social workers were on holiday and I said, 'I don't care who the hell you get. Just get someone down here and get them down here now!' They sent someone down. She was quite pleasant. I explained the problem and she asked me what I wanted to do and I said, 'I want you to go and get me a series of intercoms'. We had one in the girls' bedroom and one in our room which we could plug in and we could hear what was happening. For the next two or three nights neither my husband nor I stayed awake and we also watched the stairs.*

One might well wonder what sustained the resolve and resilience of these parents and their three older children to persevere in such circumstances, but persevere they did. Remarkably, everything seemed to take a turn for the better when the parents decided either as a stroke of intuitive genius or out of sheer desperation to take all seven children on a canal boat holiday. This is how the mother described the turn of events:

> *What actually sorted it out was that in the second week when things weren't getting any better, we booked a canal boat holiday on a narrow boat and all nine of us crammed into the boat for a week. And it was so awful that when we got back here everything seemed wonderful in comparison. It was the turning point. We were jammed together. Because we were so damned cramped, and because there was no question that the children had to do as we told them because of the danger and the safety factor, we just had to gel and we did. When we came back, although we've had our problems, they've been trivial by comparison to that awful beginning.*

2.2 A careful match and good support can work wonders

Provided that adopters themselves are realistic and have thought through the implications of adopting an older child, and provided the agency has made a careful match with adequate preparation and support, the initial phase of a placement need not be the critical trauma that it was for some families.

David, a nine-year-old of mixed parentage, had lived with black foster carers for several years before he was placed for adoption with Mrs E, a divorced African-

Caribbean mother with two birth children, a 22-year-old daughter and a son aged 13. Mrs E was a school teacher who had herself grown up in a large family. Her own mother had always looked after other people's children some of whom had stayed and lived as part of the family. So culturally one could say she was attuned to the idea of adoption. When a social worker friend talked to her about the problem of finding suitable adoptive homes for black and mixed parentage children she was, as it were, ready to take the plunge. Initially the agency wanted her to take a child with special needs because she taught such children. But Mrs E thought long and hard about it and decided that another boy of school age would best fit into her family, career and active lifestyle. In her own words:

> I knew my limitations . . . and I knew it would affect my home if I took on a special needs child . . . If I didn't work with children with special needs it might have been different.

She also knew that, despite the age difference, the arrival of a nine-year-old boy would be a challenge to her 13-year-old son, Peter, and that she would have to prepare him for it. Even so, the initial few weeks were not without incident. As she told us:

> Since he was about nine, Peter had got used to the whole house revolving around him. He had to adjust. He was no longer the baby of the family. So I had to make it clear to him that when David came David's needs had to be foremost while I got him settled in. And yes, my relationship with Peter did change for a while. He didn't talk to me as much. And he said, 'You always stick up for David,' and we had a few disagreements about that.

She then described how she had had to reassure Peter:

> I had to work on putting him really on an even keel and showing him that David's arrival didn't change how I felt about him. We just had to fit David in.

She quickly worked out a routine of giving each child, including her eldest 22-year-old daughter, a time each evening when they would have her undivided attention talking about the events of the day, etc., what she called a 'settee job'. As she put it, with regard to David:

> I had to find time for David. I had to see he had my time for himself. If he wanted to play we'd play. If he wanted to lie on the settee and talk to me he could. If he just wanted me to be there until half past eight bed time he still had my total undivided attention. Once I had put that in place he settled. He just needed some time.

But even so all this took a few weeks to work out. Initially she had had David's reaction to separation from his foster home to cope with as well as Peter's reaction to David. It appears that David was one of those children who expressed his grief about separation openly when he first felt it and it seems to have been quickly worked through with Mrs E's sensitive support. The confidence with which she handled things reflected her experience both as a teacher and as a mother. This is how she described it:

> He threw one tantrum with me the day after he'd moved into my home. It was over a ride on a bike. I sent him upstairs and he said he wasn't going upstairs so I just picked him up and took him upstairs. He jumped up and down. I said, 'Well, you stay there until you stop screaming!' And I sat outside his room for a while. Then I realised the tears weren't just a tantrum. They were also the tears of a child who had just been moved. It was his reaction to the whole process. I went in and gave him a cuddle. You can hear the difference in tears. He didn't know how to say, 'look, this is a massive, massive move in my life. I've come from this sort of family'. And you felt for the child. And we just sat and had a cuddle and then he was all right. And we've never seen another tantrum – nothing like that. Nothing.

David's relationship with his older adoptive brother Peter took a little longer to get sorted out. Very quickly this had flared up into a fight over playing with a computer game. Mrs E told us:

> Within two days they were arguing over this game. At first I couldn't believe it. All hell let loose over a silly game. I thought, 'Why in the hell are you fighting over this!' Because Peter had loads of these things. And all of a sudden this other child wanted to use one of his things. Besides there was such a difference between what Peter had and what David had. David had come with so little. I was surprised he had so little. We're a fairly big family – not rich but I hold a reasonable job and earn a decent salary. So we do all right, the kids do. And Peter has lots. But of course David wanted to share them while Peter didn't want him to touch them. So they had arguments and I had to split them apart.

While Peter was adjusting to David, Mrs E received a great deal of support from her agency social worker who appears to have provided balance, wise counsel, consistency and continuity of care over this initial phase. Mrs E found her easy to talk to; honest about what she could be expected to face in adopting an older child. She was also reported as having supported Mrs E's own children, talking them through and helping them to open up about their feelings and fears about adoption and the changes they might experience. With the agency social worker's support, Mrs E was able to work through her son Peter's feelings that she 'stuck up more for David than she did for him'. To mend things with Peter she set aside a special time after David had gone to bed in the evening to talk about Peter's feelings and the changes that were going on in his family. A turning point, and the point at which Peter accepted David, came when David had to go into hospital for an operation. This pulled them together as a family and the two boys have since become close.

2.3 Previous parenting experience, realistic preparation and agency support eases the transition to placement

Several adopters clearly felt they had been well prepared and matched for the challenges associated with the adoption of older children; parents who had thought through realistically the implications for themselves and for any other children in their family. These parents generally told us that the placement had been testing in certain respects but they had the experience and resources to cope with it.

For example, one couple wanted to adopt after the wife had had two miscarriages following the birth of their daughter, who is now aged 11. They applied to a voluntary adoption agency. After the selection process and after waiting several years (and having been disappointed once when the foster carers of a little boy they were about to have placed with them decided to adopt him instead), the family was eventually matched with two children, John aged eight and his sister Alison aged five.

John and Alison had been in care about four years and had been fostered separately – supposedly on a short-term basis. John and Alison had not seen each other whilst in foster care and by the time they were prepared for adoption had little memory of each other. Once the family had been identified as prospective adopters John and Alison were gradually introduced to each other over a six week period. It was only then that the adopters were introduced to the children. John seems to have been better prepared by the foster carers for the adoption placement than his sister who had formed an attachment to her single black foster mother (who was fostering a number of other children) and was more reluctant than her brother to move. The adoptive mother told us that originally the agency, the adoptive family and the foster carers had hoped to go at Alison's pace over the introductory period but for various reasons both children were placed within a week of their first meeting the family. This was more appropriate for John than it was for Alison.

On the day of the move a party was arranged at Alison's nursery school for the children, the foster carers and other children from the foster placements. The plan was that the adopters would pick the children up from the party, and then collect their belongings from the foster homes. Alison's foster mother did not come to the party. This is how the adoptive mother described the critical events of the day the placement began and the distress which Alison experienced:

We were invited to the party although we never saw Alison because she was

*just being carried around by everybody. Alison didn't want to be part of any-
thing at all at the party. She wouldn't speak to us that day. She just would not
speak, not even to [the adoptive father] who she usually would do before.
Well, we went to pick up John's suitcase first from his foster home and then
we had to go to Alison's and that was really traumatic. She was in such a state
that she wouldn't come to the door.*

Researcher : *Did she know you were going to her foster home?*

The adoptive mother : *No she didn't initially. The social worker said, 'Leave
them in the car and I will ask [Alison's foster mother] if she wants to see her'.
Because you see, the foster mother wouldn't come to the party. So the social
worker went to ask her if she wanted to see Alison and she said, 'Yes, I've got
a doll for her'. But she was so choked up on the doorstep about Alison's
departure and we didn't really want her getting upset in front of the children
because it was hard enough for them anyway.*

When they got to the adopters' home, the children emptied their suitcases which
were taken away in the social worker's car. This was especially important to John as
the social worker felt it would help him believe that he was finally staying in this
placement. Other adopters had been identified for him some time before and he had
been introduced to them and they were reported as having asked him what he would
like for Christmas but then he never saw them again. So the social worker on this
occasion was particularly keen to reassure him that this adoptive placement was for
real.

2.4   Inadequate preparation and inappropriate matching can quickly lead to disaster

As a fourth and final case illustrating critical transitions into placement, we have
chosen one of the saddest accounts given to us by the adoptive parents in our
interview sample. It concerns a placement that disrupted.

The background

Mr and Mrs G, a middle-aged couple, had both been married before. Mr G had a
grown-up daughter by his first marriage. They married too late to have children but
because they wanted to make a family and had a secure home and themselves to
offer, decided to adopt an older child. While they were being assessed by a statutory
adoption agency, they had made it clear that they did not feel that they could cope
with a physically disabled child or one who was violently disturbed. They expressed
a preference for a child in the 7–10 age range and expected they might well, once
approved, receive a child who had been sexually abused. Within a few weeks of
panel approval their own social worker visited to say there was a boy, Graham,

almost 10 years old, who might be suitable. They expressed interest and so Graham's social worker visited them, showed them a video and gave them some details.[2] Over a five-week period after they had heard something about Graham and seen his introductory video, they visited him and his foster carers. They took him out for a few hours on several occasions. He also visited their home with his social worker for tea and stayed with them twice overnight on a Friday evening before the placement began. On the strength of this Mr and Mrs G arranged for him to attend a local school after he had been placed.

The placement

The placement started a fortnight later. This was earlier than Mr and Mrs G had expected but was evidently because Graham's foster carers were taking on other children and wanted him placed elsewhere quickly. As soon as they collected him Graham asked Mr and Mrs G if they could buy him a hamster. This surprised them and, as we shall see, this developed into what can only be described as the first challenging event. They explained what happened:

> Mr G: *He came in and said he wanted an animal, a pet.*
>
> Researcher : *What, the minute he stepped across the threshold?*
>
> Mrs G : *Yes. We said we had no objection. It was decided it was going to be a hamster because that was what he wanted. We said, 'Well, give it a couple of days and we'll look into it. Let's get you settled in first'. But no, he wanted a hamster and he wanted it that Friday night. The shop was shut, but he wanted a hamster that night. Somebody had actually given us a cage, so he got that set up and we eventually gave in and got the hamster on the Saturday morning.*
>
> Mr G: *You see we thought that was the right thing to do psychologically: buy him a pet so he's got a mate in a new home.*
>
> Mrs G: *He wanted it in his room.*

Mr and Mrs G went on to describe how Graham wanted to rearrange the bedroom and 'played with the hamster until three o'clock on Sunday morning with sawdust all over the floor'. He was difficult to get to bed and an argument developed. Graham seems to have got into a tantrum which involved him pulling furniture around the room and at some point pulling a cupboard door off its hinges. Within a few hours Mr and Mrs G were at their wits end and their tempers were frayed. Mr G recalled:

---

[2] At this point it should be said that, after the disruption, Mr and Mrs G discovered that the agency knew a great deal more about Graham's history and disturbed behaviour than they claimed to have been told when the placement was being set up. So, as we shall see in Chapter 12, *Disruptions,* para 5, when they looked back on the placement they considered they had been badly misinformed and misled.

He was starting to get a bit awkward. When I threatened to smack him he reminded me you are not allowed to do so. He was going out towards the kitchen and I was walking by and just moved aside and he touched me. He said, 'I shall tell the social worker you touched me'. Well, you can see how quickly it got to us. It was a fiasco. At the time I could have clipped him around the ear quite happily, but it's what it leads to afterwards. You've got to be so careful.

Mrs G recalled that at some point in what seems to have been a series of defiant temper tantrums over three days, 'We tried the "you stay in your bedroom until you calm down" approach but that was when he threatened to jump out of the window sitting on the window ledge in his bedroom upstairs . . . it got to the point where we could not leave him alone'. By Sunday Mr and Mrs G were sufficiently alarmed to telephone the emergency number in the social services department. It was suggested that the following day they meet a couple who had experience of fostering difficult children. While they were meeting them, the Department arranged for another older couple which Mr and Mrs G described as 'baby sitters' to be with Graham. Mr G explained:

The Department said, 'We're going to arrange for someone to come in and baby-sit so you can meet this older couple and have a chat with them'. 'Don't give up on it yet' was their attitude. So this old couple came in to baby-sit and we went off out. But having spoken to these other people they told us, 'If we was you we'd get shot of him'. So we came back after this conversation still very unsure what we were going to do. So we came back in and this other couple who'd had him while we were out, they'd had a nightmare with him. They too had had trouble with him. The man was trying to play cards with Graham, but Graham had lost his temper and had thrown the cards about. He'd really kicked up. They eventually got him to bed and he was asleep by the time we came in . . . They said to us, 'If you carry on you are going to have a hell of a time for a long time. This is one of the worst cases we've seen.' So again we sat down and thought about it and decided 'no' we can't go on with it.

The next morning Mrs G telephoned the social services department again and although unable to speak to their own social worker, managed to get in touch with Graham's social worker with the result that within an hour or so two social workers arrived to take Graham away. Mrs G told us:

They sat him down here and they said to him, 'You didn't want to be here did you'? He said 'no'. So you see he didn't want to be here from the start and that had been his whole attitude.

Mr G described the state of complete nervous exhaustion and disappointment that he felt when Graham was collected.

When they came around here I was actually sat in the foetal position like this

over here. I never even realised I was doing it. I feel so annoyed and upset
that the chance was lost for everyone and more so for the child.

Following this disruption Graham went to live in a children's home where psychiatric
help was evidently being arranged for him. He took the hamster with him when he left
but according to Mr and Mrs G was not allowed to keep it. In Chapter 12 on disruption,
we refer to this interview again and give Mr and Mrs G's account of what happened at
the two review meetings which were subsequently held by the social services
department. But here we have to say it is disturbing to encounter such a case where,
after careful selection of prospective adopters, a difficult child appears to have been
dumped on them without adequate preparation or matching and sometimes with little
support over the critical and initial settling in stage of the placement.

2.5   Child placement practice – some old lessons from new research?

A number of points emerge from these four illustrations which we believe indicate
principles by which these critical transitions into placement should be managed –
principles which we have to say have been the basis of good childcare practice for
the last 30 years at least, and which have also been validated by Barth and Berry's
American research (1988) of stable and disrupted adoptions.[3] There are three basic
lessons that we would like to emphasise.

First, child and prospective adopters alike have to be well prepared for the
placement. This will involve such matters as ensuring that the adopters are given all
the relevant information about the child before agreeing to the placement. It also
involves ensuring as far as possible that foster carers are supportive of the idea of
the child being moved to a more permanent placement so that psychological
"release" can take place. If the child has an attachment to the foster placement,
allowance has to be made for minimising the psychological damage that could
occur by the sudden severance of that relationship.

Second, the way introductions are set up and developed are obviously crucial. In
this respect we are not just thinking of the introduction between the child to be
placed and potential adopters but also to any other children they may have in their
family. As with courtship it obviously helps a great deal if prospective adopters and
children are given time and opportunity to 'choose each other' before the final
move into placement takes place. There has to be some evidence that all the key
figures in the drama have in some measure made an initial commitment to the
enterprise, notwithstanding that there are bound to be ambivalences.

Third, even when preparation and matching have been well performed, it is clear
that during the first critical few weeks of the placement when there are so many
adjustments (practical and psychological) that are taking place, children and
prospective adopters alike need to have intensive support available to them, if they

---

[3] *Op cit* pp. 199–121.

need it, from their passage agents (i.e. child's social worker, parents' social worker or someone else). We think it is hard to understate the importance of the availability of intensive supportive help from 'passage agents' in whom the adoptive family and child have confidence during the first critical weeks of the placement. In this respect we hope the four case illustrations, particularly the first and the last, speak for themselves. At the very least, inadequate support from the social workers (for example, if key personnel are away when obviously tricky placements are being made) adds to pressure and weakens confidence in the adoption. This suggests that planning and timing of the critical move are vital. Sudden relatively short-term unexpected pragmatic moves which may be inevitable in a crisis-ridden child protection context should surely be avoided in adoption placement. Could it be that familiarity with the former context breeds contempt for the standards that should be striven for in the latter? Have some child care/adoption workers forgotten that realistic anticipation lessens the shock of potentially highly stressful changes (such as the arrival of the child) and enables children and parents alike to learn that by anticipation they can acquire some control over these events?

Who are the key passage agents?

In our postal survey of 226 adoptive parents, we asked if a particular person acted as a guide/contact point throughout the adoption process.[5] Table 10 below summarises the results.

Table 10

Person as guide/contact person throughout adoption process

	Statutory families		Voluntary families		Total families	
Adopters' social worker[4]	54	38%	53	87%	107	52%
Child's social worker	61	42%	4	7%	65	32%
Other	16	11%	2	3%	18	9%
No-one acted as guide	11	8%	2	3%	13	6%
Unsure	2	1%	0	0%	2	1%
(N. families providing data)	144		61		205	

Source: Family postal survey

[4] We learned from family responses that, in a small minority of cases, the child's social worker also acted as the adopters' social worker. We acknowledge that this was a weakness of the question.

[5] Despite this instruction, 21 families ticked more than one category and have therefore been excluded. Of the other 21 responses which we could not total because of multiple responses, typical replies included 'solicitor and link worker', 'child's social worker and link worker', 'social worker and family friend'. Of the 9 per cent in the 'other' category, four mentioned the child's foster carers and three the guardian *ad litem*.

Table 10 clearly illustrates that the social workers (either the family's or the child's) are the normal guide or passage agent. Unfortunately, we do not know from this material how well these passage agents performed their role. However, the agency set-up can either hinder or facilitate this provision, depending on whether it enforces a transfer of case accountability during the adoption process, with the case being handed over to a different social worker, or whether the same social worker remains involved throughout. This was a topic which we sought to investigate in the agency questionnaire.

Agencies were asked to identify which person normally held case accountability for the child at various stages of the adoption process. Before the adoption order, this tended to be a social worker at the agency, although in a small number of statutory agencies (6 per cent) case accountability was held by senior social work staff, or team leaders, or, in the case of one agency, post-adoption officers. However, this dropped significantly around the time of the order, since 29 per cent of agencies indicated that no particular person held case accountability during the first year after the order, and this rose to 40 per cent after that year. Fewer voluntary agencies dropped case accountability after adoption, since only 15 per cent indicated that no particular person was accountable during the first year, and this only rose to 16 per cent in the second year of adoption (and thereafter).

However, one of the most important reasons for asking this question was to establish the frequency of changes in case accountability and when these changes usually occurred. Changes in case accountability were defined as when another person becomes involved or takes over the case entirely, or when case accountability ends. We found that the worker holding case responsibility remained the same throughout the adoption process in only 15 agencies (14 per cent). In most agencies (55 per cent), there would be one change, but there could be as many as five. Figure 9 below shows the number of changes in case accountability normally incurred when children were placed with families approved by statutory and voluntary agencies.

London borough councils tended to provide more continuity for children, in that no agency had more than two changes of responsibility, whereas 11 per cent of shire counties and 20 per cent of district borough councils had more than two changes.

Figure 10 below plots when the changes of responsibility tend to occur for statutory and voluntary agencies. The most critical stage seems to be around the time of the order when 53 (63 per cent) statutory agencies and eight (30 per cent) voluntaries indicated that there would be a change in personnel. Usually, this meant that no worker was allocated to cases after the adoption order.

Figure 9

Number of changes in case accountability for the child during the adoption process: comparing statutory and voluntary agencies

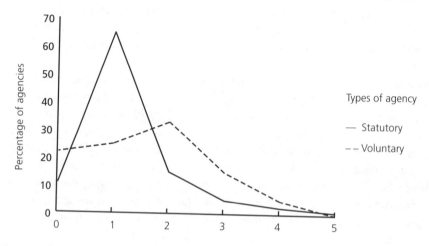

Source: Agency postal survey

Figure 10

Stages at which there is a change in case accountability for the child in statutory and voluntary agencies

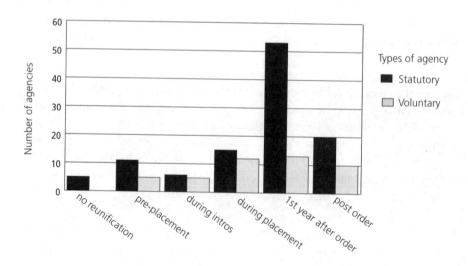

Source: Agency postal survey

Thus, in sum, social workers are often perceived to be key passage agents by prospective adopters, yet many agencies do not provide continuity in this respect, in that the same social worker is unlikely to be responsible for the case throughout the whole of the process. Rather, the case is likely to be handed over to another social worker during this time, often at a critical transition, such as at the time of placement or the adoption order.

3   Going to school

The second critical transition that older children placed for adoption usually have to make – very often at about the same time that they change homes – is changing school (or, for a few, going to school for the first time). It is probably fair to say that, in the past, concern for a child's educational attainment has not been a top priority in childcare practice. As one parent commented, 'some social workers seem more concerned with the dynamics of the placement than with the long-term educational development of the child'. Of course such a view is a false dichotomy. In terms of social adjustment, as well as education, life in school can present as many challenges to a child adopted out of care as moving to a new home, particularly if the child has experienced a disrupted educational career, has learning difficulties and/or manifests behavioural problems. The worlds of school and of home obviously also impact on each other.

It seems clearly to be a part of the culture of adoption placement practice in these circumstances for agencies to leave it to the prospective adopters to make all the schooling arrangements unless there are exceptional circumstances requiring them to do otherwise. This means that just as adoption agency staff can be seen as the key stage-managers in the placement process, so it is the prospective adoptive parents who stage-manage for the child the critical transition into school. This they have to do more or less from the moment they receive the child. In part it is a way of manifesting publicly their new found parental responsibility; a sign that the agency trusts them with the responsibility for arranging the child's educational career.

Special effort has to be made to remedy educational problems which can impact on so many other areas of a child's life. As one mother of three adopted children put it:

> Because abused children have been shoved from pillar to post they have very poor self-esteem. Once they get into a classroom – unless they are given special help – they fail continually. They fail every minute from nine o'clock till half past three. There is no escape from it. And it doesn't matter what we do at home. It doesn't alter the fact that they go in there and they have this dreadful experience five days a week.

It is significant that most adopters (141) in our survey indicated that schools had made a contribution to their experience of adoption, and 105 (74 per cent) of these indicated that their contribution had been 'helpful'.[6] This compares with respective figures for the adoption agency worker, 159 of 178 (89 per cent); for the adopters' GP, 72 of 86 families (84 per cent); for the adopters' solicitor, 58 of 65 (89 per cent); and the child's previous foster carer, 109 of 145 (75 per cent) (see Table 11 below).

Table 11

People/organisations who made a 'helpful contribution' to the adoption

	Statutory families		*Voluntary families*		*Total families*		*Valid cases[7]*
School	73	77%	32	70%	105	74%	141
Child's GP	27	66%	12	71%	39	67%	58
Adopters' GP	49	88%	23	77%	72	84%	86
Adoption agency worker	102	89%	57	90%	159	89%	178
Child's social worker	115	78%	42	69%	157	75%	209
Adopters' solicitor	40	89%	18	90%	58	89%	65
Child's foster carer	69	75%	40	75%	109	75%	145
Adopters' support group	32	89%	27	87%	59	88%	67
Other adopters[8]	38	88%	31	86%	69	87%	79
Foster carers' support group	23	74%	1	100%	24	75%	32
Other relatives	111	91%	43	83%	154	89%	174
Friends	114	93%	49	92%	163	93%	175
Church/religious organisation	39	95%	20	91%	59	94%	63
PPIAS	30	86%	25	89%	55	87%	63
NORCAP	1	33%	0	0%	1	33%	3
NFCA	10	91%	1	50%	11	85%	13
Specialist post adoption service[9]	6	75%	2	50%	8	67%	12
Other	9	75%	8	100%	17	85%	20

Source: Family postal survey

[6] If the school had made a contribution, families were asked to indicate whether their contribution was 'helpful' or 'unhelpful' (families could also state 'unsure').

[7] 'Valid cases' here refer to the number of families indicating that each particular person/organisation had made *some kind of contribution* to the adoption process.

[8] Other adopters not in support group

[9] E.g. Post Adoption Centre; After Adoption Manchester; After Adoption Yorkshire and Humberside; After Adoption Wales; Merseyside Adoption Centre; West Midlands Post Adoption Service (WMPAS); Children's Society Post Adoption Centre.

3.1   Educational issues emerging from interviews with adopters

Choosing the appropriate school

It was immediately apparent from our interviews that many prospective adopters go to considerable trouble in making schooling arrangements, having to deal with potentially tricky issues – first, the question of *choosing the right school* for the child. Here are two typical comments:

> *We thought a lot about schools and went and looked at several different ones and talked to the head teachers. We went looking for a school that was more like the background that she was used to. I did talk to the local primary school headmistress just down here but she and I both felt that it might not be the right school for her. She wasn't used to the inner city and wasn't street-wise and all that.*

> *We found out that she had never been a problem in school. She was never a problem to anyone. They loved her in school and she was very helpful but the local authority wanted to transfer her to a special school because she had been statemented. I know that school and [adoptive mother was here a qualified teacher] I said, 'not on your life'. Because I know what that school is like and she may be backward but she's not that bad. Other kids there have severe learning difficulties. Some can't even put coats on. I went to have a look and discussed it with the deputy head there and it was not at all appropriate. I then got on to my local school again and discussed it with the head there who was lovely. We both agreed that we couldn't go against what the educational authority wanted. So my husband and I then made the decision that we would have to go private which is when we decided to move house. So I know about this school and [the child] and I went to have a look, talked to the headmistress and it's all worked out unbelievably well. She's in a group lower than her chronological age but it doesn't matter because they are in small groups and that's the way they work.*

Timing the entry into school

Timing the entry to a new school can be as important as the choice of school itself.

> *The children came to us in February. We picked the date so it was the beginning of half term so that they could get used to us before going to the new school. My husband took a week off work to help them settle in and I took two or three days off.*

> *They (the adoption agency) suggested we have the two weeks at home at Easter and they suggested that I shouldn't send him to school after the holidays for a few weeks. So I kept him at home for a few days but couldn't*

really see why. I think they felt that we just needed time on our own but I think if you thrust that much time on a child it's unrealistic. He wouldn't know what to do and neither would I. So as the school is just at the bottom of the road I took him to school every day for the first few weeks and collected him at half past three. For the first four or five weeks I did all the fetching just to stabilise him. After that he was fine.

Coping with the school

The importance of parents quickly establishing good liaison with teachers is one of the major educational points to arise from our parent interviews. For example, if children were expected to have learning difficulties or to under-function because of the disturbance of their lives, most adoptive parents appreciated the need to explain the child's background to the school.

I suspected she'd perform a little below average but it was hard to tell because she had changed schools so often and she'd changed homes and everything. And indeed the first term she hardly learned anything – she just went through the motions. That's what we expected, but I discussed it with the teachers, about her IQ and how they felt she would cope with lessons, her general behaviour and her relationships with other children . . . I talked to the teachers about her background, not in detail but just basic things. They were very understanding and honest about whether they thought it was the right school for her. And I think the atmosphere of the school overcame a lot of her early problems. It was clear they had very good teaching staff and could provide her with just the right balance of ingredients.

We knew he'd seen a child psychologist before he came to us and he's seen an educational psychologist to be assessed at school, but after I'd seen the Head, he was getting all the extra help he needed from the classroom assistant. He's doing very well at school now. He's really settling down. Not doing as much work as other children there, but the fact is that he will actually sit down and try and work with the others whereas before he was very demanding on the teacher's attention and wouldn't do anything. So he's making progress.

School is potentially one of those areas of an adopted child's life where both adopters and child can find some external measure of progress and development (or otherwise, of course). Children who have been abused and neglected often lose concentration and fail to learn. As a result they can be classified as educationally backward and mistakenly labelled "dull". Yet the move to a secure, permanent, loving home coupled with a supportive educational environment obviously enabled a number of children in our sample of families to progress and catch up – at least in the view of their adopters. Here are some typical comments, first, concerning a boy of eight who, when placed, was unable to read and was in the process of being statemented because it was considered he was in need of a special school. In fact, the adopters resisted this and got him into a Junior School with a special needs teacher instead.

He got extra support for his language. Fortunately his first teacher was the special needs organiser which was great and she arranged a language support teacher to come in three times a week. A full year later he's past his age for his reading, his writing, and his English. It's marvellous. It's been really hard work because he didn't want to do it initially. He didn't want to go to school. He didn't want to do anything. So it's been hard work and a bit of a bind helping him at home with it but it paid off for all of us. He's doing so well he doesn't need the language support now. He's still doing his special needs Maths, but that too will be stopping at Christmas. Although he still doesn't like it, we all now know he can do it. In fact he's proving to be very capable. He's a very bright boy.

Parents and schools need to develop a sensitive partnership, especially when children have particular behavioural problems which may be ameliorated or aggravated in the school context. We know that children who have long careers in and out of care often have had dreadfully disrupted education and may not have learnt to read. Several parents felt strongly that failure to read contributes to a lowering of self-esteem. One mother explained that the move from an infants to a junior school can expose a child's literacy problem.

All the work in [the adopted son's] junior school presupposes literacy. In the infants he spent most of his time painting and drawing. Now in the juniors everything is written and he cannot understand what he is supposed to do. I'm having enormous difficulty getting this through to social services. I have to teach him as much as I can and he is making progress but the trouble is he isn't as fast as the other children in his stream who academically are streets ahead of him. It's a middle class area and all the other children have been together throughout their time in school. They are advanced for their age but he is so far behind.

Another educational issue which several parents mentioned concerned the child feeling the odd one out in a class because the child was so aware of not having 'a normal home background'. Some parents were able to anticipate this and forewarned the school staff. Thus, when asked how her recently placed child had been introduced to the other children in the village school, a mother explained:

I had been to see the Head and the children were all told about him beforehand. They were told he was moving to a new home and he was going to have a new Mummy and Daddy. He was the first adopted child at that school. They were prepared by the teachers who explained quite well that he wasn't living with his original Mum and Dad and they had been very accepting of him. The other children had had a lot to put up with because he has been very disruptive in class. But they have been very good, very tolerant of him. And now there are two other adopted children in the school who have been accepted. So he sort of paved the way for them.

The problem of teasing and bullying

Of course, many schools have an endemic problem of bullying to contend with but placing agencies and adopters need to be alert to the possibility that a child with an unusual background can easily be targeted and picked on by other children, teased about it, even bullied. We were told of a number of such instances which again highlight the need for close and effective liaison between parents, school and, where necessary, the adoption agency. Here is just one illustration of several such accounts of teasing and bullying at school which the parents told us.

Karen, an eight-year-old girl, had been in and out of care a number of times since she was three years old. Her birth mother had been an alcoholic and a drug addict and was separated from her birth father. During one spell while she was in care her mother was murdered by a boyfriend. Karen was placed with Mr and Mrs T, her adoptive parents, when she was seven. Within a few weeks of going to her junior school, Karen was asked by the other children about her family life and told them how her birth mother had been murdered. The adoptive mother takes up the story:

All the other children ran around the playground shouting, 'Karen's Mum has been murdered! Karen's Mum has been murdered! She's been stabbed! Karen came back home and broke her heart . . . Well, I was so upset I rang all the mothers of the schoolchildren I could think of to explain. I was thinking all these kids had gone back home distressed and told their mothers that this new girl had had a murderer in the family and her Daddy's in prison for life. Karen had made a big mistake telling them and so she was immediately cut off from the other children.

Another problem was she was overweight and she loved her food. So she was picked on because she was the tallest in the class; she was picked on because she was the fattest in the class; she was picked on because she was the only one in the class who was adopted; and she was picked on because she was the only one with a murdered mother.

Some disturbed children behave in ways at school which more or less invite children to pick on them. For example, an 11-year-old girl was described by her adopters as having long-standing behavioural problems including extreme tantrums, difficulty in relating to her peers at school, what was termed "attachment disorder", and difficulty in understanding cause and effect. Educationally she was considered to be seriously retarded. Her adoptive father told us:

> *Developmentally she's really like a three-year-old. She has extreme mood swings. She is very volatile. She blows up over nothing in a very unpredictable way, particularly when she is tired. She can't relate to her peers and tries to cover up by being demonstrative, noisy and that attracts bullying. She does it deliberately because it gets her attention and any attention is worth it. So if other children chase her around the playground at least they are noticing her. So it's better to get bullied by being chased because you get noticed rather than ignored. She consistently pursues attention-seeking behaviour which is very distractive, which winds up other children and which means they have a go at her. But at least it gets her noticed.*

Most parents sensibly took up the issue of teasing and bullying with the school staff who mostly seemed to have been able to deal with it. But as we have mentioned elsewhere in this report, there were several instances where teachers taking classes on family relations unwittingly exposed foster and adopted children to situations where they were pressurised into disclosing painful family history details. Apparently it is common at primary school level for children to be encouraged to do a "life-line" exercise, which involves them listing key events throughout their life – an exercise which can expose children unnecessarily. Another school exercise we were told of, which apparently created difficulty for adopted children, involves asking children to draw a picture of themselves and to identify features that look like their birth parents. Such school activity, unless sensitively handled, is intrusive of children's privacy and can cause acute embarrassment. We think these problematic aspects of such educational practices should be brought to the attention of the Department of Education and Science. They may indicate a need for Notes of Guidance about how to deal with these sensitive aspects of children's personal and family relations.

4   Concluding points

The older child's move out of care – usually foster care – normally involves two critical transitions: the move into the prospective adoptive home and the move to a new school. Each move involves the child in many psycho-social adjustments which would be taxing for any child but will be all the more so for children from disturbed homes with complex and often lengthy child care careers.

As far as the **move to placement** is concerned, this study highlights four important child care principles.

211

1) The placed child, prospective adopters, and any other children in their family have to be well prepared for the placement. This will involve:

- ensuring that adopters are given all relevant information about the child before agreeing to the placement;
- ensuring that as far as possible foster carers, are supportive of the idea of the child being moved to a more permanent placement so that psychological "release" can take place; and
- if the child has formed a bond with foster carers, allowance has to be made for psychological damage that could occur by the sudden severance of that relationship.

2) The way introductions are set up and developed is crucial. As with courtship it helps a great deal if prospective adopters (and any "host" children) and the placed child (or children in the case of a placed sibling groups) are given time and opportunity 'to choose each other' before the final move take place. This involves:

- allowing the key figures time to anticipate the placement, and
- ensuring that all have had an opportunity for some reality testing and have in some measure made a commitment to the enterprise, notwithstanding that there is bound to be ambivalence.

3) Even when preparation and matching have been well performed, it is clear that during the first critical few weeks or months of placement, when there are so many adjustments (practical and psychological) taking place, children and prospective adopters alike will need intensive, consistent, and encouraging support from their "passage agents" (i.e. child's social worker, parents' link social worker, or someone else).

4) Agencies should have a clear duty to ensure that transitional support is always available. This means that timing and planning of the critical move are vital e.g. key personnel should not be away when obviously tricky placements are being made.

The **move to school** is of major importance in the child's adjustment to placement. Our study shows that the primary responsibility for the placed child's education was left to the adopters. Many were so concerned about and committed to the child's educational development that they undertook "remedial" education with the child themselves. They generally dealt with the following key educational tasks:
- choosing the appropriate school,
- timing the entry into school, and
- helping the child cope with the new school experience.

This often involved parents needing to have close liaison with the school in the ongoing assessment and evaluation of the child's educational and social perform-ance, in dealing sometimes with behavioural problems, and with the problem of teasing and bullying to which children with unusual backgrounds may be especially prone. In this respect some educational practice concerning 'home life' can be intrusive of children's privacy.

It is clear that adopters and schools need to quickly establish a sensitive partnership to ease the placed child's adjustment to a new school. Adoption agencies need to prepare and encourage the less experienced adopters to establish crucial liaison with schools.

A supportive educational environment coupled with a secure caring home obviously enabled a number of children in our sample to progress and overcome earlier educational disadvantage. In this respect adoption has considerable potential in helping children overcome the under-achievement associated with being in care.

12 Disruptions

1 Introduction

First, a brief cautionary note about the definition of the term "disrupted" which can apply to both foster care and adoption. Jane Rowe (1987, p 33) has rightly pointed to some of the difficulties when determining foster care outcomes. She writes:

> . . . the term most usually applied to an unsuccessful outcome is "breakdown" but "disruption", "failure" or "termination" are quite usual alternatives. There has been a good deal of criticism of the very negative tone of the terms used, but a more fundamental problem is the lack of social worker agreement about what actually constitutes a "breakdown" or "failure".

But "breakdowns" or "disruption" of adoption placements are not quite the same kind of event as a foster care disruption, partly because the purposes of fostering and adoption are different[1], and because once an adoptive placement becomes a full adoption through the court process, legal parenthood passes permanently to the adopters.[2] Moreover one should not confuse the more general term "outcome" with that of "disruption" which we take to be more specific and limited in meaning to the act of setting aside the intended arrangement of permanent care through adoption. Any one of the principal parties involved (or any combination) may precipitate the disruption and, as Donley (1978, p. 37) observes, may have reached a judgement that the negative qualities of the placement so outweigh the positives that the decision to terminate it seems irreversible.

In the American context, Barth and Berry (1988, pp. 21–22) note that:

> A study of adoption disruptions must grapple with whether an adoptive placement has disrupted if the child is no longer living with the adoptive family but has never returned to the care of the agency. For example, he or she may be living in residential care or with a relative.

---

[1] Donley (1978) and others have, of course, pointed out that there are also distinct similarities to be drawn between the disruption of an adoption and the disruption of a foster care placement. Children, in particular, may be quite unclear of the distinction between them especially if they had not been properly prepared for placement.

[2] See Chapter 2, *The Legal Background*, para 1.1.

In their study, disruptions included cases in which the child had returned to the agency's care either before or after legalisation of the adoption or when the child was living away from the family without continued family commitment. In *our* study we follow the Barth and Berry definition, namely, the end of the adoptive placement. In practice, as far as we are aware, all the children in our family interview sample of disrupted placements left their adoptive home and returned to the care of a local authority.

To date, there is a lack of up-to-date British empirical studies focusing on disruptions of adoptive placements particularly involving older children. Our knowledge and understanding of disruptions has therefore depended first on studies of foster care such as the ground-breaking British studies of Trasler (1960), Parker (1966) and George (1970), and upon more general studies of permanent placements including both long-term fostering and adoption such as the more recent work of Berridge and Cleaver (1987), Aldgate and Hawley (1986), Fratter *et al* (1991), Borland, O'Hara and Triseliotis (1991) and Quinton, Rushton, Dance and Mays (1997a). There has also been strong reliance on American material, particularly that of Donley (1978), Festinger (1986) and Barth and Berry (1988). Perhaps the only significant British study that has concentrated specifically on disrupted adoptions is John Fitzgerald's *Understanding Disruption,* first published in 1983 by BAAF, based on an analysis of 36 disrupted adoption placements concerning 43 children from a sample of 477 placements known to the Adoption Resource Exchange covering the period 1 November 1977 to 31 October 1981.[3]

The Cardiff study

Adoptive placements that disrupt to the extent that the child returns to the local authority care usually bring much grief and distress to the families, to the child and to the social workers who were involved in setting up the placement in the first place. Our own research material concerning this aspect of adoption policy and practice, although often poignant and powerfully tragic, is quantitatively limited because we encountered relatively few such cases. Our findings in this respect must therefore be regarded as essentially exploratory and descriptive.

Although some children are resilient enough to cope with the breakdown of an adoptive placement, and according to some accounts we received, subsequently succeed in a later placement, there are others (perhaps rather more) where acutely disappointing, miserable outcomes for the child, the adopters and the agencies alike appeared to be the only lasting legacy. What can be learned from these accounts individually and collectively? What, with hindsight, might have been done by way of more effective support to forestall disruption? Alternatively, were some of them

---

[3] See Fitzgerald (1990). This book is mostly a practice text designed to encourage the use by agencies of post disruption meetings. The research material is therefore largely used to illustrate practice points. Another useful practice text is Smith's (1994) *Learning from Disruption: Making better placements.*

doomed from the outset because of inappropriate matching? Perhaps the real nagging question for which it is hard to find any satisfactory answer is: what are the longer term consequences both for the children concerned and, in our view equally important, for the adoptive parents and any other children they might have? What risks in the pattern of their future lives and wider relationships were they running by agreeing to provide an adoptive home? The emotional pain, anxiety, exhaustion and sometimes, financial expense associated with disruption, were all too obvious when we interviewed them. But how do they recover from it and reconstruct their lives after the event? In our opinion, such questions call for more extensive and intensive study of disrupted adoptions in order to increase our understanding of the effect on the adopters and any other children they may have as well as on the placed child.

We have to acknowledge that the numbers of disrupted placements in our study were relatively few (see next section below) so that in this chapter, perhaps more than any other concerning our findings, we may have overplayed from a social research perspective, the significance of single case examples. Nevertheless, we hope that it can also throw some light on the causes of disruptions and the lessons to be learned from them, and that it will make a case for more detailed investigation of the "darker side" of modern adoption practice.

2   The incidence of disruptions

2.1   No official statistics

There are no official statistics available on the incidence of disrupted adoptions. However, research such as that conducted by Fratter *et al* (1991, p 56) which reviewed permanent family placements, showed that on average about 20 per cent of adoption placements disrupted. For children aged between 9 and 11 years at placement, who were institutionalised, or had behavioural or emotional problems and a history of deprivation or abuse, the breakdown rate rose to almost 40 per cent. Rushton *et al* (1995, p 693), in a study of boys over five years of age when placed, reported a 19 per cent disruption rate after eight years of placement. A similar rate is reported by Borland *et al* (1991) in their review of disruption rates. This also showed that the older the child on placement the higher the chance of disruption; thus only 5 per cent of the two-five-year-olds disrupted while the rate was 36.6 per cent for the 11–14 age group. Nevertheless, these researchers claimed that overall, 80 per cent of the permanent placements had achieved stability by the end of the three year period covered by the study. The study also showed that almost half the disruptions occurred within the first year of placement.

2.2   Disruptions in the agency sample

Agencies were asked to indicate the number of children who were initially looked after by a local authority, placed for adoption but then removed from the adopters because of disruption. The figures they gave us represent those for the most recent year they were available. They are therefore not the same year for each agency. Agencies do not necessarily know when a placement disrupts, particularly if it does so after the adoption order, because they are not automatically informed, especially if the adopters have moved from their area. The statistics presented are therefore somewhat tentative and crude, and relate to instances when children were removed from placements (see Table 12 below). It is probable, therefore, that as a guide to disruption they represent a minimum figure.

Table 12

Number of children removed from adoptive families in disruptions for each age and ethnic group (A), compared to the number of placements made for each group (B).

	Statutory		*Voluntary*		*Total*	
	A	*(B)*	*A*	*(B)*	*A*	*(B)*
Age of children removed						
0–4 years	33	(753)	0	(127)	33	(880)
5–9 years	63	(377)	5	(102)	68	(479)
10+ years	31	(142)	6	(24)	37	(166)
Total	127	(1,272)	11	(253)	138	(1,525)
Ethnicity of children removed						
Black	9	(36)	0	(6)	9	(42)
White	100	(1,130)	9	(200)	109	(1,330)
Asian	6	(23)	0	(12)	6	(35)
Mixed heritage	10	(100)	2	(34)	12	(134)
Other (e.g. Chinese)	2	(15)	0	(1)	2	(16)
Total	127	(1,304)	11	(253)	138	(1,557)

Source: Agency postal survey

Disruptions amounted to some 9 per cent of the returns with a disruption rate of 10 per cent for statutory agencies compared with 4 per cent for voluntaries. In the statutory agencies, about half occurred in the 5–9 age group, 24 per cent in the 10+ age group, and 26 per cent in the 0–4 age group. In the voluntary agencies, 45 per cent of the disruptions were in the 5–9 and 55 per cent in the 10+ age groups, with none in the 0–4 age group. Nine of the children in the voluntary agency disruption group were white and two were of mixed heritage. However, in adoption placements of minority ethnic children by statutory agencies, it seems evident that the disruption rate is higher than for white children.[4]

Agencies were also asked to indicate when disruptions – again meaning removal from placement – occurred. These data are presented in Table 13 below. Based on a sample of 130 cases, it will be noted that 94 per cent of statutory and 80 per cent of voluntary agency disruptions occurred before the adoption order, with a further 3 per cent (statutory) and 7 per cent (voluntary) in the year following the order, and a further 3 per cent (statutory) and 13 per cent (voluntary) more than one year after the order.

Table 13

The stage at which children were removed from adoptive families in disruptions

	Statutory agencies	Voluntary agencies	Total agencies
	N	N	N
Stage children removed			
Before the adoption order	108	12	120
Within the first year after the order	3	1	4
More than one year after the order	4	2	6
Total	115	15	130

Source: Agency postal survey

2.3 Disruptions in the family sample

Adoption agencies which despatched questionnaires to adoptive families on our behalf[5] were specifically asked to include families where the placement was known to have disrupted. As far as we can tell, most did so, but six agencies reported excluding a total of 13 cases between them because the disruption was too recent and feelings too raw for a questionnaire to be timely or appropriate. It is possible that other agencies excluded disruptions without telling us.

Of the 226 questionnaires returned, 13 (6 per cent) indicated that the child who had been placed was no longer living with the adopters. Given that some disruptions were excluded from the sample, we have no way of telling how indicative this might be of a national average.

Six of those who said that the child no longer lived with them indicated that they would be willing to be interviewed. We saw three of these and a further two which had disrupted by the time the interview was undertaken. However, in six of the other

---

[4] See Chapter 6, *Agency and Family Profiles,* at para 2.6
[5] The methodology is described in Appendix A.

43 interviews, the children in those placements had experienced adoption breakdowns *before* the placement current at the time of the interview. In two of these, the children had experienced two adoptive disruptions. In a further three cases, the children had been initially placed with the parents on a short-term fostering basis. They were subsequently placed with prospective adopters but, when these placements broke down, they were returned to the adoptive parents we interviewed. *Put another way, we know that in 14 out of the 48 cases, i.e. 29 per cent where we conducted an interview, the children had experienced one or more disruptions.*

Since conducting our interviews we have learned through the *Adopted Children Speaking* study (Thomas *et al*, 1999) that one more placement has disrupted.

Piecing together the information obtained from the families, we have calculated a headline disruption rate of 6 per cent (based on 13 out of 226 questionnaire returns where the child no longer lived with the adopters).[6] But we can add a further nine cases where we discovered during the interview that the child had experienced a previous disruption plus one disruption since our interviews. These 23 cases together represent 10 per cent of the 226 in the family questionnaires. We have no way of telling how many children in the remaining 203 cases experienced adoption disruptions before being placed with the family which completed the questionnaire.

A profile of the five cases which disrupted before our interview with the adopters appears in Appendix C. Suffice to say here that all seven of the children had been taken into care in the first place because of inadequate parenting, some suffering neglect or mental, physical or sexual abuse or a combination of these. All had experienced several different foster placements and three had already experienced an adoptive placement disruption before being placed with the adopters whom we interviewed. All the children were white. Three couples had children of their own, one had already adopted a child, and one had no experience of parenting at all. The human cost to all concerned is impossible to calculate.

3   Causes of disruption

Many studies have explored a range of multi-factorial reasons for disrupted permanent placements. Here we merely report the perspectives given to us by those adopters who had experienced a disrupted placement augmented by more general views of agency staff. For those wishing to explore the matter more deeply, David Howe's (1998) recent text, *Patterns of Adoption*, is recommended.[7]

---

[6] See also Chapter 6, *Agency and Family Profiles*, at para 3.1.

[7] Howe considers both genetic and environmental influences on child development, including the influence of the pre-placement and post-placement environments on adopted children's psycho-social development and outcomes. He also develops and applies hypotheses related to attachment theory, considering different patterns of attachment relationships and notions of risk and psychological resilience (Howe, 1998).

3.1   Poor support

Family perspectives

Social work support

Perhaps not surprisingly, the families' experience of social work support was negative. It should also be borne in mind that we did not investigate the "other side" of any of these cases. A factor common to each was that the adopters felt that, had they had more support during the placement, it might have survived or at least had a better chance of surviving. Although these adopters could be said to be looking for a reason for the breakdown and, with hindsight, feel that lack of support could be blamed, the fact remains that in each of these cases they realised that all was not well with the placement and asked for help. From their accounts of what happened this was not forthcoming. Typical of the response by social workers to pleas for help was:

> They would say, 'Well, look, it's normal parenting. These are the sorts of things we told you to expect,' and that sort of thing. Therefore you think well, we've got to cope with it and we've got to move on ... She [social worker] just minimalised everything we took to her. ... it seemed like social services didn't want to help us.

Another adoptive mother who had also brought up two children of her own, said:

> But I lived with him – the social workers do not live with the child they are placing and I told them things that I felt about him – that he had been sexually abused, he was coming out with odd remarks, doing strange things and they'd all got a sexual air about them. She [child's social worker] said, 'Well, that's because he's extremely happy and he's coming out of himself'. I said, 'Rubbish, I don't agree at all, a happy child doesn't come out like that'. So the battles were there.

It was not just those who had experienced disruption but many other adopters who spoke of social workers' reluctance to acknowledge that problems existed. By so doing they were denying the adoptive parents the support they needed.

This attitude also sometimes applied to the adopters' perceived need for the child to have therapeutic help. One mother said:

> No matter how strong anybody thinks they are, there is a point where you can't take any more. That's why a tiny bit of me says if there had been the help – if it had all come pouring in – maybe [the child] would not have gone back.

Another couple who had asked for therapy to help their two boys were told there were no resources available. After leaving, the boys went to three different placements, but because none of the foster carers could cope with them they were eventually split up. The social worker subsequently told the adopters that they would begin the therapy once each boy was in a stable placement but, as the adopters said, they had thought that was the very thing they were endeavouring to give the boys.

One father told us of an argument about who would pay for psychiatric treatment for their child. The local authority said they could not afford to do so. He would have been willing to foot the bill himself but, sadly, the placement lasted such a short time that he had no opportunity to do so.

Parents who experienced disruption were not alone in their efforts to obtain treatment for their child. Many of the other parents in our interview sample experienced something similar. But the children in the cases that disrupted had chronic problems. They needed help before being placed for adoption as well as support once placed to give them a chance of coping with and settling into an adoptive placement. Risking yet another disruption in their lives in the light of their care histories appears desperate since it can only have added to the problems the children already had.

Given the above attitudes, it is little wonder that relationships between the adopters and the social workers became strained. One couple said that their social worker 'alienated herself from us', so that in the end they were not contacting her but trying to cope on their own. Another said that, of the two social workers with whom they were dealing, one was no good at communicating and the other would say, 'Well, we've got to keep this amongst ourselves'. Neither offered the adopters respite care[8] during the time the children were with them, something they considered would have helped them recharge their batteries to cope with the challenging behaviour they found so exhausting to manage.

In another case, the adoptive mother explained that the children had been seen by their own social worker once a week before their placement with her, but this reduced to once every six weeks afterwards. They then had a change of social worker, seeing even less of the new one.[9] The mother contacted this social worker for help because one of the boys was being so difficult. She would leave messages, but calls were not returned. She feels that neither she nor the children got the support they needed. The children had no help with their emotional problems.

Irregular and infrequent visits from social workers were mentioned by others. For example, in a case where the child remained with the adopters for nine months following the decision to move him on, they said that support, such as it had been,

---

[8] We discuss respite care in Chapter 14, *Financial and Practical Support*.

[9] The American study of Barth and Berry (1988, p 209) reports: 'Our families argued loudly that they were less likely to request assistance from the agency when they lost contact with the worker who did their home study (assessment). The home study is a poignant process that builds strong bonds between the workers and the family. The organisation of services should facilitate a continuous relationship between the family and the social worker.' See also Chapter 4, *The Older Child's Status Passages*, at para 2.1.

dropped off once the decision was made. They then discovered that their own son had been abused by the child but were given little support to help them cope, the social worker reportedly commenting, 'people nowadays get it all out of proportion and it has always happened in families'.

Given their commitment to wanting to succeed with the child or children placed with them, it is extremely sad that these adopters were not better supported by their social workers and the agencies. Had they been able to work in partnership then, even if the placement had ultimately failed, the damaging impact experienced by the adopters might have been reduced and more easily healed.

One adopter said that she felt that social services needed a "mechanism" whereby they checked to see how the placement was proceeding. If problems arose, help should be available before things had gone too far and total breakdown resulted. Another said:

> We were coping up to a point and then, towards the end, we weren't. And because of our inability to communicate that or their inability to see it, then a situation has happened that has destroyed both families . . . the damage to both them and us is incalculable.

Support from other sources

One mother mentioned the support she had received from the children's school:

> As far as I was concerned, the headmaster had as much right to know every-thing that would help him to cope with having these children in his school as I did in having to cope with having them in my house. So I was always quite open. The school were very, very good where the children were concerned. They were understanding, they made allowances, particularly for [the child] because of the bad time he had had.

Support from family and friends could prove problematic.[10] For instance, one adopter explained that her own mother did not see why, because the child was not born to her daughter, anyone in the family should be expected to cope with his dreadful behaviour. Consequently the adopter did not ask her mother for support. When the adoption placement disrupted, she simply explained that they could not cope with the boy and the emotional damage that he had suffered before he had been placed with them. Another described how they lost friends who considered the children to be psychopaths and did not want to socialise with them. This cut off what might otherwise have been a valuable source of support for the adopters.

---

[10] The attitude of family and friends is further explored in Chapter 7, *Changing Attitudes to Adoption*, para 4.

Agency perspectives

Several adoption workers identified lack of support as a contributory factor to disruptions. The need for support to be built into a placement from the outset was regarded as something that was essential to prevent or minimise disruption. A cry for help some time into the placement could be too late to prevent disruption no matter how much support was then made available. As a statutory agency worker said:

> Adopters need to have the support whenever they need it, not just when they ask for it. It needs continuous involvement – and from the social worker to the child . . . It's such an important question for all the parties concerned that people are not just left. Things aren't dealt with. They become really big issues – too big to be dealt with.

Another social worker stressed the importance of adopters knowing that a structure existed that would 'automatically give them ongoing help'. She thought that, by having such a structure, the agency was acknowledging that there were going to be problems. People needed to be educated to realise that adoptions of older children would not come problem free. Another, making a similar point, said that placing extremely damaged children in families and expecting them to get on with it was unrealistic. She bemoaned the fact that packages of support are not automatically built into such placements.

A voluntary agency worker stressed the importance of "listening" to adopters and not blaming them when things went wrong. Another made a similar point:

> If you try and support them by getting them to share when things are difficult as well as when things are good, you hope that it never builds into the crisis where they pack their bags and say goodbye . . . Also you try and work with them and the child as a unit and don't continue to take the child outside the situation in order to work with the child.

Whilst recognising the need for and advantages of a good post-adoption service, some raised the problem of funding. A voluntary agency worker said:

> You need very careful and thorough support and therapy for the child. That is the biggest problem: getting the local authorities to pay for good quality psychotherapy for the child. It's such a battle around that. Time and time again they leave adopters to carry on as though they are a normal family as such. Indeed they are a normal family with extra dimensions that need professional input, to help them through various crises.

3.2   Mismatching[11]

Family perspectives

In trying to fathom the reasons for disruption, adopters pointed to mismatching as a possible cause.[12] As one said:

> *You put your faith in these people because you don't think they're putting you together unless they think you're suitable.*

He wondered if the panel had been wrong to agree to the match since he and his wife had been approved for a 'non-violent child' and 'finished up with a violent child'. He saw that as a 'giant error'.[13]

In another case the adopters, having said that they would like a boy and a girl, instead had two boys placed with them. The mother said:

> *The case worker spent over 18 months with us. They are trained, surely, to be able to tell us, 'you said a boy and a girl therefore we don't think two boys will be a good idea'.*

A couple who had been approved for one child under the age of four were matched with two boys aged seven and eight who proved extremely disruptive. The adoptive mother said:

> *There was such a desperate need by social services to do the right thing for these boys and there was such a desperate need for us to adopt that both sides were looking through blinkers.*

In another case, where the adopters already had two natural children, the mother was particularly anxious that the age of the child placed with them should be between the ages of her children so that they maintained their oldest and youngest status. She has since questioned whether the boy who was placed with them was the wrong age 'for my two to fit in'. She wondered whether any of the social workers involved in matching should have discussed the implications of age for all the children more fully with her, perhaps persuading her to change her mind on that point.

---

[11] See also Chapter 10, *Issues in Matching*.

[12] In considering these adopters' comments, it should be borne in mind that they were made with hindsight, that they may be coloured by the disappointment they still felt, and that they may not have complained about the unsuitability of the match to the agency when it was proposed.

[13] Barth and Berry (1988, p 112) using a term first coined by Nelson (1985) refer to the discrepancy between a family's idea of the kind of child they initially wished to adopt and the one that they actually did adopt as "stretching". Nelson suggests that the more the family was "stretched" as a result of misinformation or lack of information, the greater the detriment to the placement and the higher the risk of disruption. This observation was confirmed by the Barth and Berry study.

Agency perspectives

One adoption worker described the process of matching as 'complex and unscient-ific' and continued, 'I don't think you can ever fine-tune assessment processes so that somehow there's a perfect matching'.

Some suggested that matching can be rushed and that in consequence any anxieties felt by the agency or the prospective adopters might then be overlooked rather than acknowledged and addressed before the match was confirmed. One social worker described a case in which it had been planned to place a black child of mixed heritage outside the family, but who, at the 'eleventh hour', had been placed with family members who were white and approved foster carers for a different agency. This placement was evidently made too quickly with the result that many 'hidden family dynamics' were not uncovered until it was too late. She described their rushed decision as 'the worst thing we could have done'.

Prospective adopters also need time to make considered decisions. As one social worker explained:

> One partner may not feel right about the child and is not being honest with themselves. When I chair planning meetings, right at the start I say, 'You've got through the panel. You've got through the linking. Now it's really exciting. You're going to meet this child and this child is going to move in with you – but hold on.' People get fed up with me really labouring this point, but if it doesn't feel right it's not going to be right. It's never, ever going to be right.

Another social worker felt that rather than concentrating on the "positives" during the matching process it was important to pay heed to the weaknesses presented by prospective adopters so that they could be acknowledged and supported in the subsequent placement.

Others raised problems associated with inter-agency placements:

> When you've counselled and assessed prospective adopters yourself you know what sort of life they are going to offer your child. With inter-agency ones you don't know them as well. You feel they can be mis-represented to you and, with hindsight, we may not have recommended this family for this child.

A voluntary agency social worker spoke of her involvement in cases with local authorities which withheld information concerning children in their care. Had the information been available at the time the parents were matched with the children, she would not have supported the match. She now routinely asks to see local authority files concerning children her agency is asked to match with parents whom it has approved for adoption.

Another problem can be the temptation to place a child of an age different from the one for which the adopters had been approved. Children being too close together in age can also pose a problem.[14]

3.3   Poor assessment, preparation and training[15]

Family perspectives

One adoptive father felt that there should have been more training for the type of behaviour with which they had to cope. He thought that the psychology of what happens should be looked at so that parents could understand why a child behaved in such a way. There should be better preparation geared to the specific child with whom prospective adopters are matched. One agency we visited prepares and trains prospective adopters first by giving them all the background information available about a specific child, and then encouraging them to learn all they can about the child's special needs and how they might be supported to cope with the problems in their own area.[16] This is clearly good practice.

Another adoptive father commented on social workers' training. He placed much of the blame for what happened in his case on the child's social worker but did not think that was the only answer. He wondered why she was in that position in the first place and why she had not, as he perceived it, been trained correctly.

Agency perspectives

Assessment and preparation of children

Careful assessment[17] of children's needs was seen as crucial in minimising the risk of disruption. It would also prevent placing children for adoption for whom it was inappropriate. Some children did not want to be adopted because they still wished to be with their birth family. One social worker mentioned the risk of placing children outside their own community, advocating that it would be preferable for the child to be long-term fostered in their own area.[18] A statutory agency worker thought that agencies tended to concentrate on the 'here and now' with children, forgetting their history and the damage done to them. Another felt that it was important to recognise that children's needs change with time. As they get older they can say, 'I don't want to be here any more'. Problems can arise when children begin to question their identity. As one said:

---

[14] Both these problems occurred in the interviews with families who experienced disruption (see above para 3.2).

[15] See further, Chapter 9, *Preparation and Training*.

[16] There is a view (with which we agree) that if people are considered suitable for the care of a vulnerable child, then they should automatically be trusted with all available information about that child.

[17] See also Chapter 9, *Preparation and Training*, para 2.

[18] This seems to us to be symptomatic of the traditional view of closed/exclusive adoption.

What nobody's been prepared for is that a child needs to change who they are and re-align their understanding and that can bring about a crisis.

Many social workers said that careful assessment should be followed by thorough preparation of the children so as to:

... Help them to understand what's happening for them, why they can't be living at home at the moment; helping them to understand that they as children can never be responsible for what's happened within their [birth] family; giving them a sense that someone is in control of their lives; helping them through difficult behaviours that they may be exhibiting because of their experiences at home ... If you don't do that way before the decision to place them for adoption is made, then, when you come to place the child – unless you've dealt with all the stuff about why they can't be at home any more – they display all the same patterns in their new family.

The preparation of existing/birth children in the adoptive family was also seen as crucial since there was a potential conflict of interests. One voluntary agency worker explained:

The preparation of those children is very important. They need to be clear about what they're taking on, what they're going to lose and what they're going to gain. Because quite often I think children go along with their parents and aren't able to express their own views.

Adopters may have to choose between the adoptive child and their own children if a conflict of interests arose: another reason why the preparation of the adopters' birth children is so important.

Assessment and preparation of prospective adopters[19]

As one social worker said:

I think you've got to have an awful lot of input into the assessment process to make sure that you stand a better than even chance of it [placement] working.

What was described as 'close work' was required since this would prevent prospective adopters 'playing a game', namely, giving answers they thought the social workers wanted to hear.

Another social worker thought that key issues could sometimes be missed. For instance, a loss in the adopters' lives such as infertility or the death of a child or partner, or difficult childhoods left unresolved could lead to difficulties during the placement. Adoption was also seen by some as a means of rescuing a troubled marriage which, as another worker said, 'could cause a lot of stress'.

---

[19] See also Chapter 9, *Preparation and Training*, para 3.

Social workers questioned whether you could ever prepare parents, adoptive or otherwise, for, as one put it:

> ... what it's actually like having a child 24 hours a day. You have moments as a parent when you think it isn't worth it. This is just awful, and it's that which makes the difference if they are adopters. There's an option there for them and some people will push through and have the level of commitment that it takes. Other people won't and I don't really know how you gauge that beforehand, because you don't see people under real pressure when they are practically on their knees with stress and anxiety and getting nothing back.

3.4   Inadequate background Information

Family perspectives

Some of the parents who experienced disruption (and others we interviewed) told us that, had they been given sufficient information concerning the child placed with them, they might have considered saying 'no' to the match.[20] They also thought that the information might well have enabled them to better understand and cope with the child and the problems that arose in placement. Depressingly, all those who attended disruption meetings[21] following the breakdown, told us that they then discovered most about the child's background.

Some of these adopters said that although they had been promised sight of the child's case history, they had never seen it. In one case, the parents were given little information, notwithstanding that in earlier proceedings, a judge was reported as having recommended that any prospective adopters or carers should be given access to some or all of the documentation concerning the children. In another case, the adopter felt that:

> ... what we knew about those boys wasn't worth knowing anyway. It was mostly extended family background about who'd been in prison and why ... so I think that was a gross misjudgement.

It was only when the child received some counselling during the placement in another case, that the adopters discovered that the agency had known that he had 'sadistic tendencies' from the age of five. This had not been disclosed to the parents. The child abused the other adopted child in the family during the placement.

Even where information is given, a common complaint (expressed not just by those adopters who experienced disruption) is that case histories are not always complete and up to date. Again, it was at disruption meetings that it became apparent

---

[20] See Chapter 10, *Issues in Matching*, para 6.1. for detailed discussion of the provision of background information generally.

[21] Discussed further at para 5.

in some cases that those involved with the child had their own fragments of information which had not been brought together to make the child's record accurate, complete and up to date. An adoptive mother who had experienced this suggested that:

> If they had strict guidelines that you've got to inform prospective parents about every move since the child came into care, why it's broken down, what's happened, a detailed history – if that was obligatory, then it may have come to light that they didn't have the information all together.

Agency perspectives

Social workers had little to say about missing or misleading background information as a possible cause of disruption. Most comment came from voluntary agency workers who found it difficult to obtain information from statutory agencies to pass on to prospective adopters. Overall, the paucity of social workers' comments on this matter is disturbing given that several authors, such as Donley (1978, p 35) and Barth and Berry (1988, pp 119–120), have identified the adopters' lack of available information about the child as a key factor associated with unstable and disruptive adoptive placements.

3.5   Problem behaviour

Family perspectives

In the five cases which disrupted, the adopters were defeated by the child's challenging behaviour. In all but one, the parents persevered for some considerable time without, as we have shown above, the support they needed. Each of the children had suffered neglect by their birth parents, and some were known to have been abused sexually or physically or both. The adopters also said they had been told that the children experienced many changes of foster placement, residential homes and disrupted adoptive placements. Given such backgrounds and in the light of the behaviour which the adopters experienced whilst the children were with them, we question whether an adoptive placement was timely or appropriate for them. Some kind of therapy and careful preparation in a less emotional setting, such as a residential unit, might have helped the children to cope with a placement in a family setting eventually.

One mother described her relationship with one of the two siblings placed in her care as 'turbulent'. She continued:

> We loved each other to death, but we didn't do living together very well. The older the child got, the more unco-operative he became. He started to question everything I asked him to do . . . I realised that he was only six inches shorter than me and that in another year I wouldn't be able to cope with him.

She also described her feelings as the placement began to crumble:

> I thought, I'm sorry [the child], I love you desperately, but I cannot go on living like this. Every day, waking up in the morning and thinking, oh my goodness, what is today going to bring? I'd get so I didn't want to get out of bed, worrying about just what battle I was going to be walking into. Picking him up from school, worrying about if I was going to get there and find the headmaster hovering – 'Mrs X can I just have a word'? Every time the phone went I thought please don't let it be the school.'

He later attacked her with a hammer and the adoptive father with a baseball bat. Another mother described something of her child's behaviour:

> He used to wander round everywhere masturbating, weeing, going from being extremely silly like a little two-year-old to being extremely vindictive and spiteful to the animals and to [other adopted child with special needs whom he sexually abused during the placement]. It sounds odd because we're big people and he was tiny – he was small for his age – but it got to the point where you became very frazzled with him. The lady he's living with this very week actually is an experienced foster mum of 15 years standing who only takes on very seriously damaged children and she can't cope with him. He was her first shock.

This represents just one small snapshot of the behaviour she described. Other parents gave equally graphic accounts of the behaviour with which they tried to cope.

Agency perspectives

Many social workers spoke of the importance of providing adopters with accurate descriptions of the types of behaviour likely to be presented by the child. Once the child was placed, it was vital to help the child understand his/her testing behaviour and to help adopters to manage it. As one worker said, 'The most damaged children tear families apart and they are the most likely to disrupt'.

3.6   Failures of attachment and bonding

Family perspectives

Attachment and bonding problems were identified as contributing to disruption. One mother felt that her husband had a problem regarding the siblings in their care as his. As she put it, they were somebody else's sons and he could not put other people's children first when they were in competition with his work and his hobbies.

In another case, where the child experienced an adoptive disruption before being placed successfully with those whom we interviewed, the adopters said that in her first placement the girl was unable to share the adoptive mother with the two natural children in the family. She was possessive of the mother and did not recognise the father and two children in the family.

Sisters who experienced two disrupted adoptive placements, after each of which they returned to the same foster carers who subsequently adopted them, had not been able to relate to the adoptive father in the second of the placements which disrupted after eight weeks.

Agency perspectives

Various attachment problems potentially leading to a disruption were described and explained to us by agency social workers. Several mentioned the dilemma posed for children who were still attached to their birth parents being expected to form a fresh attachment to their substitute family. No matter how bad their experience might have been within the birth family, children are still pulled both ways and find it difficult, sometimes impossible, to come to terms with conflicting loyalties. In such a situation, as one worker explained:

> *Either the carers can feel very threatened about that and can't cope with it, or the reality is that the child that has that attachment can't actually give anything to the carers and that's why it breaks down.*

The damage wrought upon some older children placed for adoption will, of itself, have a disabling effect on their capacity to form attachments. One worker described a case where the child 'pulled back' from the adoptive parents who had responded to his needs. The parents saw this as a 'personal rejection' and no amount of explaining succeeded in helping them to understand why the child was behaving as he did. In another case, two sisters were very disturbed having been grossly sexually abused. They had attached to each other to the exclusion of adults and appeared to see themselves as a unit.

Agency workers told us that some adopters believe that love will make everything all right but if, after some time, the child has not integrated into the family and formed the attachment which the adopters want, the placement can become vulnerable. Because attachments in these cases can take so long to form, the child may reach adolescence before the relationship has consolidated. The teenage years can produce further problems which may threaten progress in the attachment and bonding processes.

Complications can arise if the child attaches to one parent but not the other. A statutory agency worker described a case in which the child attached to the adoptive mother, but not to the father. He could not cope and became extremely jealous.

If there are existing children in a family, they may not attach to the placed child and vice versa. This can prove a difficult balancing act for adopters who may face a conflict of loyalties.

Adopters may not realise what a difficult job they have been asked to undertake and what their feelings about caring for someone else's child will be. One worker suggested that it was important that adopters acknowledged that the feelings that they might have had for a child of their own could be different from those for the child who was placed with them.

> *Getting that message through to people is really important: adoption is an alternative means of parenting a child – it's not the same as having your own.*

3.7   Contact difficulties

Family perspectives

Only one of the five adopters who had experienced disruption mentioned contact[22] as a possible cause. Contact was talked about in more general terms by the rest. This is not surprising since in two of the cases there was no contact with the birth family. In a third, contact was restricted to the exchange of birthday and Christmas cards. In the fourth, there was face-to-face contact with a sibling. In the fifth, there had been contact with the birth mother and a sister but this was terminated during the placement much to the relief of the adopters who felt that prolonged contact had added to the damage to their child.

Agency perspectives

Contact and the absence of it were both seen as possible causes of disruption. When contact was arranged, say, with the birth mother's needs rather than the child's in mind, the placement could be jeopardised. Some arrangements were considered 'onerous and costly in terms of time . . . particularly when the benefits to the child aren't quite demonstrable'. The need for and arrangements concerning contact should be made clear to adopters from the outset so that they know what they must take on. Some workers took the view that contact which may be desirable at the beginning of a placement may be less so as time goes by. One worker mentioned a case in which contact between a child and his birth parent was seen as a 'bonus' initially but subsequently became very damaging to the child, with the placement jeopardised as a result.

Others spoke of the detrimental effect of the absence of contact. This was especially so for those children who were unable to 'let go' of their birth family even though they might not have seen them for years. A social worker said:

> *If you put them [children] with families that are not inclusive . . . well, you've got a time bomb ticking away.*

---

[22] See also Chapter 15, *Contact.*

3.8   Adopters' unrealistic expectations

Several agency workers identified unrealistic expectations by adopters as a contributory factor. One said:

> *The expectation of the adopters is critical and it's awfully hard really. Because when push comes to shove it's the ability of the adopters to be patient and tolerate this slow kind of progress, the hiccups, the behaviour that they wouldn't have wanted for a child of their own. We all have our own hopes and expectations of our own children. We expect adopters to get in touch with those kinds of feelings and to be honest with themselves about it. If they're not, then that's part of the recipe for disaster really.*

Some adopters we interviewed mentioned 'love at first sight' when they first saw a photograph of the child with whom they were matched. Social workers were concerned about this because, as one said, the adopters do not move on from seeing the child as he or she might be in the picture; the reality is something different from what they expect. They may anticipate that the security and love they offer will change the child but, as one worker said, if the child had already experienced 40 moves, whatever the quality of love and security then offered, the child may very well not be able to respond as the adopters would wish.

4   Effect of disruption on adoptive families

Family perspectives

The following is an account of the experience of one family the day the child left home.

Jason, a boy aged 11, had been living with the adopters and two natural children of the family for a year before he left. The decision that he should leave was made four weeks before he physically left which the adoptive mother described as 'a hell of a four weeks', especially as Jason knew he was leaving. Social services decided it would be best if he left at half-term, hence the delay. The adoptive mother described what happened on the day of Jason's departure:

> *So [Jason's social worker] arrived on a Saturday morning four weeks later and I said to her at the door, 'I don't know how to handle this and I don't know what to say to you'. She said, 'It's all very difficult but I've seen this time and time again'. I said, 'What's the camera for?' and she said, 'Well, we must have pictures'. So I said, 'Well, we've got pictures'. She said, 'No. We've got to have pictures of him leaving'. So we had pictures of him at the front door with all of us; pictures of him with his suitcases; pictures of him getting into the cab and pictures of us standing outside the house.*

[The adoptive father] had left for work. He went into the office. He wouldn't stay here that day because he didn't agree with this . . . He couldn't handle it at all. [The adoptive father] said goodbye to Jason that morning in the bedroom and wouldn't come home until Jason had left . . . The cab waited for two hours because [Jason's social worker] had a mini and she knew that Jason had more stuff. The day he came to us he came with two carrier bags [containing his life's belongings], but the day he left he had boxes and suitcases and she knew she wouldn't be able to fit anything in her car so she hired an estate mini-cab and he [driver] waited for two hours outside. I sat over there. [Jason's social worker] sat here. Jason carried on playing in the bedroom and in the garden with the kids. I thought well, this is sheer torture for me and I just made her cups of coffee and then she got the camera, went off and took pictures. She took photographs down by the pond and did the dog and that sort of thing. It was the worst two hours I think I've ever had in my life. And I gave her lunch and then she finally decided to say, 'Well, Jason, it's time we were on our way'. And Jason left and afterwards he 'phoned us continuously for about six weeks.

Adopters described feelings of grief, pain, anger, guilt, embarrassment, shame when talking about the effects of the disruption on them and on their lives. All were still wondering if they could have done something differently and saved the placement from breakdown. One mother said:

I actually said for the first time the other day, I must go round and take the photos down, but I still haven't been able to do it. Then you start saying, could I have done something differently? Should I have tried harder? Then I look at the way that I was becoming, heading for another car accident, maybe, because my mind wasn't on what I was doing . . . it's very difficult . . . You torture yourselves with all of this.

Another couple who were still grieving for the lost child, also grieved for the lost opportunity:

The chance was lost for everybody and more so for the child. It really is a sorry story because it lost the opportunity for the child to be given what he would have liked to have thought was a very good home – and for us to enjoy as well. It's a two-sided thing.

They said that they had agreed to take part in the research because they wanted 'something done about it', continuing:

We've recovered from it but I will still regret it in twenty years time. I've mellowed now. When it happens you're very, very angry. You're very bitter that somebody's done this to you, put you through this needlessly and ruined what you were looking forward to. That fades with time . . . There is something that he [boy] left behind where he's written his name, his friend's name [in a family diary] – we just open it every now and then.

In a case where two children were placed with adoptive parents but returned, after the disruption, to their former foster carers who subsequently adopted them, the adoptive mother explained her feelings about the disruption:

I actually felt quite a lot of guilt by letting them go in the first place. People said, 'Don't be ridiculous. You took them in in the first place'. But yes, we had a responsibility to them and we sent them away in all good faith. That was the right decision at the time. But, of course, 12 months later that was the wrong decision and that's 12 months of their lives and another disruption that they wouldn't perhaps have had to have, had we known. I feel guilt because I feel responsible for that decision.

The reaction of friends and neighbours to the child's departure was mentioned by some adopters. One said:

I think when Jason left, the hardest thing was explaining to other people that it didn't work. People would say, 'Where's that young man – that little boy?' 'He's gone back.' 'Back where?' It's so cruel to say you've given someone back. I think that was the hardest part.

She added that several people, particularly her close neighbours, once they knew that the boy had left, then talked to her about his misbehaviour as they had experienced it.

Her own two children still refer to Jason as 'our brother Jason', although she thought that might have something to do with distinguishing him from other 'Jasons' in their family. Soon after Jason left, it became apparent that he might attend the same school as her son. She felt that this would have created a lot of problems for them all. In the event, and much to her relief, Jason went to a different school.

The mother explained that after the child left, a therapist whom the whole family had seen during the placement, offered to see them free of charge to help them with the disruption. This offer was not taken up, but the mother has since thought that it might have been helpful.

I make out that I'm handling it and all this sort of thing. But I don't and I know I don't. [Husband] makes out that he's handling it for me. But I know that he's not and, as I said earlier on, perhaps we should have taken the counselling, if not for me doing it for [husband] and [husband] doing it for me, then us pretending we were doing it for the kids.

Agencies had suggested to some of these adopters that they should consider adopting another child. But, as one adoptive father said,

> *It was too late. The damage had been done. We would not have dared.*

Agency perspectives

Whilst disruption was discussed in most of the interviews with agency adoption workers, particularly the value or otherwise of disruption meetings (see para 5 below), its effect on families was mentioned by some only when talking about disruption generally. Of those that did, several mentioned that adopters blame themselves for what they see as their failure as parents. One who spoke about the grief adopters experience said:

> *The whole mourning and grieving process comes into it as well. It's the 'if only' bit. The whole thing becomes a matter of emotion really that you can't cut through.*

Several said that they had tried to help adopters understand and come to terms with what had happened, some mentioning the provision of counselling as an aid to adopters.

Some social workers referred to the effect disruption can have on the workers involved, often resulting in very mixed feelings such as guilt and anger at the adopters for having failed, and making it difficult for them to support the adopters after the disruption.

5   Disruption meetings

Family perspectives

Although disruption meetings are considered desirable by agencies, they are not standard practice [see below]. Meetings were held in only two of the five cases in our sample. In the third, there was a meeting at which it was agreed that the child should be moved to specialist foster carers, although it took a further nine months for this to materialise. In the fourth case, a meeting was planned for some two months after our interview following the departure of the second sibling; a meeting had followed the departure of the first some months previously. In the remaining case, the social worker had contacted the adopters following the child's departure, but there was no disruption meeting. Two other adoptive couples whom we interviewed had first hand experience of a disruption meeting since they had attended those arranged following placement breakdowns of children whom they had initially fostered and subsequently adopted following the failure of an adoption placement elsewhere.

A common theme to emerge from attendance at the disruption meeting was that adopters discovered far more information about the child's background, reinforcing the view of many that they had been given insufficient information at the outset. One adoptive father told us:

> We were approved for a non-violent child by the panel between the ages of seven and 12. We found out that he [child placed with them] used to have a punch bag at his place (that we took him from) to go and knock the hell out of when he got annoyed. He climbed up a tree in a shopping centre and pee-ed over people as they went past. Not violent, but different. He'd been going to some aunties and uncles that acted as foster aunts and uncles who have two daughters; he'd been banned from there. To top it all, the week before he came to join us – and we didn't know about this until afterwards – he'd actually tried to sexually attack a girl at school. But he wasn't violent, this lad! So we found out more about him after the event than we ever knew about him before . . . They [social workers] read through their case histories – one where he'd pulled a knife on a little girl or something – and his ex-social worker made a statement after these things had been read out saying he's not a violent child. I said, 'Hold on, am I missing something? Is that not violent?'

His other impression, mentioned by other adopters attending disruption meetings, was that:

> Nobody had a complete picture of what had gone on in his [boy's] history, what had gone wrong and why it had gone wrong. Nobody had ever sat down and looked at the whole picture. So-and-so had a bit and so-and-so had another bit, and never the twain shall meet.

Another adopter who had a similar experience said that such a meeting would have been much more useful at the beginning of the placement because of the knowledge they gained. As it was, they just acquired fragmented information from here and there, making it difficult to build a complete picture.

In one of the cases where no disruption meeting was held, the adoptive mother felt, in retrospect, that it would have done them good to have expressed their bitter disappointment to the local authority, even though it might have sounded like 'sour grapes'. She felt that the interview with the researcher had been helpful, giving her an opportunity to say out loud things that she had not had a chance to say to anyone before. This sentiment was shared by another adopter who said:

> We need to talk. We need to sort out what we do next, where we go from here, how we feel about what's happened. We need to talk about all these things. Bottling them up inside doesn't do any good at all.

Parents also felt that such meetings might prevent mistakes being repeated and ensure a more successful future placement for the child and thereby salvage something positive from their own bad experiences.

Agency perspectives

A voluntary agency worker commented that her agency had disruption meetings 'just like any other agency would'. However, as we have already said, such meetings are by no means automatic. Some agencies do not have them at all. Others are inconsistent. A few were in the process of setting up a system.

At the time of reorganisation in one statutory agency, a policy decision was taken not to have disruption meetings, largely because of staff shortages. The worker said it was not something they ruled out altogether but, for the time being, they make prospective adopters 'aware from the beginning that disruptions occur and some of the reasons for them'. Another explained that whilst disruption meetings were written into their procedures, they did not occur because of 'inadequate resources'. A worker in another statutory agency lacking a system said that, because they had to 'gather a lot of information anyway', they would review things 'statistically' and 'there may be a kind of analysis of the things that cause disruptions' by the permanency team. She remembered being impressed by a disruption meeting she had attended some years previously at Barnardo's, commenting that 'they were more systematic and things were more seriously done'.

One worker spoke of the difficulties posed by disruption meetings for social workers which might explain in part why some agencies do not have established systems:

> Not all social workers see the value of disruption meetings because – well, I'm speculating – but one reason is that anybody who's involved in the disruption thinks they are to blame. And it's hard to go to the disruption meeting . . . The whole point is to learn from what's happened and what you are learning from are often mistakes and that's very difficult to admit to. So there has been some resistance to having disruption meetings. I hope, over a long period of time, that the culture will begin to accept that disruption meetings happen.

Several adoption workers appreciated the value and benefits a "disruption system" would bring. A statutory worker said:

> We acknowledge that it's very good practice and it's very helpful in terms of shaping your thinking and rectifying mistakes for future child care matters that you deal with . . . We need to do a fair bit of work in terms of setting up a consistent approach to dealing with disruption meetings and getting that information back to the decision-making forum . . . We want to learn from best and worst practice if you like.

A voluntary agency worker described the purpose of disruption meetings:

> It's not to apportion blame. It's to try and look at what has happened in this child's past that would help us identify the future. Hopefully, people who have cared for a child are in a good position and by analysing and looking at what

has precipitated disruptions to make sure those things don't happen again.

Several voluntary agency workers also mentioned the reluctance of some statutory agencies to hold disruption meetings. One talked about having to 'push local authorities' to do so. If they were unsuccessful, they then had planning meetings themselves. One spoke of a consortium's 'disruption code of practice' which she described as a 'well planned and well thought out process'. They kept statistics and conducted research which was fed back to social services departments highlighting the issues of which they should be aware, and from which they could learn to plan better for the child.

6   Concluding points

From the evidence presented in this chapter, admittedly on a few cases only, it is clear that the wounds imposed by disruption on adopters and their families run very deep. The healing process is clearly a long one. As with other traumatic life events, adopters' lives are changed for ever. Much the same must apply to the children, many seriously damaged before the placement and facing another move as a result of its breakdown. As we know, many children will have endured a multiplicity of moves, sometimes in a variety of settings – residential homes, foster homes, disrupted adoptive placements – prior to this. It would be unrealistic to suppose that a system could be created in which disrupted placements did not occur, but it is not unrealistic to suggest that any review of the system should take account of the lessons to be learned from what we have been told during this research so that placements can be given their best chance and the risk of disruptions minimised. Research focused specifically on disruption would shed further light on what is required in terms of both adoption policy and agency practice.

What can we learn from this study? Despite the difficulty posed by the different circumstances in each of the disruption cases in our sample, common themes did emerge from our interviews with adopters and adoption workers:

1.   Preparation of children to be placed
This involves:
- listening to what children who are to be placed hope for in an adoptive placement in an attempt to meet their needs;
- assisting children to grieve for and come to terms with the loss of their birth parents in the sense that continuing to live with them as a family is not feasible, though some form of contact may be;
- working with children to address their emotional and behavioural problems resulting from earlier neglect and abuse before placing them in a family setting with which they may not otherwise be able to cope.

If these matters remain unaddressed, the child may find it difficult to attach to his/ her new family and the new family to cope with the challenges such difficulties present as the placement proceeds.

2.   Preparation of adoptive families

It is impossible to understate the importance of working with prospective parents and existing children in the family, acknowledging the problems older children may have and the behaviour that may result with which they will *all* have to come to terms.

3.   Linking and matching

Agencies should resist the temptation to place children of a different age range, sex or sibling group from that for which the prospective adopters have been approved and/or for which they had expressed a preference.[23] This reduces the risk of prospective adopters who are desperate to have a child placed with them from being tempted to agree to a placement for which they had not been approved. This may also apply to characteristics of the child or children such as learning difficulties and physical disabilities.

4.   Background information about the child

This should be given to prospective adopters in as full a form as possible, including:

- the reasons why they were looked after
- their birth family history
- their history whilst being looked after
- reasons for disrupted foster and adoptive placements, if any
- and medical history.

Given that this is likely to be considerable, it should be presented in written form to the adopters. The information should be up to date (and kept up to date) and be as accurate as possible. Adopters will be able to make more informed decisions about whether to proceed with a match and, if they do so, it will help them understand and cope with the child once in placement. It would also give them some indication of the kind of support they might need once the child has been placed, giving them a chance to establish what is available from the agency and elsewhere before the placement begins.

5.   Support

A full and frank discussion needs to take place between the prospective adopters and the agency anticipating, before the placement, the kinds and sources of support the adoptive family and child may need and how they can be resourced. Many may not emerge until after the placement when it is essential that adoption workers

---

[23] See note 12 and para 3.2.

listen to what adopters are saying about the child and any difficulties they may be experiencing and spot the warning signs and respond to cries for help. Regular and not infrequent visits by social workers and some mechanism for checking on progress of placement are required. It is the adopters who live with the child and will know better than anyone else the problems the child is presenting and the help they need if they are to cope. All agencies need to recognise that in placing older, damaged children for adoption, their involvement and obligation does not end when the adoption order has been granted. Several agencies not only recognise this, but have developed services to meet the needs of adoptive families, building in support packages from the outset. The provision of adequate funding would do much to redress this imbalance.

6.   Therapy/counselling

This should be provided for children in need as should the resources to fund it.

7.   Respite care

The provision of respite care, and funding for it, will give child and family alike a chance to recharge their batteries when caring for the child is demanding and exhausting.

8.   Handling disruptions

When disruption occurs adoptive families will be devastated, dealing with feelings of guilt, anger, despair and so on. The adopters' marriage may be at risk, existing children in the family will suffer. Ongoing support and counselling should be available for family members to take up if and when they feel the need to help them come to terms with their disappointment and loss. Disruption meetings can help this process for those adopters who feel able to attend.

9.   Reviewing disrupted placements

Whether or not adopters attend disruption meetings, agencies should meet to review the placement, ascertaining the causes for the breakdown so that mistakes in future planning for the child can be avoided.

Some of the above suggestions necessitate an adjustment to current practice but would not result in a drain on resources. Others have implications for resources. Inadequate staffing and funding also contribute to disrupted placements. Child care, in whatever shape or form, does not come cheap. A greater investment sooner rather than later will result in savings in the longer term not just in financial terms, but in terms of damage to children and those who care for them.

13 The Legal Process

1   Introduction

Although not the main focus of our research, during our interviews,[1] views were canvassed both from agency workers and adoptive families about the legal process of adoption. Strikingly, agency workers had relatively little to say about this aspect of adoption while the adopters' main recollections and comments were about the legal process – particularly the actual court hearing – rather than about the law itself or even about individuals (except to a limited extent, the judge) involved in the legal proceedings.

The absence of comment about the law may well reflect adopters' general ignorance about it. Indeed one adoptive mother suggested that there ought to be a basic booklet 'which you can keep referring to or go back to and absorb it a little at a time, when it's appropriate'. In this respect we were told of one statutory agency that was considering devising 'some guidance and check lists and bits of papers that can be given to birth families, adoptive families and children, if the children are of age, so that they will have some idea of what's it's all about'.

For most adopters, the law and its process were something to be endured rather than questioned. As one put it: 'I think the legal system is a pain in the neck but it's there, it has to be there,' while another said: 'I hated the process, I just wanted it over and done with'. This last comment betrays an underlying anxiety, which we found was shared by many adopters, both as to whether or not they would be granted the adoption and about having to go to court. Indeed, a key finding (no doubt in part exacerbated by ignorance of both the law and its process) is the high level of anxiety experienced by both adopters and the children particularly in relation to the court hearing.[2] We therefore begin this chapter with a graphic account of one adopter's experience of the legal process which highlights many of the experiences and anxieties felt by those seeking an adoption order. We then concentrate on certain specific issues such as the length (and delay) of proceedings,

---

[1] I.e. views were *not* canvassed in our postal questionnaires

[2] For children's, at times, harrowing experiences see our related study, *Adopted Children Speaking* (Thomas *et al*, 1999).

the adopters' experience of appearing in court and the importance of ceremony to mark the successful conclusion of proceedings. Finally, we discuss the availability and use made of complaint mechanisms.

2   The courts and court proceedings

2.1   One adopter's experience

The background to this case is that the child, Lee, was placed with a couple on a short-term fostering basis (originally two weeks), when Lee was four. The original plan was for Lee to be rehabilitated with his birth family but this changed when the birth father killed the birth mother. The father had a history of violence when drunk and both Lee and the adoptive mother[3] were frightened of him. He was found guilty of manslaughter. The couple then applied to adopt Lee. The process took over two years and the birth father opposed the application.

This is the adoptive mother's account of her experience of the adoption proceedings.

> *We applied to the court and we waited some time for a date. I think that was something like July. But we got near to the court date and it was cancelled. So by now we'd been waiting something like two-and-a-half years. That's a long, long time. It's not at my age, but to a little boy who's growing up fast, it's a long time. Then we had another court date and that was cancelled because the prison wardens were on strike and the court said that the prison wardens couldn't bring his father to court.*

> *Here's this little boy, and I say we're going to court tomorrow and we don't go, and for no good reason, so that was frustrating. So when it was coming to court for the third time, well, it makes me sound like some angry person, but when you're fighting for a child if you don't stand up and fight, nobody does. I felt quite angry about it. I said, 'Look, are you all aware this is the third time?'*

> *As luck would have it, I suppose, we had a barrister for the case and he said that it would run for three days. I bought three outfits because I'm normally dressed like this. I don't wear the clothes you would wear to court. And I got to court and I was terrified. Since then I've done role play in a court case and it has helped me – I won't be as terrified again. But I'd never done anything like that. I'd never been inside a court room. I felt the guilty party. I just felt absolutely terrified, and I didn't like to tell anybody that. I wanted to look like I was confident and the right sort of person to adopt this child.*

---

[3] Before the birth mother's death, Lee's birth parents regularly visited the foster home and on one occasion threatened the adoptive mother.

> *As a child I had speech problems and I was very shy, and I would run away and hide from people. And suddenly at court I was faced with it. But little things resurface, don't they? In any case, I was going to be the first witness and I was called to the stand. My legs went like jelly and I didn't hear anything after that. I thought I've just got to get to the stand and I've got to remember and I've got to answer correctly.*

> *Apparently, as I was going to the stand, his father stood up and said, 'I can see there's nothing I can do. There's a whole army of people against me.' Well, I hadn't heard this, I was so intent on getting to the stand that I had to be dragged back.*

Once the father withdrew his opposition, the proceedings effectively ended and the adoption order was granted there and then. In fact, the mother was surprised by the sudden granting of the order. As she said, 'I didn't realise it could be. The judge immediately spoke to us and said Lee would be adopted.'

Another of the mother's anxieties was that Lee might see his father in court. As she said:

> *I was worried sick about Lee seeing his father and the effect on Lee. I had enough to worry about on that day and I told the solicitor who was there, and the barrister about it. They said, 'Look, we don't think that Lee's going to be called today so he can go back to school'. So having picked him up, we then had to take him back. That was all right. I'd rather that happened. Lee didn't see his father.*

Ironically, because of the sudden collapse of the case, Lee was not present in court when the order was granted. This disappointed the mother who had wanted Lee to talk to the judge and for the judge to tell him he was adopted. To make up for this, the family returned to the court the following day and the mother explained to Lee what had happened. They eventually got a passer-by to photograph them all outside the court building.

Although the background to this case is striking,[4] the delays in the proceedings will be depressingly familiar to many adopters. Similarly, the trauma of the court appearance, though no doubt in this instance exaggerated because the application was contested, will strike a familiar chord with most adopters, as will the mother's concern for the well-being of the child throughout the proceedings. Equally, the role and place of the birth parents in the proceedings were mentioned by many. Finally, the evident need for some kind of ceremony to mark the granting of the order was frequently mentioned by our interviewees. We now examine each of these issues in more detail.

---

[4] But, sadly, not unique. We came across other cases where the birth mother had been killed by her partner.

2.2   The length/delay of proceedings

The length and delay in adoption proceedings and the possible causes have been well documented in other research.[5] Our concern here is the impact of delay upon the parties to the proceedings and the implication that has for support. For this reason we concentrate on the adopters' view, though it is worth recording one statutory agency worker's view that delays in court proceedings generally can mean that children stay in foster placements longer than planned, during which time they form attachments and bonds with their carers and the latter are then encouraged to apply for adoption.[6]

Impact on adopters

From the adopters' point of view, the time between the application and the court hearing is obviously an anxious period during which they have to contend not only with their own fears but also those of the children. These concerns can be made worse if the adopters themselves are not sure what is happening. It would be helpful if the adopters could be kept informed of the progress of proceedings and to be given clear advance warning of hearing dates. Sadly, such information is lacking in some cases. As one adopter told us:

> It takes such a long time from presenting things to court and actually going to court . . . We might get a letter a couple of days before the court hearing and nothing in between.

There can also be a feeling of powerlessness. As one adoptive father put it:

> We just felt that the whole thing was out of our hands. We had no control over it whatsoever. The whole thing was done by the court and solicitors. But you just wonder, are they doing everything they can? You just don't know and it makes you more worried because they may not be doing all they should be doing. But it's just a concern and it just affects everybody. It affects us. It affects the children.

Another problem not infrequently encountered is the last minute postponement of the hearing. Quite apart from the need to be told about it as soon as possible, many adopters gear both themselves and the child for what some refer to as 'the adoption

---

[5] See e.g. Murch *et al* (1993), Chs 8 and 9 and Conclusions, and Lowe *et al* (1993), Chs 3 and 5. However, it is worth recording that one voluntary agency worker attributed the delay in part 'to the fact that nobody seems quite sure who does what and where to proceed' and in part because of agencies' reluctance to pay the adopters' legal fees due to tightening budgets. For other studies on delay in family court proceedings generally, see Thomas *et al* (1993); Booth (1996) and Hunt (1997).

[6] Which, in that worker's view was not necessarily a good idea. In fact, very nearly half of our sample of adopters (48 per cent) had either fostered the child in question or had fostered other children (see Chapters 6, *Agency and Family Profiles*, and 7, *Starting the Adoption Process*).

day' and arrange parties. One family explained how, having had one hearing date postponed, they had arranged to have a party after the second hearing date, only for that date also to be postponed. The mother was informed of the second adjournment by a telephone call from the court on the Friday afternoon before the planned hearing on the Monday. She was particularly upset because the adoption meant so much to the child and she was angry that she had not been given more notice about the adjournment. They held the party anyway and, in the event, the mother went with the child and her social worker to the court on the Monday that the hearing should have taken place and was able to see the judge who explained to the child what was happening. The mother said:

> If that hadn't happened, I felt [the child] would have ended up thinking it was me stopping the adoption.

Impact on the children

The effect on the children of lengthy proceedings, particularly where hearing dates are changed, was clearly a matter of great concern to adopters.[7] As one explained:

> I know [the child] has been very anxious . . . Why is it taking so long? When is this happening? When is that happening? Things have always slipped and we have always had to say, there's no problem, it's just that it takes time for the court to deal with this.

The girl in this instance was very sensitive to the developments in her case and the adopters decided that:

> It's better to tell her exactly what's going on all the time, for example, about the envelopes that came through the door . . . because she wants to know and she's always wondering what's going on any way. Like when the adoption forms came back she said, 'Why have they come back?' So I said, 'Oh, we forgot to fill in one of the questions'. We didn't really check but she actually knew it was post marked at the courts.

This mother also made the point that the format of the forms were 'cold' and certainly not child friendly. As she said:

> There's something so cold and official and threatening and big brotherish about that part of the whole procedure . . . I do not know what the answer is. It would be nice to think of some way to make it more friendly.

---

[7] See also *Adopted Children Speaking*, Thomas *et al* (1999) for mixed reactions from children concerning delays in the court process, and for evidence that social workers' and adoptive parents' verbal reassurances and explanations did not always allay children's fears and anxieties in this respect.

Being able to reassure the child is clearly important to the adopters but that is not so easy when the adopters themselves do not know what is happening. As one adopter explained:

> *It's very difficult to talk to the children, like when [the child] said, 'I'm not going to be taken away from her again, am I?' And we are saying, 'no, no, no', but you didn't know what's happening. That must have come across subconsciously. You find yourself not being so effusive about it.*

One adopter made the telling point that time scales are difficult for children in that 'every six months there's a major development for that child'. Hence delays have added significance.

2.3 The adopters' experience of court proceedings

Stress and anxiety

Understandably, many adopters recalled their court experience as something of an ordeal. As we saw in Lee's case (referred to at the beginning of the chapter), the adoptive mother was 'terrified' of appearing in court. Others recalled being 'worried sick', of being an 'absolute nervous wreck' and of crying in court simply as a reaction to the stress. There were several causes of stress. For some it was having to appear in court. For others it was the worry that the order may not be granted,[8] a concern that was obviously greater where the application was being contested, though that is not to say such anxiety was confined to contested cases. In this respect there is a clear need for some reassurance. One adopter told us:

> *When we went into court I got the impression that we didn't actually know until we saw the judge whether we'd definitely get the children. That was a bit nerve racking I think. Nobody said oh, it will definitely be alright.*

In contrast, one adoptive mother who had been assured by 'the barristers acting for us that there wouldn't be a problem because of what had gone on and because access had been terminated for quite some time', seemed more concerned for her child's social worker who was given a 'real grilling' than for herself. Others mentioned the reassurance of having a freeing order,[9] with one describing it as 'neat and clean'.

Another cause of adopters' stress, particularly but not exclusively in contested cases, is having possibly to meet the birth parents. In one uncontested case, an adoptive mother explained how, having being told that the birth mother would be in the building, though not in court, she had become an 'absolute nervous wreck' and

---

[8] Of course this anxiety may also be shared by the child which is an added worry for the adopters.

[9] A freeing order is an order (which can only be granted upon an agency application) which has the effect of ending the birth parents' interest in the child so that they can no longer object to the adoption.

how even when getting out of the car she was 'looking over me shoulder thinking, oh, I hope we don't bump into her'. Another was concerned to get away from the court after the hearing as quickly as possible because she thought the birth father 'was so violent he was going to attack the social worker outside the court'. Yet another couple told us how they wanted to avoid a direct confrontation with the birth parents and were hoping the agency would apply for a freeing order.[10]

Children, too, can have considerable fears about going to court. Underlying these can be fantasies about formidable judges; associating going to court with wrong-doing; worry that the adoption order would not be granted and about what would happen then; uncertainties about their own role in the proceedings; and the possibilities of unwanted meetings with birth parents.[11]

The adopters' attitude towards birth parents
Different relationships

Notwithstanding the above comments, it would be wrong to convey the impression that all adopters were either frightened of or wished to avoid seeing the birth parents in court. In fact, it was evident from our interviews that the inter-relationship between adoptive and birth parents varied considerably. Of course some were frightened, while others were resentful of what they saw as too much latitude being given to birth parents, for example, allowing them to appeal out of time. One adoptive mother also explained how she felt uncomfortable having treated the birth parents 'as normal people' at previous contact meetings, yet on the witness stand:

> . . . just telling them what the boys had told me. I felt I was being two-faced and I'm not two-faced. I'd rather say outright! That's what I didn't like.

Others, however, were more sympathetic. One adopter said that the birth mother 'hadn't got a clue really which was sad. We felt quite sad for her.' In another case, the adoptive mother had been lent photographs of the child by the birth mother and wanted to return them at the adoption hearing. However, because the application was supposedly opposed by the birth mother,[12] the parties were placed in separate rooms. However, notwithstanding this initial separation, the parents did manage to meet. In fact, they had coffee together ironically whilst discussions were afoot to persuade the guardian *ad litem*, who was supporting the mother's supposed opposition to the adoption, to withdraw her report. In the event the report was withdrawn and the order was made with the birth mother holding the adoptive mother's hand in court! This last mentioned case raises two other points: the first

---

[10] This is an interesting comment giving some credence to the oft cited justification of freeing, that it takes the pressure off the would-be adopters and allows the birth family's hostility to be directed against the agencies. See Lowe *et al* (1993, supra, at p. 64).

[11] See Thomas *et al* (1999).

[12] In fact, the mother's views seemed to have been misrepresented by the guardian – see further below.

concerning the practice of providing separate rooms for the parties and the second, collapsing cases.

Separate rooms

There is a well-established need for courts to provide separate rooms for the parties in adoption proceedings both to preserve, where appropriate, anonymity of the applicants[13] and to prevent direct confrontation between adoptive and birth parents. However, our interviewees had mixed experiences of and reactions to such facilities. On the one hand, the adoptive mother in the case referred to at the beginning of this chapter, told us how she had to fight for a separate room and even then, as she put it:

> We were tossed out and somebody else went in and we had to sit in the corridor where his father was.

While on the other, an adoptive mother from another case explained that she felt:

> We were shoved in a corner. I'd love to have been part of [the proceedings] . . . to actually not feel we were behind closed doors.

She also felt (perhaps naively?) that it would have been 'nice' for the 'mum' to have seen her child.

This seems an area that requires sensitive handing and a real appreciation of the relationships between the adopters and birth parents. Even then, there remains a need for caution at any rate in contested cases.

Collapsing cases

It was striking that in our sample a number went to court as being contested yet parental opposition quickly evaporated. This experience confirms earlier research findings that, in many cases, birth parents only passively oppose applications in that they do not sign agreement forms but do not really intend to actively oppose the application.[14]

Of course, the very fact that an application is being supposedly contested is likely to be more worrying for these adopters but another knock-on consequence is that the sudden withdrawal of opposition can lead to a speedy conclusion. A number

---

[13] The difficulties that some courts have in providing appropriate facilities for keeping the parties separate was commented upon by May LJ in *Re LS (A Minor) (Adoption: Procedure)* [1987] 1 FLR 302. It may be noted that in the Adoption Law Review consultation document (1992, para 40), it was questioned whether adopters' identities would automatically be revealed by their appearance in court with the birth parents and indeed it cautioned about the ease with which so-called serial number applications may be made. Our research does, however, serve as a reminder that some adopters, at least, very keenly feel the need (not necessarily to maintain their anonymity) to be kept separate from birth parents during the court proceedings.

[14] See Murch *et al* (1993), supra, at para 3.1 (b).

of adopters told us of their surprise at the sudden granting of the adoption order. For some this sudden end was an anti-climax. As one put it:

> We were all shell shocked. Literally we were in the waiting room longer than we were in the judge's chambers.

Concluding the case – the need for ceremony

It was apparent from our interviews that both adopters and particularly the children attached considerable importance to having some sort of ceremony to mark the granting of the adoption order.[15] As already mentioned, several adopters referred to the adoption hearing as their "Adoption Day" and several held family parties afterwards to mark the occasion.[16]

We were told of many positive experiences in court at the granting of the order: of judges making a special point of talking to the child or children concerned; of making sure there were enough seats in the room to allow the whole family in; of giving the child a present – in one case an old fashioned teddy done up in a little parcel with pretty bows, and to allow photographs to be taken.[17] Illustrative of these positive experiences is 'C's case' who wrote to the judge:

> It's a very special day for me. I'm having a new Mummy and Daddy and I'm eight years old. It would be nice to see you in your red coat and would you wear your wig? And my Mummy and Daddy are coming and my Grandma, my two Grandmas. All the family can't come and I've got lots of new Aunties and lots of new Uncles and they can't come. So can my Daddy bring his video camera in and film it and show all my new family?

Although the judge's clerk wrote back warning the family that all these requests may be not complied with, in fact the judge did get dressed up except for his wig. The family were then asked into a court room (rather than chambers because there were so many of them) and, in the father's words:

> So we went in the court room and whilst he can't wear his wig I do know he's taken it in the court with him. At the end of all the proceedings – which [the child] thought were a bit of an anti-climax – was a few minutes to sign a piece

---

[15] See also our earlier research, Murch *et al* (1993) at para 6.31 which also referred to the importance of ceremony.

[16] See Thomas *et al* (1999) which indicated that most children celebrated their adoption day and how some of them also celebrated its anniversary.

[17] This raises an interesting legal point, namely, taking photographs in court. We were told of one case (in the High Court) where the judge said that a photograph could not be taken because of the restriction set out in s 41 of the Criminal Justice Act 1925 though photographs were taken outside the court. While the judge was technically correct, we wonder whether s 41 was really designed to prevent the taking of such photographs with the judge's permission. For a detailed discussion of the history and ambit of this provision, see Borrie and Lowe (1996, pp 24 ff).

of paper and that was it. And then he said, 'I hear young lady you wanted to see me in my wig.' And he got this big black box and he took the lid off and he just briefly put it on so that [the child] could see it.

We heard of others who tried the judge's wig on and had photographs of it. In one case the child had since asked to see the photograph many times 'so that she can be certain that she is now adopted'. We have found in our study, *Adopted Children Speaking* (Thomas *et al*, 1999) that a number value the experience of attending the court because of the positive outcome. Also a majority had positive memories of the judge.[18]

Sadly, not all the experiences were as positive. One adopter felt that there needed to be a certificate or some such token which would have something 'concrete' for the child. In this case, as the mother put it, 'the order came in the post several weeks later, but it was just a mangy piece of paper really'. Although judges were generally praised for their handling of adoption cases, the one area where there seemed to be more of a problem is that of the contested application where the opposition suddenly collapses. It seems that while judges are readily geared up to perform a ceremony in granting adoption orders in uncontested cases, they sometimes overlook the need to do this in contested cases, at any rate in those which suddenly come to a conclusion.

3   The availability and use made of complaints procedures

3.1   The availability of a complaints procedure

Although at the moment[19] adoption agencies have no obligation to set up a formal complaints procedure in relation to adoption matters,[20] in practice most agencies do have such a procedure. According to the response to our agency questionnaire, which specifically enquired about the existence of a complaints procedure, 77 per cent of statutory agencies[21] and 92 per cent of voluntaries[22] said they had such a procedure.

---

[18] See Thomas *et al* (1999).

[19] Under cl 15 of the proposed Adoption Bill 1996 (*Adoption: A Service for Children*), each local authority will have to establish a complaints procedure. Under the Adoption Agencies and Children Arrangements for Placement and Review (Miscellaneous Amendments) Regulations 1997 (SI 1997/649), prospective adopters who have been deemed unsuitable now (as from 1 November 1997) have a right to make representations before the Adoption Panel.

[20] Cf s 26 of the Children Act 1989 which makes it mandatory for local authorities to have a formal representation or complaints procedure in relation to children being 'looked after' by them.

[21] 13 per cent of statutory agencies responded saying they had no such procedure. The remaining 10 per cent were either 'unsure' or responded in some other way.

[22] The other 8 per cent were 'unsure'.

3.2   The use made of complaints procedures

We found relatively little evidence of adopters making use of a formal complaints procedure (though our sample did not include those who had been turned down as prospective adopters where more complaints might be expected[23]). One did go to see the 'Head of Social Services', another wrote a letter of complaint and received a letter of apology. Others considered complaining: one, for example, having received someone else's confidential mail, feared that her own had similarly gone astray; another, in respect of the behaviour and attitude of the child's social worker in a case of a placement that disrupted. In the end, however, both decided not to, either because of the hassle, or, in the latter case, because it 'might look like a whole vendetta' against the worker.

We were, however, told of two instances involving guardians *ad litem* that seem instructive. In the first, the report was full of inaccuracies (the adopters rather wondered whether the guardian had confused two families) and the guardian was eventually pressured into withdrawing her recommendation that the adoption not be granted. The adopters were asked if they wanted to make a complaint but as the mother told us, 'We were so tired and worn out that we said no, we couldn't'. She added, however, 'In hindsight I think we should have done and I think possibly the social services should have taken it further but we were all just so utterly relieved at what had happened'.

In the second case, the adopter found their dealings with the guardian very distressing on a number of points (viz. the conduct of the enquiry, disclosure of confidential information, and the furnishing of a false and inaccurate report). In this instance a formal complaint was made, but not until after the granting of the adoption order, lest the complaint delayed proceedings still further. Apparently, the agency in question had not previously handled a formal complaint and it seemed to the adopter to be 'a bit at sea as to how they went about it'. In the event the Complaints Board decided to leave the complaint on file but not to determine it as the guardian had since left the Panel.

In summary, whilst most agencies had a formal complaints procedure for adoption, relatively little use seems to have been made of it. This apparent lack of use, even in those minority of cases where a complaint might well have been justified, stems in part from adopters' understandable reluctance to become involved in further proceedings on top of the court proceedings. Furthermore, many are simply relieved to have obtained the order and can see little point in pursuing complaints about past events.

---

[23] As we have said (see note 19 above) there is now a special complaints procedure for such aggrieved would-be adopters. We came across one case where, because the adoptive applicant was herself a local authority councillor, there was uncertainty as to which Panel should assess her. The mother complained 'vigorously' about the ensuing delay to the Director of Social Services who then sorted the matter out.

4 Concluding points

As mentioned at the beginning of this chapter, the key finding is the high level of anxiety experienced both by the adopters and the children during the legal process of adoption. Both need constant reassurance throughout that process – the adopters not least so that they can give that necessary reassurance to the children. Clearly, the longer the legal process the more sustained that anxiety can become and anything that can be done to minimise the delays must be welcome. Undoubtedly one contributing factor to lengthier proceedings is birth parent opposition. In that regard, we came across a number of instances where the birth parents kept changing their minds and of cases where they were reluctant to sign agreement forms even though they were not seriously prepared to oppose the application in court. We would therefore support the suggestion made in the Consultative Document on Adoption Law[24] (but which was not apparently followed up in the Adoption Bill consultative document)[25] to find some way to enable 'parents who do not intend to contest an adoption to give agreement without feeling that they are abandoning or betraying that child'. One suggestion, namely that parents be enabled to attach a statement explaining the circumstances of the adoption and indeed why they feel it is in the interests of the child to be adopted, seems to us to be well worth pursuing.

To some extent the tension and anxiety of taking legal proceedings are inevitable, particularly where the application is opposed.[26] Nevertheless, some steps could be taken to alleviate unnecessary stress. First, there seems a need for greater information both about the law and the legal process and about the progress of the case. It might be helpful if a booklet or even video could be produced which simply explains both the law and the court process. Preferably one needs to be produced for the adopters and another for the children.

There is a clear need for more work to be done to prepare both adopter and child for what the court proceedings are really like. A preliminary visit to the court might be helpful. Some anxiety undoubtedly stems from ignorance. It is also important that adopters are given clear information about the progress of proceedings: agency workers, legal practitioners and court officials all need to be aware of the likely anxiety and stress felt by the applicants and the children. Wherever possible, steps should be taken to reassure the applicants that all is well.

There is a clear need for agency workers and legal practitioners to be aware of the relationship between the adoptive applicants and the birth parents. In some

---

[24] *Adoption Law Review* (1992) paras 10.9 ff

[25] *Adoption: A Service for Children* (Department of Health and Welsh Office, 1996)

[26] Though interestingly we found in our earlier research that parental opposition to adoption makes virtually no difference to the outcome, see Murch *et al* (1993) at paras 2.9 and 2.15. Nevertheless, in such cases it is more difficult to give adoptive applicants the same degree of reassurance as where the application is unopposed.

cases, separation is essential and there need to be appropriate facilities in court buildings to accommodate this. In this regard, practitioners need to be alive to the need to keep the parties separate both before and after as well as during the proceedings. On the other hand, it seems clear that the parties do not always need to be separated though that will require deft as well as sensitive handling.

The need for ceremony does seem important to both adopters and children and all those involved in the court process need to be made aware of this. What may well be regarded by many court officials and lawyers as a mere formality, is clearly regarded by many adopters and their children as a major milestone in the adoption process. Much of our evidence in this respect underlines the symbolic significance of the final court hearing as the culminating rite of passage for the adoptive family.

It should be said, however, that overall, adopters commonly had positive experiences of meeting judges[27] who often went of their way to talk to both them and the children and to make a ceremony when making the order. The one problem area we found was where the sudden collapse of opposition to the order led to an abrupt end to the hearing and the immediate granting of the order when the vital sense of occasion and ceremony can then be lost. Indeed in some cases, the children may not even be present at the making of the order. Thought needs to be given to ensuring that the order is not seen as an anti-climax. *The Criminal Justice Act 1925*, s 41 could also profitably be amended to allow photographs and videos to be taken in court with the judge's permission.

We have concentrated on the adopters' and their children's needs since that is the focus of this research, but it would be a wrong to overlook the birth parents' needs. They too, of course, suffer stress and anxiety which also need to be addressed. In this respect, it is also worth referring to two agency workers' views about the need to pick up the pieces after the court hearing. As the first said, the birth parents need help and advice to enable them to cope with the effect of the adversarial process, while the second stressed the need for some damage limitation or reparative social work for birth parents who may well feel devastated by a contested court hearing which they have lost.

---

[27] This is not to say that other legal practitioners were not well thought of. In the adoptive family questionnaires, adopters were asked who they considered to be the key contributors to their adoption experience and whether or not these contributions were helpful: a third mentioned solicitors and, of these, 89 per cent thought the contribution 'helpful'; only 3 per cent said 'unhelpful'.

14 Financial and Practical Support

1   Introduction

In this chapter we discuss practical support by which we mean financial support such as adoption and fostering allowances or expenses; respite care; emergency support; and any other practical support such as domestic help which adoptive parents and children might need and from which they might benefit. Whereas financial support is usually obtained from a formal source – a local authority or a charitable trust – other practical support may well emanate from informal sources, for example, family and friends or religious institutions as well as from more formal sources.

The type of practical support needed can change over time, depending on where families are in the adoption process. For instance, before placement prospective adopters may require financial help in travelling to meet the child during the period of introductions but once the child is placed there may be a need for equipment or furniture. Later it may become apparent that the child needs some kind of therapy for which financial assistance may be required.

2   Financial support

The postal questionnaire asked adoptive families to indicate which, if any, types of financial support they had received. The data are shown in Table 14 below.

2.1   Adoption allowances

The legal background

As we discussed in Chapter 2, the payment of post-adoption allowances is relatively new, being originally permitted by s 32 of *the Children Act 1975* which came into force in 1982. Under that provision agencies had to submit a scheme for the payment of allowances for approval by the Secretary of State. In 1991, however, the law was changed so that instead of having a series of individual schemes, there is now uniform provision for the payment of allowances. Currently, adoption allowances are permitted under the *Adoption Act 1976*, s 57A provided they are made in accordance with the Adoption Allowance Regulations 1991.

Payments can, in theory, be made both by statutory and voluntary agencies but unlike the former,[1] the latter, if it does not hold itself out as normally paying an allowance, is under no obligation to decide whether or not to pay an allowance (see reg.4(3)) though as the Department of Health's *Guidance and Regulations* states:[2] 'it is not prevented from doing so in a particular exceptional case'. Under s 57(A) allowances are payable to those who have either adopted or intend to adopt. However, under reg 2(1) of the 1991 Regulations such allowances are only payable: a) where the agency has accepted the adoption panel's recommendation that adoption is in the child's best interests and would not be practicable without an allowance, and b) one or more of the circumstances specified in reg 2(2) exist, namely:

- where the adoption agency is satisfied that the child has established a strong and important relationship with the adopters before the adoption order is made;
- where it is desirable that the child be placed with the same adopters as his brothers or sisters, or with a child with whom he has previously shared a home;
- where at the time of the placement for adoption the child –
   is mentally or physically disabled or suffering from the effects of emotional or behavioural difficulties, and
   needs special care which requires a greater expenditure of resources than would be required if the child were not so disabled, or suffering from the effects of emotional or behavioural difficulties;
- where at the time of the placement for the adoption the child was mentally or physically disabled or suffering from the effects of emotional or behavioural difficulties, and as a result at a later date he requires more care and a greater expenditure of resources than were required at the time he was placed for adoption because there is
   a deterioration in the child's health or condition, or
   an increase in his age; or
- where at the time of the placement for adoption it was known that there was a high risk that the child would develop an illness or disability and as a result at a later date he requires more care and a greater expenditure of resources than were required at the time he was placed for adoption because such illness or disability occurs.

In short, all agencies have a discretion whether to pay an allowance at all, though as the Department of Health's *Guidance* states:[3]

> *Adoption allowances continue to be the exception rather than the norm.*

---

[1] Under reg 4(1)(a) it is *mandatory* for statutory agencies to consider whether an allowance may be paid.
[2] Vol 9, *Adoption Issues*, para 2.3.
[3] Ibid at para 2.2.

However, like the schemes which they replace, the Regulations are intended to give agencies sufficient flexibility to respond to individual needs and circumstances within this overall objective.

Notwithstanding the aforementioned discretion, statutory agencies[4] are required by reg 4(1) to consider whether an allowance may be paid and to supply information to the adopters about allowances, to give them written notice of their proposed decision, and to hear any representation from them. Regulation 4(1)(e) requires an agency to make a *decision* about allowances (and to notify the adopters of that decision and determination) *before* the adoption order is made. One leading commentary[5] advises that consideration should always be given as to whether an allowance should be paid in principle, even though initially on a nil basis, in case circumstances change after the adoption.

Agencies have a discretion as to how much an allowance should be, though reg 3(4) states that it cannot exceed the amount of any foster allowance that would otherwise have been payable.[6] There is also a discretion, pursuant to reg 2(5), as to when the allowance should be payable (i.e. at placement[7] or after the adoption order). All adoption allowances are means tested. They must also be reviewed annually (see reg 6).[8]

Given the wide discretion vested in agencies, it is hardly surprising that our research has revealed a general lack of consistency both as to the policy of whether to make payments at all and as to the level of any such payments.

---

[4] But not voluntary agencies, see above.

[5] Viz Clarke, Hall and Morrison, *On Children* (10th edtion) at **3[332]**.

[6] It is probably for this reason that adoption allowances are commonly thought to be lower than fostering allowances.

[7] But not before, see reg 2(5).

[8] Regulation 5 deals with information about allowances viz, method of payment, amount, date last payable, frequency of payment and procedure for review, variation and formulation.

Table 14
Adoptive families who received financial support

	Statutory families		Voluntary families		Total cases	
Adoption allowance	99	63%	38	58%	137	61%
Fostering allowance	79	50%	24	36%	103	46%
Travel for introductions to child	64	41%	53	80%	117	52%
Travel for contact	17	11%	14	21%	31	14%
Initial caring costs[9]	52	33%	40	61%	92	41%
Payment for loss or damage	5	3%	2	3%	7	3%
Benefits for child's special needs[10]	17	11%	10	15%	27	12%
Other financial support	19	12%	8	12%	27	12%
Received no financial support	7	4%	2	3%	9	4%

Source: Family postal survey

The adopters' perspective

Varied general experiences

Well over half (61 per cent) of the adopters who responded to our postal question-naire said they were in receipt of an adoption allowance. However, illustrative of the inconsistency between agencies concerning the provision of allowances is the experience of one mother who had adopted children placed by two different agencies. She explained that in the first:

> . . . *[their] attitude is very much you're taking on older children, difficult children who need an awful lot of support and therefore you've got enough worries without having to worry about money and they were very generous and still are.*

However, she found the second authority's approach to be:

> . . . *completely and utterly the opposite . . . I get the feeling that they're doing us a huge favour by giving us the finance in the first place. It isn't automatic by a long chalk – you have to really fight for it, or the social workers have to fight for it, every time, even in a large sibling placement (which is what this is).*

Another couple, who adopted a sibling group of three girls, had an enhanced adoption allowance which clearly made life much easier. The father explained:

---

[9] E.g. special equipment, house adaptations, etc.
[10] E.g. disability living allowance, invalid care allowance.

We drew up a shopping list of things we would like to do if we had an en-hanced allowance and gave that list to the psychiatrist . . . and NCH nego-tiated with [local authority] . . . Rather than paying for specific items they have said, 'We're going to enhance your allowance'. So we get an adoption allowance which is the boarding out rates that are applicable for foster carers less a deduction for income. Then what they've done is to enhance that by paying an addition of full boarding out allowances. So we're getting quite a lot of money at the moment . . . So that's been quite important to us at least to make life easier and enable us to do things we wouldn't otherwise be able to do. Some of those things will be a direct benefit to the kids . . . We managed when we didn't get an allowance on an enhanced basis but we only just about managed.

In contrast, another couple, who had also adopted a sibling group of three, told us that they received an initial allowance for furniture and school uniforms but nothing else. The father felt that they should have received a fostering allowance until the adoption went through. In that case, the family changed from a two wage earning unit to a family of five with one wage.[11]

Several adopters said that they found things financially very difficult, but had been given no advice or information about the possibility of an adoption allowance. In one case, where the adoptive father was out of work, it was their solicitor who first told them that they may be entitled to an adoption allowance.

In contrast, one couple were encouraged to adopt their foster children by the social worker who said they would be entitled to an adoption allowance. Another couple, who adopted a child with special needs, wanted to do certain things in their house to help accommodate her. They applied for an adoption allowance and were 'backed all the way' by their local authority. In a third case, a mother told us that: 'The social workers really sorted my financial side out . . . they fought for me and got me an allowance,' and this despite the fact that her income 'was over the allowance bracket'.

A concern to some who receive adoption allowances is the fact that they do not know how long they are likely to be eligible, or whether the level of payment will remain the same. One couple, who had to wait a long time for their allowance to come through, were worried that it would not last. This same anxiety, coupled with dissatisfaction about the level of payment in their authority, stopped another couple from adopting two of their foster children.

One father explained that when the two boys were placed initially they received £209 per week which, as they had anticipated, was reduced to £113 per week once the adoption order had been made. By the time of the interview this allowance had been reduced to £40 per week, yet the family had extended their property so that

---

[11] This begs the question of whether or not there were discussions between the family and agency about the adopters' ability to cope financially with a three sibling placement.

each boy could have his own bedroom and in doing so had doubled their mortgage. Their standard of living had suffered dramatically yet they lost their subsequent appeal to the local authority against the latest reduction. They felt particularly aggrieved because the father was near to retirement and had little or no time to recover from such a blow. Furthermore, they had ongoing face-to-face contact with the boys' birth family which necessitated a journey at some cost which they have to bear.

In similar vein a mother, who adopted a sibling group of four having earlier adopted a sibling group of two, explained that she and her husband had to buy a bigger house and a bigger car for which they had received no financial help. She continued:

> It's hampered us financially and it always will – it will obviously have a long-term effect. So now to turn round and say to us you might not actually always have this allowance, which is what happened, is I think quite horrendous and this is the battle I'm just about to start.

Annual reviews of allowances

In the postal questionnaire families were asked if their agency reviewed their financial circumstances annually. It will be recalled that under reg 6 of the Adoption Allowance Regulations 1991 it is mandatory for the agency to review this allowance at least annually. Of those who responded to this question, just over half of those approved by statutory agencies (56 per cent) said that they did, while 36 per cent said that they did not. The remainder (8 per cent) were mostly unsure whether they did so or not. Those parents approved by voluntary agencies were much less likely to be reviewed annually – probably because the major sources of financial assistance – adoption and fostering allowances – are provided by local authorities. Even so, 30 per cent of those who responded to the question said that they were reviewed, while 41 per cent said they were not. Of the remainder, most were unsure whether their finances were reviewed annually or not.

One adopter was surprised that their financial position would be reviewed on a regular basis to see if they were still eligible. She felt that was 'a bit of a cheek'. No-one had mentioned the review to her at the time she adopted her children. Another couple contrasted the approach to reviews of two authorities from which she received an adoption allowance. The first authority reviews every two years.

> The format of the letter is a very nice one, it basically only asks a couple of questions about whether our financial circumstances have changed dramatically or in a major way, either way yes or no, and do you have any extra needs which you feel aren't being met? That to me is a very positive way of putting something and I would therefore be very honest with them about what I said the changes were.

In the second authority,

> . . . it's means tested to the enth degree . . . it's every year, the form is horrible. It's exactly the same form as is given to people who are in residential care or anybody else within the system who's receiving a benefit basically. And it's a weekly amount, everything had to be copied out weekly down to the nearest penny and any savings or anything is taken into account.

Taxation of allowances

Taxation of allowances was also a worry for some. One adopter explained:

> I've had letters from the Social Services Secretary telling me that they're not taxed, but they are! They take my family allowance and take it away from my tax allowance so it is taxed. Unless I'm really strange I really think if they put things in the column and remove it from your tax allowance it's taxed, isn't it? . . . I feel that we're being penalised unnecessarily . . . I think more people will perhaps consider adopting if they knew that at some stage if they need it that there would be some kind of financial assistance . . .

She is 'fighting' with her MP to get the tax regulations changed.

Payment of allowances after the child is 18

One point raised by an adoptive couple was that their adoption allowance terminated when their son was 18. However, he wished to continue in full-time education. They were unable to pay his way through college and on to university. In this instance a solution was found by obtaining an 'after care grant'. Apparently little was known about this grant and social services was as surprised as the adoptive parents that they got it.

There is clearly a longer term implication here for those adopters whose children wish to continue their education after 18.

The adoption agency perspective

All statutory agencies which responded to our questionnaire on this point (82 out of 85) said that they operated an adoption allowance scheme but there was a difference in practice as to when allowances were paid. More than half (60 per cent) said that the allowance took effect upon placement; 21 per cent upon the adoption order; and in a further 18 per cent of cases the timing varied.[12] We asked the voluntary agencies whether they helped adoptive families to obtain an adoption allowance or other financial assistance from the local authority. All those who responded (25 out

---

[12] In two cases, agencies said that they did not pay a foster allowance during an adoption placement which could imply that they make no payment at all at this stage.

of 30) confirmed that they did so, but only 16 per cent of such agencies themselves offered financial support (56 per cent said they positively did not).

Varying attitudes and policies

There seemed some ambivalence towards adoption allowances. One social worker, for example, did not think that in his local authority allowances were communicated to adopters as a means of support. This somewhat low-key attitude was also reflected by the relative paucity of those mentioning adoption allowances at all when responding on behalf of statutory agencies to our questionnaire enquiry as to what support they offered to adopted children. A similar picture emerged from voluntary agency workers. Of course, voluntary agencies rarely pay adoption allowances. Nevertheless, it was striking that hardly any said that they discussed the possibility of an adoption allowance with the adopters and that, in answer to the question about the most common type of support requested, only two mentioned financial services.

In contrast some agencies have a well organised system of allowances which on occasion is used imaginatively. For example, one agency questionnaire respondent explained that in his authority a written agreement setting out the financial support that will be offered is drawn up between the agency and the adopters at the time of placement.

In another agency the social worker explained that finance was not too difficult for those foster carers who converted to adoptive parents because their authority had 'a well established adoption allowance scheme'. Other agencies explained that they use the adoption allowance to pay for such services as therapy or counselling for the child or to facilitate contact. One statutory agency said that in cases where the adoptive family have moved to another area in which the local authority is reluctant to provide the adopted child with a service he or she might need, they were prepared to fund whatever service may be required through the adoption allowance scheme.

Not all agencies seem as generous as this last one. For example, one agency worker explained that in her authority, unless the allowance was set up at the time of the placement, adoptive parents could not apply later. She thought that under 'their revised scheme' no allowance could be made for the possibility of an adopter being made redundant.[13]

Reviews

Although one social worker acknowledged that many adopters feel threatened by reviews, several said that they looked upon the annual review of adoption allowances as a means of keeping in touch with their adopters. As one put it:

---

[13] As a matter of law a decision about the payment of allowances must be made before the adoption order is made – i.e. it does not have to be made at the time of placement, see reg 4(1)(e) of the 1991 Regulations.

The review of the allowance would be a time every year when you would be in contact with the family anyhow and it would be part of your ongoing support of that family to look at how things were going. Both financially as well as inevitably you'd talk about how the placement was going and how you're getting on. 'Have you got what you need?' 'Are there resources which you'd hoped would be available?' 'If not, what can we do to make sure that you understand as a family that you now can come to social services?'

One problem of having to conduct reviews is where the adopters live in different parts of the country since the exercise then becomes costly both in time and money.

2.2   Fostering allowances

Agency policy, as we have said[14] varies as to when adoption allowances are paid. In fact a fifth (21 per cent) of statutory agencies said in their questionnaire response that such allowances took effect only upon the making of an adoption order. In many instances, however, statutory agencies pay a fostering allowance to the potential adopters before the adoption order is made.[15] In addition, there are those who, after initially fostering the child, subsequently adopt him/her and these parents will also have commonly received a fostering allowance. It is therefore not unusual for adopters to have received a fostering allowance before the adoption. Furthermore, by no means all adopters who have previously received a fostering allowance receive an adoption allowance.[16]

In our family sample, 46 per cent of those responding to the question about finance said that they had received a fostering allowance at some point. As with adoption allowances there is considerable variation with regard to payment of fostering allowances. One adoptive mother who was able to compare two authorities explained that whereas in the one, allowances were made over and above the fostering allowance, for example, Christmas and birthday allowances, plus an extra week's allowance; in the other, there were no extras. In this case the couple had wanted to buy a bigger house to help accommodate their child more comfortably. However, they discovered that foster care allowances are not taken into account as part of income when assessing a mortgage application – and this despite the fact that the adoptive father had payment slips going back seven years. Another couple (who were still fostering at the time of the interview) said that they had 'plenty of financial support' with the authority arranging 'for us to have anything that we need to have for him, school uniforms and bedding and that'.

This variation of practice was also reflected in the response we had from social

---

[14] See above at para 2.2.

[15] Unfortunately, our research data do not reveal how frequent this practice is.

[16] Again, we are unable to say just how many adopters had been in this position.

workers. For example, one said that his agency paid low rates and historically had always done so. He explained that a nearby authority paid more. Consequently,

> We lost out an awful lot to [authority]. They have a . . . specialist teenage foster placement scheme and they pay quite high enhanced rates. We lose a lot of people that way.

Another authority cited a case where the child needed a considerable amount of therapeutic help from a child psychiatrist. The carers had 'special foster fees', a 'very high fostering allowance'. The foster father was on a very low income and the foster mother did not go out to work. The allowance helped them survive and enabled the child to obtain the therapy she needed and to stay in the placement.

A voluntary agency told us that they paid their carers

> . . . a professional fee and they are well paid compared to around here and a part of that is they take the burden off the social worker. They bring the child in for work and take the child home and spend an hour or more . . . transporting the child.

2.3   Other financial support

There are other kinds of financial payments which might be made. For instance, expenses can be paid to prospective adopters during the introductory period to defray travelling expenses incurred in getting to know the child. Payments may also be made in connection with a child's ongoing need for therapy, for particular equipment to help children with special needs, and for furniture and clothing where adopters take on a large sibling group.[17] In contested adoptions adopters may well be given assistance with legal fees.

The adopters' perspective

Travel expenses

Just over half (52 per cent) the respondents to the family questionnaire had received help with travel costs incurred during the introduction to their child and nearly 14 per cent had help with travelling expenses for contact with birth families.

In one case the adoptive father worked abroad a great deal. During the preparation for adoption he travelled home more than usual so as to be involved with the child as much as possible. The local authority initially refused to pay his travel expenses but on appeal, agreed to pay part of them.

---

[17] Travelling expenses can also be paid to *birth* parents who have face to face contact with their children, but who can not afford the cost involved in getting to the venue. We came across one case where the birth mother needed travel expenses to enable her to see the children since it was difficult for the adoptive family to travel to see her because one of the children was severely disabled.

A family living in the country incurred heavy expenses in transporting their son from home to a hospital in a town where he was having therapy in a psychiatric unit. Before the adoption the local authority had arranged and paid for the child to be collected from home by taxi, taken to the hospital, and returned home again. When the adopters applied for an adoption allowance, they also applied for reinstatement of the taxi fares which had stopped on adoption. At the time of the interview, the mother was still waiting to hear the outcome of the application which had already taken some months. In the meantime, she was ferrying the child back and forth, which involved driving long distances and having to find someone to look after the other child whilst she was away.

Initial caring costs expenses

Forty-one per cent of families in the postal survey said they had received financial help with initial caring costs. Some specifically mentioned financial help for buying such items as furniture or clothing. A recurring complaint in this respect, however, was that the availability of such help was not made known to the adopters. For example, one mother wanted help for buying clothes and toys but was given no information whatsoever about the financial help that might be available. Another said:

> The resources are there if you ask for them. They don't offer them. If you need equipment you're not offered the money to buy the equipment. You've got to ask. If you don't ask you don't get.

She reasoned that the local authority knew them as a family and

> ... they know what we've got and what we haven't. They should have said, 'Can we help with any equipment or anything?' I would have been in there with my list.

Perhaps not surprisingly, adopters had varying experiences of what expenses could be claimed. For example, one mother wrote three letters asking for help with school uniform and other expenses incurred in extra-curricular activities, but got nothing. In contrast another got help with a clothing allowance and to 'do out' the child's bedroom. One couple told us that the local authority had been 'really supportive with equipment'. In their case, whilst the girls were still being fostered they needed new beds, but they couldn't get twin beds in the room. Social services provided 'the most beautiful bunk beds, beautiful pine ones' as well as duvets and sheets.

The costs of therapy

Several adopters mentioned their child's need for some kind of therapy. In one case, which eventually disrupted before the adoption order had been made, the prospective adoptive mother explained to the boy's social worker:

> *[The child] lives with us in the hope that he's going to become a member of our family, but you've got to help us sort him out before he does because once we adopt him we can't put him back, obviously. We're not going to take him damaged to get worse, but we'll take him damaged with help. So she went back and she said, 'Yes, they've agreed to the psychotherapy once a week'.*

Another explained that although her child's social worker had acknowledged that she needed therapy, the authority delayed agreeing to pay for it until the child was adopted, when presumably they expected the adopters to pay. The mother went on:

> *I wrote a very strong letter to the Director of Social Services stating that I didn't think that this was on. [The child] needed this therapy now – to save money in the future, she needs her therapy now.*

The prospective father said, in that case, that the benefits of the therapy the child had had so far were obvious and he would like to have paid privately for her to have more, but his income would not allow that so 'we just plod on with what we've got now'.

One family, who had previously adopted two siblings and who were now adopting a sibling group of four, realised from their first experience that it was important to obtain an agreement from the local authority about the support they were able to offer. In this case, the family went to child guidance and they ensured that the local authority had child guidance support written into the contract for as long as it was needed. The benefits applied to the parents as well as the children.

Special needs allowance

In our family postal survey, only 12 per cent said that they had received special needs costs (e.g. disability living allowances or invalid care allowances) and in only 3 per cent of cases were payments made in respect of loss or damage caused by the child. However, some interviewees told us that they were in receipt of a 'special needs allowance' because of their child's challenging behaviour, and others because of illness or disability. One mother only discovered about such payments because the social worker of two other children she was looking after wondered if she was receiving any extra allowances because the baby was 'difficult' (she had a serious medical condition). They were not. The social worker said:

> *This isn't on . . . if you're not happy with the way she's being handled here's the phone number to ring.*

The mother felt that this approach was very much 'via the back door' – her own social worker had not mentioned such a possibility.

Legal representation

Some adoption agencies paid for legal representation for adopters in contested adoptions. One couple said that they probably would not have had a solicitor had it not been for the fact that their agency (a voluntary agency) had agreed to foot the bill.

Home help

Practical help in the house was something that adopters told us they needed. For example, one adopter was finding life particularly demanding. Her son had been in and out of hospital over a period of years, her own mother was ill, and she was caring for another child. The social worker eventually said:

> *I think it's time you had home help . . . find someone that you can trust and that you know can come in and you can have her.*

She told the mother she could have 12 hours help per week which was funded by social services. It made such a difference to her.

Other parents who felt that what they needed was some kind of practical help in the house turned to their families for help. If the children's behaviour was particularly challenging it was difficult for some to ask either friends or family so it meant that they had to go without childminding or baby-sitting.

The lack of equivalent of maternity allowance or leave[18]

Some adopters mentioned the lack of any benefit equivalent to maternity benefit. Indeed, some felt so strongly about this that they had taken up the matter with their trade unions and MPs. As one adopter said:

> *One of the things I feel strongly about is allowances for the bonding period. If you have a child of your own you have maternity allowances. You have nothing at all like that if you adopt a child. You have no financial support so you're having to sort of take time off work. You either give up your job or you take on paid labour.*

This parent explained that she worked at the local health centre and the manager took up the matter with the Department of Health. They responded by saying that no allowance was available for having an adoptive child, but the health centre could make a payment at its discretion, but as the mother said:

> *Well, of course the doctors didn't want to pay me because it had to come out of their own pockets then.*

---

[18] See also Chapter 1, *Introduction,* para 2.5 note 14 in connection with the proposal to have parental leave.

These parents had two-and-a-half weeks' notice that their son was going to move in and the mother was supposed to give one month's notice at work. She had explained what she was doing and her employers were supportive of her. But, as she said, had the placement not worked out she would have had 'no job and no child'.

In another case, the adopters had a seven-year-old girl placed with them. The father felt that it was important for one of the parents to be at home with the child, at least in the early days of placement. He said:

> You couldn't say to the child, come on Saturday and there's somebody coming round on Monday to look after you because I've got to go to work.

In this case the mother took unpaid leave for a few months before returning to work on a part-time basis. She was thankful that, financially, she was able to do that but appreciated it would not be an option in some families. She felt that people should be encouraged to adopt by having proper provision for adoption leave and benefits.

The adoption agency perspective

In striking contrast to adopters little was said during the interviews with agencies about financial support other than adoption or fostering allowances. It is hard to know what inference, if any, to draw from this. However, in our postal questionnaire, 94 per cent of statutory agencies said they had funds available (and presumably used them) to defray initial costs of caring for a child, for example, to enable adopters to buy special equipment. One statutory agency specifically mentioned car loans and help with building modifications. Voluntary agencies generally said even less but help that was mentioned included giving advice on 'obscure' trust funds which might provide funding for specific purposes; loans for purchasing equipment; travel expenses during introductions; finance for attending courses; financial provision for children with special needs.

3   Other practical support

3.1   Respite care

Respite care appears to mean different things to different people. For instance, adopters who are able to go away for a weekend whilst a member of their family looks after their child or children may refer to that as respite care. Alternatively another family may consider respite care to mean care provided or arranged by the local authority when, for instance, their child may attend a special school on a daily or weekly basis, or be cared for by a carer designated as a respite carer. It is the latter with which we are particularly concerned. Although it is clear that local authorities can provide respite care, as one commentator has put it,[19] 'it is clearly a resource consonant with the philosophy of the [Children] Act', the 1989 Act and Regulations do not actually refer to the concept.[20] In view of this it is perhaps hardly surprising that there appears to be a lack of consistency in the provision of such a service. We have also found that, as with other forms of practical support, the existence or availability of respite care may not be mentioned to adopters.

The adopters' perspective

The family postal questionnaire tried to tease out what use is made of respite care. Of those who responded on this point, the vast majority, 82 per cent of those approved by statutory agencies and 73 per cent of those approved by voluntary agencies, had not used the service. Of those that had, there was an even split among those approved by a statutory agency as to whether or not the service had met their needs, but among those approved by a voluntary agency twice as many said that the service had not met their needs as those who said it had. Of those who had not used respite services, just over half approved by statutory agencies (51 per cent) and just over a third (36 per cent) of those approved by voluntary agencies said that they had not done so because they had not felt the need to do so. More worryingly, however, 28 per cent (statutory) and 35 per cent (voluntary) said that they had not used the services because either they did not know anything or enough about them. Most of the remainder were unsure.

It is evident from respondents' additional comments that some respite care was informally being offered by friends, family or other adopters. In other instances, arrangements were more 'formal', having been set up by a social worker. This resulted, in one case, in three periods of respite care during the first year of placement, and, in another, with play therapy and help from a psychiatrist for the child as well as respite care. In this latter case, the adopters had found it impossible to pick up the telephone to ask for help and it was only because their social worker happened to call them to see if they were coping that help was then made available to them. In other cases, a family link worker provided 'much needed time off each week', while in another case, the child went to a special school as a weekly boarder which gave the family 'a breather'. In contrast, one couple reported that in 17 months 'of hell' respite care was neither suggested nor offered. They felt this to be one of the reasons why the placement eventually disrupted.

In her interview one adopter explained why it was important to have respite care:

> *Ours is very ad hoc. We do it ourselves but it's essential we get away, probably three weekends a year at the moment, on our own. It's a lifeline to us and*

---

[19] Freeman (1992, p. 63).

[20] Its existence is implicitly recognised by s 20(4) of the 1989 Act and is regulated by the Foster Placement (Children) Regulations 1991, reg 9.

> *we're able to do it because we have friends who understand the children, are able to look after them, and my mother.*

She went on:

> *I think respite care is essential . . . fosterers get it but not adopters and actually I think adopters need it far more because in foster placements when things get too difficult those children move on. You don't have that when you adopt them.*

She also voiced a concern shared by others when she said:

> *The first time we did it I'll always remember they [children] were horrendous when we got back because it's a form of rejection again. But as time has gone on obviously we've come back and that's the important part.*

Even so, families we spoke to had mixed views about respite care. Whilst the need for it was not in doubt, actually putting it into practice caused anxieties so great to some that they did not go ahead with it. One couple felt that 'nobody could do it better than us anyway'. Another said:

> *No-one can give you respite care. It's a delusion. If you take a child out of the home and put it somewhere else you are getting a respite. But all you're doing is postponing it because the child you get back is not going to be any better. They are going to be worse. The only way of welding together in one family is to be together throughout the day and nobody opting out. I can quite sympathise with people who have got to the absolute limit of their tether and say, 'Look, I just can't take any more'. But taking the child away for a break is immensely damaging to the child and more importantly probably, you'll never build a relationship whilst they're getting off.*

Against this, one adopter was so desperate after what he described as a 'critical incident' that he took his daughter down to the local social services and asked for respite care.

> *In the end they persuaded us to make some arrangements with our parents. So she stayed with her grandparents for about five days.*

In the case of one placement, which disrupted, the social worker had suggested six months earlier that the adopters should have a break. In fact when they did go away they found it hard to let go of the problems. They felt, however, that had they been able to look forward to a weekend off on a regular basis that would have helped them through the hard times.

By comparison, another couple explained how their social worker was able to detect the signs of strain:

> *. . . her professional judgment and years of experience of knowing when these things are at stretch point, at a critical point.*

At such times she would tell them that they needed 'some rest, some respite' and she would come and stay with their daughter for a week whilst they had a break.

The adoption agency perspective

Of those agencies responding to our postal questionnaire about respite care, only 3 per cent (all statutory agencies) said they made no provision. So far as statutory agencies were concerned, the person indicated as being most likely to deal with the situation included social workers, either the adopters' or child's link worker, post-adoption service or, more generally the area office or foster care service. There was the additional option of families making their own private arrangements. Some said that respite care might well be discussed and agreed at the time of the panel meeting or before the order was made. The request for respite care after an adoption order was more problematic. One agency explained that there was no general policy order about this and much would depend on how long after the order the request was made. The provision of such care would be based on individual family and child needs. In some authorities respite care was limited to children with a physical or learning difficulty. One agency mentioned linking the family to special schemes appropriate to the disability. The location of the adoptive family could be a factor: if a family lived outside the local authority area it would be left to the adopters to negotiate with the local authority in whose area they resided.[21] One agency offered counselling to adoptive parents whose child was receiving respite care.

Turning to the voluntary agency perspective, some said that they would liaise with the local authority, whilst others said that the social worker would assist as would support groups and family links. One agency was able to offer a residential resource which

> ... is useful if you've got children to place with disabilities. So we can offer not only respite care for the birth families but respite care to the substitute carers as well, which is sometimes very useful ... there are a lot of services that we can call on.

Another agency said it could attempt to provide respite care from its own foster care resource, but on a limited basis. If it was needed more extensively then they would negotiate with the local authority in which the adopters resided. Support and respite care were discussed during the assessment of prospective adopters in one agency:

> Applicants are asked during assessment to consider their support systems and who they would use for respite care and their local resources. [The agency] can link families who meet at study days, etc. If possible it will be set up as

---

[21] Presumably the view is taken that application has to be made to the local authority of the area in which the family now lives for provision to be made under Part III of the Children Act 1989 concerning a child in need.

an integral part of the placement so that the child sees it as that and not a crisis measure. This is what we hope to achieve as our respite care scheme.

One voluntary agency worker explained that they have respite care provision for their bridge families, i.e. those who are caring for a child whilst he or she is being prepared for an adoption placement. She said,

There's a lot of support. We set up respite for bridge families and a lot of bridge families look after each other. They have planned weekends so there's informal and formal support there. If a family are going through it then other bridge families will come – either practically, emotionally or you can always pick up the phone.

This "system" appears to combine formal and informal respite care – formal in the sense that the agency itself may organise it, and informal in that the families work out what they need and who can provide the respite between them.

Another worker acknowledged the difficulty of coping with an older child adoption and felt it would be particularly hard for an isolated family. She said that adoptive parents of older children need to have breaks but she added:

We would like to be able to provide some respite foster carers ourselves. We don't at the moment, but we would like to be able to do that in future.

One voluntary agency social worker felt that local authorities had no tradition of building up the support networks that are needed for older, badly damaged children. They were not a priority because the local authority knew that they were going to be placed. She also thought that local authorities were reluctant to understand how extremely damaged such children are.

3.2   Support in an emergency

If an emergency[22] arises pre or post the adoption order, adopters may need some kind of practical support. Where should they turn to for help? If a placement is in danger of disruption, for example, the crisis might come at any time of the day or night. If a child should be taken seriously ill before the adoption order, to whom can the prospective adopters turn for help and what support might be available? In such circumstances, is help to be provided by local authorities, family or friends?

---

[22] See also Chapter 11, *Post Placement Issues*, para 2.4.

The adopters' perspective

Our questionnaire asked adopters if they had ever needed someone to talk to urgently or help in an emergency in connection with the adoption. Of those who responded, about half (49 per cent of those approved by statutory agencies and 54 per cent of those approved by voluntary agencies) said they had needed such help and the others did not. Of those who had needed help, most (84 per cent statutory, 77 per cent voluntary) had been able to find the help they needed but that left around a fifth (16 per cent statutory, 23 per cent voluntary) who had not.

Over 90 per cent of those responding to the question whether they had a particular social worker to act as a guide throughout the adoption process said that they had. Those adopters who had been approved by a statutory agency either named their adoption agency social worker (42 per cent) or their child's social worker (46 per cent). But the majority of those who had been approved by a voluntary agency named their own social worker with only 7 per cent naming the child's social worker. This suggests that, in adoptions arranged by voluntary agencies, the parents' own social worker played a more significant role than those arranged by statutory agencies where there was a more even split between the parents' and child's social worker.

Sources of the help received can be both formal and informal. Although in emergencies many adopters clearly turned to their families and friends, especially those who had experience of child care and adoption, several said that they had their social worker's home telephone number and some had the home number of the child's social worker. In one instance, the adopters said that if their social worker was not available in the office they were always either told where to contact her or were offered alternative counselling by her office colleagues. They also had her home telephone number. In another instance, the adopters' social worker mediated with the child's social worker in times of crisis. One mother said that she had the home number of her "support worker" and had called her at home a couple of times when she was desperate.

Although most adopters received help when needed, we were told of instances when help had not been forthcoming. One parent asked the emergency team for help – they were located 15 miles away. The duty officer explained that no-one could come as there was no-one to staff the office. The parent was advised to contact her own team after Christmas. Another family contacted the emergency duty team in two emergencies but on neither occasion were staff available to help. They coped on their own with the help of friends. But another mother, who said she was desperate to talk to someone and could not reach her link worker or her child's social worker, said that she was worried that if she turned to family or friends she would be in breach of confidentiality concerning the child's troubled background which she would have had to have mentioned in her quest for help.

As another couple explained, crises often occur "out of hours" and had they not had the experience of caring for children they may have had difficulties. One mother told us that whilst she was still fostering the child she subsequently adopted, the social workers decided that he should spend Christmas with his birth parents. She was concerned by this because both parents were alcoholics and the birth father had been violent. As she said, 'There's nobody around over the Christmas period'. She felt it was the worst possible time to send the boy home. In the event she had a call on Christmas Day to say that he had been left on his own and she therefore went to "retrieve" him.

The adoption agency perspective

Agencies were asked whether they made any provision for children, birth parents, foster carers and adopters to obtain support in an emergency. Their response is contained in Table 15 below.

Table 15

Agencies which have helplines for dealing with emergencies

	Statutory agencies		Voluntary agencies		Total agencies	
For adopters	69	86%	25	93%	94	86%
For foster carers	67	83%	8	30%	75	69%
For birth parents	17	20%	4	15%	21	19%
For older adoptive children	13	16%	9	33%	22	20%

Source: Agency Postal Survey[23]

What clearly emerges from this response is that statutory agencies prioritise the needs of adopters and foster carers at the (apparent) expenses of birth parents and older children. Voluntary agencies, on the other hand, whilst they also give priority to the adopters in the provision of emergency help, also seem to devote not insignificant resources to older children.

With regard to how provision for support in an emergency was made, so far as older children were concerned, the most common provision made by statutory agencies was via the emergency duty team telephone number: 64 per cent mentioned this. Other kinds of provision came from general access to the office (14 per cent) and giving information on specialist support services (11 per cent). The most common provision made by voluntary agencies was to give the child their social worker's home telephone number: 20 per cent of the voluntaries mentioned this.

---

[23] The table shows 'yes' responses only. The number of agencies providing data for this question: for adopters was 107 agencies (80 statutories, 27 voluntaries); for foster carers, 108 agencies (81 statutories and 27 voluntaries); for birth parents, 109 agencies (83 statutories, 26 voluntaries); and for older children, 109 agencies (82 statutories, 27 voluntaries).

Where foster carers were concerned, 83 per cent of statutory agencies mentioned the emergency duty team number but the social worker's home number was also mentioned by 15 per cent and general access to the office by 14 per cent. Provision for foster carers by voluntary agencies was via the social worker's home telephone number and the emergency duty team number, with a 67 per cent response for both. The emergency duty team number was the most likely source of emergency support for adopters, suggested by 90 per cent of the statutories; 26 per cent also mentioned provision of the social worker's home number and 14 per cent general access to the office. Nearly 6 per cent mentioned access to senior social work staff. The provision of the social worker's home number was the most likely source of provision for adopters made by voluntary agencies. Slightly fewer (60 per cent) mentioned the duty team number. General access to the office was mentioned by 16 per cent. So far as birth parents were concerned, 64 per cent of statutory agencies mentioned the emergency duty team telephone number and 14 per cent general access to the office.

4   Concluding points

Communication and information

From what families have told us it seems that the provision of information about practical support that might be available can be hard to come by. Some have told us that they came across information by chance. Support groups may play an important part in that, when talking with other adopters, it is likely that such matters as adoption allowances and other practical support may be discussed. This may not be of much help in a support group which comprises prospective adopters all of whom are new to the process and as much in the dark as each other. In Chapter 9 we discussed support as it is featured during the assessment and preparation phases of prospective adopters. There is a strong case for including information about and availability of practical support at the preparation stage. We suggest that prospective adopters should be given an information pack on all the likely sources of support, including information about adoption allowances and other kinds of financial support that might be available. There should also be a realistic appraisal of the parents' financial circumstances, especially at the matching stage when, for instance, any special needs of the child who has been identified become apparent or if a large sibling group is being contemplated. As is abundantly clear from this research, those who are willing to take on older children for adoption can face severe challenges and anxieties. Relieving them of the worry of any financial concerns would certainly help ease the situation. Obviously local authorities do not have an endless pot of gold to distribute and some families will have more urgent need of financial assistance than others. Even so, they should inform families of the range of help that might be available.

Communication between the adopters and the agency after the adoption order might be infrequent or non existent. This could well be because the adoptive family has chosen to cut its links with the agency or because the agency has no post-adoption service to speak of. However, several agencies now have annual events such as summer and Christmas parties. Others have regular study days. Many publish a newsletter, perhaps once a month, perhaps once a year. In these ways adopters can learn about the possible practical support that might be available either through other adopters attending the social gatherings or courses, or from information published in the newsletters. This can make it easier for those parents who may find it difficult to ask for help after an adoption order has been made.

Inconsistency between adoption agencies

It is clear from our data that there are considerable variations concerning the provision of financial and practical support between adoption agencies. This applies to the level of communication and information-giving that we have mentioned above. Clearly, some agencies are much better than others at informing adopters about practical support. The annual review for those in receipt of an adoption allowance is one example. Some local authorities have what appears to be an unfriendly and challenging approach which does not help the parents co-operate, whilst others have a pleasing approach which encourages parents to respond as fully as they are able. This may, of course, reflect the financial constraints under which particular local authorities are working. This may also explain why adoption and fostering allowances in one authority are higher or lower than another. The discrepancy extends to other types of financial assistance. For instance, adopters in one area may be entitled to financial help with extending accommodation for their increased family, whilst in another they might not be so fortunate. Assistance may be given for the purchase of equipment for a child with special needs in one area, but not in another.

The length of time that financial assistance might be available is another concern. Whilst it would be wrong for adopters to assume that once they had been allocated an adoption allowance it would continue *ad infinitum*, it is clear from our findings that some families have had their allowances severely reduced or terminated without much warning. It seems to us there ought to be an agreed notice period before this happens.

It seems unfair that a family living in one local authority area should fare much better or worse were they to live in another. Those adopters who have moved home resulting in a change of local authority have testified to this. We think consideration should be given to introducing a standardised system of eligibility and levels of financial support.

Differences in practical support between fostering and adoption

Many of the adopters we spoke to drew our attention to the differences in support depending upon whether the child was being fostered or adopted. This was particularly so concerning financial assistance.

One social worker was quite blunt about this when asked by adopters whether financial support would continue after the adoption order had been made. She said:

> No, sorry, all that stops because you become adoptive parents. 'So we're on our own after that?' Yes.

Another mother in this same local authority decided that she would not be able to adopt two siblings because of the financial cutbacks that would result. She explained:

> If we were to adopt these girls we would not be able to afford to pay for therapy. So these two girls are not really getting the security that they are asking for, although they know that they are not going to be moved on. It's very important to them to belong . . . but we cannot do that because if I say yes, I'll do that, out will go all the extra help.

Several of the adopters had fostered their child before adoption. They had experienced what it was like to be in receipt of an allowance and other financial payments at special times like Christmas and birthdays as well as perhaps receiving extra money for holidays, only for this to be cut right back to perhaps a 'basic allowance' or no allowance at all once the child was adopted. Some of the social workers we interviewed confirmed the fact that financial assistance could be reduced or terminated once an adoption order had been granted. We are not confident that allowances should be reduced simply because an adoption order had been made, a point to which we return in our final conclusions.[24]

---

[24] See Chapter 20, *Policy and Practice Implications.*

15 Contact

1   Introduction

Contact between older adopted children and members of the birth family was one of the most contentious practice issues which this study explored. Our purpose was to discover and to describe how both practitioners and adopters approached the matter in relation to older children.

At the outset, there is a problem of definition. Contact is an imprecise umbrella term with many different meanings, and is sometimes confused with other terms such as "openness" and "inclusiveness" (see Quinton *et al*, 1997, p 395). As a working definition, we have chosen to subdivide it into *direct contact*, meaning face-to-face meetings, and *indirect contact*, including letters, telephone calls and other forms of sporadic ongoing communication.[1] Indirect contact is sometimes facilitated by an intermediary, such as an agency "letter box" scheme. Our primary focus is on contact which is ongoing both during placement and after the making of the adoption order and not merely as a one-off "good-bye" meeting.

Drawing on data from our national postal surveys and selective follow-up interviews, we explore adopters' and adoption agency perspectives on contact (direct and indirect) between older adopted children and their birth parents, siblings, grandparents and other relatives in their family of origin – as well as with other people from their past. We uncover disagreements about the principles underlying contact, the "appropriateness" of the type and degree of contact, and the timing and management of it. We also describe the support for contact that the families themselves sought and received.

For these purposes, this chapter will focus on three groups of issues: with whom adopted children have contact, the *types* of contact in place, and the making and breaking of *contact agreements*.

---

[1] We are aware that others might use the terms "direct" and "indirect" to distinguish between non mediated and mediated contact.

2   Ongoing contact

The family postal questionnaire presented adopters with eight categories of possible birth relatives and asked whether there was any ongoing contact with them. This produced the following data (Table 16).

Table 16
Adoptive families who had any kind of contact with birth relatives

	Statutory families		Voluntary families		Total families		Valid cases
Mother	73	48%	34	52%	107	49%	217
Father	32	22%	15	24%	47	22%	210
Siblings living with birth family	24	18%	10	19%	34	18%	184
Siblings in foster/residential care	38	29%	11	21%	49	27%	181
Siblings in other adoptive families	34	26%	19	33%	53	28%	190
Maternal grandparents	28	19%	9	14%	37	18%	207
Paternal grandparents	18	13%	4	7%	22	11%	201
Other (e.g. uncles, cousins)	31	22%	3	5%	34	17%	202

Source: Family postal survey

As Table 16 shows, contact was more than twice as common with birth mothers (49 per cent) than birth fathers (22 per cent). Sibling contact was mostly with brothers and sisters placed with other adoptive families (28 per cent) and in foster/ residential care (27 per cent). However, there was also a significant number of cases where adopted children had contact with brothers and sisters still living with birth relatives (18 per cent). It was more common for children to have contact with maternal grandparents (18 per cent) than paternal grandparents (11 per cent).

In addition to the data provided in Table 16, we were also able to obtain the following information about our sample of 226 adoptive families:

- 117 families (52 per cent) indicated that their child had some form of ongoing contact with a birth parent, and in 37 cases (16 per cent), the child had contact with both.
- Contact with siblings was slightly less common, as this affected 110 families in the sample (49 per cent): 21 (9 per cent) families had contact both with siblings who were being adopted or fostered *and* siblings who were living in the birth family. One family had ongoing contact with siblings in *all three* of these circumstances.
- 53 families (23 per cent) indicated that their child had contact with a grand-parent, and there were six families (3 per cent) in the sample which had contact with both sets of grandparents.

- In total, 174 families (77 per cent) returning questionnaires indicated that they had some form of ongoing contact with a birth relative; 116 families of those having ongoing contact had already had the adoption order granted.

2.1   Contact with birth parents

Forming new attachments

In the courts, it has been suggested by Simon Brown LJ[2] that contact may well be of singular importance to the long-term welfare of the child. It can help children realise that their parents still love them and care about their welfare; it can help children to attach to their new family knowing that they have the "seal of approval" from birth parents; and it can give the child a sense of family continuity and personal identity.

This view of contact steadily gained popularity in professional opinion. Until the mid 1980s, contact was seen as disruptive, whereas now, it is usually seen as helping adopted children to settle in their new family and can be an important contributing factor to the success of adoptive placements. As one agency worker stated:

> *We've been through the same sort of evolutionary process as every other agency in terms of having a lot of children drifting in care and then getting very keen on adoption, but thinking that continuing contact was not compatible with that, and placing several children for adoption without contact where later on those placements have disrupted. A large element of that was that the child had never let go of the birth parent who they hadn't actually seen for years.*

Central to this argument is the importance of the birth parent's permission for the child to move on, and how this can be expressed through contact. Similarly, contact is a mechanism through which birth parents can be more engaged in the process – helping them to feel more positive about the adoption because they regain an element of control. Through contact, birth families can show that they still care about the child's welfare and to some extent counteract their more negative image following court proceedings. Contact may help them move on and help the child do the same. As an agency worker told us:

> *Adoption teams do tend to work with birth parents and the birth parents like it because that puts them into being a caring parent. They've been through the whole of the process of being a rejecting parent and maybe we've taken their child off them and it's never coming back, and so on. Here, in the adoption function, they can really become at least a caring parent with a role in their child's life – even if it's only about sending cards and letters – that kind of thing.*

---

[2] *Re E (A Minor) (Care Order: Contact)* [1994] 1 FLR 146, 154H-155B.

However, by the same token, birth parents can communicate their disapproval of the adoption through contact, which can undermine the placement. These messages can be communicated to the child in different ways – often unintentionally. While the more overt messages – like destructive comments about the adoption made in letters – might be easier to detect and respond to more subtle signs of approval or disapproval may go unnoticed by social workers and adopters. For example, if children see cards and presents as a token of their parents' love, their sudden cessation can be read as a sign of their parent rejecting them, or being angry with them about the adoption. This happened in one case where the birth mother stopped sending gifts to the child after the freeing order.

Some families in the sample indicated that contact actually enhanced the adopters' relationship with the child and their feelings of security as parents. Such attitudes have been observed in other research (e.g. Dominick, 1988; Fratter, 1996, p 24; Ryburn, 1998, pp 60–61). However, other stories indicated that there is a fine line between birth parents showing that they care for the child and usurping the parental status of adopters through contact arrangements. Indeed, some adopters felt that contact hindered the children's attachment to their adoptive families. One adoptive mother felt that her children needed to break away from their pasts, and that this necessitated the severance of contact while they settled in their new home. She argued that only then could they stop identifying with their family of origin and begin to identify with their adoptive family:

> If they were seeing them every week it is not that easy to distinguish who you are from who your family are. You have all sorts of feelings that are not allowed to die off [. . .] I should imagine when [the child] is old enough, he'll trace his natural family and all I can hope is that when he tracks them down and gets to know them, the gap will be long enough and sufficient enough for him to look at them and think, I have nothing in common with you any more, and move on. But then he'll have a lot more chance of being able to do that if he isn't stuck in the same labelled failure as they are.

This adopter perceived contact as harming new attachments being formed, not only for her children, but *all children* being adopted. She referred to unspecified research which, she claimed, showed that 'abused children placed in adoptive families succeed best when all contact with the past is severed until they are old enough', whereas 'prolonged contact with the birth family tends to perpetuate a neurosis and ultimately prevents identification with the adoptive family'.

Allowing children to care about birth parents

Some adopted children need to be assured of their birth parents' well-being: they may worry about them, especially those children who have actually "parented" their parents for some time before going into care. As one social worker said, 'You hear the story of the three-year-old who used to take his mum around to the Post Office to cash her giro cheque'. Children's sense of responsibility for their birth parents may well continue after placement and contact may relieve this concern. As one adoptive father stated:

> *Our biggest concern is that the children can keep the continuation because if they don't it will upset them. They want to know that their mother is all right. They feel a responsibility for their mother. I think that [the child] had a slight guilt feeling about the adoption the first week.*

However, an agency worker noted that many adopters want to protect the children from this "burden", and therefore want to limit contact:

> *They want the children almost to be protected against some of that and not take on the burden or the worry if the mum's ill. They don't want the children worried about that. Because most of our children have looked after their parents, they've been the "parent" of the parent . . . I think adopters think, like us, that they have a right to a childhood free from that worry and they don't want to leave their child because they recognise that she is the biological mother and she's got all these rights but they don't want their child going back to square one or to think 'should I go and look after her?' Perhaps there's a certain level of maturity required before you can say, 'No, I've a right to a life of my own', which I think probably is right.*

It seems that contact has the potential to either relieve this worry or make it worse. It is crucial to work out the amount and type of contact required to satisfy this need without overwhelming the child with contact so that their sense of responsibility for their parents is perpetuated.

Getting the right balance can be difficult. For example, one adopter told us how her daughter was continually blamed for everything that went wrong in her birth mother's life, and that this continued to be expressed in contact visits. In another case, a contact visit was set up by a child's foster carer (who later adopted him). The boy's father was in prison, and the carer felt the visit would be a useful way of clearing up the child's misconceptions about prisons, and answering some of his questions, such as 'where is the prison?' and 'does he have a bed?'. The adopter mentioned this to the social worker and it was agreed that he should visit his father. The child went, but after that 'he did not want to see his father again'. However, the child's social worker insisted that contact visits were to continue, against the boy's will. According to the adoptive mother he then became disturbed:

> *He'd be so distressed when he came home. He would stand in front of a wall and he would lick the wallpaper. He would pass his motions in the bath. He would be crying all night. He would be even more aggressive with me. He*

would kick the other children. He would kick the animals. He was dreadful.
They noticed his behaviour at school as well. It wasn't just me.

Despite all this, the adoptive mother had to fight social services to get the contact visits stopped. Thus, whereas a one-off visit was constructive, ongoing face-to-face contact was extremely distressing to the child.

Adopters needing to be positive about contact

A central factor in making contact arrangements work is that adopters must be positive about it, yet this can be difficult. First, some forms of contact carry with them the likelihood of having to admit the child's birth relatives into the adopters' extended family. As one agency worker stated, the preparation process should encourage families to realise that 'they're not just adopting the child, they're adopting the birth family and everything that went on before' and they need to 'own' it. This can be difficult for adopters who have a negative perception of the child's birth relatives. For example:

> *The people who have the obsession with the idea that you've got to keep in contact with the natural family tend to forget that when these kids grow up this is going to be Granny and Granddad. Are you really going to want your grandchildren left with these people? Do you really want them as aunts and uncles?*

Second, contact with the birth family threatens adopters' own sense of personal and family identity. As one agency worker stated, 'It's a reminder, and even twice a year can be a lot because it reminds them that there is another family there – that the children are not theirs'. Even when families are committed to contact in principle, they can find it extremely difficult to handle in practice for these reasons. For example:

> *There was a part of me where I just wanted . . . nothing to do with anybody. I did feel like that and that's quite selfish. I was aware that it was selfish and you have to come to terms with it. You can't do that. I had no right to do that to him. He's got other people in his life. It's like me cutting off [my wife] from anybody else – that would be wrong so you have to come to terms with it.*

Contact can be even more threatening when birth relatives themselves still see the child as a full member of their family, and this is communicated to the child and adopters through contact. As noted by another agency worker:

> *They want to treat the children as though they were still members of their birth families – which, of course, to a degree they are – but they do not understand the degree. So there's a tremendous conflict of interests where the birth family is saying to the children, 'Oh, you must come to Aunt so and so's*

> *wedding. Would you like to be a bridesmaid'? And the adopters are sitting*
> *there thinking, 'This cannot happen!' And that causes enormous difficulties.*

In addition to needing to be positive about contact, adopters also need to communicate to the child their support for the contact arrangements. From our research, it seems that some agencies have very rigid ideas about what constitutes "approving" behaviour, and therefore devise rules about what families should and should not do in relation to contact, which can place enormous pressure on adopters. For example, one adopter found it better for the children if she did not accompany them to meetings with the birth mother, even though this was not permitted by the agency. In her view it communicated to the children that she was disapproving of the contact:

> *But the last visit went really well without me there. Again, that social worker*
> *from hell doesn't know that I wasn't there – because I have to be there.*
> *Because if I'm not there it shows disapproval but it doesn't because I've*
> *talked to the kids about why I didn't go. I said, 'I think it would be more*
> *relaxed for you.' [. . .] Father went instead and it worked because he was the*
> *only father there – reducing conflicting loyalties perhaps and who to ask*
> *permission from to do/have something – but this was not approved of by*
> *social services.*

In this case, it was not the idea of contact that the adopter was finding difficult but the dynamics of the meeting, such as competing with an equivalent relative in the birth family, and the pressure this placed on the children. In another example, an adoptive father told us that the children wanted to see their birth mother, so his wife found contact more difficult than he did. He said that the children never had a father so there was no competition there – there was no counterpart in the birth family.

Not having two fathers or two mothers present at the meeting can be beneficial to the parents and children: it can reduce a sense of competition between equivalent parents and any insecurities this may generate, and prevent children from feeling confused about who has authority, or from experiencing split loyalties. It can help contact to be more focused on meeting the needs of the children. Some agencies evidently need to be more aware of situations in which such conflicts may arise. They could encourage families to show their approval of contact in a variety of ways – such as talking it through with the children and showing enthusiasm before and after visits – rather than dogmatically applying a rule that may not be suitable in all cases.

Positive attitudes to contact can sometimes be associated with the adopters' confidence about parenting the child. This helps to explain why some families found contact less stressful after the adoption order, and why others, especially those involved in contested cases, experienced difficulties (their status being more insecure). When contact is mishandled in these circumstances, insecurity can be intensified. For example, one adoptive mother had expressly told the agency that the children were not to receive gifts from birth relatives (who were opposed to the adoption), but her request was broken by the agency:

> We'd also received a book, a Christmas present. Well, we had said right along from the first, no presents because I don't want to be in competition with these people over Christmas presents, and birthday presents and stuff. I mean, there was so many hundreds of them they were going to swamp my family, because we are not a very big family.

This and other similar events led the adopters to try to stop contact altogether.[3]

2.2   Contact with birth siblings

Contact with separated siblings was an important issue for many adopters. While adopted children in 49 per cent of the sample families had some kind of sibling contact, many of the needs and issues mentioned were related to *where* the siblings were, i.e. whether they were living with the birth family, in foster/residential care, or being adopted by another family.

Siblings living with the birth family

Evidence from adopters suggests that one of the most important reasons why adopted children may need contact with siblings living with birth relatives is to know that they are not in danger. For example, one adopter told us that the child had no contact, but 'it is possible that we may in the future because a brother of our child has been returned from foster care to his birth mother and this has caused some anxiety for our child'. This highlights the need for agencies to review contact arrangements if the circumstances of siblings change and they are returned to their birth family. Although news about siblings can be passed on to children by their social worker, or by their birth parents if there is contact with them, contact with the siblings themselves may be a more appropriate means of relieving this anxiety, since trust in adults may be severely diminished for some of these children.

When siblings are returned to birth parents with whom contact had been terminated, contact with those siblings may be subsequently stopped. One family mentioned this:

> The children's brother was in the same foster placement when they moved in but shortly afterwards was given a placement which we felt at this time should never have happened. However, it did and later fell through. The children's brother then went to a relative's home and is now back with the birth mother. This is the area where we last sought help. Meetings with the brother prior to

---

[3] Gifts can be powerful symbols to children about family identity and tokens of love, and as such they can be points of contention and worry for adopters.

> *this have not been a problem. There may be none in the future but help is now being sought.*

Equally, adopted children do not always want contact with siblings living with their birth family. For example, they may not want contact if they were rejected by their parents, whereas their siblings still living in the birth family were not. This was the case for one child, who felt rejected by her white mother because she was black, whereas her baby half-sister was white and continued to live at home. She did not want any ongoing contact with her younger sister.

In sum, children's perceptions of their own situations and those of their siblings (e.g. whether they are in any danger) and the reasons *why* they are in different situations, need to be considered when assessing the need for contact with brothers and sisters living with birth relatives.

Siblings living in foster/residential care

Contact with siblings in care can reassure adopted children about their brother's and sister's well-being, and that they have not been returned to a dangerous home. For example, one adopter wrote:

> *At the time of [the child's] placement she was unaware her brother was in care. When she felt secure with us it became very worrying for her to think her brother was still with Mum so we told her he was in care and she could write to him. She has had a photo of him and we've told her she will meet him again when he's happy and settled.*

As this observation indicates, the need for reassurance might not become apparent until the adopted child begins to feel secure in their new family.

Even where sibling contact had been built into the adoption plan, many adopters encountered difficulties in relation to contact with siblings in care. Some adopters indicated that it was difficult to "pin down" the foster mother and the children's social worker to a date for the next contact visit. As a consequence, for one family, contact was not happening as often as agreed (three times a year).

There were also more worrying stories of foster carers being extremely resistant to sibling contact. This happened in two cases: in the first, the plan was for the family to adopt two brothers. After 12 months, the placement disrupted for one sibling, who returned to his previous foster carers. Since then, no contact had been made between the two brothers. As the adopter told us:

> *Our child misses his brother desperately and needs to see him. However, having said a while ago that he wanted to see him he has now said he doesn't. We believe his foster parents have an influence over this. [The child] did not get on well in this foster placement. We are trying to get the boy's social worker to sort it out for our child's sake.*

In a similar case, two sisters were separated, with one continuing to live with their foster carers. Problems with sibling contact were attributed by this family to difficulties in the child's move from the foster to adoptive family, and the resulting tensions between the two families. Preparation for the move, and a smooth process, may be an important prerequisite for ongoing contact with siblings still in the care of, or returned to, the adopted child's previous foster family.

Another difficulty faced by adopters concerned siblings in foster care having contact with the birth family when the adopted child had none:

> When C was placed with us we were given to understand legal decisions had been made severing any contact except with a half-brother in local authority care, which we were encouraged to maintain. On the event of taking [her] to her first visit with her brother, we were informed contact had been re-established between her brother and their birth family. At adoption – three years after placement – we were left to make very difficult decisions about C having contact with her birth family. We received no help.

This, again, highlights the need for agencies to review both sibling contact and parental contact when siblings' circumstances change.

Siblings placed for adoption elsewhere

Many adopters believed that contact with siblings being adopted by other families was important for their child. It can also be a valuable source of support for other adopters, providing them with an opportunity to discuss the children and how the adoption is progressing. As one adopter told us, 'We would talk about the problems that they were having with the boys'.

However, identifying the child's need for contact with adopted siblings was not always straightforward. Caught up in this is the difficulty of distinguishing apparent needs for contact from other dynamics related to the adoption. For example, desires for contact can be mixed with feelings of guilt which might emerge when the child is beginning to feel happy and secure, but fears that his/her separated siblings are not. Matters may be made worse if children hold themselves responsible for the fate of siblings. For example, one couple we interviewed were adopting two half-sisters, but their brother was placed separately, in another adoptive family. The mother told us that her daughters expressed new desires for contact when his placement disrupted. She explained this as a reaction to their guilt because they had not wanted to be adopted with him.

On the other hand, adopted children can find contact difficult if they are in the early stages of placement and do not yet feel secure. This may be exacerbated when their siblings are not in the same insecure situation. As one adopter described:

> Initially, she was very jealous because he had a family and she didn't have a permanent family, and I think there was a certain amount of that. Now she feels

> *more secure perhaps, she's more able to write to him, because I did say every*
> *so often, 'Would you like to write to [her brother] because [the social worker]*
> *can send it to him?' She started a letter and she never finished it. But now she's*
> *actually written a letter and drawn him a picture. So she's moved on.*

As this account shows, although children may not want contact early on in their adoptive placement, they may do later when they feel more secure. Agencies should therefore aim to keep the option for sibling contact open. This could be achieved by asking siblings to write letters and keeping them on file until adopted children are deemed ready to receive them.[4]

When siblings are placed separately for adoption, it can be difficult for families and their social workers to agree on what is in the best interests of the children regarding contact. Even when it is agreed and is part of the adoption plan, one adoptive family might change their attitude to contact. For example, one adopter stated:

> *We have requested contact with the birth brother and have made many repre-*
> *sentations, both verbal and written, agreeing to meet in a neutral place –*
> *park, etc. But the other family refuses on the grounds it will upset their*
> *adoptive child. It is a very sore point with us as our child has indicated he*
> *wants to see his brother and we were originally quizzed before he was placed*
> *with us that we would allow this. Previously his adopted brother's family had*
> *agreed prior to adoption, so they have changed their minds. The social worker*
> *has tried, as has his foster parent, but all to no avail. We won't give up,*
> *however, and intend to continue sending letters, videos, photos, cards and*
> *presents until either they allow contact or his brother reaches 18 and seeks*
> *him out as we and social services are certain he will.*

In such cases, it is important for agencies to try to establish *why* the adopters of the siblings had changed their minds.

Adopters suggested several reasons for the reluctance of other adopters to maintain sibling contact. First, it was argued that this was due to the attitude that sibling contact could threaten the stability of a placement. For example,

> *The adoptive parents of his brothers didn't want [the child] anywhere near*
> *them because it had taken them so long to get the two lads settled. They felt*
> *now they've got a good stable relationship and a good family building. He*
> *could just wreck the whole thing. So they didn't want to know.*

Adopters may consider sibling contact even more of a risk if that sibling had been involved in a placement disruption. Second, it was thought that some adopters

---

[4] Some agencies do this to keep the channels for contact open with other birth relatives, such as parents and grandparents.

refused sibling contact because they feared that contact could rekindle painful memories about the child's past which the child (and perhaps the adopters) may rather forget. As one adopter told us:

> We now receive help from the adoption agency in maintaining contact with siblings adopted by another family. This has become necessary because their adopted mother has been very reluctant to facilitate contact as she believes this is not necessary to the well-being of 'her' children. She also has concerns that they will learn details of their past which she would prefer them to forget.

It is commendable that, in this case, the agency recognised the attitude of the other family and had intervened.

However, it was not only adopters who placed obstacles in the path of contact between siblings who had been placed separately for adoption. One family had considerable difficulty in getting the social worker to arrange sibling contact. It was only after six months of persuasion and being 'forceful' with the social worker that this was finally arranged. In the adopter's words:

> Six months was five and a half months too long. What they say is, 'You've got to let the children settle'. Well, I'm afraid I think that's rubbish. The children cannot settle if they're worrying about their brother or sister. They settle better if they have much more contact.

Another family recalled that even where social services had made commitments to children about ongoing sibling contact, these were later broken. To quote the adopter:

> Social services made a lot of commitments to those children like they would always be able to see each other, social workers would support them, would make available transport. They would make sure that even if they were adopted at the end of all this process that they would still be allowed to see each other. That it would be part of the adoption agreement. All of this they tried to go back on afterwards but that's sort of four years down the line.

In addition, one family told us that problems were caused by the family's solicitor who assumed that the two adoptive families of separated siblings had not wanted sibling contact, when this was 'totally untrue'. Another family reported how the child's guardian *ad litem* had opposed contact and the adoption in general. The guardian had persuaded the birth family to contest the adoption because the adopters might not keep to the contact agreement:

> I think that was the guardian's own ideas pushing her because she didn't like adoption. I can remember the first thing she said to me; she said, 'There's no such thing as an open adoption,' you know, which is where the child has

*contact. She said, 'Once the child is adopted it's a closed adoption,' she said
'and nothing that's said in court makes any difference'.*

2.3   Contact with other birth relatives

Other relatives (such as aunts, uncles, and cousins, but particularly grandparents)[5]
can be key players in the adoption, sometimes making more demands for contact
than the children's birth parents.[6] However, the value placed on contact with such
relatives varied. Some adopters believed that contact with relatives who had not
been "key people" in the children's lives was unnecessary. Others stressed the
importance of it. For example, one family told us of how contact was initiated with
the child's paternal aunt and uncle so that, when she was ready, she could find out
more about her father (who had died):

> *So, in the list of things that [the social worker] and I agreed after the
> adoption, one was to get more information on the natural father. It took her
> the best part of a year to track down people, but she did actually come back
> to me with a whole lot of details. And contacting his family for us to contact
> when [the child] felt ready to have information. I think his sister and his
> brother were willing to actually talk to [the child] and meet [her] and were
> thrilled to bits that somebody had finally remembered that they existed. So
> she did actually do that but it took a lot of doing.*

In another case, a child met her half-sister – with whom she'd lost contact 12 years
previously – by accident. The adoptive mother claims that this was good because
she turned out to be 'the most sensible in the family and it's actually helped to settle
her down'.

Indeed, contact with relatives who had *no relationship at all* with the adopted
child can also benefit the child. In one case, the child's birth father did not even
know he had a daughter until he was approached to sign the consent form. Although
the child had never met or had any contact with her father, contact initiated through
the adoption process showed signs of being positive for the child:

> *We didn't know that her father was a really nice guy. He was such a nice guy
> that he sent photographs back with the guardian ad litem and he said, 'Tell
> [the child's] new parents if they would like me to see her, or if they would like
> me to come to see them. If [the child] wants to see me, she doesn't have to
> wait till she's 18. I'm never going to bother her – I'm just happy that they've
> found someone nice for her to be adopted by. I'm happy for her. I've never,
> ever supported her and through no fault of my own. No-one ever told me that*

---

[5] For the incidence of such contact see Table 20 at para 3.3 post.

[6] One adopter told us that the child's grandparents' application to court for unsupervised contact had been
extremely problematic for themselves and social services.

I had a daughter or a son. Nobody ever got in touch with me until a couple of years ago when they sent me a form to sign.' [. . .] We've written to him and sent a photograph to him and I couldn't see anything wrong in that. And that turned round to [the child's] advantage because she thought she had a wicked, wicked father that never wanted to see her, never wanted anything to do with her, wasn't interested in her future at all – just signed her away – and that wasn't true at all. And all that negative information that she'd had, we had to turn it all round.

2.4   Contact with other people from the child's past

The child's previous foster carers

Contact with previous foster carers can be extremely important for children once placed for adoption. As an agency worker said:

It might have been the most stable home that they had for their whole lives mightn't it? In my view, it's sometimes more important to look at that contact and that link than it is to look at birth parents' contacts and links.

For example, if something important happens in the child's life, their previous foster carers might be the people they need to discuss it with. One adopter told us that the child wanted to tell the foster family about his new school:

He could phone them any time he wanted. The number was written for him by the phone. One night apparently he phoned them up at twelve o'clock when he first moved in. [The foster carer] just listened to him saying, 'I'm going to school next week, it's just down the road I can see it from my bedroom'.

Another adoptive family visited the foster family every three months, and the children in both families wrote to each other regularly. The adopter said, 'We wouldn't want to change that because it is a big chunk of their lives and we enjoy it as well'. Another parent described the child's previous foster carer almost as if she were an extension of the adoptive family: she had continued to be the child's 'Nan', and had even become a kind of 'Nan' to the other boy in the adoptive family.

However, many adopters experienced problems around contact with the child's previous foster carers. One family explained that contact with foster carers had 'actually been more of a difficult issue to deal with than issues about contact with birth parents'.

One problem was where families felt that there was too much contact and it was difficult to limit (in one case, the children were having lengthy telephone calls with various members of the foster family every week) or they were put in a position where they felt they were "competing" with the foster carers. Other problems were related to the child needing contact but foster carers being unresponsive. One adoptive family sent cards and gifts to the foster carers at Christmas, but this wasn't reciprocated. Consequently, the child felt they had forgotten about her as soon as she was placed for adoption.

One agency worker explained that problems around contact with foster carers could be due to either 'the adopters wanting to draw a tighter boundary and feeling everything is secure' or 'the foster carers not really dealing with their separation or loss'. The run up to the move, and the way this was handled, seems to be crucial in this. In one case, on the day of the move,[7] the prospective adopters rather than social workers collected the children from the foster home. Because they were the people who physically moved the children, they were made to feel like "kidnappers". This negative image of the adopters as "baddies" was perpetuated when they tried to curtail contact with the foster carers, even though this was reduced very gradually and over a long period of time.

One family had contrasting experiences of contact with foster carers when adopting their sibling group of three: the two girls were previously placed in one foster home, and the boy in another. The girls' foster carers had no previous fostering experience or guidance from social services; they rarely saw their social worker, and had become extremely attached to the children. As a result, the adoptive mother told us, the introductory period was rushed 'because the situation was spinning out of control' and 'it was fairly obvious that it had to be moved fairly quick before it all fell apart'. Thus, instead of working through these issues at the time, they rose to the surface five or six months into the adoptive placement, when social services encouraged the adopters to take the children to their foster families for a "farewell visit", to reassure the children that the foster carers were okay. As the adoptive mother recounted:

> We agreed to this initially because we hadn't realised what a lethal mess it would be. Then, having agreed to it, I felt that I had to stick to the agreement for the sake of our relationship with the children really. We put a high premium on truth in the family and I don't tell lies to the children. I said they could go back to visit at Christmas and so we went. It was a disaster. We actually left. The foster carers were bitter. They kept dragging off the children to whisper to them. I'm driving away, this kid in the seat with me, there's some chap running along the window saying to me, 'Promise me you won't hurt them, promise me you won't hurt them'... God! I wish we had never done that. I should never, never have gone back.

By contrast, the adopter felt that the boy's foster carer was far more experienced and she had fully prepared him for the move. Consequently, contact was far more positive and the child seemed to need it less. The adoptive mother described what happened during the contact visit:

---

[7] See Chapter 11- *Post Placement Issues*, para 2.3.

[The child] by that time had started to learn the guitar. He brought the guitar along to show them what he'd done. He came in. He sat down. He showed them the bit on guitar. The foster carers said, 'Hi' and 'How are you doing' and he was chatting away to them. His foster Mum said, 'Are you going to kiss me then?', and he said, 'No'. He didn't want to know and came and sat on my lap. So he'd made the adjustment: 'these were just friends of mine, this is now my family'.

The child's adopters or prospective adopters after disruption[8]

Sadly, a proportion of adoptions do not work out, and 13 families (6 per cent) responding to the postal survey indicated that the child was no longer living with them. Some of these families, and evidently children too, felt the need to maintain some form of contact after the child returned to care.

When [the child] first left he carried on phoning us which the supervisor said he would have to do and I said I'd be quite happy with that. He would have to have the reassurance that because we gave him back it didn't mean that we didn't want to see or speak to him anymore, and I said I understood that. So he would phone every night the first few weeks.[9]

Telephone contact with his foster carer was also a valued source of support for this adopter, in that she could find out about the child's progress. However, contact in such circumstances need not be limited to telephone contact. An agency worker told us about a case where, after disruption, the child went back to live with birth relatives, but that her previous adopters were offering her respite care.

While the agencies involved in these situations seem to have handled contact positively, this was not the case for all the disrupted cases we investigated. In one case, contact was denied when the children returned to care, even though the adoptive mother felt that one of the children (who remained in placement for longer) in particular needed contact:

It's like I know for a fact that he's very upset because he's away from me. He is asking if he can phone, and they've told him 'no' – their argument being that talking to me is going to unsettle him. But I know [the child]. It will upset him, yes, but personally I think he is going to be a lot better if he can continue to have contact with me, than he is if they just try and cut us apart.

When a social worker came to collect the rest of this child's belongings, the adopter asked how the child was. She said the social worker ignored her questions and 'kept changing the subject'.

---

[8] See also Chapter 12, *Disruptions*.

[9] These telephone calls continued (but less frequently) after he was found a new adoptive placement.

It is important that agencies establish both the child's need and the adopters' need for contact after disruption, as this can sometimes ease a situation that is difficult emotionally for both parties to bear.

3   Types of contact

Where some form of ongoing contact with a birth relative was indicated, families were asked to describe the kind of contact the child had. From these data it emerged that, although most families had some degree of contact, the types of contact arrangements varied enormously, from fortnightly visits to annual letters. These were regrouped into two broad types of contact: "direct contact" and "indirect contact".[10] Although we only asked about the relatives with whom the *child* had some form of contact, some families stated that the child had no contact but there was some kind of exchange between the adults of both families (classified as 'other contact'). Again, these data were collected in terms of each birth relative (Table 17).

Table 17
Types of contact with birth relatives

	Families with direct contact		Families with indirect contact		Families with other contact		Total with contact
Mother	43	42%	56	54%	4	4%	103
Father	17	37%	28	61%	1	2%	46
Siblings living with birth family	18	56%	14	44%	0	0%	32
Siblings in foster/ residential care	35	83%	6	14%	1	2%	42
Siblings in other adoptive families	36	71%	14	27%	1	2%	51
Maternal grandparents	23	70%	10	30%	0	0%	33
Paternal grandparents	13	68%	5	26%	1	5%	19
Other (e.g. uncles, cousins)	27	90%	3	10%	0	0%	30

Source: Family postal survey

---

[10] Contact which included face-to-face contact was defined as "direct", and contact which excluded face-to-face contact (e.g. letter-writing, telephoning) defined as "indirect".

Eighty-nine (39 per cent) families had direct contact, and 113 (50 per cent) of families had non face-to-face contact, with at least one birth relative. Direct contact was more common than indirect contact for every type of relative except birth parents. Face-to-face contact was especially limited in relation to birth fathers, where only about one third of the cases with contact included face-to-face meetings.

Interestingly, direct contact with the immediate birth family was less common for families approved by voluntary than statutory agencies,[11] yet there was not much difference in relation to the other categories of birth relative. Is this due to difference of policy, or because direct contact with the immediate birth family is easier to manage when the placing and approving agency is within the same local authority? These are among the questions to be explored in this section.

3.1   Ongoing direct contact (face-to-face)

Whether agencies encourage/facilitate direct contact

In relation to policy regarding direct contact, agencies were asked if they normally encouraged or facilitated ongoing direct contact between the child/adoptive family and birth relatives. The data relating to this question (Table 18) provide a somewhat different picture of the statutory/voluntary split regarding direct contact from the family data (Table 17), suggesting that voluntaries are more supportive of direct contact than statutories. This is difficult to explain. Are the different pictures given by adopters and practitioners on this topic due to chance, or could it be that agencies are saying one thing and doing another?

Table 18

Agencies which encourage/facilitate direct contact with birth relatives after adoption

	Statutory families		*Voluntary families*		*Total families*	
Yes	31	40%	16	62%	47	45%
No	18	23%	2	8%	20	19%
Unsure	0	0%	2	8%	2	2%
Other	29	37%	6	23%	35	34%

Source: Agency postal survey

---

[11] Responding families approved by voluntary agencies were 11 per cent less likely to have face-to-face contact with the birth mother, 35 per cent less likely to have face-to-face contact with the birth father, and 32 per cent less likely to have face-to-face contact with siblings living with the birth family, than families approved by statutory agencies.

Many agencies were reluctant to state whether or not they encouraged or facilitated direct contact after adoption (accounting for the large number of "other" responses), because it depends on the needs of the child, the agreement drawn up pre-adoption, and other case circumstances. One agency stated that direct contact occurred in about one third of cases, while another wrote that this had only happened in one case so far but that practice was gradually changing. One agency rarely "encouraged" direct contact as such, but would support it if such arrangements were required by the adopters.

How agencies encourage/facilitate direct contact

Agencies which encouraged or facilitated direct contact (even if only occasionally) were asked how this was achieved. This question generated a variety of responses, indicating the complexity of maintaining direct contact between birth and adoptive families. The usual means was via written contact agreements (24 per cent), but this was far more common for voluntary (48 per cent) than statutory (16 per cent) agencies. Next was the provision of social worker mediation or supervision of meetings, and contacting parties to arrange meetings (both 17 per cent). However, there were wide differences between statutory and voluntary agencies in both of these provisions. Supervision was three times more common in voluntary (33 per cent) than statutory (11 per cent) agencies, and the difference was nearly as wide for organising meetings (29 per cent of voluntaries, and 13 per cent of statutories). However, the largest difference was regarding the venue of meetings. Whereas, overall, 13 per cent of agencies which facilitate direct contact provide or organise a neutral venue for meetings to take place, this figure was 29 per cent for voluntary agencies, but only 8 per cent for statutory agencies. Other provisions mentioned were agency 'contact registers', although only two statutory agencies cited this provision. Only one agency mentioned the payment of travel expenses for contact when answering this question.[12]

Four of the 104 agencies responding to the question stated that they aimed to be involved in direct contact only in the early stages of the adoption process, expecting it to tail off after the order, with the families managing it themselves. During the period before the order, when contact is supervised, it is hoped that 'relationships will form between the two sets of parents and that will no longer make it necessary'. However, 49 per cent of agencies answering this question (56 per cent of statutory and 29 per cent of voluntary agencies) stated that practice is extremely variable in the way that direct contact is facilitated, and a large proportion of these provided no further details. In addition, two statutory agencies stated that the provision was rather patchy and needed some improvement.

---

[12] Although the equivalent questions in the family postal survey suggested that this form of support was more widespread. See Chapter 17, *Agency Workloads*, at para 2.4.

Deciding whether direct contact is appropriate

Agency views

Agency interviews provided more detailed information about agency policies on direct contact and, in particular, the criteria agencies use to decide whether direct contact is suitable or not. One agency worker stated that, while there wasn't a written policy on contact, the agency's "professional view" was that:

> *. . . in every case we ought to look at what contact is right for that particular child. Unless you can actually give evidence to the contrary, you should be talking about direct contact and the minimum you should be talking about is indirect contact.*

'Evidence to the contrary' was defined by this worker in terms of the following:

> *I quote social workers who keep saying there are two distinct contra-indications to direct contact. One would be if the birth parents see it as a way of achieving custody some time in the future [. . .] The second would be if the birth parents are not able to make the psychological shift from being the parent [. . .] That would apply whether you were talking about the birth parent, the birth grandparent, or whatever. If those two aren't there, and unless you can say that the contact is actually detrimental to the child, then it's given very serious consideration.*

A similar view about criteria for direct contact was shared by a voluntary adoption agency:

> *. . . I always thought the criteria (certainly the evidence in the High Court) for direct contact work was that the birth parents had to be in full support of the adoption plan and of the placement, and secondly of a sufficient maturity to accept a different role in their child's life – such as more of a godparent.*

However, in contrast to the first social worker, she added:

> *The trouble is, I don't think we often have those criteria in place. If we did, we often wouldn't be placing the child for adoption [. . .] If you really feel the child's interests need a lot of direct contact then perhaps you ought to be looking at fostering and not trying to get foster parents on the cheap. It's a very, very difficult area.*

This is an interesting point given the number of adoption placements made with direct contact, and the more so when one considers the evidence from the family study which suggests that direct contact *is* arranged for birth families who *do not* meet these two criteria.

Adopters' views

Many families told us that their children had direct contact with birth relatives who clearly *did not* approve of the adoption. One adopter stated that, 'birth parents were often known to pass improper information to the child' during contact visits which meant that a social worker had to be present at all times. Another family told us that a social worker was always required to control meetings at the Social Services 'Contact Centre', to prevent the birth family 'making destructive comments about the adoption, the children, us, etc'. Yet another described visits with the birth mother as 'very traumatic as she is against the placement for the children'. There were even cases where contact had to be supervised because birth parents had previously absconded with the child.

We also have evidence of contact being granted with birth relatives who had not accepted their new role in the child's life. Take the following example, where children had direct contact with their grandparents:

> *After the first few contacts, the grandparents started being plain awkward, stirring things up during contact in front of the children when the time should have been about children. Mainly, 'Granny' has not come to terms that her grandchildren have been adopted and have their own lives. Neither children seem to need this contact. But it's an ongoing, difficult situation, which there is no end to until the children are a lot older.*

Supervising contact visits

Several families complained about the inadequate supervision of contact visits. One parent felt that she did not get the support she needed from the children's social worker during the first contact meeting:

> *The meeting took place in Social Services offices. The child's social worker was around and helped set up things. She then disappeared for ages and wasn't there when I needed to end the meeting. I think she was on the phone for ages. It was a little upsetting because the situation could have been difficult and I needed to know someone was there to help out.*

In another example, the birth mother began to act inappropriately with another child brought to the meeting by the adoptive mother. The adoptive mother felt that the children's social worker had not sufficiently controlled the situation:

> *When we met his mum we were horrified. We met her at Social Services but it was a hot day and we all sat outside. We had (other child) with us, obviously, and he was in his buggy because he's not mobile, wearing shorts [. . .] Knowing that she abuses little boys [. . .] she honestly was going, 'Ooh, I like this one. This is quite cute.' She tried to ignore her own son, which, as we said at the time, we can understand why he didn't want to see*

her. She hardly said two words to him. She sat next to our son on the floor and said, 'Ooh, I really like this one,' right up his leg . . . with the social worker sitting there.

The social worker's response to this concern was that it was merely the birth mother's 'way of showing affection'. Clearly direct contact with birth parents, whether supervised or not, can spark off complex emotional reactions in all the parties. Birth parents, as well as the child and the adopters, may need support to enable them to cope positively with it. This should be an important consideration when contact is being negotiated between the parties.

Resource implications of supervising contact

Of course, supervising contact is viewed as an enormous drain on resources in relation to other aspects of the service. As one voluntary agency worker said:

We offer ongoing supervised contact for the child with the birth parents and that, in terms of our time, is an enormous commitment. But we've had to offer that because there hasn't been an alternative. We're struggling now with what to do in the future for those children who have been adopted. We can't, with a small staff group, go on offering supervised contact for ever or until the child is adult enough to take it on. So we're considering things like training volunteers to supervise it or any other ideas that people have – it's difficult.

Direct contact is not so resource-laden for agencies who believe that it should be as non-interventionist and as "normal" as possible. While contact visits may be supervised initially, the agency's involvement tails off and is expected to be managed by the families after the adoption order. For example, here are comments made by practitioners in two statutory agencies:

We don't think it's appropriate to be involved in that. The whole idea of adoption is that the responsibility is transferred to the adopters and they take that responsibility in managing contact if they want to. I don't think it's appropriate for social workers to go whizzing down three times a year or whatever and take the child away. Because the whole idea is for the child to be rid of social services or whatever and to be as normal as possible.

The intention of any openness and contact is that it should be as non-social work interventionist as we can make it, otherwise you begin to defeat the object of the adoption. One of my prime objectives for kids is to get social workers out of their lives and get back to the sort of real world of having parents and family and friends. Not the social worker people who come in and somehow have some rights in your life when they don't actually mean anything to you. It normalises it. So in a sense one wants to try and develop an open system that can be as least involving of us as possible.

Another practitioner stated that supervision took 'the sense of being parents away from the adopters'. For such agencies, "normalisation" is the key concept for not supervising direct contact after adoption – not its resource implications.

Feedback, counselling and support

The need for support before and after contact visits clearly varied between adopters. Some families managed very well on their own. Take one family, for example, who used their voluntary agency's Contact Centre for meetings with the birth mother and grandmother. When asked how the meetings affected the children, the father replied:

> *Delightful. Actual angels for two days [. . .] One of the first visits we had, we had them about three months and they had a visit. When they came out the first time [. . .] they seemed so glad to be back in the car and they were wonderful. I really felt that they seemed so glad to see us, to be with us again [. . .] They come out of those usually very well behaved and completely nice for a couple of days, and then they really seem to want to be welcomed back almost. I think it almost feels as if they'd slipped back into their previous existence and they want to come back out again and are sort of really keen to please and to be nice. They really make an effort. It's wonderful you know. So it doesn't distress them. People said that visits sometimes cause a lot of distress but it doesn't seem to do that. It seems to be the opposite. They seem to be quite well balanced about it.*

In contrast, other families needed support because of the impact direct contact had on the child. Several reported behavioural difficulties which coincided with contact visits, resulting in contact being reduced. One family told us that 'very high levels of distress' were triggered by contact visits, which lasted 'in excess of two weeks each time'. In another case (which had disrupted), the adopter told us that the child became 'very sexualised' after contact visits with his birth mother (who had abused him) and 'extremely aggressive' seeing his sister who was being adopted by another family. As the adopter told us:

> *We realised at a later date that it was because no sexual contact had taken place with her. A direct result of this was that he went on to sexually abuse three younger boys at school.*

Another family stated that 'because of emotional problems caused by the contact, the child was seen for six months by a play therapist'. To begin with, the child visited the birth mother fortnightly, but it was reduced to once a month because of the distress it was causing the child. Eventually, the social worker had to go to court to get the contact stopped altogether, but this took a year. The time that it takes to reduce direct contact when it seems to be detrimental to the child in these ways was often a problem for adopters.

We noted one example of particularly good practice regarding support for direct contact. When asked about the support they had received for contact, a family wrote:

> *Main help has been from the children's social worker. Both he and our worker from [approving voluntary agency] have given much moral support and helped us cope with our feelings about the visits. Both have consistently followed up each visit with phone calls to check the children's reactions (and ours!), how we felt the visit went, and any problems that occurred and/or needed ironing out before the next visit.*

In addition to social work support, agency groups can be important forums for peer support, and contact was an issue which often arose in these settings. One voluntary agency was particularly innovative in this respect because it provided group support for children in the adoptive family as well as adults. If there were enough children (whether birth, adopted, or foster children) in adoptive families, this agency ran a separate preparation group for children. The agency also ran a 'Young Network' for adoptees over the age of 13, which included camping activities. As the agency worker told us, at the last camp, 'there were little conversations like "do you see your mum or dad?" '. Talking about contact to other children in similar situations in an informal environment like this can help children work through contact issues. The agency was now exploring setting up a group for the under-13s, precisely because of the need for support around contact:

> *A lot of the children at sixish we are placing with indirect contact, with the comment that one day that will probably turn into direct contact. And adopters are beginning to say to us, 'Well, they're getting to the stage where they're probably going to need to see their mums soon. When's Younger Network going to start?'*

3.2   Indirect contact (letterbox and telephone)

Whether agencies had an exchange system for indirect contact

For many families, direct contact is not deemed appropriate. Practitioners were asked if their agency had an exchange system, such as a letterbox scheme, whereby such families could pass on information to each other via the agency. This question was asked in relation to indirect contact with the child's previous foster family as well as their birth family (see Table 19 below).

Table 19

Agencies which had a system for the exchange of information between adoptive families and the child's birth and foster families respectively

	Statutory agencies	*Voluntary agencies*	*Total agencies*
Exchange with birth family	78 94 %	26 96%	104 95%
Exchange with foster family	46 55%	19 70%	65 59%

Source: Agency postal survey

Only one agency stated that it did not have an exchange system for communicating with *either* the child's birth or foster family, while five stated that this provision was being developed or under review. Exchange systems were nearly twice as common for contact with the child's birth family than they were for contact with the child's previous foster family. This is partly because some agencies encouraged more informal contact with foster families, such as writing or telephoning directly (seven statutory and four voluntary agencies specifically mentioned this qualification).

Practitioners in 11 per cent of responding agencies indicated that their "systems" were rather idiosyncratic or ad hoc, depending on the initiative of individual social workers involved in adoption cases rather than set agency procedures. Indeed, 15 per cent of agencies indicated that the system was still being developed, or that it needed to be improved in some way.

The *family study* suggested that letterbox contact with birth relatives could involve letters written wholly by the adopters (with or without the knowledge of children), by adopters on behalf of the children, or by the children themselves. This depends on the child's age and literary abilities, but also the *reason* for ongoing contact. For example, adopters may write letters to birth parents to keep communication channels open – in case the child needs contact in the future – rather than to meet their current needs. One agency asked adopters to send a regular update, so that even if birth parents did not want to receive information about the child, they could, if they changed their minds later.

Preparation for indirect contact

Preparing adopters

Several adopters were having difficulties composing information to send birth relatives. One family stated that, 'It was very difficult to write without going into detail'. Keeping the family's identity and whereabouts anonymous was a key concern for some families. Similar issues about the information forwarded to birth parents were identified in the Social Services Inspectorate (1995, p 28) report on post-adoption contact:

For adopters in particular, it requires considerable skill and sensitivity to provide information about a child that does not over-emphasise the value of the adoption and the resultant progress of the child or over-emphasise the nature of a child's problems, which might inadvertently create hopes and expectations in the mind of the birth parent.

Although it is important that agencies give adopters guidance in communicating with birth parents, only 3 of the 113 families, who had indirect contact, all approved by voluntary agencies, mentioned that they received such help. The first family stated that they received 'support from the adoption agency in preparing information for birth parents'; the second received guidelines from the agency about the information to send which helped them to write the initial letters which were very difficult; and the third received a 'detailed sample letter giving examples of the type of information to include in a letter to birth parents – provided by the adoption agency social worker'. These are examples of good practice which could be more widespread.

Preparing birth relatives

Birth relatives also need to be prepared for indirect contact. Many adopters said that they had received letters from birth relatives containing material that was unsuitable for the child. Mostly, this was due to the emotive content of letters, which could make the child feel guilty or confused. Vetting information is not common agency practice, being associated with difficult questions about who should do the work and how it is to be funded. Accordingly, preparation may be the cheaper way of minimising the exchange of improper information between families.

Birth relatives may find written guidance on this subject helpful, particularly since obtaining support as issues arise may be difficult: they may no longer have an allocated social worker after the adoption order and, in any event, many do not want to approach their local authority for help regarding contact. As one agency worker stated:

Birth parents, I'm afraid, get the same raw deal as they get in every other part of the process. Although help would be available for them, they're not going to be very inclined to see the placing team of the local authority who've removed their child to talk about how they could write this letter or how they could see this, that or the other. Very difficult.

However, this seems to depend on how support is organised within the agency.[13] In the one quoted above, support was provided by children and families' social workers in area offices. Other agencies, which have specialised fostering and adoption

---

[13] See Chapter 19, *The Organisation of Adoption Services.*

teams, are more likely to be a source of support for birth parents for contact.

A worker in a statutory adoption agency – which was a centralised, specialised unit – claimed that his agency was able to offer support for birth families about the adoption through contact mechanisms:

> *In effect what you are getting is counselling and helping birth parents with the fact that their child has been adopted. Some of the dissatisfactions that they may have about quality of information that is coming through – letterbox wise – is almost certainly not about that information but about their feelings about the adoption . . .*

He explained that this was possible because the adoption agency develops 'links with birth parents at the beginning of that process' as they were 'going to be their point of contact with the department, with their child's life'. This involved meeting birth parents, explaining how letterboxes work, and generally including birth parents in planning for the child:

> *We work with the social worker in helping them through the adoption process – part of that is to ensure that social workers are aware of precisely that issue – which is the inclusion of birth parents in the plan. Obviously it's to do with wishes and feelings about families but also meeting adoptive parents, setting up letterboxes, and this, that and the other.*

It seems that this approach can enable birth families to get help regarding contact issues, and the adoption in general.

In the case of inter-agency placements, the agency which approves the family may be the more suitable organisation to prepare birth families for contact and provide support. As a voluntary agency worker stated:

> *We are having more contact with birth parents now because of the contact after adoption. We are finding that the birth parents often find it easier to have contact with us than they do with their local authority because there's often been 'fights' in court with the local authority. In fact we have actually struck up relationships and ended up in informal counselling of birth parents really. I think that will happen more and more actually.*

Vetting material sent by birth relatives

Some agencies did not read or even open mail from birth relatives, but simply forwarded it to the adopters. For example:

> *From times gone past I still get letters from relatives of children who've gone for adoption to be forwarded to where they've been adopted. I wouldn't open those. That's very much up to the adoptive parents to do that. I wouldn't wish to interfere with whatever the contents of the letter were – I just forward them.*

However, as one agency noted, 'There's always the risk that somebody might try and slip in "Oh, come and see me," or that kind of thing which may be inappropriate,' and with this system, responsibility for controlling this risk is shifted further down the line to the adopters. If families experienced difficulties in the content of mail, some agencies then began to monitor it. Two families mentioned that they had to ask the agency to check letters before sending them on because of their emotive nature. One family also stated that the agency was, in addition to vetting, regulating the mail because it was very erratic.

Some families told us that letters and cards were handed direct to the child, without any vetting by the agency *or* the adopters. As one adoptive mother told us:

> *She'd come in with bags of tat, pictures of the abuser, all sorts and just handed them to the kids without going through me! I just said to her, 'Look, you can't do this. You have to let me decide when it's the right time.'*

There was also an incident reported by one family where the guardian *ad litem* bypassed the agency and took the child a letter from her birth mother. This was against the advice of the child's social worker, therapist, and adopters.

It is essential that, if agencies do not intend to vet mail, they explain this to adopters. Even then, guidance should be given to adopters in handling this role. Ideally, all this should be stipulated in a written agreement. This may then prevent later misunderstandings, which can be of great cost to the child. For example:

> *[The children's social worker] brought a letter from their mother which basically was a page and a half of 'I'm so guilty, I've destroyed your life,' really emotive. It was appalling. It was shifting the guilt on to the kids. We gave these letters to the children because [the children's social worker] had said it was a 'good luck to the family' kind of letter. . . . I was cooking and [the oldest child] was in floods of tears and [the youngest child's] got her letter but she couldn't read it. It was the worst thing I've had to do because [the youngest child] said, 'Well, read mine'. I couldn't not read it and we had these kids distraught. 'We thought, how can you have done this, you stupid woman? I rang her up and she said, 'I never thought to open it, [the birth mother] said it was a card'. I said, 'Bloody hell! I gave them to the kids because you told me it was safe.'*

Other agencies vetted mail to some extent, but mailboxing was primarily treated as an administrative task and conducted by administrative personnel (such as the adoption panel clerk) at the agency. This is how the system worked in one agency:

> *It is actually done by a central post box administrator, but only the mechanics of it if you like. Any problems she sends out to us. She reads the mail as it comes in and we set up the contact agreements and all that. She has copies of them. Stuff comes in to her. She opens it, and if she thinks the letter is going*

to cause problems in wherever it's going to, she refers it to the area. Then we dig it out and deal with it.

Social workers were only involved when administrative staff spotted a problem.

In contrast some agencies treat vetting as a social work task, or sometimes part of the duties of a post-adoption worker:

> *We'd seen the post-adoption person in each district being responsible for each letter box but having half an admin. worker for general support. We have a very clear belief that it is a professional task and not an admin. task because of checking out the information. We did actually think at one time about getting the adoption panel clerk to be the letterbox for the whole county, but it wasn't right. It didn't feel that an admin. person would have the right skills and understanding of the information to know whether it was appropriate or not.*

Another practitioner pointed out that it was a social work task because, when information is not appropriate, 'you have to go and either talk to the birth parents about that information or talk to the adopters about how they receive that information'. Of course, there are resource implications when letterboxes are allocated to social work rather than administrative staff.

Difficulties in managing letterboxes

Practitioners' main worry about agency letterboxes was the sheer volume of the work. For example, one agency had received 60 parcels (as well as cards) for onward transmission at Christmas. This agency felt that the volume of the work, together with its confidentiality element, had quickly outgrown the structure which was managing it:

> *We have a Headquarters structure that had not been dreamed of ever being administratively geared to address any of this and we were suddenly confronted with something that's going through the roof and is not going to diminish. We do not yet know what the ceiling is going to be.*

Confidentiality is another important issue in letterbox work. As one agency noted, 'It's highly confidential because all this onward transmission is the point at which the key connection is made'. The experience of one agency illustrates why it is necessary to be extremely careful:

> *The letter went. It didn't go recorded delivery. It went normal post, and for some reason it didn't arrive. The GPO – or whatever they're called now – opened it and returned it to the sender. The sender being the birth parent, who then had at least an idea . . . she knew it hadn't arrived, but she had an idea of the area in which her adopted child lived. Now she hasn't pursued that in*

any way and we, with another agency involved, have been able to reassure the adopter. But it was a lesson for us that that might have had much worse consequences. So now we're having to produce a system that's got special stickers on that say if undelivered it must be returned to this address or we send stuff registered or recorded.

Some problems with managing letterboxes seem to be associated with certain types of agency structure. Several agencies mentioned difficulties when letterboxes are held at local offices. As one practitioner explained:

Almost all our placements involve letterbox contact now and we've got all that number at local offices. At the moment the social workers say, 'You send me a photo once a year and a letter, and you contact me once a year and I'll give you it'. In three years' time the social worker's gone. Nobody knows where the file is, and some poor person is going to come to the district office and say, 'You're supposed to have a photo for me,' and the duty social worker is going to say, 'Who the hell are you?'

Two agencies found it necessary to invent a provision to safeguard against this: when social workers leave or change position in the authority, they hand over the files and agreements for contact to a 'central aid'. However, as one worker who was taking over the letterboxes in these circumstances stated:

I think that before too long I'll have to set up a proper system for it because it's just growing, and growing, and growing, and it will just get too big for me to handle.

3.3   Sporadic (non-ongoing) contact

Even if ongoing contact is minimal or non-existent, many adopters may need to have sporadic contact with people from the child's past. For example, in the early stages of the adoption process, a one-off meeting may be set up by social workers between adoptive and birth families. A second example is where something important happens in the birth family about which the child or adoptive family has the right to know, such as when a birth relative dies, or a sibling is born, or when a birth relative develops a serious illness which could have implications for the child's health. Conversely, the birth family may need to know of important events in the child's life, such as if the placement disrupts and the child is returned into care. These issues were mentioned in several ways in the postal surveys.

Meeting birth relatives during introductions

The first and most common type of non-ongoing contact which we investigated was meeting the child's birth family during the stage of introductions. Indeed 80 per cent statutory agencies and 89 per cent voluntary agencies stated in the questionnaire that they normally encouraged families to meet each other. Half of the adoptive families responding to this question in the family questionnaire had met the child's birth mother, and 21 per cent the birth father.[14]

There are all kinds of reasons why it may be useful for the families to meet. For example, meeting the child's birth parents in person may give the adopters the opportunity to find out more about the child's background. Also, it could be argued that, if the child is to have contact with a birth relative, it may be particularly helpful for the adopters to have met him or her beforehand. This is perhaps especially important if the adopters – rather than the adoption agency – are to take a key role in managing contact arrangements.

To explore this proposition, we looked at whether adoptive families who had met birth relatives also had ongoing contact with them or not (see Table 20 below). This table suggests, perhaps not surprisingly, that adopters are far more likely to have a meeting with birth relatives if there is going to be some form of ongoing contact. For example, whereas over two thirds of adopters who had ongoing contact had met the birth mother, this dropped to less than one-third for adopters who did not have any contact.

Table 20

Families who had met birth relatives who (a) had ongoing contact with them and (b) did not have ongoing contact with them.

| | *Families who had met birth relatives* | | |
| | *With* | *Without* | |
	Ongoing contact	*Ongoing contact*	*Total*
Mother	75 72%	33 30%	108 51%
Father	29 63%	14 9%	43 21%
Siblings living with birth family	18 56%	39 29%	57 34%
Siblings in foster/residential care	35 76%	27 23%	62 38%
Siblings in other adoptive families	31 66%	7 6%	38 23%
Maternal grandparents	29 85%	9 6%	38 20%
Paternal grandparents	19 86%	5 3%	24 12%
Other (e.g. uncles, cousins)	31 80%	8 5%	39 20%

Source Family postal survey

---

[14] See Chapter 10, *Issues in Matching*, at para 5.2, for further discussion.

In general it was difficult to discern the adopters' view of whether meeting birth relatives hindered or facilitated ongoing direct or indirect contact arrangements. However, as one would expect, families who did not want contact with birth relatives often did not value meeting them. For example, one adoptive couple did not want to meet the birth mother and only did so when she requested it. The adoptive mother recounted:

> We had preparation with the social worker before meeting the birth mother. The actual meeting was a farce. I felt totally frustrated listening about how wonderful this person felt her children had turned out, knowing how little input she'd had in it all. She wanted the meeting, not ourselves. We also had to be persuaded that contact (by letter or a birthday card, twice a year) would be in the best interests of the children.

On the other hand, adopters who were committed to the idea of contact, tended to find the meetings useful. As one adoptive mother put it:

> It also helped me to be candid, for the simple reason that I have met her mother. She is not some sort of dragon phantom from the past. She's just an ordinary human being who then didn't probably make the good choices at certain times of her life. If I felt that if I couldn't go and talk to her mother, that for some reason her mother and that family was unacceptable to me because of what they'd done, then that wasn't going to be of any assistance whatsoever to the child. Actually it helped me considerably to meet her mother and it helps too, because when [she] wants to talk about her mother I know who her mother is now. I didn't know who her mother was before – that's invaluable.

However, it is clear that when such meetings are set up, good preparation and support are essential. Adopters found the attendance of their own social workers to be especially helpful, in what was described by one adopter as 'nerve-racking for all concerned'.

Funerals

One issue which arose during family interviews in relation to sporadic direct contact was where the adopters learned that a birth relative had died. Adopters had to make the difficult decision about whether the child should attend the funeral, and thus have face-to-face contact with birth relatives. Would attending the funeral help the child to grieve or would it stir up acrimony between the families? An adoptive mother talked about this in relation to the death of her daughters' birth grandfather:

> Yes, they were upset but they hadn't seen him for years. He was not a key figure in their lives. I didn't think it was a good idea. Thinking about the funeral, I felt very guilty about should I let them go? But I felt I'd get a lot of aggression from the family.

But what if the person *was* a key figure in the child's life? One adopter told us how her child's birth mother was killed by his birth father while he was in her foster care. In this case, social services wanted the child to attend his mother's funeral, even though his father (who was contesting the adoption) would be there. The adopter refused to take the child to his mother's funeral. Instead, she arranged an informal service away from his relatives:

> *What we did was we went down to the crematorium here. I spoke to our minister and said could we have some sort of funeral service down here which obviously you can't, but just sort of something to mark it for [the child]. So we went down to the crematorium. We had flowers, and we met the minister from the crem. And we had our minister, and we had some friends of [the child's]. And we went behind the hedge, had a service, put the flowers down, and said a little prayer. We marked the spot mentally so that if [the child] wanted somewhere locally to go and remember his Mum (you know, I explained that you can remember people anywhere), if he wanted anywhere particular, he could go there.*

In some situations, it may be better for social workers to encourage this kind of informal ceremony since, unlike a formal funeral, it is non-confrontational.

Updating adoptive and birth families about important events in each others' lives

Agencies were asked in cases where there was no ongoing contact whether they had a provision for *updating the birth family* about developments in the child's life or the adoptive family (such as placement disruption, or the child's death, or onset of serious illness), and a provision for *updating the adoptive family* about developments in the child's birth family (such as the death of a birth parent, or the birth of a sibling). The resulting data are contained in Table 21 below.

However, the large number of "other" answers suggests that there is some ambiguity in this provision. Most agencies answering in this way stated that the provision was not a formal one: it usually operated on an ad hoc basis or depended on case circumstances. These agencies would usually take steps to inform the other party but the information is not collected or forwarded in a systematic way. Moreover, it depends on *both* families maintaining some sort of contact with the agency. This can be difficult since contact may be lost with birth families once they no longer have an allocated social worker. Similarly, once the adoption order has been made, the adoptive family is under no obligation to stay in contact with the agency or the child's local authority, or even inform them of any change of address.

Table 21

Agencies which had systems for updating families about important life events where there is no ongoing contact

	Statutory agencies		Voluntary agencies		Total agencies	
UPDATING THE BIRTH FAMILY						
Yes	42	51%	20	74%	62	57%
No	21	26%	3	11%	24	22%
Unsure	2	2%	0	0%	2	2%
Other	17	21%	4	15%	21	19%
Total responses	82		27		109	
UPDATING THE ADOPTIVE FAMILY						
Yes	44	55%	19	70%	63	69%
No	18	23%	3	11%	21	20%
Unsure	6	8%	1	4%	7	7%
Other	12	15%	4	15%	16	15%
Total responses	80		27		107	

Source: Agency postal survey

Agencies were also asked about the kind of information they collected and passed on in this way. Overall, the most common reason for getting in touch with *birth families* was if the adopted child died (27 per cent). However, this was much higher for statutory agencies (35 per cent) than voluntaries (8 per cent). The next most common reason was if the child's placement disrupted, but again this was more than 10 per cent higher for statutory agencies. The least popular reasons cited were if the child developed a serious illness or if there was a change in the adoption plan.

The provision was slightly more even between statutory and voluntary agencies regarding the information that was collected and passed on to *adoptive families*. Twenty-five per cent of agencies which had a provision for updating adoptive families, informed adopters when a birth relative of the child died (17 per cent of statutories; 27 per cent of voluntaries). Only 8 per cent informed the adoptive family when a birth relative developed a serious disease or illness (7 per cent of statutories; 9 per cent of voluntaries). This figure seems low considering that some diseases could have implications for the child's future health.

One agency suggested a solution to this problem, namely, to write into a contact agreement how this information is to be collected and handled (if at all). This would have the benefit of flagging this up as a potential issue and would give all parties the opportunity to discuss how they would like it to be resolved if it were to arise, and to work out what information they are and are not willing to provide or receive from the agency.[15]

4 Making and breaking contact agreements

4.1 The process of planning and agreeing contact

The process of "negotiating" a contact agreement can be a long one with certain critical points along the way. The first critical point is around the time of *approval*. By this time, the child's contact plan should have been worked out and contact issues should have been covered in the preparation of adopters, giving them some idea about what they can and cannot handle in terms of contact. This preparatory work should be evident at the matching panel, where written agreements about the child's needs regarding contact are considered in respect to the particular family's ability to meet those needs. As one agency social worker said:

> *Our expectation would be that the child's social worker has quite a clear plan in relation to future contact and how that contact might change over time. They need to have a clear idea of what it is going to be like just after placement, and then what it should be like after that. It is necessary to ensure that the carers have had work done with them about that and that their expectations are right in relation to what's actually likely to happen.*

One agency had learned to take extra precautions at this stage to ensure that there were no misconceptions about contact, and to prevent problems from emerging later.

The second critical point is the run up to the proposed placement – the planning meetings – in which 'contact arrangements often come up repeatedly'. Some agencies told us that, at the point of placement, a written agreement between the parties is drawn up, setting out each worker's field of responsibility, the support to be offered, along with any plans about the child's education, health and contact with the birth family.

Agencies identified various systems they had developed, or wanted to develop, in order to make contact arrangements work in the long term. A voluntary agency involved the agency's post-adoption worker in linking meetings and, immediately after the matching panel, he or she would start picking up the work regarding planning for contact:

> *The post-adoption worker will visit all the parties to see what their thoughts are and will talk through the implications and what is right, and not only in*

---

[15] We have since been told of one area which does this.

relation to birth families but previous foster carers (the scenarios are endless), and realistically, what adopters can manage because they've got their own life and they want to do their own thing as well.

Another voluntary agency told us that they would like to be involved more in the planning stage because local authority social workers often have 'unrealistic requests' for the level of contact, and expect the approving agency to provide them with what they want:

Sometimes they invite us, but not as much as we would like to be invited. It feels like they have more of the power and sometimes I think they're asking for things that haven't always been thought out.

4.2   Issues in negotiating contact

Failing to make the child's interests paramount

Many families reported the lengths to which local authority social workers would go to get a "good deal" for birth parents regarding contact. This seems particularly likely when the child's social worker is also allocated to the birth family. Several adopters suggested that the social worker's history with the birth family can make them over-sympathetic to birth parents – particularly where their children had been removed against their will – with contact being seen as a means of alleviating that loss. One adopter told us that she was given conflicting messages from the children's social worker about how important it was that the adoptive family sent letters and photos to birth relatives, due to 'the problem with the same social worker wearing different hats, basically, because he's obviously trying to help [the birth mother]'.

Over-identification with the birth family can lead to misguided decisions about contact. An agency practitioner identified this as a problem:

I think it's the old problem of the social worker identifying with the person they're trying to help so, of course, the social worker is identified with the birth family. Maybe the problem stems from the birth family and the child being lumped together. Their interests are not necessarily the same.

In fact, contact was often seen by adopters as serving the interests of birth parents rather than those of the child, with some believing that contact was actually detrimental to the child. One case, mentioned earlier in this chapter,[16] was where the child was forced to visit his father in prison against his will, despite showing signs of severe psychological distress. In the words of his adoptive mother:

Well, I did force him to go, the once, and when he came back and he was so sad, I thought no. I honestly felt as though I had to fight Social Services.

---

[16] See para 2.1 above.

That's the truth of it. I don't feel that I had the support from them at that time. I felt that the father had the support and the sympathy and I didn't.

In another case, the child said himself that he wanted contact to end, and the adopters believed that contact was affecting him negatively because his language and behaviour became increasingly sexualised after seeing the birth mother. Contact was eventually terminated after the child's referral to the Tavistock Clinic. Despite this, the child's social worker still wanted contact to be resumed in the future. In the adopter's words:

She still says, 'Oh, I feel he should still see his mother,' but I mean, let's be honest . . . If people like the Tavistock say 'no way' then surely you've got to . . . and the school even said to her on one occasion 'in whose interest are you dealing – [the child's] or [the birth mother's]?'. Oh well, I feel very sorry for [the birth mother].

According to some adopters, sympathy with birth parents may not be the only factor affecting negotiations for contact. Both the adoptive mothers quoted above also thought that the birth parents inspired fear in their local authority workers. In the latter case, having contacted their adoption agency to put pressure on the child's social worker to reduce contact, the child's social worker finally told the birth mother that it could no longer go on.

When she actually rang up, she said, 'Oh, I've told [the birth mother]'. She said – and it didn't dawn on me until then because she came out with some comment about 'Oh, she accepted it very well, I thought she would have attacked me like she has before' . . . and [the birth mother] evidently is also physically violent and that's what the social worker thought was going to happen when she told her that she couldn't see [the child]. She thought she was going to be attacked and that's why she didn't want to say it.

Contact as a condition of the approval of adopters

The Children Act 1989, s 34, by providing for a presumption of reasonable contact between the child in care and his or her family requires local authorities to plan for contact; indeed, 'the court may require a local authority to justify an adoption plan which excludes it' (Richards, 1996). Similarly, adopters can feel pressured to *agree* to contact plans. Some agencies raised an expectation of contact at the very beginning of the adoption process, as part of the preparation of adopters. As one practitioner told us:

We would be advising all prospective adoptive parents that they must con-sider contact and this is something very important. It's not something they can ignore and say, 'We don't want any contact'. That won't do; if you're going to be like that then you're going to be a long time waiting for a child and the chances are you'll never get one!

One family stated that they had been led to believe that their level of contact (meetings with the children's birth mother every three months) was normal, so they had not questioned it at the time. It was only much later, having spoken to other adopters, that they realised that their case was quite unusual, and that perhaps they could have had 'more say about it'. At other times, the pressure to agree to contact came after matching. A family said that, although they were told that 'no contact was envisaged' when the match was made, 'now after a few months they were beginning to put pressure on us'.

However, when agreement to the principle of contact is a condition of the approval of prospective adopters, or a requirement for specific children to be placed with them, families may agree to contact without fully taking on board its implications. Indeed, the problem of assessing how serious and committed to contact adopters really are, was a concern for several agency workers. For example, a voluntary agency worker stated that it is difficult during preparation, planning pre-placement, and even in the early stages of placement, 'to know how good prospective parents are going to be' regarding contact. He continued:

> *Some of the ones who say all the right things are usually the ones we are chasing up [. . .] Others, who are quite fearful of it, will go and change and actually be able to cope with it. So I think it is extremely difficult. I think it's a very difficult area for us to be able to assess.*

Workers in two separate statutory agencies argued that it does not matter how much the contact message is reinforced during the preparation and training process. Once prospective adopters get a child placed they start 'backing off' – it is a case of 'they'll do anything to get the child'. One agency informed us that they used a questionnaire, developed by their consortium, to establish what adopters felt they could offer in terms of contact. However, while this might be a useful tool in matching, it is unlikely that agency workers will have any real way of telling how reliable – in the long term – the answers will be.

When adopters agree to contact, it is important that this is sincere, as a contact agreement will often persuade birth parents to agree to the adoption. As argued by one writer:

> *Given that an offer of contact will often influence a birth parent's approach to consent at the time of the adoption, it is not acceptable that adopters should say one thing and do another [. . .] Since, however, the law does not allow parental agreement to adoption to be subject to a condition that contact be subsequently allowed, the giving of consent must be an act of faith, and if subsequently that is seen to be betrayed by the adopters, conflict shifts further*

down the line, to the detriment of, if not outright risk to, the child. (Richards, 1996, p. 178)

Contact as a condition for birth parents' agreement to adoption

Some adopters argued that contact was used as a bargaining tool to 'ease the passage of adoption', i.e. to persuade the birth parent to sign the consent form or to deter them from actively opposing the adoption in court. One adopter believed that this was why contact was initiated with her son's birth father:

> *To begin with, he said he would agree to the adoption. Then he wouldn't agree. This was the kind of man he was, you see. It was put to me that if we agreed to [the child's] father seeing [him] four times a year, then he might approve or give his permission for the adoption.*

This type of practice has been noted by professionals in adoption. Richards (1996, p. 178) argued that, for many practitioners, 'contact is inevitably regarded as a means of facilitating adoptions; not the *quid pro quo* exactly, but a way of enabling birth parents to accept what would otherwise be unacceptable in order to achieve the best possible outcome for the child'. In the words of one practitioner:

> *Don't contest and you can have some contact. It's newish in that the judges are latching on to openness and contact now. They're not all the same from the point of view of the child but from 'well, this poor woman. What can we give her, or how can we make it up to her?'*

One adopter commented that 'contact with the birth mother is complicated as it has been used as a condition to deter her from contesting the adoption when it comes to court'. It certainly seems that contact in adoptions where birth parents are not in full agreement with the adoption plan can be more difficult to manage than when they are in agreement. Part of this may be the threat of the non-agreeing parent to the adopters, and their worry that they might prevent the adoption from going ahead.

Yet, when there is no threat, contact can work well. For example, in one case cited by an adoption worker, the birth mother had a terminal illness which made her unable to care for the child:

> *A child who we've placed at a very young age, his mother had some terminal illness, debilitating illness, and wasn't able to cope. Although very unhappy about relinquishing the care of him she agreed to the adoption. In that case I understand that the adopters have even taken mum and the child on holiday together. There's definitely still a role for her as well, while she's alive.*

Or, in other cases, where the birth parent is unable to care for the child because of the child's disabilities:

The adopters for those kind of children are a very rare breed. They are always open to contact and they're even willing to give their home address to the birth family. To say, 'Look, if you're passing by you can drop in and see your child. We've got no problems.' Because the circumstances that that child has been given, those circumstances are not going to change. That child is not going to go back to the parents. So they feel fairly secure that this is going to be their child and the threat of that child going back is minimal really. We find those kinds of families a lot more open to face-to-face contact.

In both of these instances, the birth parents accepted the adoption. It is the security of knowing this, and that the situation will not change, which seems to enable the adopters to accept contact and make it work.

Unreciprocated contact

Fourteen families had required help from the agency because birth families were not writing or visiting as often as agreed (this occurred equally in relation to direct and indirect contact). As one parent stated:

We needed help to encourage us to gather photographs and information to send to various members of the birth family. This is because it has always been a one-way communication although we have been promised photographs/information from them. We get rather depressed when we are the ones putting all the effort in – or so it seems.

Another family stated that one-way letterbox contact had been going for three years and that they had never had anything back. In such cases, it is important that social services re-establish contact with birth relatives, and make them realise how important it is that they keep to the agreement.

While most families struggle to meet their side of the agreement in such circumstances, others may decide that *broken* contact agreements are more damaging than no contact at all. Then they may dispense with the contact agreement because the birth relatives have already done so. For example, one family reported that children became 'emotionally disturbed on the many, many occasions grandparents missed coming'. One adopter told us that, 'It's detrimental to arrange a visit and not have them turn up – that's even worse than not having a visit – so we have the right to cancel if they don't appear'.

4.3   Written contact agreements

A study on post-adoption contact by the Social Services Inspectorate emphasised the importance of written contact agreements:

> *The study found without doubt that the process of negotiation leading to the preparation of written contact agreements, and the agreements themselves, proved invaluable in reducing conflict, establishing a clear understanding of the expectations of all parties, and forming a basis for subsequent review and, where necessary, amendment. Use of such agreements should become a standard element of agency procedures.* (SSI, 1995b, p. 33)

An additional advantage is that the existence of a written agreement may avoid more formal action in the courts (ibid p. 13). The report also argues that these should not be seen as written in stone; rather they should be reviewed, and review procedures should be made explicit to all parties involved. Finally, 'consideration should also be given to establishing a system for monitoring compliance with agreed arrangements and the agency should be clear as to the extent to which it will become involved in situations of non-compliance' (p. 34). However, in a more recent report, research found only 'isolated examples' of written agreements, and they 'tended to reflect the initiative of individual staff' rather than agency practice (SSI, 1996, p. 47).

Families with written contact agreements

This section examines some of these assertions in relation to data collected in the family and agency studies, first by looking at the extent to which written agreements have become standard practice in adoptions with contact in England and Wales.

The family questionnaire asked adopters who had contact to state whether the arrangements were set out in writing, such as in an explanatory letter from the agency, a contact agreement, or a contact order. The resulting data are set out in Table 22.

Sixty-four (39 per cent) of those who had some form of contact with at least one birth relative had a written contact agreement. The majority of families which ticked "other" stated that they had unwritten "informal" or "voluntary" agreements which were made and maintained by the families themselves, with a minimal or non-existent agency role. Some pre-order families stated that the agreement had not yet been drawn up but that it would be before going to court for the adoption order.

Table 22
Families which have contact arrangements set out in writing

	Statutory families with written agreement		Voluntary families with written agreement		Total families with written agreement	
Yes	42	36%	22	45%	64	39%
No	66	57%	23	47%	89	54%
Other	5	4%	3	6%	8	5%
Unsure	3	3%	1	2%	4	2%

Source: Family postal survey

So why are contact agreements drawn up in some cases and not others? First, it seems some types of agency use contact agreements more than others. Contact agreements were 9 per cent more common in families approved by voluntary agencies than their statutory counterparts. It also seems that certain types of statutory agencies more commonly use written agreements: 42 per cent of families approved by shire counties had written agreements, compared to 39 per cent of those approved by inner/outer London boroughs, and only 17 per cent of families approved by district borough councils. Third, the use of written agreements did not appear to be spread evenly across regions: whereas 31 per cent of families approved by agencies in London and the South East had written agreements, no families in Wales and the Northern region had contact arrangements in writing.[17]

However, there was no evidence to suggest that any agency used written agreements for *all* the families with contact which it approved.[18] This suggests that their use may be dependent on other factors, such as with whom contact is proposed. Data from the family survey showed that around 50 per cent of the families which had contact with birth parents had written agreements, whereas this dropped to 44 per cent for grandparents, and to only 36 per cent for siblings.

In addition, it seems that the type of contact is also significant. One agency worker told us that written contact agreements were used 'only for indirect contact'. For direct contact, they would use part of the 'care file', though she thought that more formal recording of arrangements for direct contact needed to be considered. However, this worker pointed out that, for indirect contact, 'You can make the decision about what it's going to be, and really to a large degree leave it at that, but you cannot for direct contact'. Thus, written agreements were more likely to be

---

[17] However, it should be noted that the response samples for these two regions are far smaller than those for other regions.
[18] Where we had questionnaire responses from five or more families which had been approved by the same agency, there was often a 50–50 split between those who had written agreements for contact and those who did not have them.

used for indirect contact arrangements because the arrangements are less likely to change. Another agency stated that contact agreements were developed with indirect contact in mind, but the agreement form could be adapted for the purposes of direct contact. Indeed, when the issue arose, most agencies spoke of written agreements in relation to indirect contact.

Ensuring compliance with contact agreements: comparing written contact agreements with court orders

It is clear from our research that agencies differ in the steps they are willing to take when agreements are broken by birth or adoptive families. One agency stated that they would chase up the party who failed to meet the arrangement, and ask why. Several agencies sent out reminders and one voluntary agency had introduced an acknowledgement system:

> One of the things that we're doing now, that we didn't do when we first started, is to ask birth parents to acknowledge when they get their annual letter and photograph. Because what was happening was that the adoptive parents were giving the information that they'd contracted to do and [the birth parents] weren't doing anything. They didn't even know, in some cases, if the letter was reaching the birth parents. And I didn't know that it was reaching the local authority social worker because we didn't get any confirmation that it had actually been received. So we are certainly trying to get that for them if we possibly can. And that seems to be helping them to go on to the next year.

Another agency had set up a working party to develop a system which would be more proactive in the way that contact agreements were monitored. Copies and examples of contact agreements were being collected and analysed, so that existing contact forms could be refined. Thought was also being given to computerising records so that agreements and reminders could come up automatically, which seems a good idea.

However, ultimately, written contact agreements are not legally binding. Several agencies indicated the necessity to make clear to families that the contact agreements are voluntary. This is precisely why some agencies prefer the term "agreement" to "contract" (although we did find evidence of the latter term being used in a few agencies). It was because contact agreements only operate "in good faith" that some agencies preferred to pursue contact orders which are (in theory anyway) binding and enforceable. For example, one statutory agency worker told us that they would hope that birth relatives made an application for a contact order:

> Because our view is that if they don't do that at the time of the adoption order, it's more difficult (it's not impossible, but it's more difficult) to do so afterwards. It's the child's right to have contact if it's in their best interests. But

unfortunately what has happened is it's been very easy for contact to be pushed to the side or to the bottom of our adopters' agendas without recognising that it's the thing that can help the child with openness about their birth family and that would give the placement stability and security. So rather than being at the bottom it ought to be very much near the top. We feel that a contact order is probably the best way of ensuring that for the child – providing we can get agreement between all parties. We work very hard to get agreement between all parties about the contact order in general terms. If we couldn't get a contact order we'd like to have a written agreement built into the adoption order. So that when we go to court the judge is under no illusion that contact will be taking place by mutual agreement at this stage, in this form.

However, contact orders also have disadvantages, which could leave some practitioners in a dilemma about which method to pursue in order to ensure that contact agreements are adhered to. For example:

The difficulty with not having a court order is that if there is no court order the adopters can say, 'Well, we said we'd do it but we're not going to. It doesn't suit us. There is nothing you can do about it.' So if there is a court order you've got problems because then, of course, you're stuck with administering the order. If there is no court order, you're really dependent on goodwill. I suppose I like to go for goodwill every time. But once in a while one happens and it always will and I don't honestly think we know enough about it. I don't think again it's well enough understood or appreciated.

The "goodwill" element of contact agreements gives positive messages to the adopters and the birth relatives about the trust invested in them in maintaining the agreement. When all parties are agreed and a contact order still goes ahead,[19] it suggests that one or both parties cannot be trusted to keep to the agreement. This happened to one family we interviewed where, even though all the parties had agreed to contact and the arrangements had been working for a year, the family had just been informed that the agency was going ahead with a contact order. This action shocked both the adopter and her solicitor.

I said very strongly at this meeting yesterday, 'I've agreed to contact with this mother and I will stick to it'. This is what drives me up the wall because they don't trust me. They obviously think that as soon as she's out of the picture that we're going to shut the door on [the birth mother]. How could we do that when it's to the kids' detriment?

---

[19] Though, as a matter of legal practice, the order is unlikely to be made. See *Re T (Adoption: Contact)* [1995] 2 FLR 251, discussed at Chapter 2, *The Legal Background*, para 1.2.

An agency worker succinctly summarised this issue:

> It's a kind of a crazy notion that, on the one hand, we entrust this child to the
> care of these people and then, the court slaps an order on them. It's a
> contradiction. If contact is going to work, it's going to work on an informal
> basis. If it's not going to work on an informal basis – it's not going to work.
> So there's no need for it – an order is irrelevant really.

The prospective adopter quoted previously backs this view, suggesting that the
agency's rationale for using a contact order was flawed anyway. She stated, 'I think
it's very naive to think that because there's an order we'll stick to it'. This throws
some doubt on whether contact orders do, in fact, provide a more effective means of
ensuring that contact agreements are adhered to, because they are forcing contact
on an unwilling party. This was the view of one practitioner:

> I think that is why we are a bit cagey about contact orders on the basis that if
> everybody's agreed, then they shouldn't be making an order. And if
> everybody's not agreed, then an order which imposes arrangements is going
> to be imposing arrangements on an unwilling party at the outset . . . So we
> do try, and we haven't always succeeded, but we do try very hard to find
> adopters who are happy with, as opposed to just willing to tolerate, the
> contact plan that we've got for a child.

In addition, three agencies we interviewed preferred written agreements because
they avoided more formal action in the courts, such as contact orders. For example,

> I think we have got lots of contact arrangements but very few of them are
> actually written into the order. They are very flexible. We've got them worked
> out. There's a contract that's done in each case that's worked out before it
> goes to court. That's presented to the court, and the judges are saying at the
> moment, 'The contact is there so I do not need to make an order', which I
> think is wonderful.

While in some cases the simple fact that the contact has been agreed by parties is
not enough,[20] if it is agreed there usually will not be a contact order or a condition
of the adoption order.

Some families and agencies preferred written contact agreements because of
their *flexibility*. The (alleged) inflexibility of contact orders is at odds with the
nature of contact.[21] By 'laying down arrangements which might no longer reflect

---

[20] One agency reported that judges sometimes challenged the details of written contact agreements, such
as the type or frequency of contact, and asked parties to 'go away and agree something', or they may write
it into the order.

[21] It seems to us that some of this anxiety is misplaced given that court orders can simply be made to
provide for reasonable contact, leaving it to the parties, in suitable cases, to work out the details.

the child's needs as time goes on', contact orders may give misleading messages. To quote one practitioner:

> *I think the other thing is that contact is being seen as something that will last for ever. I don't think you can see contact like that. I think contact is to be something that's maybe annually agreed – three years at the most. Because everybody changes – particularly the children end up saying, 'I do not want contact,' and if that's written into an order . . .*

Other social workers were reluctant for anything to be written into the adoption order or contact order (and it was argued that solicitors shared this view), because it means that you need to go back to court every time contact arrangements need to be changed. Furthermore:

> *It just brings in another power game, and all of a sudden people start quibbling and you have to go back to court and all sorts of things.*

By contrast, if done properly, written contact agreements acknowledge the possibility of change and give guidelines about what parties should do if the need for this arises. As one practitioner told us:

> *All these agreements are reviewable and changeable. It's written into the contact agreement that if anyone wants to change it then they approach the post-adoption worker who will re-negotiate it in recognition that circumstances have changed. The same is true of face-to-face contact.*

Certainly, written contact agreements themselves should remind families that the agreement is not written in stone, and that any changes should not be made in isolation but in consultation with the agency. In other words, when one agreement becomes outdated, it should be replaced by another, more suitable agreement, rather than being dispensed with altogether.

5   Concluding points

The purpose of this chapter has been to explore the range of problems and issues concerning the various forms of contact between the child and other important figures in the child's life before and after adoption. However, we should make it absolutely clear that we are by no means committed to the view that any form of contact between the child and birth family is always in the child's interest. On the contrary, we take the view that the issue of contact has to be governed by the welfare of the particular child (including taking into account the child's own wishes and feelings) in his or her circumstances which may change from time to time. What has to be avoided is the imposition of inflexible rules based on doctrinaire policies. What we have therefore set out to do is to indicate some of the conditions precedent which, from our evidence, would seem to facilitate workable and beneficial arrangements.

Notwithstanding our general view, we have found that contact affects the vast majority of adoptive families. First, overall, contact was seen as potentially important for the child's sense of identity and knowledge of their family background. Second, it can reduce their feelings of being rejected and birth parents can show that they still care for the child's welfare. Third, it can help the child settle in and attach to their adoptive family, and it can help relieve any anxiety that children may have about the well-being of birth relatives (although a few families believed that contact could harm new attachments, and can perpetuate the child's sense of responsibility for birth relatives). Contact does not necessarily need to be with close relatives for these purposes. In some cases, contact with relatives hitherto unknown to the child can have a positive influence on the child and the placement. It may be worth agencies investing time in tracing relatives for this purpose, especially in cases where children have no contact with any other birth relatives. It is also important not to overlook the child's possible needs to maintain contact with their previous foster carers.

It seems that several conditions need to be in place for adopters to feel comfortable with contact and see the benefits for their children. First, birth relatives must approve of the adoption and not make destructive comments to the children about it. Second, adopters must accept that the child has birth relatives and may need to continue to see them and to some extent admit them to the adoptive family. For some families, a particularly negative perception of birth relatives can make this difficult, making them want to shield the child (as well as themselves) from the birth family. Third, contact can be threatening in situations where there are any insecurities about the adoption, but it can work well in cases where the birth parent consents to the adoption, believing it to be in the best interests of their children. Involving birth parents in planning for the child and providing independent support can help achieve this. Finally, adopters need to be positive about contact – to see the value of contact for their children and for the adoptive family as a whole. They also need to communicate that they approve of contact with the children, but not necessarily in the way prescribed by inflexible agency rules.

It must be recognised that needs for contact may change. Children's perceptions of their own situation, and those of their relatives, need to be considered when planning for contact, but these may have to be revised as children's understandings develop, or the situations of their relatives (especially siblings) change. Also, the need for contact may not become apparent until children feel settled in the adoptive family. Equally, they may need contact to begin with, but this may tail off. In this context, written contact agreements can be useful because, unlike contact orders or conditions for contact in the adoption order, they do not give inappropriate messages about the rigidity of contact agreements. Building a clause into the agreement which says that it is variable will remind families of this and may help prevent families from straying from agreements. Yet less than half of the adopters had their contact agreements in writing.

Contact with siblings in other families can be complicated yet many children need this. In the case of siblings placed in other adoptive families, for contact to work *all families* must be committed to contact, and this was not always the case. When contact with siblings being adopted elsewhere works, it can be an important source of support for the adopters as well as the children. Contact with siblings placed with foster carers seems to depend largely on whether the adopted child had a positive previous relationship with the foster carers. If the child had been placed with the foster carers before the adoption, much depends on whether they had been well supported and able to deal with their loss. It also depends on whether the move was well managed. These conditions apply, not only for contact with siblings living in foster care, but also for continued contact with the foster carers themselves, which many children may need once placed for adoption. Contact with the child's foster carer can also be an important source of support for adopters, if these conditions are right. When they are not, handling contact with foster carers can be more problematic for adopters having to cope with than parental contact. Contact with the child's foster carer after disruption can ease the adopters' anxiety for children if they are returned to care.

Many families indicated that they valued good supervision of direct contact. However, many agencies pointed out that supervision was a considerable drain on resources, or that they believed in "normalisation", so supervision was often not built into arrangements. Other agencies were investigating training volunteers to supervise contact visits. Some families also needed feedback about direct contact, to talk about any arising issues. Other families need more intensive support because direct contact seemed to be distressing the child, perhaps requiring some therapeutic input, or psychiatric assessment of the effect of contact. Some families needed to stop contact altogether for this reason, yet this sometimes was met with resistance from social services and took far too long to achieve.

Families which had indirect contact highlighted the importance of practical preparation for writing letters and sending other information to birth relatives. Sample letters are particularly useful. Preparing birth parents for indirect contact is also important. Good preparation may lessen the necessity for agencies to vet correspondence sent between families. The agency's role in vetting mail should certainly be made clear to adopters. Contact material should not be given directly to children by social workers, guardians, or others without going through the adopters first, especially if the agency has not checked the mail.

Talking to peers about contact can be an important way for families to measure the "normality" of their situation, and to discuss any issues arising from contact. It may also help families who are experiencing difficulties to see that contact *can work*, and thus encourage them to persevere. Agency support groups or networks for all parties to the adoption (including children) are an important source of support in this context.

Finally, the *child's* needs must always be the priority when planning for contact. Sometimes, the needs of the child get confused with the needs of birth parents, especially when the same social worker is allocated to both. Granting birth parents contact to alleviate their loss, or to persuade them to agree to the adoption, can have negative implications later, and can cause conflict at other levels.

16 Adopters' expectations – were they met?

1 Introduction

We conclude this part of the study, which considers adopters' and agency practitioners' views of the adoption process, with an examination of material, obtained from our family postal questionnaire, which invited adopters to reflect on their experience and to consider the question: How far do you think the *information* you obtained on your adopted/prospective adoptive child's background gave you/ your family a *clear/realistic picture* of what to *expect* from the adoptive placement?

This question, combined with another which asked whether they had found the information they received about the child helpful or unhelpful, produced a rich crop of replies, showing whether or not their expectations had been met or even exceeded. Perhaps mistakenly, we did not ask a direct question about the overall level of their satisfaction with the adoption support services, but this particular question produced qualitative replies which, in our opinion, in many instances give a clear indication. We have classified 168 replies to the particular question out of the 226 questionnaires received, according to whether or not they were essentially positive or negative. Table 23 below indicates the proportionate classification.

Table 23
Whether the information on child's background was clear/realistic (N = 168 families)

	Positive response		Negative response		Mixed response		Other	
Whether information on child's background was clear/realistic	61	36%	56	33%	22	13%	29	17%

Source: Family postal survey

As can be seen, there was a slightly larger proportion – a little over a third – who thought that the information they received had been clear and realistic, and a third who did not. Of the remaining 30 per cent, most of the mixed positive/negative responses veered to one side or the other but with some qualification, whilst those

327

in the "other" category made comments which did not precisely relate to the question.

2 Reflective experience compared with initial expectations

An examination of the qualitative replies indicates there are some whose expectations were exceeded; a number who felt that the reality broadly matched what they had expected; and others who were disappointed, amongst whom there were some who felt they had been misled. As one would expect, those falling into the last two groups contained the saddest and most poignant replies. Overall, the picture received covered a wide spectrum of experience from joy to disillusioned anguish. To give a flavour of this material we have chosen a representative selection from the large number of replies.

2.1 Expectations exceeded

A significant minority of parents (about 20 per cent of the 61 "positive" replies) wrote of their surprise and relief that having been warned of potential difficulties, they either did not materialise or quickly disappeared. For example:

> We understood the background. [The child] was six years old when he came to us a very hurt, disturbed and frightened child. He had, however, worked through a lot of his problems before the adoption with us. We are very pleased now. He is a 12-year-old, bright and well adjusted boy who is still in contact with his birth mother and his siblings.

In similar vein two other adopters wrote:

> It was a reasonably clear picture from the standpoint of behaviour. However, the difficult behaviour didn't take very long to sort out, and the child that has emerged has become just more delightful than I would have thought possible from the information I was given.

> We feel we have been very lucky indeed. We appear to have a settled (if only the school was better!) and friendly lad, far better than the social services led us to expect. But we think they were absolutely correct to drive home the likely pitfalls.

One parent, who had adopted two children with learning difficulties, cited medical information in particular:

> Most of what I was told by the medical profession was very pessimistic particularly. I've had to face that before and found things were not as bad

as painted. Both children far exceeded what was expected for them to achieve.

Another said:

When first presented to us, prior to meeting the children, the formal language used made things sound much worse and gave us much more concern than necessary. It over-emphasised areas which in reality were fairly minor. For example, [the child's] sister was supposed to have "wetting" problems, but they were nothing like as severe as suggested. We do know from talking to other adopters that we have been very lucky in having had two older children placed with us with relatively minor behavioural problems.

2.2   Expectations matched by reality

A considerable number of replies – about 70 of the 168 – indicated that adopters considered the information they had received gave them a clear, realistic picture of what to expect. We quote first from some where the adopters felt that things were working out well:

Knowing all that I know about her background through her social worker and mine, I knew exactly what I was taking on. Emotionally the child's trust in mankind had been dwindling very fast because she's been moved around so much and her self-confidence is nothing compared to other children of her age. But the information they gave us has helped a lot and we are building confidence in each other and this is making us very close. She tells me when she is having a problem of some sort, and I explain to her how I think the two of us should work it out with the help of one of the social workers.

One person with previous experience of adoption wrote:

We already knew from experience what we were letting ourselves in for and went into this adoption with our eyes wide open and fingers crossed because we felt we could give [the child] the security he needed.

It may also be significant that a number of these "satisfied adopters" had previously fostered the child. For example:

[The child] came into our home as an emergency foster placement and the information was gathered over a long period, mainly for therapeutic work for the child. By the time we had adopted her three years later, we had a very clear idea what to expect.

[The child] came to us in foster care when he was four-and-a-half years old. He had been in previous foster care elsewhere. Adoption was first considered when he was nine years old and finally achieved when he was 12 years old.

> *He was a contested case because his natural family did not agree, but it was*
> *fully supported by Social Services and it was what [the child] and all our*
> *family wanted.*

2.3   Expectations disappointed

Placements that had proved harder than expected, or which had even disrupted, understandably prompted the most comment. We quote from these more extensively partly to convey the anguish they reveal and partly because they underscore so many of the practice points concerning careful matching, the provision of truthful information, and supportive preparation which we have made in previous chapters. On the other hand, we caution readers not to think that these distressing accounts outweigh the number of more favourable replies. As pointed out they represent only about a third. Nevertheless, they testify to the considerable challenges and risks involved for families who are willing to engage in an adoptive placement for older children. Broadly there were four kinds of disappointed expectation: first, those who experienced problems different from those that were anticipated; second, those who anticipated difficulties but did not imagine their severity despite receiving good support; third, those who felt problems had been understated or simply not recognised; and fourthly, those who considered they had been deliberately misled.

Anticipating the wrong problems

Amongst the "disappointed" group were those who found that some of the antici-pated problems did not materialise while other unexpected ones did. For instance:

> *We received a very negative view from [the child's] social worker as it was*
> *anticipated that she would be very distressed at having to leave her foster*
> *mother (she had been at the foster placement for four-and-a-half years). The*
> *older child, we were told, would not be so difficult. In effect the opposite was*
> *the case. There were problems which we did not expect and those we expected*
> *did not materialise. Sadly, none of our numerous social workers seemed able*
> *to offer any constructive help.*

Similarly adopters of three siblings wrote:

> *Not enough was made of the emotional damage that children who have been*
> *in care for a long time suffer. We adopted three siblings at the same time (aged*
> *eight, six and nearly five). The social workers tended to paint a rosy picture*
> *of how well they got on together and left a lot unsaid. They have tremendous*
> *sibling rivalry which can be very wearing and tiring at times.*

'Nothing can prepare you for the reality'

There was group of replies which indicated that, despite having received excellent background information, the adopters faced great challenges which they were only surviving with support, as one explained:

> The information we received provided an extremely clear and realistic picture of [the child] and what to expect. Unfortunately, although we were prepared for living with an emotional time-bomb, in reality it is far harder to cope with the daily screaming and confrontational behaviour which is increasing now that he is in the middle of play therapy. He is a child suffering extreme grief, separation and loss and, in reality, nothing and nobody could really prepare a family for this. The continuing support from his social worker so freely given has held us together for now. If the adoption agency had the resources available to provide ongoing social worker contact to support the family without having to request it, this would greatly relieve the family strain.

Another couple who, in common with others, thought that no amount of information could necessarily prepare them for what lay ahead, described the effect of the placement on their family:

> Nothing prepares you for the impact of taking on a miserable, angry teenager from a different background to your family. Our children were very generous in welcoming [the child] but he has found it hard to mix – and no report could have prepared us for this. We took in a teenager 250 miles from his home ground and no-one envisaged the problems this culture shock – hard northern town to small, middle-class Home Counties village – would have on [the child]. He is still struggling to adapt two years later. Also, we were not prepared for the lasting wounds [the child] still felt from being moved on from place to place. These show themselves in many ways including [the child] expecting us to get rid of him every time there is a problem. When he reversed the car into the house knocking out a porch support he expected us to show him the door. When we did not, he started to believe us. We wanted him to stay.

These adopters, like so many others who have written or spoken to us, display commitment to the adopted child despite all the difficulties. A single parent adopter who felt that she was given 'huge amounts of information about her [child's] behaviour' before meeting her, told us that the child had been considered unplaceable having spent five years in a children's home because she could not be placed with foster carers. The adopter felt that, whilst this prepared her some way for the adoption, she nevertheless found it

> ... much harder than expected. We are both doing great, but it has been at great personal cost to me. I feel that the local authority should have thought through the process better and feel that they should not expect you to hold

down a full-time job and be a single parent. Perhaps the adoption allowance should reflect this.

Problems understated or not recognised by the agencies

Amongst the disappointed group were a number of adopters who felt that their child's problems had been understated or not mentioned at all. Many of these commented that, in the absence of accurate information, they had simply had to 'learn as you go'. Others mentioned specific issues in the information they had received which was misleading, for example, over the level of the child's educational attainment. Thus one couple were told that their child could read and write, but when he was placed with them aged eight, 'we found he couldn't read a word'.

Another adopter wrote that:

> *The emotional problems were understated and her educational report from school was totally inaccurate. We were told she had settled well in school and was making good progress, but when she started her present school her new teacher said it was as if she had never been to school.*

Likewise an adoptive mother wrote:

> *We were told our child had 'developed into a happy, healthy child who was developing along normal lines and making good progress'. True, she was a happy child but she was extremely insecure which showed in an abundance of ways. She was not really developing along normal lines. She had behaviour problems which she still displays (although not as bad as before). We are now seeing a child psychologist to help us with regards these problems. She was definitely not progressing well with her school work. At five years of age she couldn't count to three, say a, b, c, or even identify a number or a letter. She didn't even know her colours. We have had to work very hard together with the school to help her attain the level she is today, which is still below average. We feel our child should have been encouraged and stimulated more in her previous foster home. She lived there for two vital years and academically she was not taught anything. We have made our feelings known to social services and this foster carer has since been removed from Social Services' list of foster carers.*

Yet another wrote:

> *The information given to us was brief, incomplete and seriously underplayed the effects of separation from her siblings in foster placements and the subsequent problems in reuniting them. It also ignored the consequences and facts about the widespread sexual and physical abuse encountered by [the child] from many members of her birth family. We felt that this was either known to social services or strongly suspected by them yet not discussed with us. A*

police investigation based on disclosures was later necessary. Educational ability was overestimated with her statement being out of date. Overall, I think that the information failed to give either a realistic or clear picture of [the child's] needs or the challenges we and our other children would face during the placement.

Being deliberately misled

Nothing hurts aspiring adopters more than the feeling that they had been deliberately misled. We quote from four separate replies.

Given that a child is said to be disruptive and seeks attention can give a wrong picture, unless it is also stated that there have been several place-ments, some only a matter of weeks, and some without any visits of 'getting to know you' sessions. This does not give a child a sense of belonging or of being loved and wanted, or any self worth. A natural reaction, therefore, is to 'get what you can' before you are moved. This created problems when the child was placed with us and he could not understand why, when major trouble was caused, we were not throwing him out but explaining that con-sequences must be faced and lessons learned. We felt that the agency did not make adequate support available to us at this time, leaving us to use our own knowledge and abilities to see us through the crisis.

After two years with us the children are undergoing stress therapy (the need for which should have been identified before placement) which shows them to be very disturbed. The agency insisted that these were two normal children and ignored all our calls for help, in fact making us feel it was in some way our fault. We have been extremely traumatised by the lack of preparation and support from the agency who have left us to struggle on alone.

If the educational psychologist's initial feelings are correct, our son may be suffering from a condition which is thought to have a genetic origin, and if social services had taken heed or acted upon some of the stories that the foster carer apparently told them, they would have discovered this fact some two years before we came onto the scene. Of the two years our son should have been attending school before he came to us, he had attended for less than six months in total – though the time was spread over the two-year period. Social Services apparently did not know this, and didn't seem to be particularly interested in why. They were happy to blame the foster carer . . .

[The child] had been in the care of more than 20 different carers. I was only informed about the longer term care which was five placements. She was presented as a child who was fairly stable, but this turned out not to be true. Many of her carers had given up in despair. I was not told about this until the

adoption broke down. [The child's] behaviour was extremely disturbed and included lying, stealing, bed-wetting, soiling – all the symptoms, in fact, of attachment disorder. I had received no information to expect any of this. She also regressed to a baby stage for about two months which I had not been warned about. It was impossible to take my eyes off her for one moment. She displayed very dangerous behaviour, for instance, in the kitchen when I was cooking. It was extremely difficult for a single parent to cope with this be-haviour. I could not relax even when she was in bed as she usually began to search my room for items to steal or break when she was upstairs by herself, or she would sing extremely loudly in a raucous voice for hours and hours, sometimes starting to do this at 5 a.m. She woke up very early and made sure she woke me too. I was exhausted and very unhappy from the moment the placement began until she left my house.

RESEARCH FINDINGS – SYSTEM

17 Agency Workloads

1   Introduction

The agency survey aimed to discover the scale and variation of adoption work in England and Wales. While this task was important in itself, it also reflected a fundamental question about what level of workload in adoption generally, and in respect to older children in particular, is necessary for agency viability. While we are not in a position to answer this question in this research (since it will partly depend on other factors in central and local governmental policy which we are not in a position to evaluate), it is important to flag it up as an issue and provide some relevant information and indicators which may aid its discussion and analysis. To explore this matter we needed, first, to establish the basis upon which agencies collected and maintained workload statistics for management information purposes, and second, to discover whether such data were compiled in such a way as to permit inter-agency comparison.

We knew from the reconnaissance phase of the research, in which we asked agencies to send us their most recent annual report (or any other reports relevant to adoption work, such as those prepared for social services committees or adoption panels), that the extent to which agencies kept up-to-date statistics, and the form that statistics took, varied considerably. We tackled this problem in the postal survey by first, asking agencies to state whether they compiled statistics and, if so, to indicate the most recent period covered. Second, we asked for data on numbers of children and families approved for adoption by agency panels, and the number of placements made by agencies in that year. As we explain in Chapter 6, we received replies from 115 agencies comprising 85 statutory agencies and 30 voluntary agencies.[1] These responses form the basis of this chapter.

---

[1] See Chapter 6, *Agency and Family Profiles*, paras 2 and 2.1.

2   Agency statistics on adoption work

In the postal survey, agencies were asked if they compiled statistics of their adoption work. While all 30 voluntary agencies indicated that they did, only 92 per cent of statutory agencies said they did. Of the seven authorities which could not positively say that they compiled statistics, five were district borough councils.[2] Thus, whereas compiling statistics of adoption work was almost universal in shire county councils (98 per cent), and common in inner/outer London borough councils (94 per cent), 19 per cent of district borough councils still need to develop this practice.

Even where agencies had some kind of system for compiling adoption statistics, there was variation in how statistical periods were defined. This hindered the construction of an accurate picture of adoption workloads. Agencies were asked to indicate the most recent year for which adoption statistics were available, and the exact period the statistics covered. Most agencies (71 per cent) defined their statistical year by the financial year (1 April–31 March), but a significant proportion (25 per cent) based statistics on the calendar year (1 January–31 December). There were no major differences between statutory and voluntary agencies in this regard. The remaining agencies, all statutory, defined their statistical year in alternative ways (e.g. October–September, July–June, etc.).

There was also variation in the degree to which adoption statistics were up to date. Bearing in mind that questionnaires were dispatched to agencies in September 1994, 56 per cent of agencies which compiled statistics each financial year had returns for the year ending 1 April 1994 (this figure was 64 per cent for voluntary agencies and 54 per cent for statutory agencies). Four statutory agencies, however, did not even have statistics for the year ending 1 April 1993. On the other hand, agencies which collected statistics on a calendar or alternative basis tended to be more up to date, with all such agencies, whether statutory or voluntary, having statistics for 1993 or later.

The above-mentioned variations need to be taken into account when interpreting the statistics provided in the forthcoming discussion about agency workloads in terms of children and families approved for adoption and the number of children placed for adoption.

3   Children approved for adoption

3.1   The national and regional picture

Statutory agencies were asked to indicate the number of children (*of all ages*) which were approved for adoption by their panel in the year specified. Overall, a total of

---

[2] It is to be noted that four of these indicated that limited statistics were available, but they were not collected systematically or with a specific focus on adoption.

2,036 children were approved by panels in the 79 agencies responding to this question. However, as illustrated in Figure 11, there was considerable variation in the distribution of referrals between regions, with almost half of the children made available for adoption coming from the Midlands and London and the South East.

Figure 11

Number of children approved for adoption by LAs: Regional makeup of approving statutory agencies

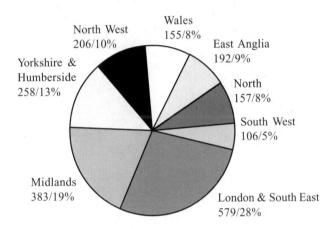

Source: Agency postal survey

Of course, this does not necessarily mean that agencies in the Midlands and London and the South East have the largest workloads in terms of the number of children referred for adoption. To answer this question, account needs to be taken of the number of agencies in each region. By dividing the number of children approved by the number of agencies in each region, we were able to estimate the average number of approvals made by agencies in each region (see Figure 12).

Although agencies in London and the South East approved the most children for adoption, as this region had the largest number of agencies to carry out the work, the mean average of agency approvals was fairly low, at only 21 children per year. By contrast, 258 (13 per cent) of the total number of children approved for adoption were approved by agencies in Yorkshire and Humberside, but since there were only six agencies in this region, the mean was much higher at an annual rate of 43 children per placing agency.

Figure 12

Regional adoption workloads: Average number of children referred for adoption by LAs in each region

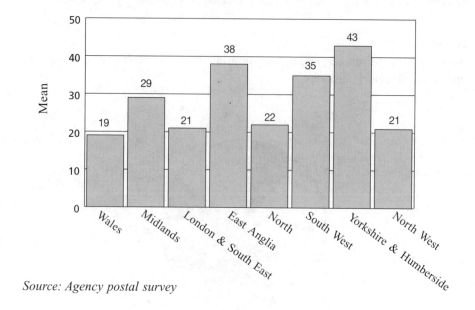

Source: Agency postal survey

3.2   Individual agency workloads

Statutory agencies

Analysing the statistics on an agency rather than a regional level, it can be said that 67 per cent approved under 30 children in a given year, but the picture is variable, with panels approving between 1 and 91 children for adoption. This to some extent reflects the type of agency. Of the 2,036 children approved for adoption, 1,311 (64 per cent) were approved by shire counties, 483 (24 per cent) were approved by district borough councils, and 242 (12 per cent) were approved by inner/outer London boroughs. While the overall mean was 26 per agency, it was 35 for shire counties, 21 for district boroughs and 13 for inner/outer London boroughs. Thus, shire counties typically approved nearly three times as many children for adoption as London boroughs.

As Table 24 shows, 28 per cent of London boroughs, and 30 per cent of district borough councils, approved less than 10 children for adoption in the given year. When agencies have such small numbers of children referred for adoption, questions are raised about their viability to provide an adequate service. Such small numbers may not merit specialist adoption workers to be employed by the agency, necessitating adoption work to be done by either generic child care social workers, or by specialists brought in from other organisations.

Table 24

Number of children approved for adoption by statutory agencies: comparing shire county, district borough, and Inner/Outer London borough councils

	Shire county		*District borough*		*London borough*		*Total*	
Approved 0–9	4	11%	7	30%	5	28%	16	20%
Approved 10–19	3	8%	7	30%	10	56%	20	25%
Approved 20–29	9	24%	5	22%	3	17%	17	22%
Approved 30–39	13	34%	1	4%	0	0%	14	18%
Approved 40 or more	9	24%	3	4%	0	0%	12	15%
(N. agencies providing data)	38		23		18		79	

Source: Agency postal survey

Voluntary agencies

The questionnaire asked voluntary agencies how many children (of all ages) they had matched or agreed to find adoptive families for in the year specified. This resulted in a total of 360 children: 43 per cent of agencies had matched or agreed to match 0–9 children, 39 per cent 10–19 children, and 14 per cent 20–29 children. Only one voluntary agency had matched or agreed to match more than 40 adoptive children. The mean average for the number of children on agency caseloads was 13. Thus voluntary agencies typically had half the adoption caseload of statutory agencies (with the caveat that the caseloads of statutory and voluntary agencies were defined slightly differently: data provided by statutory agencies concerned children approvided for adoption by their Panels, whereas the data proved by voluntaries related to the number of children for whom agencies had found, or agreed to find, adoptive families).

3.3 "Looked after" children approved for adoption

Local authorities were also asked to indicate how many of the children approved for adoption by agency panels in the given year were "looked after". This information was only obtained for 1,424 children. Of these, three-quarters of the children approved for adoption were looked after under a care order, and one quarter were accommodated under the Children Act 1989, s 20. Table 25 below shows the regional breakdown of these figures.

The largest proportion of children in care who were approved for adoption was in the Midlands (23 per cent of the national total of 1,071), and the largest proportion of accommodated children approved for adoption was in London and the South East (25 per cent of the national total of 353). However, Wales and the northern regions in England had the highest proportion of children in care in relation to the children accommodated. In the North, Yorkshire and Humberside, and the North West, at least 80 per cent of the children approved for adoption were in care.

Table 25

Summary statistics for looked after children approved for adoption by statutory agencies in each region

	Children under care order		Children accommodated		Total
Wales	87	68%	41	32%	128
Midlands	251	76%	78	24%	329
London and South East	230	72%	88	28%	318
East Anglia	48	67%	24	33%	72
North	126	80%	31	20%	157
South West	67	63%	39	37%	106
Yorkshire and Humberside	212	83%	44	17%	256
North West	50	86%	8	14%	58
Total	1071	75%	353	25%	1424

Source: Agency postal survey

A similar enquiry about the previous status of children was made of voluntary agencies. Of the 360 children on voluntary agency caseloads nationally about whom information was given, 269 were looked after by local authorities, with 225 under care orders, and 44 accommodated. The regional breakdown of looked after children for whom adoptive families were found by voluntary agencies is shown in Table 26 below.

Of the national total, the largest proportion of looked after children being found adoptive families by voluntary agencies was in London and the South East (33 per cent). However, children in care constituted over 90 per cent of the total children being found families by voluntary agencies in the Midlands and East Anglia, and all children in the South West.

Table 26

Summary statistics for looked after children being found families by voluntary agencies in each region

	Children under care order		Children accommodated		Total
Wales	8	62%	5	38%	13
Midlands	46	98%	1	2%	47
London and South East	74	82%	16	18%	90
East Anglia	33	92%	3	8%	36
North	13	72%	5	28%	18
South West	20	100%	0	0%	20
Yorkshire and Humberside	11	73%	4	27%	15
North West	20	67%	10	33%	30
Total	225	84%	44	16%	269

Source: Agency postal survey

4 Families approved for adoption

The questionnaire asked agencies how many applications by prospective adopters were approved by their Panel in the most recent year for which they had statistics. Overall, a total of 1,932 applications from prospective adopters were approved by agencies responding to this question, comprising 1,539 approved by 77 statutory agencies and 393 by 28 voluntary agencies. Figure 13 below shows the number of families approved in each region.

Again, far more families in London and the South East and the Midlands were approved for adoption than in other regions. However, on average, agencies in these regions approved 15 and 25 families respectively, whereas the figure was higher for Yorkshire and Humberside, and East Anglia, where agencies typically approved 31 families per year (see Figure 14 below).

The number of adoptive applicants approved by agencies varied considerably. Three agencies (two statutory and one voluntary) approved no families in the most recent year for which they had statistical information, whereas one agency had approved as many as 67. The mean average for statutory agencies was 20, compared with 14 for voluntary agencies. However, the modal average was considerably lower: most statutory agencies approved between 10 and 19 families in one year, whereas most voluntaries approved under 10 applications from prospective adopters (see Figure 15 below).

However, the number of families approved for adoption also varied according to the type of statutory agency. Shire county councils typically approved the most prospective adopters per year, with 71 per cent approving more than 20 families in

Figure 13

Number of families approved by statutory and voluntary agencies in each region

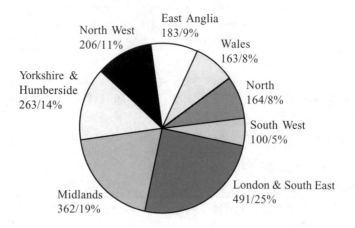

Source: Agency postal survey

Figure 14

Regional adoption workloads: Average number of families approved per agency in each region

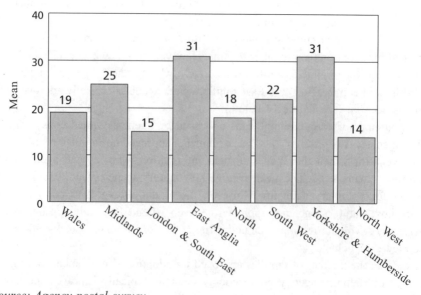

Source: Agency postal survey

one year, although there was one county council in Wales which had approved no families in the last year for which statistics were available. District borough councils tended to approve between 10 and 19 applications (48 per cent), whereas London boroughs mostly approved under nine (59 per cent) (see Figure 16 below), with one approving none in the given year. The mean average for each type of agency was 28 for shire counties, 15 for district boroughs and nine for inner/outer London boroughs.

Figure 15

Number of families approved by agencies in their most recent statistical year: comparing statutory and voluntary agencies

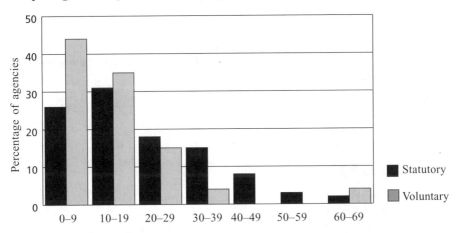

Source: Agency postal survey

Figure 16

Number of families approved by statutory agencies in their most recent statistical year: comparing types of statutory agencies

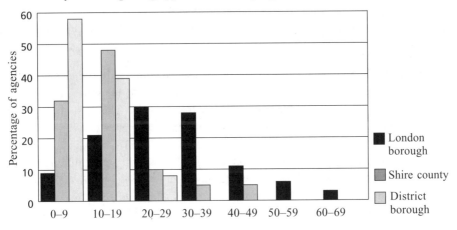

Source: Agency postal survey

345

4.1   Comparing the approval of families with the approval of children

A comparison of the figures on families approved for adoption with those children shows a close match (within 6 per cent) in all regions except London and the South East, where there were 579 children approved for adoption but only 491 families – a difference of 15 per cent. Only three regions – Wales, the North, and Yorkshire and Humberside – approved more families than children in the last year for which statistics were available.

On a more micro level, 27 of the 76 statutory agencies (36 per cent) which provided figures for both children and families approved by their Panels, approved more families than children for adoption in the most recent year for which statistics were available (see Figure 17).

Figure 17

Comparing the number of children approved for adoption with the number of families approved for adoption by each statutory agency

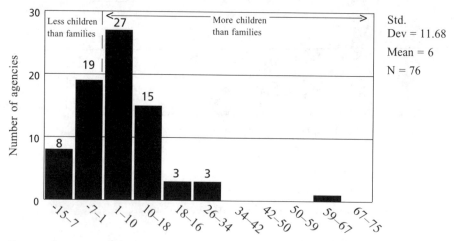

Source: Agency postal survey

More specifically, 19 (25 per cent) approved up to seven more families than children, and eight (11 per cent) approved seven or more families. At the other end of the spectrum, one agency approved 66 more children than families. This raises questions about how placements were found for these children. The agency may have relied heavily on inter-agency placements for their children. Alternatively, the agency may have had a substantial backlog of approved families waiting for children, or the agency could have delayed matching while more parents were approved, both of which have implications for the support of families and children. However, most agencies approved between 1 and 10 more children than families, with a mean of six more children made available for adoption in the year specified.

4.2   Details of families approved for adoption

The questionnaire asked agencies to state how many applications were approved for families which included at least one prospective parent who was black, Asian or of mixed heritage. In total, 180 of the 1,932 approved applications were for minority ethnic families, which constituted 9 per cent of the total.

Minority ethnic families constituted 7 per cent or under of the total number of families approved in each region except London and the South East, where the figure was more than twice as high at 18 per cent. Statutory agencies approved 120 applications from minority ethnic families, which was 8 per cent of their total workload, and voluntary agencies approved 60, which was 15 per cent of their total workload. Twenty-six (36 per cent) statutory agencies and 10 voluntary agencies (37 per cent) had approved no applications at all for minority ethnic families, whereas one voluntary agency had approved as many as 10. More commonly, agencies approved one or two, with the mean average being two for both statutory and voluntary agencies.

Agencies were also asked how many applications their Panel approved for gay/ lesbian prospective parents. Only three were approved in total (0.2 per cent), all of whom were by two county councils in the Midlands.

Finally, agencies were asked how many applications were approved for prospective parents living without a partner or spouse. In total, 96 applications were approved for single parent applicants, which constituted 5 per cent of the total number of applications approved.[3] Seventy-three were approved by statutory agencies, and 23 by voluntary agencies. Fifty-five (56 per cent) agencies in total – 43 (59 per cent) statutory agencies and 12 (46 per cent) voluntary agencies – had approved at least one application from a single parent in the given year. While 44 agencies had not approved any single parents, three statutory agencies and three voluntary agencies had approved as many as four in one year. There was no significant difference between statutory and voluntary agencies in the proportion of approvals for single parents in terms of their overall workload, the mean average number being one per year.

---

[3] This finding was higher than in *Pathways to Adoption* in which it was found that only 2 per cent of court applications for adoptions were by single applicants (Murch *et al*, 1993, at para. 2.6) but less than in our family sample where the figure was 9 per cent, see Chapter 6, para. 3.2. See also the analysis of our interview sample at Chapter 6, para. 4.2.

5   Children placed for adoption

Hitherto, the focus of this chapter has been on agency workloads as defined by the number of children and families that agencies approved for adoption in one year. However, it is also important for any analysis of workloads to look at matching, or more specifically, the number of placements made during that period. Thus, the agency questionnaire also asked agencies to provide data on the number of looked after children placed with adoptive families in the specified year. This enabled us to build up a picture of the adoption workloads in terms of placements as distinct from approvals, and how this varied between regions and agencies. Moreover, a focus on placements enabled us to extract more detailed case information about the children who were being placed for adoption, in relation to their age, ethnicity, and whether or not they were placed in sibling groups. In addition to the data provided by agencies on this topic, we will also refer to data from the family questionnaire on occasions in this section because it also helped to build up a profile of the types of children who were being placed for adoption, and the types of families they were being placed with.

A total of 1,557 children were placed for adoption in the year specified. The regional distribution of the children placed for adoption is shown in Table 27. The largest number of placements was made by agencies in the Midlands, which also had a relatively high average workload of 20 looked after children placed for adoption per agency, superseded only by Yorkshire and Humberside where the average was 26 per agency.

Table 27

Number of looked after children placed for adoption in each region

	Sum		*Mean*	*Minimum*	*Maximum*	*N. Agencies*
Wales	144	9%	16	0	53	9
Midlands	362	23%	20	0	79	18
London and South East	321	21%	9	0	36	34
East Anglia	80	5%	10	0	28	8
North	188	12%	17	0	46	11
South West	100	6%	17	6	41	6
Yorkshire and Humberside	207	13%	26	0	78	8
North West	155	10%	10	0	31	15
Total	1557		14	0	79	109

Source: Agency postal survey

Of the 1,557 placements that were made, 1,304 (84 per cent) children were placed by statutory agencies and 253 (16 per cent) were placed by voluntary agencies.[4] The mean average number of children placed by statutory agencies was 17, but only eight were placed by voluntaries; 11 (13 per cent) statutory and seven (23 per cent) voluntaries made no placements at all, so their adoption workloads in that year consisted entirely of approving and preparing new cases, and supporting placements made previously. At the other end of the scale, 12 agencies placed more than 30 children for adoption, the most placed by any statutory agency being 79 and by any voluntary agency 40. In short there is significant variation between individual agencies in the number of children they placed for adoption.

5.1   Age of children placed for adoption

Agencies were asked at the outset of the questionnaire whether they place children aged five years and over for adoption. All 85 statutory agencies returning the questionnaire indicated that they did, but three of the 30 voluntary agencies stated that they did not. However, all agencies, including the three agencies which only found families for babies and infants, were required to give details about the age of children placed for adoption in the most recent year for which they had statistics (as well as their age and the number of siblings in each placement). Agencies provided the age of the child in 1,525 of the 1,557 placed, which are shown in Figure 18.[5]

Figure 18

Number of children placed for adoption in each age group in the most recent year for which statistics were available: Comparing statutory and voluntary agencies

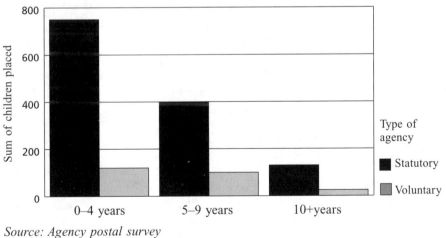

Source: Agency postal survey

[4] Some cases may be duplicated here, i.e. those children approved by statutory agencies in the sample for whom families were found by voluntary agencies in the sample.

[5] Ages of 32 children were not provided by statutory agencies – these cases were excluded from the analysis. Again, the absence of this information raises the issue of the reliability of statutory agencies' records of adoption work and their value for management information.

Eight hundred and eighty (58 per cent) placements were of young children (babies and infants aged under five): 753 (86 per cent) of these were placed by statutory agencies and 127 (14 per cent) were placed by voluntary agencies. The mean average number of younger children on the caseloads of statutory agencies was 10, and four for voluntary agencies, compared with a general mean of 17 and eight respectively.

Focusing on the older children placed for adoption, 645 placements were made for children aged five or more, constituting 42 per cent of all children placed for adoption: 519 (80 per cent) were placed by statutory agencies, and the remaining 126 (20 per cent) were placed by voluntaries. Of these children, 479 (74 per cent) were aged between five and nine years, and 166 (26 per cent) were aged 10 or over. The mean number of older children placed for adoption was six per agency. The mean average number of older children placed for adoption by statutory agencies was seven, compared with four by voluntary agencies. However, if we turn to the differences between statutory and voluntary agencies in terms of their overall placement workloads, we can see that older children constituted 41 per cent of statutory agency caseloads, whereas they constituted 50 per cent of voluntary agency caseloads. Thus voluntary agencies tended to be more involved with the placement of older children than younger children relative to statutory agencies, especially children aged 5–9 years.

Table 28 below shows the regional distribution of older children placed for adoption by agencies in their most recent statistical year. The highest concentration of older children placed for adoption in terms of the overall number of children placed in one region was in Wales, where they constituted 49 per cent of the children placed for adoption. The lowest concentration of older children was in the North West, where they formed 30 per cent of the total placements made by agencies in that region. On average, agencies in East Anglia and London and the South East placed the smallest number of older children, at three and four per agency, whereas agencies in the Midlands and Yorkshire and Humberside placed the most children on average, at 10 and 11 per year respectively.

5.2   Ethnicity of children placed for adoption

Agencies were also asked to state the ethnicity of looked after children placed for adoption. We knew from the annual reports sent to us in the reconnaissance phase of the research that agencies classified the ethnicity of children for statistical purposes in different ways. Thus, to be as accurate as possible, we asked agencies to state the ethnic origin of each child placed for adoption, and to be as specific as possible in doing this. We then reclassified the answers given into five main ethnic groups.[6] We found that, of the 1,557 children placed by adoption agencies, 1,330

---

[6] We used the ETHQ-2 classification tool for this purpose, as advised by the Department of Health.

(85 per cent) children were white, 42 (3 per cent) were black African-Caribbean, 35 (2 per cent) were Asian, 134 (9 per cent) were of mixed heritage, and 16 (1 per cent) were from "other" minority ethnic groups. In other words, 227 (15 per cent) of the total number of children placed had minority ethnic origins, the majority (59 per cent) of whom were mixed-heritage.

Table 29 below shows the regional distribution of children placed for adoption by their ethnic origins. Minority ethnic children constituted between 3 per cent and 20 per cent of the total number of children placed for adoption in each region. Agencies in London and the South East placed the largest proportion of minority ethnic children, followed by the Midlands and the North West.

Table 28

Number of looked after children aged five or more placed for adoption in each region

	Older		*Mean*	*Minimum*	*Maximum*	*N. Agencies*
Wales	71	49%	8	0	31	9
Midlands	165	46%	10	0	49	17
London and South East	132	41%	4	0	14	34
East Anglia	25	31%	3	0	10	8
North	65	41%	6	0	28	10
South West	40	40%	7	2	13	6
Yorkshire and Humberside	91	44%	11	0	32	8
North West	47	30%	3	0	12	15
Total	636	42%	6	0	49	107

Source: Agency postal survey

Table 29

Ethnicity of children placed for adoption: summary statistics for each region

	Black	*Asian*	*Mixed*	*Other*	*Subtotal*		*(Total)*
Wales	0	2	10	0	12	8%	(144)
Midlands	8	6	38	7	59	16%	(362)
London and South East	31	14	41	7	93	29%	(321)
East Anglia	0	1	5	0	6	8%	(80)
North	0	1	6	1	8	4%	(188)
South West	0	0	3	0	3	3%	(100)
Yorkshire and Humberside	1	1	21	0	23	11%	(207)
North West	2	10	10	1	23	15%	(155)
Total	42	35	134	16	227	15%	(1557)

Source: Agency postal survey

Figure 19 below shows the number of minority ethnic placements made by statutory and voluntary agencies which provided information about the ethnicity of children placed for adoption (117 agencies in total). Of the agencies which provided data, 25 (32 per cent) statutory agencies and 14 (47 per cent) voluntary agencies placed no minority ethnic children for adoption at all. The largest number of minority ethnic placements made by any agency was 14. Indeed, for this statutory agency, *all* placements made in that year were of minority ethnic children. More commonly, agencies tended to place two minority ethnic children in one year (this was the mean for both statutory and voluntary agencies).

However, if we look at the difference between statutory and voluntary agencies in terms of the total number of children placed by them, we can see that, as with older children, minority ethnic children constitute a greater proportion of total placement workloads in voluntary agencies than they do in statutory agencies. Whereas 174 (13 per cent) of the 1,304 children placed by statutory agencies were black or minority ethnic children, the proportion of those placed by voluntaries was much higher at 21 per cent (53 of the 253 children placed).

Figure 19

Number of minority ethnic placements made by agencies the most recent year for which statistics were available: Comparing statutory and voluntary agencies

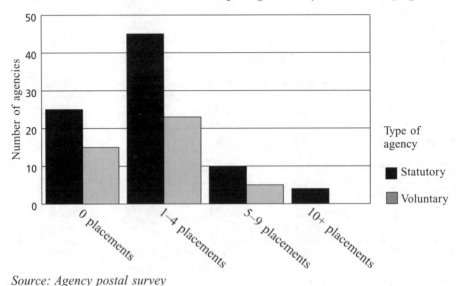

Source: Agency postal survey

5.3   Sibling groups placed for adoption

Agencies were also asked to indicate whether each "looked after" child placed for adoption was placed individually, in a sibling group of two, or in a sibling group of three or more. Unfortunately, we did not receive replies to this question for 204 placements. This could be a reflection of incompatibilities in the way some agencies keep records or compile statistics (e.g. whether a placement of three siblings consists of one or three placements), or errors in the way the questionnaire was completed. However, it was clear from the data relating to the remaining 1,353 children, that a significant number of children were placed in sibling groups: 496 children – 37 per cent of the total number of children placed for adoption – were placed in sibling groups. More specifically, 25 per cent were placed in sibling groups of two, and 12 per cent were placed in groups of three or more. Table 30 shows the regional distribution of children placed in sibling groups.

Table 30

Number of looked after children placed for adoption in sibling groups in each region

	Children in groups	Regional total	National total	N. Agencies
Wales	38	44%	6%	7
Midlands	146	45%	24%	16
London and South East	108	38%	21%	32
East Anglia	23	26%	7%	8
North	68	37%	14%	11
South West	19	22%	6%	6
Yorkshire and Humberside	59	32%	14%	8
North West	35	29%	9%	14
Total	496	37%	100%	102

Source: Agency postal survey

Of the 102 agencies providing information, only 23 (32 per cent) statutory agencies and 14 (47 per cent) voluntary agencies made no sibling group placements in the given year. However, looking at the number of children placed in sibling groups in relation to those placed individually reveals that 35 per cent of the children placed by statutory agencies and 43 per cent of children placed by voluntary agencies were in sibling groups. Thus sibling groups tend to constitute a slightly larger proportion of the workload of voluntary agencies than statutory agencies.

The picture of sibling group placements provided by the family postal survey showed even more of a difference between statutory and voluntary agency workloads.[7] From these data, only 27 per cent of those adoptive families in the sample approved by statutory agencies had a sibling group of children placed with them, compared with 51 per cent of the families approved by voluntary agencies. Furthermore, only 4 per cent of families approved by statutory agencies had more than two siblings placed together, compared with 19 per cent of families approved by voluntary agencies (see Figure 20).

Figure 20

Percentage of families which had children placed with them individually or with siblings: comparing families approved by statutory and voluntary agencies

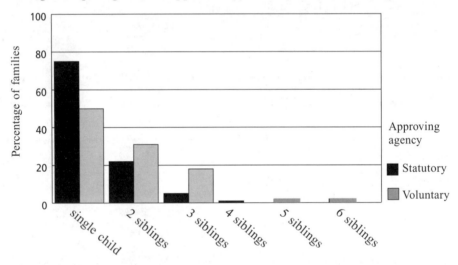

Source: Family postal survey

6   Concluding points

The evidence from our agency questionnaire highlights the considerable variation in general adoption workloads, in relation to both the number of children and families that panels approved for adoption, and the placements made by agencies in their most recent year for which statistics were available. The region in which agencies are located, and the type of agency are important considerations in explaining this variation. Indeed, some general patterns have emerged which can be summarised here. First, it seems that the voluntary sector tends to be more involved with children

---

[7] See also Chapter 6, *Agency and Family Profiles*, para.3.2.

who are more "difficult" to place, in that older children, minority ethnic children, and sibling group placements represent a greater proportion of their overall adoption workload than they do of the overall statutory agency workload.

Secondly, it is extremely worrying that not all agencies kept adoption statistics and that those which do vary in their method of compilation: these two findings alone must call in question the reliability of national adoption statistics. There is an urgent need for a standardised form of data collection for management information purposes, using the same categories and statistical periods, so that adoption work can be compared across agencies. This would have several distinct advantages. First, it would enable research to establish a more accurate picture of the level of adoption nationally, and make clear comparisons about adoption work between agencies and regions. Second, it would enable agencies to monitor their own work in relation to other agencies. Third, it would provide an important source of information about levels of adoption work, and expertise in certain kinds of placement, for other agencies and interested parties.

The Social Services Inspectorate has already stressed the importance of this, and has suggested a framework for adoption management reports (SSI, 1996, Appendix B). For example, the framework suggests that, for all children for whom adoption is the likely plan, reports should document their age, gender, ethnicity, legal status, and whether the child is alone or one of a sibling group. We would also argue that, within this, standardised categories need to be used to permit cross-comparison between agencies. This issue arose especially in relation to ethnicity when analysing adoption workloads in this research.

However, there are also other, more hidden factors which vary between agencies in the way that workloads are defined. These need to be made explicit if there can be any attempt to standardise statistics on agency workloads. For a standard system to assess agency workloads, we identified at least four variables which need to be clarified at a national, regional and agency level:

Case load   the number of children and families referred to the agency and the key characteristics of these children and families

Case flow   the turnover of cases and how long each case takes to complete

Case closure when a case ceases to be a case, e.g. whether cases remain open after the adoption order

Case division when a case is one case, i.e. whether a sibling group of three children is counted by the agency as one case or three.[8]

This chapter has looked at "case load" but not at the other factors, although some of them will be discussed in the following two chapters. While each of these variables

---

[8] In addition to the caseload variables, there is a strong case for recording systematically the annual number of placements known to the agency which disrupt, and to standardise or at least make explicit how disruptions are defined.

is determined by many other factors, such as the number of people available to do the work, the time they are able to devote to it and the priority given to adoption work, it is necessary to look at them if services are to be reorganised in any way.

18 **The Impact of Agency Resources**

1   Introduction

This chapter is concerned with the impact of resources of staff (including their experience, skills and availability) and finance on adoption services. Agency resources, though not expressly included in the agency questionnaire, were frequently referred to in comments made by agencies and families in the postal and interview surveys. The general message from agency workers was that there seems to be little understanding, on the part of senior managers and politicians, of what a time-consuming and resource-laden activity adoption work is. Much work goes into finding the right family for children, and then supporting the placement to ensure that it is a success - all of which has resource implications.

It was evident from the process of negotiating help from agencies at the outset of the research that many local authorities, and a few voluntary agencies, were experiencing difficulties regarding staffing.[1] One agency worker told us that, not only was she under extreme pressure, but her morale was so low that she could not cope with the anxieties that the questionnaire might generate by highlighting the shortcomings of the service.

As we shall see, some of these messages have filtered through to families, with many appreciating the difficult circumstances in which social workers try to meet their needs and those of their children. This can make families ambivalent about asking for support. While they know that they need to get a particular service for the sake of their child or the placement, they may find it difficult to be persistent in requesting that service because they know how much pressure the local authorities are under. However, there were also many families (and indeed workers) who argued that deficiencies in the adoption service are not always due to pressures of time and money, but a reflection of the skill and professionalism of workers, and the structures that are in place to guide them in their tasks.

This chapter focuses on how adoption work and the provision of support are affected by the resources available to agencies as outlined below:

---

[1] Nearly all those agencies who were unable to respond, or whose response was late, explained this with reference to the agency being too short-staffed, or that workers did not have enough time, or that no suitable person was available due to staff sickness.

- It explores issues raised by families and agencies about staffing and the availability of workers to undertake adoption tasks and support families;
- It looks at areas of work which are affected by the other duties of practitioners, and examines the availability of specialist staff to work with minority ethnic children and families;
- It considers the issues related to funding services for adopted children and families, such as specialist support and general post-adoption support, and the types of services which are restricted when money is tight;
- It discusses skills and expertise of adoption agency staff, outlining the areas in which skills are lacking, and how agencies seek to improve these through staff training and supervision; and
- It examines the links between agencies, viewed as a potential resource in meeting families' needs.

2   Availability of social work support

As we have seen in earlier chapters, a number of families felt that they were not well supported in terms of the time that social workers were able to allocate to their case, particularly during the critical early stages of placement. For example, one family had been given a list of telephone numbers but this did not compensate for the lack of visits.

Another adopter, drawing on her experience of adopting two children at different times through the same adoption agency (as well as working for Social Services herself), stated that these pressures had become worse. Whereas she was well-supported the first time she adopted, the second time she was not. She said:

> Social workers just don't have the time now. They don't have the money. We have only been in it five or six years but things have changed out of all recognition just in those few years. And where the social worker could drop everything and come to see us in the early days if we had a problem, that's just not possible now. They are so overworked, so understaffed, that I would hate to be doing it now to be honest.

One adoptive family said that if they had relied solely on the help of the child's allocated social worker, the necessary work would not have been done because their child was only one of hundreds in care, and 'they are all overworked and understaffed'. They added that the placement would have almost certainly disrupted without the help of the Principal Officer at the child's previous residential unit. She was able to dedicate much time to the child, whom she had known for five years, and therefore was a good source of support for the family. However, as this input was not sanctioned by the agency, the Principal Officer did the work voluntarily.

One family did not see a social worker for two-and-a-half weeks after four children were placed with them for adoption. They had telephone contact, but this was not enough to help them deal with the problems they were having. The adoptive mother explained that 'there was a sense of they're placed and they're safe and obviously they've got more serious cases still to be dealing with'.

These cases illustrate that the limited availability of staff can result in families not having the general social work contact that they require, or in specific pieces of work not being done. They also indicate some of the reasons why social workers are not available to dedicate the time required to support the placement: their *adoption* caseload can be too high; or their *general* child-care caseload may be too high, with other types of child care work taking priority over the adoption tasks.

It is striking that all families who commented on the lack of social worker contact did so in relation to *local authority* social workers, especially those with case responsibility for the children. No one complained about the insufficiency of social work support in voluntary agencies.

Staff availability will now be examined in relation to adoption caseload, the impact of other work, and how agencies make special provisions for specialist staff to work with black and minority ethnic children and families.

2.1   Adoption caseload

Work which could be improved with more staff

Post-adoption support

Many practitioners complained that there were not enough workers to give a satisfactory amount of time to each adoption case. The most prominent issue here was the lack of support *after* the adoption order. For example, one district borough council which made about 25 placements a year had a team of five practitioners with one more post being created. That team had to recruit, assess, support and review all foster carers and adopters. Consequently, 'by and large the cases are closed' after the adoption order 'because we don't have the staff to follow it through for ever'.

Many statutory agencies stated that they offered very little post-adoption support because they just had not got the staff. But this experience was not confined to local authorities. One voluntary agency commented:

> *Many of our families that are in need ring up and say, 'Please come,' and we will go. It doesn't matter how long after the order it is, we will do that. But where we are in difficulties is really in doing any sort of lengthy piece of work with people. Doing a few visits isn't a real problem but there are four social workers, three of them are part-time, and I'm the fourth and I've not really got a lot of time for social work. So the social work time we have in the agency is very limited.*

Thus, ongoing work after the adoption order is often sacrificed. In particular, supervised face-to-face contact was an issue for one agency, which was considering training volunteers to supervise contact after the adoption order.

Working with birth parents

Many agencies wanted to develop their work with birth parents, including counselling, because they saw the value of doing this work from within adoption and fostering teams rather than in area social work teams.[2] However, here too, they felt that there were not enough resources to take on this extra work; an issue which particularly concerned practitioners in district borough councils. For example, one such told us:

> *Maybe the person who's been involved in the removal of that child isn't the best person to help that birth parent with the process of adoption. But the idea of bringing in another worker is met with horror in my agency because they see it as more pressure on limited resources. So I think the chances are that it just won't get done. We won't help birth parents cope with relinquishing – whether that's voluntary or involuntary – we won't help them.*

And in another agency:

> *If we had more staff, then I would like to see the counselling of the birth parents from here as well. I don't think we ought to be taking over responsibility for the children but certainly it's a very skilled job counselling birth parents especially when the district social worker's involved. They'll see them as the child's social worker so that seems an issue, especially if it's a contested case.*

A third worker stated that, while on a few occasions they had the opportunity to do individual work with birth parents, it was an area in which they were sadly lacking. She continued:

> *I think that the level of support and preparation of birth parents is something that sooner or later we've got to address, but it's quite difficult to see it as an area that needs money spent on it, and we just haven't the man hours to do it.*

On the other hand, voluntary agencies are perhaps better resourced to do this work, in terms of experience in birth parent counselling.

---

[2] As other studies have observed, counselling and preparing birth parents can be difficult if there has been a dispute between the parents and the authority (e.g. SSI, 1992a, p. 25). In such circumstances, counselling may be more effective if provided by someone other than the children's social worker (SSI, 1997, pp. 41-42). See also Murch *et al* (1993, p. 245).

Controlling the number of adoption cases

Several voluntary agencies commented on the problems caused by fluctuations in caseload. For example, the number of children waiting for placement in one agency (which had only been in existence for five years) jumped from 3 in one year to 15 the next. The agency felt that there were not enough staff to do this work properly. By contrast, another voluntary agency actually approached the Welsh Office to pull out of adoption because of their fall in caseload: they had only made one placement (of a sibling group) in one year. They continued to do adoption work, however (section 51 counselling and tracing),[3] and in the next year the number of placements made went up again. Clearly, fluctuating caseloads can have implications for the availability of staff to provide support.

However, as one statutory agency worker noted, local authorities can have even less control over caseloads. She pointed out that whereas voluntary agencies can limit how many cases they take on, and thereby control caseloads so that the availability of social workers to support families is not undermined, local authorities cannot:

> *I think being a local authority, by definition, makes it more difficult because as a local authority, our first response invariably is to the demands of the here and now. It's the kids, it's the child protection, it's the fostering services, it's all those things. It's the fact that we cannot, again as a local authority, say, 'Well we work with this many cases,' in the way that voluntary agencies say, 'Well, we can't take on that many'.*

In fact, voluntary agencies are more likely to worry about the opposite problem – not having enough adoption cases – without which many agencies might cease to exist. As one worker stated, 'Basically, if we don't "sell" the families we approve – we would go down the chute'.

Controlling the flow of adoption cases

Size of adoption caseload and availability of staff can also influence the order and pace of the adoption process. As one voluntary agency worker told us, this may affect preparation days in relation to assessment, and whether or not they are optional:

> *In some authorities that's obligatory. But we can't make it obligatory really because we are only placing perhaps 12 children a year. So you're either going to keep people waiting until you've got enough people for a group or somebody's interested in a child and you're going to get on with the assessment anyway. So it's not possible. A local authority will wait until it's got a number of people and then have preparation groups and then do a*

---

[3] Discussed below at para. 2.2.

general assessment. But we won't wait if there's people. We'll get on with it.

Another agency stated that the home study (part of the work which results in the completion of Form F) may start at any time during the preparation course depending on the availability of staff. In other words, staff availability may affect the timing of assessment in relation to the preparation of adopters. It can also affect who is allocated what tasks. For example, one county council worker said that 'the question of who does the preparation of the child is decided at the planning meeting and it's an area for negotiation – basically who is available to do the work. Not always who is the most appropriate.'

2.2   The impact of other work on the adoption service

Child protection and crisis work

In many local authorities, adoption is not separate from child protection work, in that the same social workers are expected to carry out both tasks, particularly in statutory agencies with small adoption caseloads. Take the following example:

> *There isn't such a thing as an adoption team - that's the first thing! [This county council] doesn't have a specialist adoption service. It is an adoption agency which has an Adoption Officer, which is myself, who also does child protection work. I'm a Child Protection Co-ordinator. That's my day job, if you like, and I deal with as much as I can on the adoption work.*

While merging adoption work with child protection may be understandable in agencies which have very few referrals for adoption (the above county council had only one in 1993), it also occurs in local authorities which have larger adoption caseloads. For example, one district borough council had 14 children referred for adoption in 1993 and all this work was done in children and family teams whose main workload was child protection.

Observations have been made elsewhere that 'child protection is eroding services for disabled children' (SSI, 1995c, p 8). This report claimed that many local authority workers viewed child protection as dominating child care services: 'The role of social worker as investigator and corrector of abuse is eclipsing the broader based child welfare role' (p 9).[4] We touched on a similar issue in our research, where many practitioners commented on how adoption work is often accorded lower priority than child protection work.

---

[4] For a similar conclusion, see also Murch *et al* (1993, pp 118–9).

Drift[5]

When a worker has responsibility for child protection in addition to adoption, the former has higher priority and a higher profile. As one worker noted:

> *By the time you're at that stage in the process of the child moving towards adoption, it's a low priority because of the crisis work, the child protection work.*

Once children have been placed safely in foster homes and it has been decided that the plan for those children is adoption, their foster placements will often be allowed to drift[5] while finding temporary residence for other children takes priority. An adoptive mother was told by her social worker that, because there are so many children and not enough staff, once children are out of a dangerous environment and in a foster home, they are left until next week, but 'next week never comes'.

Inadequate direct work with the child

Failure to undertake direct work with children[6] in order to prepare them for adoption is another consequence of the low priority attributed to adoption work in some social services departments. This work is usually the responsibility of children's local authority social workers, who are sometimes inexperienced in adoption or are unable to do the work because of other pressures on their time.[7] As one voluntary agency worker told us, direct work is often not done as a consequence, and this can cause problems for the placement:

> *I think that the way things are going in local authorities these days there just doesn't seem to be the time to do thorough preparation. Unfortunately with some of the older children that we've placed, we have been told that the work has been done but find once the placement has been made that it hasn't. And we really have a struggle when the child is initially in placement to get over some of the issues that we feel would have been helped enormously by a more thorough preparation time for the child [. . .] Because we find that the preparation work with older children, particularly with those who have been abused, is very, very time-consuming. It takes more time than local authority*

---

[5] See also para 2.2 post for organisation factors contributing to drift.

[6] See also Chapter 9, *Preparation and Training*, paras 2 and 3 for a fuller account of the many problematic issues which this research has uncovered concerning the preparation of children for adoption – a crucial issue highlighted in the recent Court of Appeal decision, *Re M (Adoption and Residence Order)* [1998] 1 FLR 570. See also paras 2.3 and 4.1 post.

[7] Ideally, direct work begins when the child is first taken into care or accommodation, although at that point it is often not clear that the child will be placed for adoption. Once adoption has become the plan for the child, a specialist worker in adoption, working alongside the child's key worker, may help to ensure that adequate direct work with the child to prepare them for adoption is completed to a satisfactory level.

> *workers seem to be able to give to it at the moment, and it is so important that it's done thoroughly.*

However, practitioners in local authorities also recognised this shortfall, and some directly linked this to the impact of child protection work on fieldwork teams. For example:

> *The fieldwork division tends to involve itself more or less with child protection issues and doesn't get involved in doing any direct work with children. So often, children will have been in care for say three years, they transfer into this team with no life story work done, no understanding of why they are where they are. They end up here in a very adult-focused service, where their childhood needs if you like and their long-term needs haven't really received the attention they require.*

A county council worker told us how her department had been directed to give priority to child protection cases and assessments for court, 'so the preparation of a child for adoption, a weekly session that was promised, all the life story book work that was to be done, hadn't in fact gone ahead'.

Irreconcilable roles [8]

Adoption work and child protection work are arguably irreconcilable in some respects. Workers responsible for both types of work are likely to feel a double-edged pressure: they have to give crisis work higher priority, yet if they fail to dedicate time to do work with children who are being adopted at the right time, they or others may have to 'pick up the pieces' later. For example, one practitioner said:

> *I still deal with quite a bit of child protection and if something crops up on child protection everything else goes by the board. In my view, that is wrong. But I accept it's urgent, child protection. But so is a five-year-old who's stuck in a fostering placement who equally needs that attention to get them moved on.*

And another:

> *I just have this feeling that social work is focusing much more on protecting children or at least removing children from situations where they're in danger and just leaving them. I think if you do that then when you come to place the child, unless you've dealt with all the stuff about why they're not at home anymore, they display all the same patterns in their new family.*

Furthermore, since both roles involve different ways of approaching the child's situation, i.e. looking at the short-term or the long-term needs of the child, social

---

[8] See also Murch *et al* (1993 p 126).

workers may have difficulties in making the necessary role adjustments, or they may be skilled and experienced in one role and not the other. As one worker put it:

> There's always going to be some perhaps inexperienced, perhaps less motivated workers who maybe enjoy the bulk of child protection work but are not particularly good at the long-term stuff or seeing situations for longer.

Organisational factors

Some local authorities attempted to reduce these problems through internal departmental reorganisation.[9] One county council, which had a higher than average number of children approved for adoption (51 in 1993), distinguished designated child protection workers from general child care workers. Even so, one worker told us that, 'I still find that adoption issues and family placement issues are always put on the back burner: there's something more urgent which needs doing'. Thus, even though roles were separated in staff designations, the reality was that general child care workers continued to be mostly involved in child protection duties.

The potential for child protection and crisis work to impede adoption work depends very much on the management of workers. In particular, staff morale and motivation are often linked to the status that management attaches to an area of work. This will affect how adoption is seen in relation to fostering and child protection:

> I think that the priority that your employer gives to the service that you provide has a filtering down impact on the service that's offered really – not only in terms of time, staffing, resource, visits, provision, but also morale because it does give you a feeling that the service that you're involved in offering isn't valued by the agency. I think it does have a hugely filtering down effect really. Then for children to be even the lowest in the pecking order within your own division is disconcerting. I'm sure it's the case in a lot of authorities but here because it's so small, it's so much more visible. It feels like all the effort is going into child protection and not into work with children and families.

If differences in priority are coupled with differences in skill and motivation, adoption cases are even more at risk of not receiving the attention they need by children's social workers who are also responsible for child protection.

One practitioner suggested that some agency structures are better than others in preventing drift. In her agency, adoption work was done by outpost workers managed in area social work teams, which meant that the centralised adoption team

---

[9] For the impact of local government reorganisation and recurrent internal departmental reorganisation see also Chapter 19, *The Organisation of Adoption Services*, para 4.

continually had to chase up children's social workers to keep adoption cases moving:

> *I also think that because the workers are generic we do have some battles.*
> *They do the preliminary work. They get the child settled in a foster home. They*
> *decide that adoption is the plan. Then it all stops because there's other things*
> *that become a priority. And so we spend our time saying, 'Come on, come on.*
> *You've got to get this done you can't leave this child sitting there. Yes, we*
> *know they're safe, but their long-term future's not safe.'*

The practitioner linked this situation to decentralised management, and suggested that if the outpost workers were managed centrally by someone with an adoption focus, this could ensure that the progress of the child's placement for adoption would not be hindered by conflicts about other priorities.[10]

Management structure also affects the deployment of resources for adoption services. In another agency, a worker explained that his department had a highly devolved structure and that district managers were responsible for everything. In his view, this structure resulted in adoption being given lower priority than fostering, since managers were 'willing to put time and resources into fostering because their social workers are desperate for foster homes on their own patch'. This is less likely to occur in relation to finding adoptive families for children. He continued:

> *There is a problem that adoption doesn't get the same priority as fostering. A*
> *part of that is to do with the fact that developing adoption resources is likely*
> *to be meeting the needs of some other manager and not your own staff.*

Developing skilled and experienced adoption practice

It is clear that when workers in local authorities have other priorities, they cannot be immersed in adoption the same way as, say, workers in voluntary agencies. Some practitioners suggested that direct work may be better done by voluntary agencies precisely because they can dedicate more time to preparing the child because there are fewer competing priorities. They argued that immersion in adoption work is important to develop the skills necessary to prepare children adequately. To quote one voluntary agency worker:

> *Having worked in all sorts of settings, I think that that kind of immersion in*
> *an adoption team (that's what it felt like) is how you actually learn about the*
> *process of adoption. You don't learn that from being in what is basically a*
> *child protection team because there are different priorities.*

Alternatively, some practitioners suggested that, at the very least, preparing children should be done by specialist adoption workers in local authorities rather than area

---

[10] See also Chapter 19, *The Organisation of Adoption Services*, at para 2.1.

social workers. Yet there seem to be obstacles to this: first, it was argued that local authority adoption services are "adult focused" in that they may not have the necessary skills to work directly with children; and second, even where there are such skills in adoption teams, they are not utilised. One practitioner explained that while there were several workers in her adoption and fostering team who had special skills in working with children, such as getting at their feelings about things through play, they are not permitted to do this work 'because they are meant to be working with the carers'.

However, it is also clear that links with child protection and crisis work should not be lost. Some practitioners said that experience in this work informs their work in adoption, and should be viewed as a resource in adoption work. Thus one explained, there is a 'terrific pressure' of children languishing in placements which 'obviously isn't a pressure for voluntary agencies'. She continued:

> *I think that sometimes means a lot of energy is taken out of our service on the fostering side. But I still think that I would rather have it that way really because it does keep you rooted in reality about what's coming in, and the sorts of kids that you are getting, and the problems that they have got. It puts it in a context that isn't so rarefied, that adoption becomes not actually realistic. That's the sort of worry that you have. You can actually talk to adopters with confidence, I think, about the sort of grot really that there is. You get a real feel for the sorts of problems that they are going to have to cope with. So that's the other side of it, a kind of balance really. Neither I suppose is ideal, but I'd rather have it this way than things just being completely encapsulated in adoption and adopters only.*

A voluntary agency worker similarly told us that she valued working with social workers involved in child protection because it informed the adoption service:

> *I personally have found it very helpful to have worked with children who are in the care system right now and to be working closely with people who are actually removing children from families and the child protection work and seeing that intake work going on. That's where I've just come from. I think it informs this work.*

Without that, adoption work could become somewhat of an 'ivory tower'. Thus the dilemma is whether child protection should be undertaken by those who also do adoption work, or linked to it in other ways. For example, a specialist adoption worker could be linked to those children needing direct work when adoption becomes the plan for the child.[11]

---

[11] Indeed, a specialist team could be linked to children needing direct work *wherever* they are in the system.

Section 51 counselling and tracing

Several agencies told us that birth records counselling and requests for tracing relatives constituted an increasing area of work which imposed resource difficulties. One county council worker stated that more than 50 per cent of adopted children wanted information about their birth families.[12] Other agencies told us that birth parents were increasingly contacting the agency because they wanted to find out about their child who had been adopted – some wanting contact – and this was consuming significant resources. One agency in particular was experiencing difficulties, having inherited responsibility for the cases of two former voluntary agencies – some 30,000 files which people were always trying to access. One worker suggested that the increase in such enquiries was due to growing media coverage about tracing relatives, while another suggested that, 'everybody knows that if you are adopted you can trace your parents from the age of 18'.

Tracing work is far from straightforward, and resolving dilemmas about what information should be passed on can have a significant impact on resources. One practitioner talked at length about how tracing work had got out of control, with agencies responding to the work in very different ways:

> It's horrendous! We are now receiving an increasing volume of requests to find brothers, fathers, siblings, mothers. Our powers are restricted by the adoption agency regulations and there are limits to what we can do. We have a voluntary sector making up its own rules (and that's no criticism). For instance, The Children's Society have now decided they will contact adoptees direct and we are asked to complete something called a non-disclosure agreement which seems to me to breach adoption agency regulations and I can't get myself past that fact. There is nothing in the Bill about it, because I checked, and yet we have no code of ethics. We have private agencies cropping up here and there and one of these days somebody is going to come the most awful cropper. Because of the pressure you are under, people are in a constant state of extreme anger, anxiety and distress. The information you have is dynamite.

Despite the resource implications of section 51 counselling, many workers recognised its importance, not only for the children and families involved, but also for informing future adoption practice: they saw this post-adoption work as an important means of feedback. Indeed one voluntary agency worker argued that since voluntary agencies have been involved in this work for so long, they are better equipped to prepare children and families for adoption:

> I feel very strongly that that has to influence the practice of today and unless you're doing those two bits of work that almost follow in a cyclical basis, I

---

[12] Cf the earlier findings on tracing birth families by Stafford (1993, pp 4–5).

think that adds to your expertise too. So people who are out in teams, out in social services departments probably don't know what section 51 counselling is. If they're not hearing what people are saying, how can they prepare people who are coming through now – either in respect of adopters, children who are likely to be adopted, and birth families?

This worker illustrated how counselling had informed current work with adopters and birth parents *during* the adoption process:

I think we're learning now from birth mothers of the past who are coming back to us. This has an effect on how we work with birth parents today: How much more involved they are in the process; how far they are involved in choices about couples; how far they are involved in looking at what sort of attributes they want and they're going to have a choice of maybe two or three couples that they can pick; they meet prospective adopters who are going to have their child. We have an information exchange going on. Last year I think we had about 180 exchanges of information.

However, many agencies had difficulties in keeping up with this kind of work. In particular they found it difficult to balance this work with other priorities, such as finding families for children.[13] As one worker said:

I've just had pointed out by the clerk to me today that we've got eight on the waiting list and at the moment I've got nobody with any space to take them. And of course, people who are making that first foray and waiting for counselling, it's taken them a long time to get to that stage and they find it very difficult when we say, 'Well, we're going to have to wait now perhaps another couple of months'. But that kind of work, although the adoption workers would love to make it a priority, in departmental terms has to be fitted in. It cannot take over from the needs of today's children. So that's a problem.

One agency, where adoption and fostering teams were managed at an area level, told us that due to higher priority work such as fostering, section 51 counselling was undertaken by people almost on a voluntary basis, but that a new system had to be devised if enquiries continued to snowball:

I'm trying to get a separate arrangement for post adoption. I'd love to see a post-adoption unit because we've got all the section 51 counselling which at the moment is done by all sorts of staff, effectively – not in theory – but effectively in their own time, as an addition to the job that they are doing

---

[13] The low priority of services for adopted adults, as well as the lack of monitoring systems and defined quality standards, were observed in a recent SSI report (1997, para. 9.10).

because they are interested. But they don't often get any time allowed out of their other jobs to do it. That's just about containable and is going on at a level that we've had for the last few years. But what we've got now is a lot of birth parents coming to us and saying, 'I had this baby 25 years ago,' which we didn't have a few years ago. We've always had a trickle but we've got a flood now.

A practitioner in another agency felt that they kept abreast of all post-adoption work compared to other agencies (some of which allocated this work to students in social work due to the backlog of work). This seems due to the helpful provision of having allocated a half-time Post Adoption Worker in each of its five district teams. Before these posts were created, social workers had to squeeze section 51 work between all other fostering and adoption work. So instead, it was decided that post-adoption workers would do all section 51 work, in addition to enquiries by birth relatives, contact issues and supporting "wobbly" adoptions.

Bureaucracy

While families tended to explain the low availability of staff in terms of under-staffing and high caseloads for individual social workers, two workers in the same voluntary agency identified increasing bureaucracy as a factor in this. The first pointed out that bureaucratic duties increasingly eroded the time allocated to adoption-related tasks in local authorities:

More and more the whole bureaucracy seems to be taking over. You spend more time in meetings and discussing procedures and I don't know whether this is a sort of response to the fact that there aren't the same number of people to do the work – perhaps there's a feeling of some safety in this. But there seems to be a diminishing amount of time actually to do the work.

A similar point was made by the other worker, referring to her own experience of working in a local authority:

Because we don't have a double dose of the bureaucracy that the local authority would have, we are clearly providing a service which is being bought by local authorities. That feels a lot cleaner to me. I came from a local authority where I was Service Manager and it was just passing the buck the whole time. In fact, I forgot really what I was supposed to be doing because it was meeting after meeting to argue all kinds of silly, silly points the whole time.

2.3   Staff sickness and turnover

A prominent issue arising from family interviews was the importance that families attributed to the continuity of social workers involved in adoption work.[14] This in itself can be thought of as an important element of support for families. Social workers who knew them and the children they were adopting were more able to anticipate and respond to their needs.[15] One adopter clearly saw the value of the low turnover of staff in her agency's adoption unit. She adopted children through two county councils and she stated that she was 'very lucky' with the second 'because the people in charge have been there for so long'. The two senior members of the home finding team had been there for 20 years. The adopter knew most of the home finding team and the Principal Social Worker, and she said that, 'If we ever needed anything – equipment, help, support, anything at all – they've been absolutely wonderful'. However, this situation is comparatively uncommon in relation to social workers with case responsibility for children, since they rarely stay in one position for long periods of time. For example, one family told us that, over two years, the child had had three different social workers from his local authority.

Inadequate direct work with children

The family just referred to felt that as a result of various staff changes at the child's local authority, including the post of Team Manager, their adoptive child fell "victim" in that he received insufficient preparation for the adoption. This was also identified as a problem by social workers. One suggested that areas of direct work which focus on emotions, such as dealing with grief and loss, are particularly difficult to achieve in child care teams due to a high turnover of staff:

> That's the kind of work that takes time and takes knowing a child well, building up a relationship. That's difficult if field workers are either changing a lot, which they do, or they are being asked to set their priorities elsewhere.

Indeed some workers believed that work with children ought to be done by adoption and fostering staff who typically stay in post longer than children's social workers:

> A big problem for this authority – we've had a huge staff recruitment problem. Staff tend to stay longer in places like the adoption teams. This is, I suppose, why I would rather see child work done within the adoption team because I think there's a better chance of that than in the mainstream team.

---

[14] See also Chapter 4, *The Older Child's Status Passages,* para 1.
[15] See also Masson, Harrison and Pavlovic (1998, p 44).

Inadequate knowledge of the child and his/her background

The information the above-mentioned family had received about their child was inaccurate: 'It presented a very difficult child with serious behaviour management problems – the child is nothing like that.' Again, the adopters saw this as a consequence of staff changes at the agency:

> I really felt they didn't know anything about the child. I think that the problem could be that the whole family he came from had had a series of social workers, so nobody actually knew the file or knew the family properly. It kept being passed on all the time. Over the time that I started to hear of the child to the time when I actually adopted him I was on my third social worker. So it makes it very difficult. You're always retracing your steps.

She believed that things could have gone badly wrong had it not been for her own determination and the fact that she had a good social worker (from a voluntary adoption agency) who supported her throughout the adoption process.

This highlights the problem that when a child's social worker changes, vital knowledge about the child's current needs and background can be lost. This can be especially problematic in inter-agency placements because the child's social worker is the family finding agency's key link to any case information they will need in order to prepare and support the child's new family. As one worker explained:

> If that social worker leaves, that creates problems for us in that we don't really have anybody definite who can tell us the history of the child if we need to know more about it – who knows the child personally.

Other problems associated with staff turnover

A child can regress because of a change of social worker, especially if the change occurs near a critical transition, such as when the child goes to live with the adoptive family. As one worker said:

> There's no doubt that a change of social worker does have an effect on the child because just like moving from one placement to another, it puts the child back a little bit and the child regresses. Similarly, a significant person going out of a child's life does have an effect on him or her. Nobody can actually measure that in any way, but we know from the child's behaviour that it's having an effect.

In contrast, one worker pointed out that while a low turnover of staff may be positive for children and families, it can be problematic for social workers. She explained that the longer a worker remains in one agency, the more their caseload continues to accumulate:

Given the nature of the children that are being placed nowadays, a lot of them don't ever go away. So the longer a worker is in the team, the more work they have, because they end up with a huge backlog of work they constantly carry with them as well as all their current work.

2.4 Staff who work with minority ethnic children and families

Our agency postal survey suggested that 9 per cent of families approved for adoption included at least one parent who was black, Asian, or of mixed heritage.[16] The questionnaire also asked agencies whether they made special provisions in choosing staff to work with black or minority ethnic children and/or families. Nearly half (46 per cent) of the agencies stated that they had no provision (47 per cent of statutory agencies and 44 per cent of voluntary agencies). Four per cent of both statutory and voluntary agencies indicated that they were unsure. Only 35 per cent answered "yes" to this question, with another 15 per cent answering "other", indicating that they had a more limited provision. Of these, several explained that they were developing this provision, perhaps 'seeking to use sessional time to be part of the approval'. Others said that *recruitment* of staff reflected the ethnicity of clients, rather than the *allocation* of staff to cases. They had staff of a variety of ethnic origins, but there was no specific provision which allocated them exclusively to children and families of the same ethnic group. One agency stated that while they would allocate minority ethnic staff in principle, this was rather ad hoc in practice, due to a 'highly devolved management structure'.

Predictably enough the presence of this provision seems directly related to the number of minority ethnic families[17] the agency approved for adoption (see Figure 21 below). Whereas only 57 per cent of those agencies which had approved 1–4 families had some kind of provision, this rose to 77 per cent for agencies which approved between 5–9 families, and to 100 per cent for agencies which approved 10 or more minority ethnic families for adoption. Furthermore, the type of statutory agency seems to be relevant: shire county councils had the poorest level of minority ethnic provision at 43 per cent; district borough councils were slightly better at 50 per cent; whilst inner/outer London borough councils were most likely to have a minority ethnic provision, at 61 per cent.

---

[16] See Chapter 17, *Agency Workloads*, at para 4.2.
[17] A "minority ethnic family" was defined as where one or both parents were black, Asian or of mixed heritage.

Figure 21

Agencies with staff provision for minority ethnic children and families

By number of minority ethnic families approved

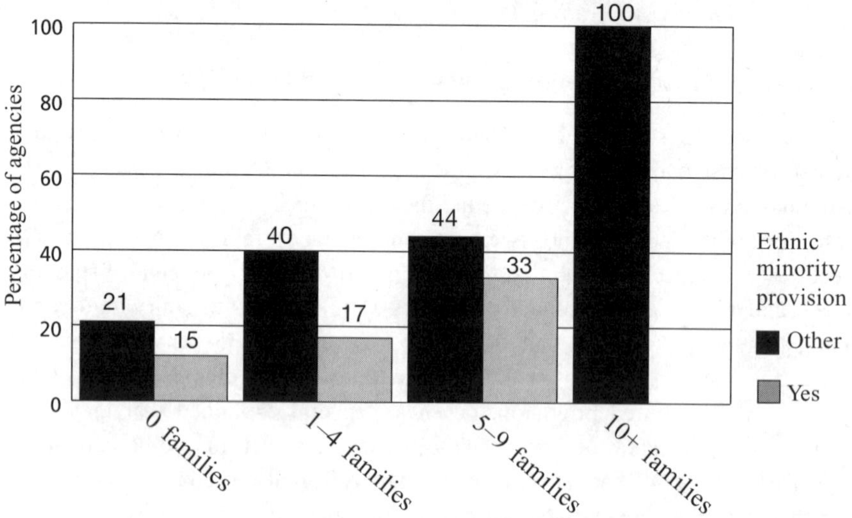

Source: Agency postal survey

Employing minority ethnic workers as permanent staff in the adoption team

Agencies were asked to give further details about their provision and to state the ethnic origins of workers where possible. With regard to allocating workers with a similar ethnic background to clients, our data showed that only 23 (42 per cent) of the 55 agencies with a minority ethnic provision appeared to employ social workers from minority ethnic groups (there was no significant difference between statutory and voluntary agencies). While several agencies did not state the ethnicity of these workers, 15 agencies stated that they had at least one black worker, and 12 had at least one Asian worker doing adoption work: only two agencies indicated that they had workers of mixed heritage.

The number of minority ethnic workers available to work with children and families was a problem identified by many agency workers. One explained that their adopter preparation groups had always been of a very even mixture ethnically, but that the staff were all white women, which the agency identified as problematic. This was particularly frustrating for one voluntary agency which wanted to expand its work with minority ethnic families but felt that it could not do so without having minority ethnic members of staff, or at least access to them.

Many agencies had sought to recruit staff from minority ethnic groups, and some had applied for funding for this under section 11 of the Local Government Act 1966.[18] One agency stated that they were awaiting funding for this, and three indicated that they had tried to recruit minority ethnic staff but had experienced some difficulty in filling these posts. These difficulties need further investigation.

There is the further problem of keeping the workers once they had been recruited. One adoption officer explained that they had only one black social worker in the whole of the county. Black social workers would move from areas like Birmingham and London thinking that it would be a nice place to live, but then would experience racism: 'It is a very xenophobic county'. The officer stated that the high turnover of black workers may also be due to frustration with policy statements which seemed to go no further than anti-discrimination policy and anti-racist training.

Another problem voiced by agencies was that the number of different ethnic groups serviced by the agency was too large to be reflected in staffing. Hence, although 42 per cent of agencies employed at least one minority ethnic worker, they could be working with families of many different ethnic groups. As one statutory agency worker said:

> *Another side of the problem is the mixture of races that we deal with here. So we can't say, 'We've got a huge Afro-Caribbean population or we've got a huge Bangladeshi population'. We've got the population but not in those volumes. I think that's why we have to get creative; get off the tram-line.*

Another adoption officer pointed out that simply employing a single minority ethnic worker does not guarantee access to all religious communities that might be needed by an agency:

> *We have employed a section 11 worker[19] for a full year and he has not got me one referral out of that group. So getting in culturally into that is in through the community. They're skilled workers, the section 11 workers. He's not a fool by any means - he has a degree and he's a well educated man. But because he has a different religion (he's a Hindu), he has just not been able to get into the Muslim community. It's been an absolute waste of a post.*

In other words, a worker's "race" may not be as significant as their religion or their language. Indeed, one statutory worker reported that while their agency had a minority ethnic provision, it had not been used because all children referred for adoption had been white and that the Welsh language was more of an issue in that particular local authority.

---

[18] Under this provision local authorities can claim from the Secretary of State the cost of making special provisions in the exercise of any of their functions because of the presence in their area of substantial numbers of immigrants from the Commonwealth whose language and customs differ from those of the majority community.

[19] Viz one appointed under s 11 of the Local Government Act 1966, for the explanation of which see note 18 above.

Employing minority ethnic workers on a sessional or voluntary basis

This evidence suggests that even where there are minority ethnic workers in the adoption agency, there is sometimes a need for alternative provision, such as involving appropriate people from outside the agency. One agency, which dealt with a mixture of ethnic groups, was beginning to explore the idea of involving volunteers from various communities for this purpose:

> We are terribly, terribly short of black workers and I would have thought that one would have the aspiration – if you cannot get a black worker then maybe we have to use the expertise of Barnardo's in generating black volunteers. Because I really think that if you're a birth parent and you've given your kid up to adoption to this white-dominated agency – not to have a single, understanding black face to link to must be awful.

Another agency had appointed a black worker sessionally who was a local university student. She had remained with them for eight years and was responsible for identifying the needs of black children referred to the agency and for finding black families. However, these alternatives did not seem widespread. More commonly, agencies "borrowed" minority ethnic workers to work with the child's social worker. These workers could be from other teams in the local authority, Inspectors, or "bought" from outside (such as workers from other adoption agencies and BAAF). Only eight (15 per cent) agencies which considered themselves to have minority ethnic provision stated that they did this.

While this practice may be good for accomplishing certain tasks, such as assessing children and families, life story work, and planning placements, these workers are not necessarily available for children and families for ongoing support throughout the adoption process. This was noted by one London borough council worker who considered her agency "lucky" because it had many people working for the authority who were linked to community work with different ethnic groups and who were keen to get involved in adoption where appropriate. But while this was a useful resource, the practitioner believed that the agency also needed experienced black family placement staff. The fact that the team was an all-white group was perceived as problematic because the agency had many black families to whom they provided support. This view was shared by a voluntary agency worker who employed sessional black workers, but had none as permanent members of staff.

Training and consultation for white workers

Six (11 per cent) of the agencies which had a provision in allocating staff to minority ethnic children and families did not appear to employ any workers who themselves had minority ethnic origins, either on a permanent or sessional basis, to work directly with children and families. Instead, these agencies explained their provision in terms of using consultants to advise on issues of "race" and ethnicity, or emphasised the experience of white workers in working with ethnic minorities, and specialist training, such as "race awareness". These agencies sought advice and consultation from a range of bodies, such as specialist units in local authorities (e.g. Black resource teams, Jewish Manchester Social Services), race equality officers, and even minority ethnic guardians *ad litem*.

In summary, 52 per cent of voluntary agencies and 50 per cent of statutory agencies had some kind of minority ethnic provision. Nevertheless, at least 47 (26 per cent) of the 180 minority ethnic families who were approved by agencies in our sample in one year, were approved by agencies which stated that they had no provision. Furthermore, of those agencies which had some kind of provision, only 42 per cent employed minority ethnic social workers for these purposes, 15 per cent brought in workers from elsewhere to work with the children's social worker, and 11 per cent used consultants to advise on ethnicity issues or relied on white social workers who had extensive experience or training in working with minority ethnic clients.[20]

3   Funding services to adopted children and their families

This section considers issues raised by families and agencies in connection with funding services to adopted children and families.

A practitioner told us that 'with budgets tightening', some agencies had decided not to pay adopters' legal fees. Indeed, one adopter told us that the agency advised them to get legal aid to go to court and apply to dispense with parental agreement to the adoption. The agency knew the adoptive father was unemployed so the family would get legal aid, and this would save departmental funds. The adoptive mother stated, in relation to this, that:

> *Everything now with fostering and adoption is money. They deny it to the hilt, but it was all to do with money . . . They're running out of cash very fast, and so for them to actually take everything to court would cost them more money.*

Inadequate funding was seen to restrict other kinds of work in adoption, including recruiting adopters. One family we interviewed had already adopted one child, but when they approached the same agency to adopt another, they were kept waiting and then finally, after four years, they were turned away because the agency could not afford to assess them.

Most of the funding issues centre around specialist support, such as psychotherapy and general post-adoption support.

---

[20] Cf. SSI, 1997, para. 5.5.

3.1   Funding long-term or specialist support

Identifying the need for specialist support

Family interviews suggested that many adopters were well aware of the significance of the adoption order in terms of the support they could expect from the placing or family finding agency. More specifically, they believed that if the placement needed any form of support which involved the local authority spending money, this needed to be done or agreed before the order, even though problems may not arise until afterwards. Some agencies tried to overcome this problem by using adoption allowances to secure funds for families if specialist support was required after the adoption order:

> *If a placement is made and, for instance, it's one of our children and we know that there might be an issue in relation to counselling later on, then we are very much using the adoption allowance situation where you can have agreements in principle. So if we feel that maybe the child's not ready yet or the situation has not warranted any – what I would call very detailed counselling – then they may get an agreement in principle that the child may need counselling at some point in the future, and we're willing to fund that counselling at some point in the future. And that is being used a lot more, not just by us – by everybody.*

This means that the child's potential needs have to be identified early on which may not always be possible.

Battles between families and placing agencies

Funding psychiatric help seems to be a provision which is unavailable to families when local authority budgets are tight, even when the need becomes apparent before the adoption order. For example, one boy was assessed by a psychologist at a local hospital as needing psychotherapy twice a week. The psychologist wrote to the child's local authority informing them of this. However, they refused to pay for the support because 'money was tight' – the family would have to pay for it themselves. In response to this, a battle ensued between the family and social services, with the adopters taking their complaint higher each time. Eventually the local authority agreed to pay for it once a week. This all happened before the adoption order, when the local authority still held parental responsibility for the child.

Another family told us that the placing agency had agreed that the child needed therapy but were delaying organising it. The adopters believed that the agency was waiting for the adoption order to come through because then they would not have to pay for it. The adopters had to take their request for specialist help to the Director of Social Services before they were able to get the service they required:

> *They were saying, 'Yes, [the child] needs therapy,' and they were hanging out*

and hanging out. The reason again is finance. Because once she was adopted
we would have to pay. I wrote a very strong letter to the Director of Social
Services stating that I didn't think that this was on. The child needed this
therapy now. In order to save money in the future she needs her therapy now.
I wasn't just an over-anxious Mum. I'd been through this with several other
children before and I knew when a child needed help. And eventually I got it.
We were told she could have just six months, at one hour a week for six
months. But we got it.

In another case, the family needed support after 12 months of placement (before the adoption order). Yet despite the fact that the agency had warned them that this was the most likely time that they would need support (i.e. after the "honeymoon period") none was forthcoming. The only support the family were able to obtain was from the child's previous residential unit. While this support was clearly valued by the family, as it almost certainly saved the placement from breaking down, the child's local authority refused to pay for it.

Many families and voluntary agencies spoke of local authorities 'trying it on' in terms of not funding support. Often, authorities will informally agree that specialist support is required, but when it comes to organising it, they say that they cannot fund a service because the money is not there. However, if pressure is continually applied by families or allied professions they will often find the money from somewhere.[21]

Battles between placing and family finding agencies

Several voluntary agencies noted the reluctance of many local authorities to pay for specialist psychotherapeutic help. One voluntary agency had a particular difficulty with a London borough when a child had to go to hospital. The borough did not seem to understand that the child was adopted (they treated the adopters as suspected abusive birth parents) and it was very difficult to get the authority to fund the services required. In fact, we were told that if it had not been for the persistence of the hospital in arguing how much the child needed their help, he probably would never have got it.

Another voluntary agency worker told us of a child who had been placed with one of their families and who had a lot of problems which needed specialist residential help without which, in their view, the adopters would not have been able to cope. They recommended "sharing" the child, so she could be "residential" during the week, and go home to her adoptive family at weekends. The child's local authority social worker agreed with this and recommended it to her director, who rejected the arrangement. In the experience of this voluntary agency, the occasions

---

[21] See Chapter 14, *Financial and Practical Support*, at para 2.4.

when local authorities over-ride their recommendations nearly always come down to resources and funding.

Short-sighted priorities

One voluntary agency worker attributed the lack of funding for specialist support to the agency's practice of reacting to crises once they have happened rather than preventing them occurring in the first place:

> *Specialist workers still do some good work, but what happens now is that they're the very last resort after the disruption, and then a particular local authority will regard it as 'there's no way out of this, we'll have to spend the money'. And the shame of it is if it had happened earlier on . . .*

In addition, pressures on local authorities to stay within their annual budgets enforces a short-sighted view of adoption funding. To quote a voluntary agency worker at length:

> *But there's no-one in social services that looks at three year budgets! We have to look at three year budgets otherwise we don't get approved! Local authorities can't look beyond the end of their nose. £12,000 in this financial year means that they're £12,000 down. It doesn't actually indicate that that £12,000 could be paid for in years 8, 9, 10, 11, 12, 13, 14 up to 18 and they don't see that! They see £12,000 in the debit column in that year. But what they don't see is the £90,000 in five years time or the £400 a week bed that we've got to have in an emergency at 4.30 p.m. on a Friday afternoon that no other provision will provide because they know people will pay to get it out of their hair. I find it extremely frustrating that local authority purchasers just can't see beyond annual figures. Until they do that I actually feel that agencies like us are in jeopardy.*

Refusing to fund specialist support seems one way in which local authorities can cut corners in order to save departmental funds. For example, a voluntary agency worker told us that her agency used to do a lot of preparation work for children as part of the inter-agency package for statutory agencies in its consortium, but the demand for this work had dwindled. She felt this was a reflection on the budgets available to local authorities.

Finally, there are often disagreements in local authorities about whether long-term or specialist work deserves funding or not, perhaps especially in teams where adoption is under the remit of an area manager. For instance, one county council practitioner told us about a case where a social worker was doing life story work with a child but this was stopped 'because a certain manager didn't agree that resources were being spent appropriately'. This was despite the fact that the work was markedly benefiting the child. For example, the child used to rock her head violently in her sleep. After six months of direct work this behaviour ceased, but when the work stopped the head rocking apparently started again.

3.2   Funding general post-adoption support

It is evidently becoming increasingly difficult for agencies to fund their growing post-adoption work, particularly in relation to contact. Besides paying for travel costs for face-to-face meetings, contact was an area of work that we were told demanded more and more staff time. As one agency worker explained, if agencies are required to monitor and review the contact needs of children, this has funding implications – 'its not a no-cost piece of work'. It could include social worker visits to three or four different sets of people, which then needs to be written up.

In response to increasing post-adoption work, one agency wanted to provide a post-adoption worker in each district with administrative support, who would be responsible for letterboxes and the like. This was shelved because balancing the budgets was given priority:

> Where are you going to get your hours from? We haven't got hours. We're having to carry this huge vacancy factor at the moment – we're trying to balance the budgets. So every time somebody leaves they don't get replaced. It's just bad news at the moment. We've just got nothing and we know that for the next financial year (in two weeks' time) the budgets are standing still. They're not even having inflation increases put on them. So they're going to be exactly the same as they were last year. So there is absolutely NO development whatsoever. Yet we're expected to provide the same level of service with less resources. Crazy!

One practitioner told us that her agency and others in their local consortium wanted to develop a post-adoption service, but 'it's been hit on the head so many times because of funding'. But even when such services were set up, they could not be assumed to be permanent. One agency was helping to fund the West Midlands Post Adoption Service until 1996, but they did not know what would happen thereafter, 'because obviously within this financial climate it's difficult to say we can remain financially involved with anything for very lengthy periods'.

Another agency described how their children and families used to get help from the Manchester Post Adoption Service, but now that the agency no longer makes financial contribution to the service, they are turned away. The issue here is that families approved while the service is being funded may be under the impression that they can access good post-adoption support. Yet when they seek to use it several years down the line, they can find that the independent service is no longer available to them, and that their local authority has no comparable service.

Other problems associated with developing post-adoption services were also noted. One agency worker stated that because they were in the 'early days' of post-adoption issues, 'We haven't seen yet the full panoply of what this is going to mean over time for the agency for ongoing help and I do think that we are ill-equipped at this moment to deal with those things'. Instead, they respond in an ad hoc way. Another practitioner commented on how the allocation of resources in adoption do not necessarily keep pace with changing models of adoption. As one adoption agency manager stated:

> *Part of the problem is that the managers have got to fund these things. When they were social workers there was no such thing as an open adoption, or post-adoption services. So they take a hell of a lot of convincing that this is not some fad.*

Voluntary agencies also face problems around funding post-adoption support. While they may get charitable funding for post-adoption services for those adopted through the agency as babies, because it is 'easily identifiable', we were told that it is not readily available for older children and their families. This means that although voluntary agencies, on the whole, are willing to undertake post-adoption work, it needs to be funded by the local authorities who looked after the children before their adoption. And because they are working with all kinds of local authorities across the country, they find their willingness to finance post-adoption support 'enormously variable'.

Indeed, at the time of our field work, the Consortium for Voluntary Adoption Agencies was proposing that, from April 1996, a standard fixed fee would be attached to the interagency fee to address post-adoption support. This would pay for 'a sort of core menu of services which are fairly basic services and not long ongoing,' such as post box, telephone advice and short-term counselling. But the problem with this is that many local authorities already see the inter-agency fee as prohibitively expensive in relation to their budgets.[22]

4   Staff skills, training and supervision

4.1   Lack of skill and understanding

Direct work with children

Several adopters told us that children's social workers were unskilled in direct work with children. For example, one said that although the children's social worker had sympathy and anxiety for the children, she did not spend enough time doing direct work with them. After the placement, the children had disclosed previous sexual abuse. The adoptive mother felt that social services must have at

---

[22] See para 5.2 below for a discussion of the use of voluntary agencies.

least suspected this, but evidently this problem had not been addressed. The work that *had* been undertaken suggested that the social worker's understanding was superficial, and did not properly get to the roots of the problem. The adopter suggested that this social worker, like many others, lacked training in dealing with sexual abuse.

Experience in adoption

Other adopters emphasised the inexperience of some social workers in adoption, and their lack of understanding of the issues, for example, how it differed from fostering.

> *She thinks she has the right to treat us like foster parents in her employment. That's why she's failed to do things like ask us to be involved in giving the children stuff from her mother. She's not acknowledged that – that this is a permanent relationship and it's not for money. I think they should have special training to be able to look at the difference.*

Similarly, another adopter stated that improvements needed to be made in relation to the 'lack of openness and honesty in the process' and in 'treating the people who are adopting as equals'.

Lack of understanding of newly-qualified social workers who had not been trained in adoption work was particularly identified as a problem by some agency staff. One said:

> *There's a whole new generation of social workers who are coming out of college and universities and social work training who don't understand that adoption is still one of the main real options. They don't actually understand what adoption is about.*

Furthermore, decentralised agency structures can create a situation where local policies are made by experienced and skilled adoption workers, whilst those implementing them tend to be unskilled. This problem was neatly summarised by a voluntary agency worker:

> *Yes, I think there are some local authority social workers who've got experience of childcare and are communicating with children. They maybe have a Family Placement certificate or things like that but sometimes they are working in teams where they now can't work with the children! It strikes me as rather ludicrous and I think that in some local authorities the people who are coming in at the lower level don't know very much about adoption. People who are managing that maybe know a little bit, but the people who are at Principal Officer level probably do know about adoption and they probably have done quite a lot of adoption in the past. But there's a tremendous gulf between those two bits. So you've got authorities that*

*are making policies about adoption up there but they're not actually being
carried out by the people down here.[23]*

Care and consideration for adopters

Another adopter described how the child's social worker had been careless
throughout the adoption process. One described a situation in which a social worker,
having set up meetings, would be poorly prepared, and on one occasion failed to
turn up at all. The adopter had asked for her family details to be kept confidential,
but she later discovered that they had been sent out to another family by mistake –
she had received somebody else's. On another occasion, the adopter was told that
the birth mother was planning to have the care order revoked and for the child to be
returned home. This caused her great anxiety which was made worse by the fact
that no-one in the local authority was able to clarify the situation:

> *We were very upset at home. It was very traumatic. We never thought that was
> going to happen. That message shouldn't have been passed on with very little
> information to back it up. It was really quite a distressing time and I event-
> ually phoned my social worker. She was appalled that they'd done that
> and went to keep badgering them to get some information as to what was
> happening. I think they weren't as helpful or as caring as they could have
> been.*

Another adopter found the 'casual attitude' of social workers disconcerting,
especially during assessment. He felt that they had little understanding of the
tension experienced by adopters during this time. Meeting their social worker for
the first time was a nerve-racking experience, compared with social workers who
were dealing with this every day. Yet they evidently turned up in a 'dirty car' and in
'shabby clothes'. In his own words:

> *Social services are coming to assess you as prospective adoptive parents. You
> do your housework. You make yourselves presentable. The least they could do
> is make the same effort.*

More generally, this adopter felt that this image of social workers militated against
the respect applicants should have for the social worker, especially given the negative
image of social workers portrayed in the press. He strongly felt that this needed to
be addressed by agency staff to generate adopters' confidence in their skills so that
they can feel properly supported. The approving agency subsequently invited the
adopter (who was a managing director) to run a workshop on self presentation for
agency staff, teaching them how to 'sell themselves' to children and families.

---

[23] This problem has been identified in our previous research – see Murch *et al* (1993) at para 117–127.

Social work ideas about "the family"

One adopter told us that social worker training needed to question some of the ideologies behind current adoption practice, such as stereotypical views about age, marriage and parenting, and what constituted "the family". Practitioners, too emphasised how these could be perpetuated by children's social workers in area teams, particularly if not trained or skilled in adoption, because they have a lot of power to thwart efforts made by the adoption team, thereby making decisions based more on prejudice than skill. This was also noted by a voluntary agency worker in relation to single-parent adopters:

> Quite a few local authority agencies are approving single people as adopters. I can think of one authority that has approved quite a few, but very sadly one or two have withdrawn because they've waited so long and haven't had a placement. So there's a discrepancy within the authority. In other words they are approving them and yet their own workers have prejudices against them. It never gets passed. The basic grade social worker has so much power at the stage when she is selecting the family.

4.2   Training social workers

The agency postal questionnaire asked agencies to describe the training available to staff providing support to children and families. Twenty voluntary agencies (67 per cent) and 37 (44 per cent) statutory agencies encouraged staff to attend external courses and conferences on specialist issues, or they bought in training from external sources. Such training was usually provided by BAAF and less often by the Post Adoption Centre, NFCA, PPIAS, NORCAP, other adoption agencies, or adoption consortia. One statutory agency had received secondment training from the Tavistock Clinic for a term.

Twenty-four (28 per cent) statutory agencies and five (17 per cent) voluntary agencies indicated that in-house training was available to adoption workers. In one agency, all personnel assessing prospective carers had in theory to complete the agency's in-house training, but it was suspected that this did not always happen in practice. Reasons for not providing in-house training were linked to the size of the agency (i.e. too few staff to warrant a course) or the experience of staff (i.e. staff were very experienced and had been working at the same agency for a long period).

Management assumptions and priorities

Practitioners told us that training reflects the priorities of management. In some statutory agencies, instead of training being specific to adoption, it tends to focus on emergency and short-term work such as child protection and more general issues such as partnership with parents and working with abused children. Little attention is given to the long-term needs of children in care or those who are being adopted.

Training programmes also reflect management assumptions about what skills are required. A black social worker stressed that working with black children and families, especially preparing black children for adoption, involves difficult tasks which few people can do properly. However, the skills involved are often not appreciated by managers responsible for training budgets:

> *White managers don't realise they're doing it. They're assuming because I'm black I can do the work. You have to question that all the time. Don't just allocate it to a black social worker because the worker is black! They must have a sound knowledge base, a sound skills base, and a sound personal development base just as they would be expected to have if they're working with a white child who has difficulties about what went on in their own family. I don't think there's enough understanding of that.*

Consequently, those working with minority ethnic children and families may have to push hard for training opportunities, without the support of senior staff:

> *It's hard to criticise workers in that respect but certainly I have always taken charge of my own learning and development in relation to that because that's what I wanted to do. It's important for all black workers in social work to do that, but you do need to be motivated, you do need support and those aren't necessarily there. Because a white manager may not see it in the same way as you see it, they think that you're spending too much time, etc. without actually thinking, 'Actually, this is a very detailed piece of work and you've got to spend time on it'.*

Linking training to practice

The way adoption work is organised in an agency may affect the ability to identify training needs and to evaluate the effectiveness of training programmes. Central adoption units often have a function to develop a common philosophy and practice standards and, within that, to provide training for district teams on such matters as open adoption, life story work, and preparing children. Yet one senior manager stressed that linking training to practice in a coherent way can be difficult if adoption work is done in separate districts rather than a central office.

Avoiding discontinuities of support for families

While it is important that adoption workers be trained, absence from staff duties necessitated by training courses can produce discontinuities of support for families. One family told us that her social worker was constantly going on courses in one year which meant that other social workers were taking her place. This can make families feel that they do not actually have a social worker, as such, on whom they can rely for support. Clearly, the implications that training leave has on the cases allocated to staff should always be considered.

4.3   Supervising social workers

Adoption social workers need to be not only well trained but properly supervised. The postal questionnaire asked agencies to describe the supervision available to staff who provide support to children and families. It could take the form of individual line management supervision, team supervision, often both. It tended to be fortnightly to monthly, although in one statutory agency it occurred only twice a year. As one agency worker stated, the quality of supervision depended on the knowledge and experience of supervisors which was often considered inadequate.[24] As a Social Services Inspectorate report observed:

> *Inspectors found that although line management provided regular supervision to child care social workers, it was not always informed. First line managers were themselves often no more familiar with adoption work than those staff seeking advice from them. This reinforced the importance of having specialist personnel or quality practice and procedural advice available to staff.* (SSI, 1996, p. 18)

An agency worker pointed out that the experience of supervision varied widely because their services were so generic. In other cases, line management support and supervision were not given high priority. By contrast, some voluntary agencies had highly innovative supervision systems. For example, in one, staff were supervised every month by their team leader and a psychologist.

4.4   Consultative help for social workers

Agencies were also asked to describe the consultative help available to those staff[25] who provide support to children and families in the adoption process. The resulting evidence suggests that consultation generally took the form of peer support and support from specialist workers or teams within the agency, rather than from professionals outside it. The use of external consultants (from organisations such as BAAF and NFCA) was only mentioned by 19 agencies.

Similarly, only a small number (around 10 per cent) mentioned that experts in law, medicine, psychology and therapy linked to the agency had a consultative role in supporting staff.

---

[24] See Murch *et al* (1993, p. 126).

[25] We distinguish here between supervision and consultation, regarding the former as a management control function whereas, with the latter, consultants assume no responsibility for case management. See also Caplan (1970, pp. 19–34).

Consultative links with psychological/psychiatric specialists were more prominent in voluntary agencies. One such had a weekly workshop facilitated by a senior psychotherapist for discussion of practice issues as well as a facility for individual consultation. Two other voluntary agencies said that they needed help from psychological consultants but had not yet found any, and another found it increasingly necessary to use psychiatric staff for consultancy. Whilst only three statutory agencies stated that workers were supported by psychiatric experts, none indicated a gap in this kind of support for staff.

Use of educational specialists as consultants to adoption services was unusual; only 3 per cent of agencies mentioned it. This confirms the findings of the Department of Health's Social Services inspection of local authority adoption services which highlighted deficient educational advice and support in most local authorities. It was suggested that this was associated with reduced local educational authority influence over schools which was a growing concern given the numbers of older and more difficult children being referred for adoption (SSI, 1996, p. 12). Under their new autonomy, some schools were found to be reluctant to enrol older children with educational difficulties who had moved to their adoptive placement (ibid. p. 76). Some of these children may have been statemented.

4.5   Training time-limited foster carers

Training is intended to improve the overall quality of an agency's staff resource, including its foster carers.[26] One agency worker told us that there was a need for understanding the foster carers' sense of separation and loss when children are placed for adoption. This was necessary even in those agencies where foster carers were getting good support from link workers and support groups. For example, a practitioner in another agency said:

> *I think when you go to their home and try to have interviews and counsel them through it, it's very intense. In an information group it's more detached, more academic. They can stand back a little bit and actually look at the issues in a wider sense rather than being in their own particular situation.*

One local authority adoption worker stated that while there were some very skilled residential workers in the authority, most were under-qualified, yet access to in-house training on preparing children was limited, and even then, only optional. The same applied to foster carers. Three agencies attributed shortfalls in training for short-term foster carers to poor resources. However, there are also other factors which militate against training foster carers. These are outlined below.

---

[26] The importance of foster carers to the success of the adoptive placement is discussed in Chapter 10, *Issues in Matching*, paras 4.2 and 5.1 and Chapter 11, *Post Placement Issues*, para 2.3.

Inconsistent attitudes to the relationship between fostering and adoption

Several practitioners told us that training for foster carers stresses the importance of preparing children for adoption placement, but some district social workers undermine that objective. For example:

> We have some workers in the district who, once a child is in a foster placement and they can see a child doing well there, actually give messages which are undermining the direction we want to go.

Furthermore, district teams of social workers can differ in their attitude to adoption by foster carers. Thus one worker stated that foster training reflected the view of research which suggested that, while foster placements developing naturally into a *de facto* adoption may be permissible, fostering children deliberately in order to adopt is not. Yet, he knew that some social workers subscribed to the contrary view transmitting it to foster families.

> I've been to an introductory meeting for foster carers and heard specialist fostering social workers saying to prospective carers, 'If you want to foster long term we always advise people to do a short-term placement first to see if they like it.' Well, it seems to me to be absolute cobblers because the motivation is different, and if what you really want to do is look after a child permanently then you are not going to make a good job of handing the child over to whoever it has got to be handed over to.

Updated training for well-established foster carers

Several agencies recognised the need to update the training of well-established foster carers. In one agency, foster carers approved a long time ago had not received any training and little social work support because it was low priority work:

> Prior to our reorganisation, fostering training was almost non-existent and foster parents got individual assessment only. It was a lower priority on the practice teams because we were concentrating on child protection. Relatively unskilled social workers would be assessing foster parents. No wonder we've got the legacies that we've got.

Since restructuring, untrained carers were being taught "on the hoof". They now had far more contact with staff, they were reassessed every year, and had much more support.

However, other agencies described difficulties in training long established carers to bring their skills in line with changing models of adoption practice. While some agencies gave foster carers the opportunity to attend training sessions on, say, attachment and contact issues, they were not always receptive to it. In some agencies, it is not compulsory anyway. In the words of one practitioner:

> *Within our training of all our new foster carers, we talk very much about the sort of fostering that we're asking of people. Being time limited it's very much part of the task of foster carers to move children on. But we have many foster carers who were recruited and approved a long time ago, many years ago, pre Children Act, for whom we've offered updated training. But it's been very difficult to get these people to come to our training sessions. We have a problem within our system that we need to use foster carers who maybe are not in tune with some of the modern thinking. We need their places but sadly they really are not in tune with the more modern thinking which leaves a lot of pressure on the district social workers and the fostering link worker to try to ensure that they stay on task. But it's not always easy, is it? We have many children staying inappropriately with foster carers.*

In some authorities many time-limited foster placements may be left to drift, sometimes for years. In such circumstances, it is difficult to expect foster carers to prepare children for moving on, and not become attached to the children themselves, especially when the prospect of a move to an adoptive placement seems more and more remote. It is not surprising that such attitudes can be transmitted to new foster carers in foster carer support groups and networks. As one worker told us:

> *Within support groups, new foster carers sadly are getting messages from the more experienced foster carers that some children have stayed in placement. So, it's about shifting that culture, which is difficult. I think really until we do a lot to replenish our stocks of foster carers and actually be moving people on who, with the best will in the world, cannot work to the Children Act requirement. Until we actually move to a newer stock we're going to be struggling.*

5   Links with other adoption agencies

Collaboration with other agencies can itself be perceived as a resource. Under the Adoption Act 1976, s1, local authorities are required to provide, in conjunction with other agencies in their area, a comprehensive adoption service relevant to the needs of the local community.[27] There is a requirement for collaboration with the authority's other social services and with voluntary agencies in their area, and that they should explore opportunities for joint action. Potentially such collaboration has many advantages. It can allow for specialisation to meet particular needs which

---

[27] See Chapter 2, *The Legal Background*, at para 2.2.

would otherwise be too uneconomic for a single agency to provide. It can facilitate training and the dissemination of good practice. It provides greater flexibility in the deployment of resources particularly for those agencies with small adoption workloads whose viability might otherwise be called into question. As the 1996 SSI Report observes:

> *Consortia can help an agency's approach to adoption to be informed by wider professional developments in adoption: it is a forum whereby workers involved with adoption can consider adoption issues, promote shared regional activity in training, recruitment and placement* (SSI, 1996, p. 12).

Developing strong links between agencies in a given region is therefore essential. This seems to be achieved largely in two ways: through regional consortia and so called "service agreements" between agencies.

5.1 Adoption agency consortia

Agencies in consortia

The questionnaire asked agencies whether they were members of a consortium, network or association of adoption agencies: 58 (69 per cent) statutory agencies and 25 (93 per cent) voluntary agencies stated that they were. Of the statutory agencies, district borough councils were most likely to be in a consortium at 88 per cent, compared to 65 per cent of shire counties, and only 50 per cent for inner/outer London boroughs. There were, however, considerable regional variations. While over 90 per cent of agencies in the Midlands, the North, the North West and Eastern Counties were in a consortium, this fell to 83 per cent for agencies in the South West, to 67 per cent for agencies in Wales, to only 50 per cent in Yorkshire and Humberside and 47 per cent in London and the South East. Many agencies were members of several consortia, and one agency was a member of six. Seventy-one per cent of statutory and voluntary agencies which were members of a consortium, were members of general adoption and fostering consortia organised on a regional basis, such as the Greater Manchester Consortium of Adoption Agencies.[28]

In addition to regional consortia, many agencies were also members of national networks or associations such as BAAF. Some voluntary agencies were also members of the Consortium of Voluntary Adoption Agencies and organisations such as Catholic Children's Welfare Agencies.

---

[28] In answering this question, agencies mentioned a total of 18 consortia organised on a regional basis (listed in Appendix D).

The advantages and disadvantages of adoption agency consortia

Agencies in consortia were asked to list those provisions which consortia provided but which the agency did not. The variety of answers to this question suggests that adoption consortia can be important to adoption practice in many ways. These can be summarised as 12 main functions which are listed in Table 31.

There were several differences between the way that statutory and voluntary agencies answered this question. In particular, twice as many voluntary agencies as statutory ones emphasised the importance of consortia as a means of collective bargaining, co-ordinating an approach between particular agencies, and of providing issues-related information. This perhaps highlights the more proactive role of many voluntary agencies in developing adoption policy and practice.

Table 31

What services consortia provide in the view of agency members

	Statutory agencies		Voluntary agencies		Total agencies	
Greater access to children and families	40	68%	8	33%	48	58%
Training material, courses, conferences	17	29%	10	42%	27	33%
Co-ordinating approaches between agencies	14	24%	11	46%	25	30%
Sharing skills, abilities, perspectives, experiences	21	36%	8	33%	35	29%
Issues-related information/publications	8	14%	8	33%	16	19%
Professional development – policy and practice	10	17%	5	21%	15	18%
Professional support	8	14%	3	13%	11	13%
Maintaining links with other agencies	5	8%	4	17%	9	11%
Collective bargaining power	3	5%	4	17%	7	8%
Independent services	4	7%	1	4%	5	6%
Post-adoption support initiatives	3	5%	1	4%	4	5%
Access to specialist agencies/workers	2	3%	1	4%	3	4%

Source: Agency postal survey

Pooling resources

Pooling resources, in terms of matching children to families, was the most popular function of consortia cited by agencies. One practitioner described how the 11 member agencies of the consortium paid a one-off standard fee to cover rent, administration and so on, rather than exchanging money per placement (the figure was approximately £3,000 for statutory agencies and £750 for voluntary agencies).

This means that children are placed with adopters in the same region but in a different authority, with the advantage of placing some (but not too much) distance between the child's origins and the new family. There can also be distinct advantages of pooling adoptive families in consortia for specific tasks, such as preparation.

The same consortium pooled minority ethnic families so that they could receive ethnically relevant preparation for adoption.

> We have run a separate preparation group for black families by black workers, with that group being conducted in . . . to be quite honest, I'm not sure which language it was, whether it was Gujarati or whatever. That's one of the advantages of the Consortium in that we were able to work with one authority in particular and gathered families in. Not just from [this authority] but from elsewhere. Because at one point nobody's going to have sufficient families whose first language isn't English basically. We might have one or two because we have got a significant Asian population, but we wouldn't have six or seven. So we actually co-operated and worked together on that. So the preparation was different.

A similar arrangement regarding the specialist preparation of Asian adopters was mentioned by a voluntary agency which had strong links with several adoption agencies in Yorkshire and Humberside. When they are about to run the groups, they write to these agencies and ask if they would like to buy any places on the course.

However, several disadvantages were noted in relation to this system. First, the number of placements could work out very unevenly for agencies. For example:

> I buy one off you and you buy one off me maybe the next week. No money changes hands – which is slightly different to most other local authorities who pay each other. I hope that might change soon. It's on their agendas. Because we've certainly realised that some are winners and some are losers. Why the heck should they provide 43 placements for another local authority next door when they have only taken 14 of their kids!

Secondly, the pooling of resources in such a consortium can involve a certain loss of control as noted by a worker in another agency:

> Part of the negative side of being in a consortium is that you're actually out of control of your own families. In simple terms, our families go into a pool and are fished out by social workers from other agencies – not by our social workers. Whereas if we were operating independently you would almost have some input into that process, wouldn't you? Whereas with this, we don't have any!

Understandable though this view might be, some might consider it unduly narrow and parochial.

Common standards in policy and practice

In addition to pooling resources, a second function of agency consortia was co-ordinating a complementary approach to policy and practice. Common standards can be extremely useful in settling disputes between agencies:

> *Both consortia have actually got agreed standards and they have been in existence for a long time. That, to me, is very good and very positive and therefore we know that if you have a disagreement or something you know who to contact.*

This practitioner pointed out that agreed standards can be particularly useful for settling disputes between purchasers and providers in those authorities where the people who purchase and handle the finance do not know very much about adoption. However, another agency worker highlighted the risk that the common standards developed in consortia can be dysfunctional if they become too rigid. This was based on her experience of making inter-agency placements with agencies in the Consortium of Voluntary Adoption Agencies:

> *We're not very enamoured with the Voluntary Agency Consortia. You have to take this support package. You can do a bit of negotiation around the edges but not about money, about philosophy, about contact, and things about social work supervision. It seems like the consortium has an overall policy and procedure which they don't want to break ranks on. So we're not very enamoured with that because we don't think that that always meets individual children's needs.*

Consortia can play an important part in developing links between agencies in order to complement each other's work, such as collective planning and joint recruitment campaigns, and to ensure that there are no gaps or overlaps in the local service. For example, one county council, which was a member of the Catholic Child Welfare Agencies consortium, had a tradition of working with two voluntary agencies. The council wanted to develop the links further so that the voluntary agency's work complemented its own even more closely:

> *There are two voluntary agencies that we've a long tradition of working with. I won't bore you with the details but it's part of my ambition to try and get to a position where we fine tune what they do, very much to complement the work that we do. There is quite a bit of duplication at the moment and we're working on that but I think that is the way to go.*

Such arrangements might well be a way of achieving a more coherent adoption service relevant to the needs of a local community.

Independent services

Adoption consortia can also be a means of establishing independent post-adoption services. One North West county council wanted to develop the authority's support after adoption. Their adoption officer thought that people may be more likely to take advantage of this provision if they could go to a "neutral" office from the one which approved them as adopters, even if it was connected in some way to the approving agency or the child's local authority.

Elsewhere, for example in the Midlands, we were told of local post-adoption services which provided counselling. While they are currently funded by local authorities, the service is looking to expand and perhaps become an independent charity.

Other agencies achieved this kind of provision through developing strong links with a particular voluntary agency. For example, an agency we interviewed in the North told us about a pilot project which they had initially funded, but which is now resourced by the Henry Smith Foundation, specifically for the support of birth parents of adopted children. Again, this was very much a service for counselling rather than advocacy: helping parents deal with their loss and anger, and enabling them to move on and achieve a more realistic view of their future involvement with their child. All parents of children referred for adoption by this county council are given a leaflet about this service, and the people running it are involved in training adopters.

Sharing information and expertise

Finally, consortia were cited as important because they can provide an arena in which workers can share information and expertise. For example, one agency told us that its consortium had produced a leaflet on adoption issues and that this was included in the adoption information pack given to adopters. Others told us about consortia newsletters for adopters, and even a magazine for older children. Some felt there was a good scope for this type of consortium.

A voluntary agency worker felt that more could be done by her organisation to improve formal links between projects to enhance the sharing of skills, yet there had been some discouragement from head office. She was not sure why. We were told also of attempts to share expertise in the development of training materials. These also had been thwarted. In one instance, a London borough adoption agency had begun to assess and train adopters in-house, and had encountered difficulty in designing suitable material for preparation groups concerning permanency. Being worried about 're-inventing the wheel', they approached other agencies so they could learn what they had done. However, they found that while some agencies were 'quite helpful', others were 'quite protective of their material'. They thought this was because many agencies are in direct competition with each other and sharing materials with competitors would result in loss of contracts and revenue.

5.2   Service agreements

The use of voluntary agencies to find families

Many statutory agencies regularly place children with families approved by voluntary agencies. They have different policies about how this should be done. For example, one local authority made numerous inter-agency placements because they needed families who lived outside the borough. Their worker stated that they would 'always much rather buy a family from a voluntary agency because they have better post-placement support systems'. But more commonly, statutory agencies make more selective use of voluntary agencies in their recruitment of families. For example, in one statutory authority in which most children placed for adoption were of school age, the authority usually turned to voluntary agencies to provide families for them. Inter-agency placements were a 'heavy cost' to the agency, but they were a burden that they had to bear.[29] In the words of another agency worker:

> In adoption practice it's always been the case that you don't necessarily feel you have the resource within your area. Although inter-agency placements are expensive and it's much better if you have the family to match a child, ultimately if there isn't a match within your authority, there isn't a match, and you can't create a match. You shouldn't be minimising the needs of the child in order to be financially expedient. Certainly, I've been around adoption and fostering for six odd years and, in my experience, team managers just bite the bullet and pay the money. They do. They don't necessarily go within their own authorities because it's cheaper.

Developing strong links with voluntary agencies

Given the fact that local authorities from time to time need to 'buy families' approved by voluntary agencies, many recognised the importance of developing and maintaining strong links with them. One statutory agency worker explained this meant knowing how the voluntary agency worked and developing negotiating strategies on how to get the best from it:

> Because the section works with other agencies a lot, it builds up a knowledge of how those agencies work and an expertise of working with other agencies and negotiating with them and a knowledge of where best to go for any particular child.

Other workers stressed the importance of appreciating the quality of work done by the other agency. As one voluntary agency worker asserted, 'It's better to have

---

[29] See also Chapter 19, *The Organisation of Adoption Services*, at para 3.6, for further discussion of the use of voluntary agencies.

worked with a local authority that we've worked with before because we know roughly the sort of input and the level of preparation'. Similarly, knowledge about the agency's post-placement support was cited as an important factor when deciding which agencies to approach for a family.

Advantages of service agreements

Some local authorities enter into long-term service agreements with voluntary agencies whereby they pay in advance for a certain number of placements each year. This brings financial advantages for both agencies: statutory agencies are able to make placements at a cost significantly less than the standard inter-agency fee, and voluntary agencies are guaranteed a minimum annual revenue which many need in order to survive as an enterprise. For example, one county council had a service agreement with a voluntary agency, which committed them to pay for 10 placements at the beginning of the year, whether this number of placements was used or not. This benefited the authority because they were paying £4,000 less than the standard interagency fee per placement. The worker we interviewed in this agency stated that the voluntary agency also benefited from the contract because their existence wholly depended on the revenue generated from inter-agency placements. Since they never knew how many placements they would get in one year, the arrangement gave them an 'element of stability in their budget'. We were told of one voluntary agency that had been doing some research on these kinds of agreements, which evidently found that local authorities who make the most placements with voluntaries 'are those that have some form of service agreement with the voluntary or voluntaries in their area'.

Service agreements may also help to address problems encountered by some agencies in standard inter-agency placements. For example, a local authority reported an incident where an inter-agency placement only lasted three weeks, yet the voluntary agency which approved the family insisted on the agreed inter-agency fee, even though their family was no longer providing a service to the local authority. Voluntary agencies may be more flexible if they have a service agreement with the placing authority which provides a stable minimum income.

We encountered other types of service agreements. For example, one practitioner described how his county council had a contract with a small voluntary agency to prepare, assess and review foster carers. This situation was unusual in that placements involved no monetary exchange at all because the authority had seconded two of its workers to the voluntary agency – in what he described as a 'gift relationship'. He sensed, however, that this relationship may soon change because the charity supporting the voluntary organisation had recently appointed a development officer, and it was felt that they wanted to do 'other things'. Nevertheless, this is an alternative to service agreements which some agencies may like to consider in relation to adoption.

Disadvantages of service agreements

While we found several examples of such agreements working well, one agency, a London borough council, had terminated its contract with a voluntary agency to provide adoption placements because families approved by that agency did not have a 'desirable attitude to contact'. Since 1992, wherever possible, the local authority therefore sought to recruit, assess and train their own adopters who would be expected to agree to some contact with their child's birth family.

There was also evidence that some agencies seem reluctant to enter into service agreements, even though they could save money. A voluntary agency worker told us about some of the problems he was having in negotiating such arrangements:

> We have one local authority in our diocese (who will remain nameless) who I'm sick of writing to, telling them what we do – often very appropriate pieces of work – asking for some sort of service agreement with them. They don't even have the courtesy to write back to us. Yet three weeks later we place three children for them on an inter-agency basis. It's cost them probably £10,000 more than it might have cost had they had some sort of agreement with us. It would have made it a far better service. Anyway, that's their loss.

6   Concluding Points

This chapter has considered factors which limit the effective deployment of resources in adoption agencies. As a result of under-staffing, some children have missed out on vital direct work, and some adopters have been deprived of support after placement. Post-adoption support – to birth parents as well as adopters – was an area which social workers saw as needing improvement, but there were often insufficient staff to facilitate it. It is not just a question of lack of money and under-staffing. Fluctuating caseloads can affect an agency's ability to provide the right level of social work support. Furthermore, *who* is allocated what task and *when* often depends on the availability of staff rather than their suitability to do the work, or when it should be done.

Problems seem especially prominent in local authority agencies where social workers doing adoption work also hold responsibility for child protection and crisis work. Adoption work appears to have lower priority than other child and family work, and this is reflected in the *time* staff are able to dedicate to making and supporting placements, doing life story work, and developing skills through well supervised adoption practice and training. The low priority attached to adoption work takes it toll, not only on the resources channelled into that service, but also on the morale and motivation of those doing the work.

Whereas adopters are usually prepared and trained for adoption by specialist social workers, children tend to be prepared by children and family social workers, often unskilled or inexperienced in adoption, or who have little time to dedicate to the case due to competing priorities. For these reasons, there seems to be a strong case for encouraging adoption teams (in both statutory and voluntary agencies) to be more active in the preparation of children for adoption, and in certain types of direct work. This could also ensure greater continuity for the child since adoption teams usually have lower rates of staff turnover than area fieldwork teams. In addition, through working more closely with children, agency staff may acquire better knowledge and understanding of the children for whom they are finding families. This should help them be informed when matching and supporting families and to support families more effectively.

While social workers specialised in adoption may need to be involved more directly in work with children, social workers specialised in working with minority ethnic groups need to be made available to support relevant children and families. Only half the agencies had any kind of specialist social work support for minority ethnic children and families, whether by employing workers of various backgrounds on a permanent or sessional basis, or by making appropriate consultancy and training available to white workers. This was an area which many agencies saw as problematic in their adoption service but which they were having difficulty in solving.

Another area of concern was the availability of specialist services, such as psychotherapy, for which many local authorities are unable or unwilling to pay. Some local authorities even seem to use delaying tactics, so that the burden of payment is transferred to the adopters after the adoption order. Continual pressure may need to be applied by families, or by other agencies on their behalf, before social services agree to pay for this kind of support. This in itself may deter families from trying to get the specialist support they need. Unfortunately, it seems that many local authorities are prepared to pay for specialist support only after a crisis, rather than taking more preventative action.

The underdeveloped state of post-adoption services in many areas was often seen as a reflection of inadequate resources resulting from a lack of managerial appreciation of its importance. Much post-adoption work is time-consuming, especially contact work. While several authorities wanted to develop this area of work, they had been unable to obtain the necessary funding. This is partly because resource allocation does not necessarily keep up with changing models of adoption, and the fact that post-adoption work – including section 51 work – is regarded as being of low priority, since it concerns work with children the agency looked after in the past rather than the present.

Families felt that staff training should address the problems arising from inade-quate skills in direct work, inexperience in adoption issues, undue care and consider-ation for adopters, and outdated models in social work. However, social workers explained how developing skills in such areas is rarely straightforward. Training programmes reflect the priorities of management, and linking training to practice can be difficult in some organisational settings. Supervision can also be inadequate, and most agencies do not make use of consultants in law, physical and psychological health, or, particularly, education, to guide social workers involved in adoption.

By contrast, links with other adoption agencies – another resource dimension – tended to be good. The majority of agencies had developed formal links with other agencies, either regionally or nationally, often via consortia (although local consortia were lacking in some regions). These were seen as useful for widening the scope for matching children to adopters; preparation and training; developing common standards in policy and practice; complementing each other's work in collective planning and joint recruitment campaigns; access to independent services; and sharing training materials and expertise. In some areas strong links had also developed between individual statutory and voluntary agencies in the form of service agreements which also brought financial advantages to participating agencies.

In summary, most agency practitioners felt that their adoption work was under-resourced[30] and some areas of the work in particular, such as specialised input and post-adoption support, were vulnerable when money was tight. We were drawn to the conclusion that the availability of good quality adoption services was something of a lottery, largely dependent upon the willingness and ability of individual local authorities to resource it.

---

[30] It might be thought that many of the deficiencies to which we have pointed can only be resolved by an increase in resources. That may be the case in some instances, and should not be forgotten, but the re-organisation of services may achieve a more efficient and economical use of available resources targeting them more appropriately where they are needed. In particular, we are concerned that agencies may not always be making the most appropriate use of staff skills and experience. We discuss the more general question of possible reorganisation of adoption services in Chapter 20, *Policy and Practice Implications*, para 5.

19 The Organisation of Adoption Services

1 Introduction

In this chapter we consider a number of issues related to the way adoption agencies, *particularly statutory ones*, are organised. In doing so we mostly draw on material obtained from agencies themselves. At the outset we should emphasise that it was not our task to *evaluate* these arrangements: we were in no position to consider in detail financial management matters or the ways in which agencies balance their adoption service responsibilities with competing priorities. Rather our aim was simply to obtain an overall picture of how adoption services are organised in particular parts of the country, dealing with such matters as whether adoption work is centralised; the introduction in some areas of internal markets – the so-called purchaser/provider split; the recurrent issues of agency reorganisation; and the adaptation of organisations to take account of particular geographical considerations.

2 Centralised/decentralised teams in statutory agencies

It was evident from the reconnaissance phase, that the way adoption work was organised into central and local teams in statutory agencies was complex. There is a profusion of different management models. To obtain a clearer picture of agency structures, our postal questionnaire asked practitioners to describe how adoption work in their agency was organised in terms of district offices and/or a centralised office. Rather than relieving some of the confusion, the responses to this question added to it. It soon emerged that it was not helpful to classify an agency as either centralised or decentralised because the differences between agencies were so wide.

This problem forced us to clarify what we meant by "centralisation". There seem to be several issues relevant to this concept. First, there was the geographical/spatial issue, in that the adoption unit would be concentrated in one place (such as County Hall) rather than being dispersed across several autonomous units (such as area offices). Second, there was the managerial issue, in that adoption work would be governed from one centre, rather than by several autonomous sites. Third, there was the issue of whether workers and their managers were specialised in adoption or family placement. But within these parameters, it is possible to distinguish some general organisational models under which adoption work is carried out by statutory agencies.

- **The centralised model**
  Agencies classified by this model had only one central family placement unit which did all the work relating to adoptive families, such as recruitment, assessment, and support. In addition to a central team, some agencies also had specialist family placement workers in the districts, but all were centrally managed by the family placement team (rather than from area offices). In other agencies, the centralised family placement unit comprised more than one team which was concerned with adoption. For example, there could be one team which focused on recruitment and assessment and another which focused on ongoing support. The role of district teams was generally confined to children – assessment, formulating a plan, direct work and support.

- **The combined model**
  In this model, adoption work was split between a central family placement team and workers in area teams, who may or may not have been specialists in adoption. Tasks were split between the two in various ways. For example, the central team might recruit, assess and train, whereas the workers in area teams undertook matching and provided ongoing support to families or vice versa. Area workers were managed by general area managers rather than by managers specialising in family placement.

- **The decentralised model**
  Under this model, apart from a limited amount of centralised co-ordination (including advice, publicity, policy and planning, record keeping and panel administration), all adoption practice was carried out by area-based family placement teams. Some agencies even administered their panels locally rather than centrally. One agency differed from all others in this model in that its adoption work was undertaken entirely by general child care staff (rather than family placement specialists) in area teams. The only central role was that of professional adviser to the adoption panel.

Within each of these models, agencies may have specialised teams based on specific groups of children, such as black children or children with special needs. Sometimes, these were centrally based, but in other agencies a specialist unit was based in an area office and was managed by that area, even though the service served the whole of the authority.

While there were many individual differences in agency structure, most could fit into one of the three models outlined above, although the "combined model" did not seem to be as widespread as the centralised or decentralised models. For this reason, the rest of this discussion will focus on the two contrasting models of organisation, and what the practitioners working in these settings had to say about how organisational structure affected adoption work.

2.1   The centralised model: the pros and cons

Matching and recruitment

Workers in centralised agencies considered their system facilitated more efficient matching. One worker gave an example: the agency had three girls with special needs, and through attempts to find a family for one of the girls it found families for the other two. It was suggested that this would not have happened if the girls, from separate districts, were being found families separately by workers in their local team. She also believed that they would end up recruiting families for specific children rather than making general assessments. Another agency made a similar point:

> *From our perspective it's a tremendous advantage because everybody's aware of what other children everybody else in the team has. When staff are advertising they think not only of their own child.*

Similarly, centralised services can serve larger numbers of children who could be grouped in certain ways, such as by their special needs or their ethnicity. This was seen as having two advantages. First, one agency had different workers responsible for different groups of children, for example, black children. This involved 'going out into the black community and raising the profile of adoption and getting prospective adopters interested'. Secondly, it meant that when talking to adopters about black children, the social worker would have all black children across the authority in mind, rather than only those in one area of the borough. In decentralised areas, that might have only one or two black children to place, it would be more difficult to justify this work. In sum, matching and targeted recruitment seem better done in small authorities by centralised teams, because numbers of children and families in local teams will otherwise be too small.

Support for adopters

A centralised adoption team was seen by some as better able to provide support for adopters. For example, one worker told us that it would not be possible to offer the same degree of training, workshops and support if they were run on an area basis because there were only one or two adoptive families in each. In addition, a centralised family placement team was more helpful to adopters because it provided a tangible, fixed place which they could approach for help: 'We're certain that a centralised team has great advantages from the point of view of the work we can do with adoptive parents and the fact that they have a place to come back to if they want'. One worker went so far as to say: 'My gut feeling is that if you want to understand family placement issues or issues for adopters, then it's got to be centralised'.

Voluntary agencies, too, when asked what they thought about centralised teams, usually preferred it. One of their workers pointed out that an advantage was that workers can support each other more easily because team members have a greater degree of contact, know what is going on, and are more familiar with each other's caseloads. If anyone is away, there is always someone to pick up the work so that families are never left feeling no-one is there for them.

Specialist skills and expertise

Many workers thought that centralised adoption teams facilitated the development of specialist skills and expertise more readily than decentralised teams. Furthermore, it was argued that a centralised family placement team could help develop the adoption skills of children's social workers. One agency worker described how a centralised family placement team (which recruited, assessed, prepared and supported adopters), established in her agency in 1989, had developed a common, authority-wide approach to adoption:

> The existence of a centralised team helps to develop practices and transfer those practices into the department and into district teams. We work hard in doing that. We organise training around, for example, open adoption or whatever it happens to be. My belief is that you've got to share a common philosophy. There's no point in us having some kind of philosophy about the approach to work and feeling very comfortable with it if the district teams are off in a completely different way.

This worker explained how developing a common approach had been helped by children's services being split into 'reception/intake' and 'longer term' work when the centralised team was created:

> That helps in the sense that, for adoption work, we're working with a smaller number of social workers who are therefore gaining experience in adoption work. Prior to that the social workers would do an adoption here and an adoption there, whereas now it's more focused. That is really helpful.

Another advantage of centralisation was that workers usually had specialist supervision.[1] One agency worker told us that the family finding unit was mostly centralised but there were also three outpost workers specialising in adoption and fostering who were in the districts. She thought they would be better supervised by herself rather than by line managers who had other priorities. A similar point was

---

[1] See Chapter 18, *Agency Resources*, at para 4.3, for further discussion of staff supervision.

made by a voluntary agency worker. She too argued that, in her experience, outpost social workers interested in adoption should be able to access specialist supervision because their area line managers might not know anything about adoption.

Specialised teams within a centralised unit

Some centralised adoption agencies had several teams specialising in different aspects of the work. For example, one agency had three teams: the first focusing on support of long-term foster carers and adopters; the second on support for short-term foster carers; and the third on recruiting and training both adopters and foster carers. Workers from each team were located in four different offices, but the teams were responsible for county-wide services and they were "line managed" by their respective team managers (no matter where they were located).

One worker thought the advantages of this system were, first, it enabled the team to

> . . . focus in on the needs of long-term carers in a way that was quite difficult under the old system where it was getting increasingly difficult to be abreast of everything.

Second, it was easier to be more flexible with the budget. However, she acknowledged that there could also be problems associated with such highly specialised, centralised units because those in the recruitment and training team after a while might lose touch with the realities of managing a caseload. Also there was a loss of continuity in casework with families. As one worker said:

> One of the biggest problems is that you get a relationship with a carer through assessment, see them through and then pass them on to another team.

Relationship with district social workers and managers

A more general problem associated with centralised teams was the tension between those teams and child care social workers in district offices.[2] As one worker told us, adoption work in her agency was done by a centralised team but the authority was questioning whether its workers should be shared among the areas, since adoption workers were seen by district teams as 'a thorn in their side' because they were constantly making demands upon them. She explained:

> I think they feel that communication would improve, but my worry is that our ability to recruit as a team and prepare carers as a team would suffer. I'm frightened that we would just get absorbed into this big child protection hole.

---

[2] This problem has been noted in other studies, e.g. SSI (1992b, p 62).

The agency was supposed to have a system where members of its centralised family placement team were nominated to each of the three sectors in the authority. They found that, whereas some sectors used this link positively – using their nominated family placement worker as a "sounding board" (as somebody who has specialist knowledge) – others really wanted to exclude them. Much depended on the attitude of area managers.

However, we have found that this problem is not confined to centralised units. It is perhaps more related to specialisation than centralisation since difficult relations between adoption and child care workers were encountered in an agency which had a "combined model" of organisation[3] (in that it had a central team *and* family placement workers in area teams). A worker in this agency stated that, 'Tensions always exist between a children's fieldwork team and a specialist team ... that sort of tension and rivalry – "you've got it easier than us" – things like that'. She believed that such rivalry hindered the development of adoption skills in the field work teams:

> *The benefits for this team are that there's an ability to concentrate on a much more specialist area of work and develop skills and knowledge. And the optimum result of that is that you end up with a specialist resource which the fieldwork teams can tap into if only they can get over their feelings of resentment and rivalry. I can say that because I was in Children and Families for seven years before I went into adoption work so I do know what it's like!*

2.2   The decentralised model: the pros and cons

Another way of organising adoption work was to have specialist adoption workers in dispersed local teams. One such agency told us that local teams were essential because the county was 50 miles wide in places, and their central unit could not have coped. Each team, or "group base", served a population of around 300,000, which is larger than some London boroughs. Each district needed its own adoption provision and panel, with one specialist family finding unit in each of the districts. As one of its workers said: 'By generating comparable specialist systems in each group it then becomes possible to pull each specialist together to generate common thinking between them'.

Several workers discussed the benefits of this structure. First, it was argued that local adoption and fostering teams enabled specialists to work with and support *birth parents*. Interestingly, one of them observed that birth parents seemed to prefer working with experts in adoption rather than district social workers involved in child protection, who perceived them as 'the "rejective parent"', whilst also helping the child make the transition to a permanent placement. Secondly, since the

---

[3] See para 2.1 ante.

local groups were "roughly coterminous" with district council boundaries and health authority boundaries, it was easier to align services.

However, several agencies highlighted some of the areas of practice which needed improvement in this type of agency setting.

Work with children

Whether or not adoption is organised on a centralised, decentralised or combined basis, work with children to be adopted was generally done by area social workers in children and family teams. Only one centralised family placement team told us that they routinely became involved in working with children. There were no decentralised teams which did so; this despite the fact that there could be more scope to involve adoption workers in decentralised agencies because they were locally based – often even based in the same building as the social workers with case responsibility.

One worker in an authority which had five adoption and fostering teams indicated that, although it was traditional for the children's social worker (in children and families teams) to do direct work, this situation was far from ideal. She explained that since the major role of children's social workers was child protection, they had less time to devote to life story work and helping children to move on. She felt that adoption and fostering teams should have a larger role, working collaboratively with children's social workers and perhaps linking more closely with other related services, such as residential care workers, especially those who specialised in preparing young teenagers or sibling groups for family placement.

Consistency – the need for central guidance

Another area needing improvement was how to make local teams more consistent. One large decentralised agency had a number of adoption and fostering teams which operated 'fairly autonomously'. Since the various elements of adoption were carried out both by children and family teams as well as fostering and adoption teams, a total of 20 teams was involved. When adoption work is spread across so many teams, it is obviously difficult to maintain the level and quality of service. We were told that, although the differences were subtle rather than major, they were large enough to affect how the teams recruited and trained families. For example, a recruitment hotline had been set up, as well as a standard pack of information for adopters. However, when the agency began to receive complaints from enquiring families, it became evident that workers in the various teams had understood the process differently.

In this very large decentralised agency it was also very difficult for the Policy and Planning Adviser, the person we interviewed who was the only person with a central role, to liaise closely, not only with team managers, which she did in monthly meetings, but with field workers in each team whom she could only meet about once a year. Furthermore, her role in giving ongoing advice to individual workers had been reduced because she had too many other calls on her time.

Another county council had two regional family placement teams, each of which served seven practice teams. The adoption service was decentralised, with the only centralised element being Adoption Panels. We were told that although this worked better than the old system (which pivoted on a Principal Fostering and Adoption Officer), workers still needed more centralised input and adoption policy guidance, for example, concerning the recruitment of families for children aged from 10 years upwards.

Similarly, decentralised adoption services may have problems with collating and disseminating information throughout the authority as a whole. For example, we found that in some of the decentralised agencies there was no central person to whom we could send the questionnaire, nor anyone who had access to agency-wide information. Instead, a separate questionnaire had to be sent to each area-based team. This suggested that practice between teams differed. Furthermore, there often appeared to be no centralised body which collected information, such as adoption statistics, about the work in each team.

Another problem faced by decentralised agencies, which perhaps inhibits the development of consistent county-wide services, are area variations in demand for an adoption service. For example, one decentralised adoption team worker told us that 'unlike fostering, which is immediate, urgent, and always necessary, developing adoption resources is likely to be meeting the needs of some other manager and not your own because the scale of the work is less and so variable'.

3 The purchaser/provider split

3.1 The concept

The so-called purchaser/provider split was much in vogue during the period of our research. Yet such a model had long been established in the inter-agency context, in which the child's local authority is the purchaser organisation, and the family finding agency (either a voluntary agency or another local authority) is the providing organisation. The amount of money paid for this service, and the exact services provided, depend on the agencies which enter this contract and the negotiations which take place. And, as some agencies have pointed out, voluntary agencies too sometimes need to purchase services from elsewhere on occasions.

What is new, however, is to split the function within a single local authority. In this model, the purchaser is the area social worker with care management responsibilities, and the provider is usually the internal adoption and fostering team, which recruits, assesses, trains, and supports adoptive families, and links them to the children referred to it for adoption. In this respect, the area social worker with responsibility for the child can choose whether to approach the internal provider for a family, or to go to another adoption agency altogether.

In this section we summarise issues concerning the purchaser/provider split emerging from both our agency questionnaires and from follow-up interviews with agency personnel. Workers in statutory agencies were asked to confirm whether their authority was split into purchaser and provider organisations. The resultant picture was extremely confusing. Some workers admitted that they did not know what the term really meant. Other workers confirmed that their agency had the split, yet the arrangements they went on to describe varied enormously from agency to agency. It soon emerged that the term "purchaser/provider" meant different things to different people.[4]

3.2   Scenarios

The range of internal purchaser/provider scenarios was large and difficult for us to grasp as outsiders. At one extreme, there were agencies which had a highly developed purchaser/provider split. One agency in particular had achieved a more complete split than any other agency we encountered. All of its departmental functions which could be identified as service provisions – such as old people's homes, children's homes, recruitment and support of foster carers and adopters, home care, day centres, family centres – were taken away from the control of local district managers and placed within the provider organisation. This organisation had a separate management structure and its own Assistant Director. It was only at Director level that the purchasing and providing organisations came into contact, in that both Assistant Directors were responsible to the Director.

On the other hand, some agencies were less enthusiastic. For example, one agency had "shelved" a proposed purchaser/provider split for 12 months to have a closer look at its implications. But even then, the proposed split was thought to be more 'a shift of emphasis' rather than a major change, given that in this agency clearly delineated internal and external markets were not going to be set up.

3.3   Experience, skills and priorities

There was some disagreement about the potential effect that the purchaser/provider split could have on specialist skills and expertise. On the one hand, some thought specialist skills would be lost. One worker, whose agency had not split into purchaser and provider, believed that the split would put pressure on the agency to become a family finding agency, whereas she saw the adoption unit as much more than that.

---

[4] This conceptual confusion has been noted elsewhere. For example, the SSI Report, *Children in Need* comments: 'It was clear that the terminology of purchaser/provider separation described very different arrangements regarding organisational structure, staff deployment, delegation and budgetary control in different local authorities. Discussion was therefore characterised by confusion' (SSI, 1995, p 15).

Alternatively, the agency could contract out the family finding service to the private and voluntary sectors. Both scenarios carried negative risks to other work undertaken by agencies (including elements of support):

> *The extra bits – the consultative service to social workers, the section 51 work, the birth family counselling, and all the general other work that comes in to us – would go back to the child care teams and would not get done. To be fair to them they struggle. As with other local authorities, the child protection comes first and last. So all that work would all be lost.*

In this authority people requiring these services, as well as general adoption enquiries, went directly to the adoption and fostering team, but if the adoption unit was a "provider", they would presumably need to go to area social workers who might be less skilled and informed. Similarly, another agency worker described how the purchaser/provider split had, in the experience of her agency, caused 'interface problems'. Purchasing teams were 'the front door of the organisation'. These people were often inexperienced in child care work – let alone adoption – and the agency worker was sure that they had lost potential adopters because of that. As another worker pointed out, work with birth parents was going to be removed from the family placement unit because of the purchaser/provider split. Yet, she argued, field social workers may not be the most appropriate people to deal with this work. Not only are they less experienced and knowledgeable in this area, but they have many other demands on their time, working at the "sharp end" of child protection.[5]

On the other hand, some said that the purchaser/provider split had brought advantages in terms of the development and deployment of specialist skills and expertise. For some agencies, the split led to the creation of specialist fostering and adoption teams for the first time, concentrating specialist skills and expertise. One county council worker also believed that reorganisation in terms of a purchaser/provider split, and the formation of seven family placement teams, had helped to develop the authority's commitment to family placement services. Furthermore, they were seen to be providing a good, skilled service which was being acknowledged far more than it used to be.

Thus, the purchaser/provider split has the potential to raise the profile of adoption work. However, an adoption agency manager in another agency thought that while the move to specialised teams was a welcome development, it had not occurred for the right reasons or in the most appropriate way. Workers interested in adoption and fostering had long been suggesting that specialist posts would improve adoption services, but this development only emerged as a by-product of the concepts of "community care" and "purchasing and providing", rather than as a good way of organising adoption work in the department in its own right.

---

[5] See Chapter 18, *The Impact of Agency Resources*, at para 2.2, for discussion of the impact of child protection work on adoption work.

3.4   Increased bureaucracy

One concern in agencies which had adopted a purchaser/provider split was with the amount of time absorbed by bureaucratic matters. In one county council for example, once the Adoption Manager had calculated what the agency needed in terms of adoption and recruitment, it took four months to get the purchasing managers to agree, and then a further nine months to calculate the costs. This was followed by an argument between the purchasers and providers about whether the costings were reasonable. In sum, it took nearly two years to work out the costings for the adoption service, and even then this could not be finally agreed until the same had been achieved for fostering. Part of the reason for this delay was that each of the five district managers had to be involved in negotiations, with each having to decide what they wanted in terms of adoption services, and how much they were willing to pay. The adoption unit had been under pressure by purchasing managers to reduce costs, but this tended to be in terms of the number of placements required rather than the amount of money calculated for each placement in terms of time and support. Indeed, several agencies pointed out that while an amount of money allocated to a child is good, in that it may increase options available to child care social workers about the kinds of service they can buy for the child, it can also generate problems for the actual running of fostering and adoption services, such as knowing how many carers to recruit.

Where purchasers and providers are separate departments, each with separate line management, there can be consequential delays in the decision-making process. As one agency worker (whose authority had been split into purchaser and provider organisations for one year before reorganising again into one department) argued, sometimes decisions needed to be taken by a single person who can both assess need and decide the level of resource to meet it – a person who can say, 'This is what I've decided, as opposed to two people of equal status sitting across the fence negotiating *ad infinitum*'.

3.5   Boundaries and inflexibility

Statutory agency views

Another issue raised by agency workers was the way that tasks were divided between purchasers and providers. For example, in one agency fostering work had split into an assessment team and a maintenance team. The worker thought that the purchaser/provider split would introduce further divisions of responsibility. She stressed that she would resist this division in adoption work because once the family was approved they would be handed over to yet another team, and that post-placement support, crucial as it is, would be provided by strangers to the family. Furthermore, knowledge of placement support informs approval, and this knowledge would be more difficult to draw upon if the tasks were split between different teams or workers.[6]

A worker in another agency explained how the purchaser/provider split had created more boundaries and more divisions which in themselves aggravated demarcation problems:

> One of the criticisms that I have of the organisation that we've got is that, although we seem to be sorting out our problems in terms of work, we've created an organisation with lots of boundaries, and the moment you create a boundary you get boundary problems, and a lot of management time has to go into sorting things out.

Creating boundaries can also result in more inflexible ways of working. For example, one agency worker told us how the imposition of the purchaser/provider split caused children's social workers and adoption social workers to 'grow apart'. Before the split, it was agreed that children's social workers should be involved in preparation courses and support groups. Afterwards this became more difficult because social workers were seen as providing the purchasers of services. This meant that they rarely became involved in family support which was thereafter, regarded as the responsibility of the provider.

It certainly seems that one implication of the purchaser/provider model can be that people on either side of the split feel they belong to entirely different organisations, which can bring into play all kinds of dynamics around competition and policing boundaries. For example, an adoption unit manager told us how workers in his agency no longer saw themselves as working in the same department. He told us: 'The Director keeps saying we are one department, but the trouble is nobody, except me, believes him'.

Voluntary agency views

Mapping boundaries and responsibilities in local authorities which had split into purchasers and providers can be extremely difficult for voluntary agencies. For example, some told us that they found it difficult, when working with local authorities which had this internal split, to discover who the budget holder was. As one voluntary agency worker put it:

> It's quite hard sometimes to find out who has the budget and where it is. Sometimes it's the child care manager and sometimes it lies with the adoption and fostering team – and they are providers, you see, so they are sanctioning the budget for a rival.[7]

---

[6] This problem, about over-specialism, has been noted in the previous section.

[7] Of course, the latter scenario brings into play all kinds of competition between internal and external providers.

Another told us that they would often get to the planning meeting stage where they thought they had been talking to the right person, only to discover that the person who had come to the meeting and signed the agreement was not the designated budget holder. The apparent reason for this is that voluntary agencies usually negotiate with family placement workers in local authorities, now located in provider organisations. Yet the child's social worker is usually the purchasing budget holder and may not make contact with the voluntary agency until later, for example, when they visit the adoptive family.[8]

Another voluntary agency stated that they now had to work with area teams rather than fostering and adoption teams in purchaser/provider agencies, and area teams are often less experienced in fostering and adoption issues. In these circumstances, the agency would contact the authority's family placement unit for advice, only to be told that, 'No, we can't have any actual input into the situation because it's the area team who is holding the purse strings'. This worker concluded that the purchaser/provider split had 'made it more complex for the voluntary agencies in trying to untangle what's happening in local authorities'.

3.6   Power and skill

Another problem faced by one agency was that the adoption unit, as part of the provider organisation, had to respond to the demands laid down by the purchasers in local teams: they had no power themselves to tell the Director what resources or quality standards they needed. The provider organisation had no budget of its own. Instead it was left to the area managers, who held budgets, to decide what they needed. The worker believed that, as a result, the provider organisation will lose its specialist staff: 'the logical conclusion is that they will eventually float off into the private sector or the voluntary sector'. Even though the workers in the provider organisation were on the payroll and part of the local authority, it was expected that eventually they would have no budget – only service contracts. In order to pay staff, buy stationery, etc., the provider organisation would therefore have to negotiate contracts with the purchasing organisation.

A voluntary agency worker believed that the increasing incidence of the purchaser/provider split had adversely affected the composition of her local adoption consortium. Ten years ago, it was made up of skilled and experienced workers in adoption who were often senior managers. These specialists were now being replaced by purchasers of services such as service and budget managers who, she thought, 'don't actually know very much about adoption'. Moreover, the adoption specialists tended to have decreased influence over management.

---

[8] This certainly seemed to be one voluntary agency's experience of working with London borough councils.

Such developments explain why some adoption workers are reluctant to lose their power to purchase services from *other* agencies. To one adoption worker, in an authority moving towards the split, it was going to be important that the adoption unit was equipped with its own budget, and a purchasing arm. She argued that this was because the section had a lot of experience of working with other agencies, and 'knowledge of where best to go for any particular child'. She explained her concern:

> *We've yet to have the nitty-gritty arguments, but my argument will be that we, as a unit, need to have a purchasing arm of our own so that children are actually referred to us, but we'd choose whether to go and purchase else-where. I would be very concerned and wouldn't feel it would work very well if the commissioning arm of the department were commissioning all over the place, i.e. they'd got their child and they'd choose whether to ask us to find the placement or whether they'd go to some other agency, somewhere else directly. That's the thing that would concern me most I think.*

Another worker described this kind of arrangement, as the family placement unit being a kind of "broker" to the purchasing teams.

Other agency workers claimed that the purchaser/provider split brought too much power to the purchasers and not enough to the providers. One told us that the reorganisation proposals for his agency were going to create an imbalance in the relationship between social workers with care management responsibilities in local teams and centralised adoption staff, in that essentially more authority and power was going to be invested in the former.[9] Another agency, initially reorganised into purchasers and providers, abandoned this arrangement after a year because there were some aspects which were not working. For example, the area social workers felt that, as purchasers, they could choose what placements they wanted without really taking much guidance from the adoption unit. This was considered unsatisfactory.

As far as exerting influence on the purchaser is concerned, a voluntary agency worker told us that they could refuse to provide a family for a child if they considered that the assessment of that child was inadequate, or that the child's local authority was being unreasonable, over the level of contact with the birth family. Other voluntary agencies found that some local authorities exerted their influence, as purchasers, over other aspects of the adoption process. Thus one voluntary agency found that some local authorities were now insisting that *their* panel did the matching, rather than the voluntary agency's panel.

---

[9] The agency did not go down that route in the end.

414

3.7   Use of the voluntary agencies

Other issues were raised about the impact of the purchaser/provider split on voluntary agencies.[10] As a voluntary agency worker stated, although local authorities are encouraged to use voluntary agencies to provide services, they are also under pressure to get "value for money". This means that they do not use voluntary agencies if they think it can be cheaper to provide in-house. However, as another voluntary agency worker pointed out, this depended on the type of local authority and very often its organisational setting. This agency had done its own research into inter-agency contracts, concluding:

> *We have a theory that the Southern authorities are more into the purchaser/ provider split than the more Northern, traditional Labour-controlled authorities, plus the fact that we think that the Northern authorities are 'poorer' than the Southern authorities. But we have another theory which extends out of that, that the Southern authorities being further down the line are now further into a review of that, and are maybe actually starting to do some of the work themselves, i.e. rather than buying three placements they may appoint another social worker and try to recruit three placements themselves.*

He continued:

> *Authorities that have split understand more about the cost that an inter- agency placement involves. So therefore the actual fee that we charge as voluntary agencies is not such a shock. They have worked out that their costs are maybe more – all told. So it isn't a huge jump to place with a voluntary.*

4   Reorganisation

Reorganisation was not tackled directly in the agency questionnaire or interview survey, but clearly at the time we conducted our fieldwork it was a major pre- occupation for many agency workers.[11]

4.1   Local government reorganisation

One result of large authorities breaking up into smaller ones, such as county councils being split into several unitary authorities in April 1995, is that new authorities may

---

[10] See also Chapter 18, *The Impact of Agency Resources*, at para 5.2, for further discussion of the use of voluntary agencies.

[11] Indeed, one county council which participated in the agency survey told us that they would have liked to help us with the family study but that they could not because of the pressures brought about by local government reorganisation. They had already had to produce a lengthy briefing document within a matter of days, and reorganisation itself was going to be 'chaos'.

have reduced adoption caseloads which may be too small to justify specialist teams. In other areas of the country, there was some evidence of local authorities pre-empting some of the anticipated upheavals of local government reorganisation. We were told of one county council which had a working group to explore setting up adoption panels in each district because it was likely that some of the districts were going to become unitary authorities. It therefore made sense 'to be looking towards them having their own adoption panel or their own family placement panel'. Yet one worker in a Welsh authority observed that local government reform in Wales was going to create 23 unitary authorities. He was sceptical whether 23 separate adoption agencies could be justified by the overall level of work. Instead he suggested the following arrangements:

> *I think you might have to have consortia type arrangements whereby people set up an adoption agency arrangement and maybe provide a specialist service supplemented by social workers from individual unitary authorities doing individual pieces of work, but a specialist service being available to a group of unitary authorities working together. I could see that could work.*

However, a recent SSI report into local government reorganisation in Wales observed that, while unitary authorities initially wanted joint arrangements, this interest dwindled with time. The Review stated that this was due to a concern that financial imbalances between neighbouring authorities could jeopardise future arrangements, and a worry about the impact of differing approaches to service delivery which would inevitably develop. There were also concerns about accountability and quality assurance (SSI for Wales, 1996, p 6).

4.2   Internal reorganisation

Reorganisation can bring about positive changes. It can force people to re-evaluate old, possibly outmoded practices and to adopt new, more effective and economic ways of doing things. One agency worker reported that departmental reviews can be helpful, because 'people come closer together' and share more information and ideas. One of the 'good' things they were doing in the review was to examine and standardise assessment practice in their family finding teams.

Another agency told us how restructuring led to their family placement service developing 'a wider package than just finding families', for example, taking over responsibility for the child before the end of the court process. Yet such changes in case responsibility can also cause confusion unless clearly managed. As one worker said:

> *Obviously, the preparation of the child for adoption is essentially very child-focused in the early stages. That's the responsibility of the practice team social workers. Interestingly though, when we reorganised in January of 1993, quite a number of people were under the impression that family*

placement would be taking over some of that work. It was never formally part of reorganisation but led to some frustration and confusion.

Whether or not reorganisation led to a general slump of morale in many agencies was hard to judge, but we were told of a number of adverse consequences for local authority adoption services.

Reduction in the range of services

During the agency interviews, we discovered that many social services departments reorganise on a regular basis. The problem with this is that there is some evidence of adoption provisions being lost or suspended. For example, one agency worker told us that, because of reorganisation and staff shortages, 'there was a policy decision made that meant that we would discontinue holding disruption meetings. Instead someone independent would gather information, interviewing the people involved in the case'. While this is clearly better than nothing, the support that some families get from a disruption meeting should not be minimised.[12]

Discontinuity in family support

Discontinuity of support for families can be another consequence of reorganisation. One agency worker told us that she was 'lucky in reorganisation' because she was allowed to hang on to a lot of her original cases. However, this seemed to be more of an exception than the rule. One family we interviewed explained that there had been a 'shuffle' of social workers, so that at one time they did not even know who the child's social worker was.

One of the strongest messages from agency interviews was that, irrespective of all the advantages and disadvantages brought about by reorganisation, much anxiety and chaos characterise the transition – not only in the run up to reorganisation, but in its aftermath. As one worker said, 'There has been a big improvement in the last three years but it's been very hard work and the anomalies that existed before are still in some cases around and difficult to shift'. Another worker noted: 'It will be easier when we've tidied it up. Part of the problem is that we're still dealing with the remnants of a very messy structure.'

Loss of skill and experience

One of the most worrying aspects of reorganisation was the adverse effect it can have on skill levels. For example, one worker described how it resulted in some very skilled people going into management, leaving those at the ground level needing to develop skills from scratch. Other workers suddenly found themselves

---

[12] See Chapter 12, *Disruptions*, para 5.

working alongside new people who had little or no experience of adoption.[13] One practitioner who had worked in child protection for 12 years was transferred to family placement. She thought that her previous skills, like those of other workers who had moved into management, would gradually reduce as she lost touch with that sphere of work. She also described how, with reorganisation, she and her fellow adoption workers felt 'totally devalued', explaining how all of the social workers who had entered family placement teams had previously been senior social workers. Yet social workers in practice teams 'were made practice managers and given two increments more'.

Some reorganisation evidently forced people into jobs that they did not want. In one authority, although many wanted family placement jobs, a number did not get them, and ended up instead with their second or third preference. This situation seemed partly due to the fact that job allocation was not based on suitable criteria but on length of service. As our informant observed: 'It wasn't done on skill which was unfair to a lot of workers, and a lot of skills were lost that would have been good in a family placement team'.

5   The geographical area covered by agencies

The geographical location both of the adoption agency and of the families which adopt the children referred to it has important implications for the adoption process and support provision. In particular, the size of area which the agency recruits from, as well as other characteristics, such as density of population and tightness of community, can affect adoption practice and sometimes create difficulties for workers. In addition, the placement of children with families who live outside the child's local authority brings into play such issues as who has responsibility for providing or paying for support.

5.1   Size of area served by agencies

There is considerable variation in the size of geographical areas covered by adoption agencies. Some county councils serve large areas compared to small district borough councils. Some voluntary agencies approve families living all over the country. One of these agencies, which is based in London, also recruited families from Scotland and the North of England, and the resulting distance made supporting those families difficult. Instead, they had to rely on the help of local authorities for funding which they found 'extremely variable'.

Other agencies were finding that distance from their families was increasingly

---

[13] Similar comments were made about the affects of restructuring into a purchaser/provider split. See para 3.2.

becoming a problem. One agency found that it was having to 'widen its net' and go further afield than a 100 miles radius, in order to reach enough adopters, since fewer people were coming forward for adoption. Other voluntary agencies reported the effect that neighbouring agencies could have on the geographical area covered. One, based in Essex, recruited most of its families in Suffolk because there were fewer agencies there than in other counties. Similarly, a Cambridgeshire based agency recruited families from Norfolk as well as Cambridgeshire because they had arrangements with the local authority there, and because the only voluntary agency based in that area had closed.

Implications for ongoing support

One county council worker told us that direct work with the child after placement depends on where the adoptive family lives, as well as upon the expertise of the staff and any prior relationship with the child. In another shire county, social workers were not supposed to travel more than 100 miles a day without special permission, which meant that they had to do some geographical splitting of their work to make link visits feasible. While this may be adequate for routine visits which can be planned in advance, it does not make allowances for families in a crisis who need support from their social worker. As another worker said, the problem with supporting people at a distance is that workers often cannot visit the family the same day that they telephoned for help.

Another problem associated with large catchment areas is that it can be difficult for agencies to link with community services. For example, one agency with a catchment area of 50–60 miles radius, told us:

> The difficulty with us, I suppose, is that we are not geographically confined to one small area so we are not able to build up the community networks that perhaps we would do if we just operated in a small borough. However, that doesn't stop us and we do build up community links with Child Guidance or the local adoption medical adviser, or whatever we feel is necessary we should link into. But I think that's harder for us because we have to start from scratch.

The size of the area covered by the agency also made it difficult to network with neighbouring colleagues in adoption. One adoption officer felt extremely isolated in his work, in terms of keeping up to date with issues, and getting advice about difficult cases. He was the only adoption specialist in his large rural county, and specialists in even the closest counties were far away. In his words:

> It's the geographical factors which sometimes make it impossible for you to think of the job and the agency as being anything other than a bureaucratic organisation. The problem in these circumstances is humanising it, personalising it, making sure that the people out there think yes – it isn't just

> *an amorphous organisation which has no tangible place or people I can refer to and relate to.*

Preparation and support groups for adopters

Statutory agencies operating over a large geographical area can find it particularly difficult to organise group preparation and training for adopters. For example, for several agencies in Wales covering a large, thinly populated area, it was impractical to do so. One agency had only 20–25 adopters across the five areas of the county. As the worker stated:

> *We haven't done anything like enough group work to support a group of people who are going through the assessment process. Because of geographical factors, it is difficult to have enough people in one area to make a group worthwhile.*

Instead, preparation comprised individual social workers working with individual adopters who were encouraged to do much of the preparation themselves, such as through reading and attending Open University courses run in the area.

This problem was also faced by a number of voluntary agencies. For example, one which recruited families from West Yorkshire, and parts of South and North Yorkshire, told us that adopters initially expressed an interest in support groups, and group training on specific issues such as contact and managing difficult behaviour. However, because people were travelling from so far afield, it was difficult for people to make it although they tried, and usually came once or twice. 'After that the interest just faded away and eventually folded up – purely because of that'.

Another voluntary agency, with a religious affiliation, which experienced similar difficulties tried to compensate by putting adopters 'in touch with one another'. They also used their links with local churches to link families into a support network. But the agency worker stated that while this made it easier for some people to go back to the agency for support, for others it made it more difficult. They also asked local authorities if their families could attend their groups: sometimes they were told 'yes', sometimes 'no', and sometimes 'yes – but only if you pay'.

Another agency told us that the number of people attending their agency study days was not particularly high, because their catchment area was 100 miles radius of central London. Even so, they found that the families of children with disabilities usually attended, as well as making use of whatever was going on in their area. Supporting those families who could not attend those study days was more difficult, because they were dispersed. However, in the agency's experience, these families tended to get involved in their own local networks. If families ran into difficulties in doing this, the agency would help by asking PPIAS or the Post Adoption Centre if they knew of any other adoptive families living in that area with whom they could be put in touch. Telephone networking was another promising idea this agency was considering. The worker commented:

> *I have all these ideas about groups and can't get people into them because they can't come. We're going to explore using telephones more where you can link people up. I'm going to find out about that to see if it's a possibility as a way of sometimes holding meetings.*

5.2   Types of communities served by agencies

Apart from size, other aspects of the agency's catchment area, such as whether there are "tight" or "loose knit" communities, can also be important in relation to practice and support. As one rural county agency worker told us, there were some areas which had 'a very strong family community' where people would rally round and support families who were struggling. This had several implications. First, it meant that fewer people from such communities came forward to adopt. Secondly, it meant that fewer children were referred for adoption. (This particular agency only placed one child and approved five families for adoption between January and December in 1993.) Strong community networks, combined with the impact of the Children Act 1989 (which, as they saw it, encourages local authorities to avoid moving children from families if at all possible), meant that the county council was often able to place children in alternative ways. However, this only applied to families who had strong links in the community: families which moved into such areas from outside were often 'isolated' with no relatives for the agency to 'tie into'.

6   Where the adoptive family lives outside the agency area

6.1   When agencies approve families living outside their authority

Geographically compact authorities faced the problem of how to make sure that the birth family and the adoptive family did not live too close to each other. This led many agencies to recruit routinely from outside their area. This particularly applied to minority ethnic children such as Asian, Jewish and Greek Cypriot children who came from close-knit communities where they might be easily identified.

Several issues were raised in relation to supporting families who do not live in the area covered by the approving agency. First, as one worker argued, it was more difficult to liaise with other organisations than it was for agencies which recruited within their authority. So, if families were having problems with schooling or health, or they needed help from Child Guidance, the agency had fewer established links with those local services. After the adoption order, matters could become even more complicated. Even getting the help of the family's local social services could be difficult. As one worker pointed out, local authorities have their "own" families to support. There is a tendency to parochialism here which disadvantages children and families supported by agencies external to the particular local authority in which they live.

One family we interviewed seemed to be caught in this trap. They had been approved by a different local authority from the one in whose area they now lived. They had applied to court for the adoption but the hearing was still pending. When they asked their adoption agency whether financial and social work support would continue after adoption if they continued having problems with the children, the reply was that all that would stop. The family would be on its own after the order, but they could write a letter to their local authority and explain things to them. This was not successful since they had already been rejected by them (after three years of agency preparation and assessment as prospective adopters, the family's application was turned down by Panel).

6.2   When adoptive families move out of the placing or approving authority

Problems can be experienced when adopters live outside the area of their approving and placing agency. One such said that they had received very little social work support after they had moved and none at all after the adoption order was made. The adoptive mother thought that this was because they had 'fallen through the net' because the local authority in which they were living neither vetted them nor looked after the children prior to adoption. Even so, some agency workers who mentioned such problems, took the view that in most instances agencies should 'finish' what they started because they have a moral obligation to do so, especially if the children have behavioural problems or other difficulties. Indeed, some authorities actually do provide support after adoption where the family lives outside their area. For example, one district borough council had a provision for children who had been sexually abused, through its adoption allowance scheme, to pay for counselling in whatever area they live. The worker said that, even though such a child is no longer legally their responsibility, support – or at least the finance for the support – should come from the placing authority. Only then can the placing authority be sure that the family will get the service that they require. This admirable attitude does not seem to be general practice.

6.3 When the adopter's approving agency is different from the child's local authority

The use of the BAAF inter-agency standard contract

Of course, some of the issues outlined above – about who is responsible for support when families do not live in the child's local authority – are also relevant to inter-agency placements. Our agency postal survey asked agencies whether they used the BAAF inter-agency contract (now Form H1/H2) to negotiate which agency provides support for children and their families in inter-agency placements: 92 per cent of agencies answering this question did so. In addition, several told us that they had developed their own form based on the BAAF form. Some use the Voluntary Agency Consortium contract as well as the BAAF form. However, even when these agreements are used to plan support, some families involved in inter-agency placements reported problems regarding support after the adoption. Several workers, too, were aware of the problems of support in inter-agency placements, especially after the adoption order.

For example, one family had been approved by a voluntary agency and lived a fair distance from their adopted children's local authority. They had approached their local county council about using its post-adoption services, but were told that they could not use them because the children were not adopted through that council. (This, despite the fact that the family had read in an agency leaflet that the service was for *anyone* who was involved with the adoption). They were told that responsibility for post-adoption support lay with the local authority which were looking after the child prior to the adoption, and the voluntary agency which approved the family. However, the adopters' voluntary agency had evidently provided all they could within their budget, and the placing authority were less accessible. In the end, the only support they were able to obtain was from a generic social worker – not well versed in adoption and who knew neither child nor family – who had been allocated to them by the local authority in which they were now living. They were not optimistic about her support because they felt they needed specialist help.

Comment

There is clearly scope for ambiguity and disagreement regarding who is responsible for supporting families who, for a variety of reasons, reside outside the child's local authority. This is a problem which needs to be recognised nationally. At the very least, it needs to be fully discussed and agreed by the agencies involved, and understood by families, before they agree to the adoption. The issue was neatly summarised by a worker in North Wales from a voluntary agency:

> Gone are the days where I think local authorities can place for adoption and go, 'Phew! Another one off the caseload!' I think there have to be issues about local authorities recognising whose responsibility it is. If we place a child for

423

[the local county council] and they're still in [that area], then that's OK. But what about the child who is placed from another authority who comes up to live in [this county]? Whose responsibility is it? Is it ours or is it theirs?

7   Concluding points

The material considered in this chapter suggests that the way an agency is organised has major implications for the development of a comprehensive adoption service. It has been argued that centralised agencies are more efficient in matching and recruitment, and they are more likely to be able to offer group preparation and training. Other advantages of having one adoption office are: there is a tangible place to go back to for support; it is easier to pin people down; communication and contact between social workers are likely to be better; and it is less likely, therefore, for gaps in the service to emerge. In addition, workers in centralised teams are more likely to have specialist knowledge about adoption and access to specialist supervision. However, there can sometimes be rivalry between centralised adoption teams and fieldwork teams which can hinder the development of adoption practice across the authority.

On the other hand, area-based adoption teams can have the advantage of smoothing the child's move from one type of placement to another within the authority.[14] But decentralised adoption agencies often felt that consistency in the level and quality of service between area offices needed improvement, as did the co-ordination of local services and the collection of authority-wide information about adoption (e.g. adoption statistics).

There were mixed feelings about the purchaser/provider split. While some workers argued that the split brought about positive changes, such as raising the profile of adoption work and creating specialist family placement teams, others criticised the way that this was handled. Workers were cautious about the new powers vested in the purchasers of services, and the fact that area field work teams rather than adoption units, would be the front door to adoption enquiries, mainly because area fieldwork staff tend to be inexperienced in adoption and have many competing priorities. Others believed that the split introduced even more bureaucracy and 'boundary problems' into adoption, and more rigid divisions between adoption social workers and children's social workers.

Geographical factors, in addition to organisational ones, are also important in explaining varying types of adoption practice and levels of support, for example, the size of the geographical area covered by the agency; the other agencies operating in that area; density of population; and tightness of community. These factors affect

---

[14] Local authority teams are generally set up according to function, such as a child care team and an adoption team.

the extent to which agencies are able to build up community links, network with other experts in adoption, and provide general social work support – especially in an emergency, or through preparation and support groups for adopters.

Adopters who live outside the jurisdiction of their approving agency may be particularly vulnerable to poor support because there is ambiguity about which agency is responsible. Because of this confusion there is a danger of the child falling between two stools, with neither agency being prepared to take financial responsibility for continuing support. In our view this confusion needs to be removed. We recommend that the placing agency should retain responsibility for supporting the adoptive family even where that family moves out of the agency's area. Of course, there will be occasions when it would be more practicable for support to be provided by the agency nearer to the family. All we are suggesting is that *financial* responsibility rests with the original placing agency.[15]

Overall, the most salient message throughout this chapter has been the substantial degree of variation in the way in which agencies organise their adoption work. Furthermore, the terms which social workers and researchers use (such as centralisation/decentralisation, and purchaser/provider split) to describe these structures are somewhat inadequate in accommodating these differences. In particular, the structure of a single agency – how adoption work and responsibilities are shared among its workers, and its various points of entry – was also difficult to grasp at times. This was despite having collected a significant amount of information from such agencies. This raises the question: how must these agencies appear to their clients? How clear a picture do families have of the agency's organisation so that they know which door to knock on to meet their particular needs at a given time? We know that the organisation of many agencies is far from straightforward, with adoption work sometimes being bolted on to other areas of work which bear little resemblance to it.[16] It is ironic that the children, whose lives are often marred by chaos and unpredictability, are looked after by such large, confusing organisations, almost as if they mirror the children's disordered past lives.

It is not only adopted children and families who need to have an understanding of the organisations with which they are dealing: many professionals involved in adoption work also need to have a clear idea of the people involved, their powers and responsibilities, what they can mobilise, and so on. These include the courts, solicitors, guardians *ad litem*, the Department of Health, and, in particular, those who work in other adoption agencies and allied professions. The fact that agency

---

[15] This suggestion is no different from the system of 'designated authorities' under s.31(8) of the Children Act 1989 in relation to care orders. Query, however, whether it should be possible to permit formal transfer of responsibility from one authority or agency to another.

[16] In small populated areas, the management of local adoption and fostering teams was sometimes combined with other functions, such as residential children's homes, or the placement of adults with learning disabilities.

structures vary so much cannot make it easy for other professionals who have to work with local authorities. This mystification is further perpetuated by the fact that local authorities are continually reorganising.

While these highly complex organisations may embody sophisticated frameworks for dealing with client needs in adoption, it is clear that some have evolved into their present state as a result of other considerations, in particular, financial ones. Such complexity could be due to the fact that adoption is only a small part of the work of social services departments, which in themselves are extremely complex because of the range of other functions they perform: adoption is only one of many competing demands. However, it is also possible that some highly complex systems developed to act as protective devices to shelter them from the outside world. To outsiders the system is baffling, with many being deflected or giving up pursuing the services they need. In this way, complex systems can act as covert rationing devices, as a means of restricting the distribution of resources. Accordingly, as we propose in the following Conclusion, the line of accountability should be clearly stated in adoption agreements between the agency and the adopters.

Part IV

CONCLUSIONS

20 **Policy and Practice Implications**

1   Introduction

It is not our intention in this final chapter to repeat in any detail the conclusions and recommendations that we have made in earlier chapters. Instead we concentrate on what we believe are the main implications for law reform, policy change and practice development arising from our research findings.

The current law and structure of adoption services are still essentially based on the Houghton Committee's recommendations made in 1972.[1] At that time the adoption of babies and infants dominated practice and thinking. Since then, however, the whole nature of adoption work has changed, becoming smaller in scale but more intensive and complex. Adoption of babies has become almost non-existent (just 4 per cent of all adoptions in 1996) while the adoption of older children out of care, the subject of our report, has grown to be a major part of adoption practice – approaching half of all non-relative adoptions. Many people now seeking to adopt a non-relative are likely to have placed with them a child aged five or more. Because most of these children have complex family backgrounds and ties – the implications of which for children and adopters by any standards take some managing – there is likely to be a continuing need for support even after the making of the adoption order.

It seems to us that, notwithstanding the change of adoption practice, the prevailing "mindset" is still, in a number of respects, associated with the adoption of babies, inasmuch as it is still often seen as the last and irrevocable act in a process in which the birth parent has "given away" her baby via the adoption agency to the adopters, who are then left to their own devices and resources to bring up the child as their own. This mindset, however, sits uneasily with the adoption of older children.[2] There needs to be an acceptance that, at the very least with regard to older children (if not for all children), adoption is not the end of the process but only a stage (albeit an important stage) in an ongoing and often complex process of family

---

[1] 1972 Cmnd 5107 – outlined in Chapter 2, *The Legal Background*. Ironically, the mandatory obligation upon local authorities to provide an adoption service (under s 1 of the Adoption Act 1976) was not implemented until 1988.

[2] This theoretical perspective is developed further by Lowe (1997, pp 371–386).

development. We think that the adoption of older children out of care is best understood as some kind of informal "contract" between the birth family, the child and the adoptive family – a "contract" which brings with it a pattern of reciprocal obligations between the "parties" and the adoption agency, which performs a brokering role as well as providing continuing support, while the court holds the ring in this process and puts an important symbolic and official seal to the arrangements.

Although in places our report deals with instances of poor practice and problematic support which make depressing reading, we should emphasise that, in both statutory and voluntary agency placements, we have seen a number of adoptive families where the children are thriving. We have come across many instances of careful and imaginative matching, where placements have been well supported, where adoption agencies managed the whole process expertly, and, where necessary, mobilised a wide range of community support. We have also been extremely impressed by the dedication and commitment of many of the agency professionals involved.[3]

Even under optimum conditions of good practice, because of the imponderables of the human chemistry factor, adoption involves a variety of risks. Nevertheless, our overriding impression – taken as a whole – is that a number of placements seem to succeed in spite of the system rather than because of it. Lack of resources, structural weaknesses in the system, inappropriate mechanistic and inflexible management, excessive pressure of work (often resulting from competing respon- sibilities), and inadequate training and experience all too often mar the service provided and detract from the potential value of adoption support which can sometimes make the difference between a placement succeeding or disrupting. All this has led us to concentrate our thinking on what improvements should be made to the existing system.

2   Law reform[4]

2.1   The obligation to provide post-adoption support

Consistent with the general thesis that adoption should not be regarded as the end of the process, the State cannot consider its obligations towards such children as being *ipso facto* discharged by the making of the order. In other words, its duty to support these needy children and those who take on the task of looking after them, must *prima facie* continue even after the adoption order has been made. Accordingly, it is

---

[3] Exemplified not least for their unfailingly patient help and support for our project.

[4] For other legal reforms relating to the court process see Chapter 13, *The Legal Process,* para 4, and for tightening up regulations for the provision of information see post, para 3.

simply not good enough for the legislation only to impose an *implicit* obligation upon local authorities to provide post-adoption support as part of the general adoption service. The legislation should be changed so as to make provision of post-adoption support an *express* duty. Furthermore, it will be necessary to accompany this change by providing, in subordinate legislation, guidance as to more precisely what is expected of a post-adoption service.

2.2   Adoption allowances

With regard to adoption allowances, it is not acceptable that (a) they should be regarded as the exception rather than the norm, (b) they should be lower than fostering allowances, or (c) they should be dependent upon individual agency policy. We maintain that there is a compelling case for society to continue to bear the costs of looking after these especially vulnerable and frequently highly damaged children, particularly those who had previously been removed from their birth families into care on the basis of 'significant harm', and whom the state undertook responsibility to look after into adulthood. At the very least, these children should be entitled to the same level of financial support as if they continued to be fostered. The adoption process should not financially disadvantage such children (nor their adopters). We recommend that a national standardised system of eligibility and levels of financial support be introduced, possibly, by means of a state allowance rather than one paid by the adoption agency. Ideally, we would like to see financial considerations removed from the question of adoption so that decisions can be made based entirely on the welfare of the child.

3   Practice improvements – refurbishing the system

We consider there are a number of steps which need to be taken to ensure a much higher overall standard of adoption agency practice – measures which need to be underpinned by well-informed professional supervision and consultation and backed by more rigorous management information, for example, to monitor case progress and to avoid drift. We suggest below a number of *quality assurance improvements* which should be made.

3.1   Providing prospective adopters with reliable information about the placed child

Although, as we have stressed, we have encountered many examples of good practice, we have nevertheless on occasion been appalled by rank bad practice. For example, we have been alarmed in some instances at what can only be described as the deliberate concealment of relevant information from prospective adopters. In its worst form, information about a child's development is either withheld or concealed from the prospective adopters. We have come across at least four cases in this study where the adopters discovered only after the placement had disrupted that the placing agency had not told them the full story. Quite apart from the question of whether this withholding of information is actionable,[5] it is clearly unacceptable practice.

In particular we should emphasise that as a minimum *parents* need:[6]

- A reliable and up-to-date care history of the child, including the reasons for being in care, the number of previous placements and why they changed.
- A medical history of any illnesses suffered and treatment received, written in lay language.
- The child's educational record including schools attended and copies of school reports.
- A record of behavioural difficulties including the propensity for violence or sexual abuse.

Also unacceptable is the apparent reluctance, at least in some agencies, to give information about what practical (including financial) support is available. Indeed it was our impression that this reluctance was at least in part motivated by a desire to reduce the level of demand upon the service

Children, too, need reliable information about their care plans and about prospective placements. Our related study, *Adopted Children Speaking* (Thomas *et al*, 1999) reveals that many are confused and worried about what will happen both to themselves and to their birth families, when they are placed for adoption.

3.2   Appreciating the risk factors

As part of what we consider to be good practice, careful thought needs to be given to what is an "acceptable risk" in placing a child with potential adopters. Although our research did not specifically focus on "risk factors", our assessment of the experience of the families in our interview sample nevertheless enables us to sketch out some of the more obvious indicators.

---

[5] Cf *W v Essex County Council* [1998] 3 All ER 111 in which the Court of Appeal upheld Hooper J's ruling that a social worker had a duty of care to provide foster carers with 'reasonable' information about the child and that a local authority could be vicariously liable for a breach of that duty. Accordingly, four children who were sexually abused by a teenager fostered by the family were given leave to sue the council.

[6] Under the current Adoption Agency Regulations 1983 there is no express obligation under reg.12 to provide prospective adoptive parents with background information upon placement for adoption, while the new reg. 13A only obliges the agency to 'provide the adopters with such information about the child as they consider appropriate' *after* the adoption order has been made: in our opinion this obligation should arise *before* the placement.

High risk factors

- Length of time in care coupled with the number of moves and broken or fractured attachments.[7]
- A child known to be violent and/or sexually abusive to other children – the apparent precipitating cause of all the disruptions in our sample.
- Breaking a settled attachment with a foster carer.
- Splitting up children who are part of a settled sibling group.
- Where adopters have their own children living with them, especially if they are of a similar age to the placed child, a point that emerges very strongly from Parker's study of foster care (1966).[8]

Factors that can diminish risk

- Orphaned children who can be adopted by relatives.
- Children who have obviously become attached to, and who may have had a part in the selection of the adopters – classically children who wish to be adopted by their foster carers.
- Children who have been well prepared by their foster carers for adoption elsewhere.

3.3   Other good practice points

- Achieving an appropriate balance between the number of children available for adoption and the number of approved adopters.
- Better pre-placement preparation of children, adopters (and any other children they may have) and foster carers, as well as greater care in the timing of placements (see Chapter 9). In particular, there is an art in finding the 'right tempo' suitable for both child and adopters when making the placement. As our related *Adopted Children Speaking* study (Thomas *et al*, 1999) shows, some children appeared to need longer "courtship" than others.
- Ensuring appropriate continuity of personal support for both children and adopters by *key passage agents* over the critical transitions out of care, into placement and during the initial settling down phase.
- The provision of 24 hour emergency back-up support and, where necessary, respite care for adopters having to cope with particularly challenging behaviour.

---

[7] Our sample included one child who had experienced no less than 32 moves.

[8] Parker R (1966). See also Packman J (1975) at p 33.

3.4 Recommendations

To achieve these and other improvements suggested by the study, we recommend that consideration should be given to introducing a number of measures into agency policy such as:

- The provision of some type of *Adoption Agreement* (or possibly *Charter*) for both adopters and children setting out the kind of support upon which they should be entitled to rely. Under such an agreement the placing agency should *inter alia*:
  a) give the adopters an information pack explaining precisely what support is available, including information about adoption allowances and other financial support, and how and from whom it can be claimed;
  b) guarantee that the information about the child is complete and up to date (and that it will continue to be updated) and is clearly explained to the adopters;
  c) respect the adoptive applicants' own wishes (viz. as to the type of child they wish to adopt), and to only depart from this by agreement; and
  d) continue to offer support both after adoption or even after the child has left, if the placement has disrupted.
- Agencies should be required to formulate plans about how best to achieve continuity of personal passage agent support for children and adopters during critical transitions such as placement, changing schools, recommencing or terminating contact, and, where necessary, after the making of the order. In this last respect, we were struck by how relatively unusual it was to keep the same social worker once the order was made (see Chapter 11). These could be made the subject of regulations such as those proposed in the Adoption Bill under which local authorities would be required 'to prepare and publish a plan for the provision of' their adoption service.[9]
- All agencies should ensure that the adopters (and, where appropriate, the child) understand not only the nature of the agency's responsibilities but also how the lines of accountability within the agency work so that all can know clearly who is responsible for what.[10] A similar obligation should be owed to other service providers involved in the adoption process.
- An attitude of mind in agencies needs to be cultivated which should ensure that children, adopters and foster carers are always kept in the picture and are well informed about how the agency is approaching key stages in the adoption placement process. In particular, they should be the first to know if there are likely to be delays and changes in the plan. The reasons for unexpected turns of events should always be quickly explained to them so that they are not left in limbo or made to feel that their role in the process is merely passive.

---

[9] See cl.3 of the proposed Bill attached to *Adoption: A Service for Children* (1996).
[10] This issue is considered further, post, at para 5.1.

- The interests of other children involved such as the adopted child's siblings, and any other children the adopters may have, should also always be considered. Where appropriate they should be consulted. After all, their welfare may be as vital as that of the placed child and indeed placing agencies may well be held to owe them a duty of care.[11] Under the present system such children often seem to be left out of the reckoning.

3.5   Safeguarding the child's education

Education is obviously important to any child but for those who have been adopted out of care it poses special challenges. As we know from previous research[12] many children who have been looked after by local authorities for any length of time experience disrupted education and low educational attainment. In addition, the child placed for adoption usually has to contend with the challenges of starting a new school in a new neighbourhood. We know from our research how much importance adopters place on the education of their children and many go to great lengths to make up for the child's previous educational deficit. Many children, once they are settled in their placement, exceed expectations in the progress they make. Furthermore, educational progress is often seen by the adopters as an important indicator of success in the placement. Indeed higher educational attainment could well be one of the key benefits of adoption.

Paradoxically, the future education of the child once placed for adoption does not seem to figure large in agency thinking and planning. Indeed it is our impression that this is regarded as a matter for the adopters alone. While we have come across instances where this approach seems to work, we think education is too important an issue for agencies to ignore. Under the current law their sole obligation is to inform the relevant local education authority of the proposed placement.[13] We think this obligation should be strengthened by requiring agencies to formulate with the adopters, and where appropriate the child, an education plan with provision for any specialist support that may be required.

In the light of our evidence from some parents and from our related study, *Adopted Children Speaking* (Thomas *et al*, 1999), there is a need to monitor the child's progress at school and, in particular, to be alert to the risk of bullying and teasing.

---

[11] Particularly in the light of the recent decision in *W v Essex County Council*, supra.

[12] See Jackson S (1987).

[13] Adoption Agency Regulations 1983, reg. 12(2)(d).

4 Reframing the approach to adoption support – should it be seen as educational?

The success of the policy of placing older children out of care for adoption depends in part on how well children and adopters learn to live together. Should adoption support therefore be viewed essentially as an educational rather than as a social work process? After all, the primary purpose of adoption *support* is to enable adopters to learn the very special parenting skills and understanding that they will require. Children, too, have to learn how to settle into the new adoptive home. Many adopters view the process as a pathway to a "normal" family life, not one which is to be supervised and supported by "the welfare". This perception comes from an understandable wish on their part not to be seen or labelled in any way as social workers' "clients". What some adopters fear about the conventional approach is that adoption support is covert supervision. Indeed this may well be what some agency social workers assume too. Of course, it is recognised that there is a legal obligation to supervise the child's well being while in placement.[14] Nor can it be denied that there must be an element of protection for the child until the adoption order is made. Nevertheless, given the careful selection process of adopters in the first place, one would have thought that there should not normally be a need for close supervision (as opposed to support) particularly after the initial settling-in period.

Of course the skills and insights of social workers/ doctors/ lawyers, particularly in relation to child and family psychology, play an important part in the placement process but we would argue that sight must not be lost of the learning task in adoption. Viewed in this way, the primary task of adoption support should be defined as enabling adopters to learn as rapidly as possible the skills of parenting children who have experienced extraordinary and often turbulent childhoods. Accordingly, we suggest that consideration be given to changing the regulation by substituting the words 'safeguarding and promoting' for the word 'supervise' the child's well being.

We think that once one begins to move away from a traditional social work or even psycho-therapeutic mindset to a more educational approach, the provision of adoption support services begins to be seen in a new light. One immediate effect of this would be, in our opinion, to create a more equal partnership between the adopters and their children on the one hand and the professional service providers on the other, in which all are engaged in the common enterprise of establishing a well functioning family. Accordingly, we recommend that the notion of partnership should be expressly written into the adoption regulations in much the same way as it is in regulations issued under the Children Act 1989.

---

[14] Adoption Agency Regulations 1983, reg. 12(2)(g).

5   Rationalising the system

In this final part we focus on the structure of adoption services. It seems to us that there are three key issues by which to evaluate the success or failure of the overall system: first, how coherent in terms of the allocation of responsibilities and the provision of clear lines of accountability is the organisational structure both to those who work within the adoption service, and to those who use it, not least to adopters and their children? Secondly, what scale of adoption workload (in terms of both the numbers of children placed and families recruited annually, as well as the provision of continuing support for previous adoptions) is required to provide a minimum viable organisation offering a genuinely comprehensive service? Correspondingly, is there a maximum level of work beyond which the organisation of adoption services begins to lose efficiency? Thirdly, how effective are agencies in deploying the scarce skills, experience and knowledge of their staff in providing an adoption service, particularly for families of older children adopted out of care?

5.1   Accountability

As we have seen in Chapter 19, the lines of accountability, particularly in statutory agencies, are diverse and complex. Each agency seems to have invented its own structure and uses a wide variety of official designations. In the research we came across 38 separate designations of workers who completed our agency question-naire.[15] Quite apart from any suggestions for radically altering the structure (see below) there is an urgent need to clarify for the benefit of adopters and their children, agency by agency, who is responsible for what. Moreover, as we have already suggested, lines of accountability should be clearly stated in our recommended Adoption Agreement.

5.2   Viability

Given the relatively small scale of current adoption work there seem to be too many agencies – both statutory and voluntary.[16] From our information about agency workloads, we question whether very small operations (i.e. those placing annually just a handful of children and recruiting a relatively small number of prospective adopters) which are not involved in consortia are best placed to provide the comprehensive service required by law. In contrast, the larger and more stable services seem better able to recruit and retain highly skilled and experienced adoption workers. Related to scale are the crucial questions of economic viability

---

[15] See Appendix E.

[16] Since completing our research, local government reorganisation of larger metropolitan boroughs and county councils into smaller unitary authorities can only have exacerbated this problem.

and cost effectiveness. On the face of it there is an overwhelming case for rationalisation and amalgamation. We therefore think there should be a Government Review to establish a minimum level of adoption agency viability and to consider reorganisation.

5.3   Options for restructuring the system

In thinking about restructuring the system much depends on how one defines the tasks and the boundaries. Should adoption stand alone or should it be seen as part of the integral provision for the placement of children away from home, which would therefore also include fostering and residential care? Alternatively, should the key task boundaries include the local authority child protection function in order to facilitate the continuity of care for the child? Even if one could agree on the appropriate boundaries, there is still the related question of how best to maximise the deployment of specialist skills in an informed and sensitive way. We do not profess to have definitive answers to these difficult questions, but in order to inform a considered debate about them we outline below the following options.

The pros and cons of disentangling adoption services from local authority social services departments

Our material certainly provides a case for arguing for the removal of the adoption function from local authorities. The principal reasons for this are:

- There is a need for a clearer demarcation between local authority child protection work and the child placement function. Our study, *Pathways to Adoption,*[17] and our current research have provided ample evidence that this is a problematic association in that, for example, the priority tends to be given to child protection; there are incompatible differences in the pace of work for each task; and there is a tendency for many practitioners to confuse the regulatory supervisory function of child protection with the essentially more supportive one of child placement.

- There are endemic problems of local government administration and finance which seem to bear down unhelpfully on many aspects of statutory adoption work. For example, there are the annual complicated budgetary arrangements, the politics of which often seem impenetrable to the outsider. There is the recent confusion over the introduction of internal markets and the purchaser/provider split. In many areas there is staff turbulence and recurrent reorganisation. There is the inevitable tension that arises in large hierarchical management structures between administrators and professionally trained field workers. Extended chains of command risk slow decision making. Relatively small specialist areas of practice such as adoption can sit uneasily in departments providing a large scale general social work service.

---

[17] Murch *et al* (1993).

- There is also staff morale to consider. Apart from the fact that many social services personnel feel pressurised and beleaguered, a number of specialist adoption workers, at least in certain agencies, have told us that they feel their work is marginalised and devalued by colleagues who do not understand the nature and requirements of adoption.
- To outsiders, such as adopters, local authority adoption services, in contrast to those in the voluntary sector, seem more complex and bafflingly bureaucratic. The lines of accountability and the range of potential services on offer are more difficult to perceive.
- Some would also argue that local authority social services have acquired a long-standing stigmatic association with the "welfare" social control function. More-over, removing the adoption function from local authorities is not quite as revolutionary as it might sound, because there is already in effect a hybrid system by which local authorities can opt to contract out their adoption functions to the voluntary sector.

Notwithstanding these arguments there is also a case against them:

- One immediate difficulty is how would the removal of the adoption function relate to the continued local authority child placement function through fostering? Why should adoption be singled out for special consideration in this regard? Although it is legally different, the skills and understanding required for both are much the same, particularly, as on our thesis, adoption should not be seen as ending the agency responsibility to provide support.
- If adoption were totally hived off from local authorities there is a danger that their planning for children might ignore adoption as an option altogether.
- Wholesale hiving off could be taken as an expression of public dissatisfaction with the current service. This would be a further blow to the morale of local authority staff and might lead to a loss of expertise currently found in many authorities.
- Unless carefully planned, hiving off could increase the risk of discontinuity of care for children and associated changes of personnel so that children and families would lose the chance of passage agent support at critical transitions.
- The current system for all its structural defects does at least offer potential adopters a degree of choice of agency which might be lost in any wholesale restructuring.

These counter arguments have convinced us that the complete severance of the adoption function from local authorities, as recently advocated, for example, by Patricia Morgan (1998), is problematic in itself. Moreover, it does not address the question of what system would best replace it. There are various options all of which would need careful consideration. For example, there could be a newly established National Adoption Service, akin to recent proposals to establish a unified court welfare service for the family justice system. That would involve national funding and central government regulation. Also it would be necessary to determine the optimum and minimum levels of local/regional viability and how best to balance the requirements for minimum national standards of good practice and quality assurance with the need to allow for experimental innovation and the tailoring of services to meet local needs. It may also involve the wholesale recruitment and relocation of staff – itself a potentially expensive exercise.

Alternatively, adoption could be vested solely in the voluntary sector. Not all areas of the country are adequately covered by voluntary agencies at present. Although they could be encouraged to expand their activities, it is not at all certain that they would wish to do so. Some large children's charities, for instance, have withdrawn from adoption family finding activity and others would be worried that taking on the whole adoption task would skew and possibly overshadow their other existing charitable functions. Also, unless one was careful, expanding voluntary agency workloads could again lead to cumbersome bureaucracy.

Less radical options

Although we think there is no escape from the manifest need to rationalise the service, there are less radical approaches to doing so.

First, regional consortia could be more systematically developed so that statutory agencies, not thought to be viable, would be required to amalgamate their resources with other agencies in their area or region. It should be acknowledged, however, that the history of consortia in adoption and other fields (for example, the provision of the guardian *ad litem* service) has not been entirely problem free, largely because of the complexities of local government finance and the problem of how to achieve equitable arrangements. There would therefore have to be careful central government regulation to ensure the delivery of a good service.

Second, local authorities could be released from the *mandatory* duty to provide an adoption service but again there would need to be centrally imposed safeguards to ensure that a comprehensive service is available throughout the country as envisaged by the Houghton Report.

5.4   Broader policy considerations

Inevitably, consideration of these structural options will become embroiled in the broader debate about the future of local authority social services departments. This debate, fuelled periodically by disturbing findings from child abuse inquiries, by a large and growing body of childcare research, and a recent study revealing serious shortcomings in social work training and the lack of supervision of newly qualified local authority staff,[18] has been given added impetus in the adoption and childcare field by the publication of Morgan's challenging polemic[19] and by various pronouncements by the previous Minister, Mr Paul Boateng.[20] The Government is evidently considering whether to seek a closer alignment of local authority community care with the health service and of their childcare responsibilities with local authority education services.

Our concern is simply how best to raise the overall effectiveness of adoption support services and through this research to inject the perspectives of adopters and their children[21] into that debate. Accordingly, we support the Department of Health's decision to set up a committee under the chairmanship of Professor Roy Parker to consider and refine messages for practice arising from this and other recent adoption research. However, we think that a focus on practice development alone is not enough. Law reform and structural change, insofar as they set the context for practice, are of fundamental importance and, as we have sought to demonstrate, also need to be addressed.

---

[18] Marsh and Triseliotis (1996).

[19] *Adoption and the Care of Children*, op cit.

[20] At, for example, the Department of Health's Conference for Directors of Social Services and their elected Members, London, 16 December, 1997.

[21] See our related study, *Adopted Children Speaking* (Thomas *et al*, 1999).

Part IV

APPENDICES

Appendix A

Outline methodology

1   Research Advisory Committee

The project's Research Advisory Committee was chaired by Carolyn Davies of the Department of Health. The Committee's membership comprised: Michael Brennan, Department of Health; Joan Fratter, Barnardo's; Pennie Pennie, Lambeth Social Services; Jim Richards, Catholic Children's Society (Westminster); Julia Ridgway, Department of Health; Alan Rushton, Maudesley Hospital; Phyllida Sawbridge, ex Post Adoption Centre (retired); June Thoburn, University of East Anglia.

The Committee and the Research Team met approximately four times a year.

2   Purpose of the research

To examine the need for and provision of support services for families adopting children aged five years and over who had been previously looked after by a local authority.

3   Aims of the research

- Gather empirical evidence about the use and organisation of adoption support services and plans for their development within statutory and voluntary adoption agencies in each of the BAAF regions (as they were in 1994) in England and Wales. A postal questionnaire to be sent to all adoption agencies in England and Wales with selective follow-up interviews.
- Conduct a postal survey of families adopting older children previously looked after or accommodated by a local authority followed by interviews with a sample of families drawn from those responding to the postal survey. Their evaluation of support in terms of their expectations and experiences to be recorded.
- Explore the application of certain theoretical models to illuminate our understanding of the provision of support during the adoption process.

4   Stage 1: Preparation and reconnaissance

During this phase all 177 adoption agencies (116 statutory and 61 voluntary[1]) in England and Wales listed in the BAAF's *Adoption Agencies Directory: 1993–94* were sent a letter in April 1994 informing them about the research. The letter also asked them to send any information they may have concerning the provision of support services for families involved in adoption by their agency, such as an annual report or panel report, and to nominate a person with whom the researchers could liaise when the national postal survey was conducted. This letter was followed by telephone calls to those agencies who had not responded.

Figure 22

Type of documents sent by agencies during the reconnaissance phase

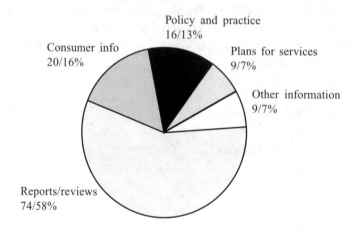

Policy and practice
16/13%

Consumer info
20/16%

Plans for services
9/7%

Other information
9/7%

Reports/reviews
74/58%

A total of **103 (58 per cent)** agencies responded to our request by sending information about adoption services – **65 (56 per cent)** statutories and **39 (64 per cent)** voluntaries. The type of information sent is shown in Figure 22, and Figure 23 (below) shows the response rate for each region. This material was utilised in clarifying research questions and designing the postal questionnaire. This process was also aided by input from the *Social Services Inspectorate* (the Project was presented and discussed at their meeting in May 1994) and by reconnaissance visits which were made to a number of voluntary and statutory agencies and adoption consortia.

---

[1] Throughout this research, individual satellite projects within one voluntary adoption agency (such as New Families Projects in Barnardo's, or Children's Society offices) are counted separately.

Figure 23

Response rate for agencies in each region for sending documents during the reconnaissance phase

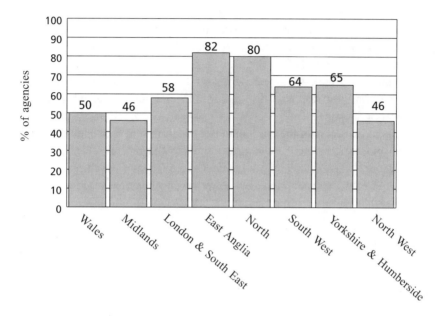

The *Association of Directors of Social Services* (ADSS) was informed about the Project and in due course its Service Evaluation, Research and Information Committee decided to recommend the Project to the Social Services Departments. This decision proved to be critical in obtaining the participation of many statutory agencies.

A 100 per cent response rate was achieved in relation to establishing a link person with whom to liaise during the postal survey. We also learned from the reconnaissance that some offices or projects listed in the BAAF Directory had since closed, thus producing a list of **116** statutory and **51** voluntary agencies in England and Wales. These **167** agencies comprised the sample of the next phase of the research: the national postal survey.

5   Stage 2: The agency study

This part of the research was split into two parts:
a) a national postal survey of *all* adoption agencies in England and Wales; and
b) an interview survey of a sample of adoption agencies (both statutory and voluntary) located in each of the regions

5.1 National postal survey of adoption agencies

In June and July 1994, questionnaires[2] containing comparable questions were drafted – one for statutory agencies, the other for voluntary agencies. These were circulated to members of the Research Advisory Committee and the agencies visited in the Reconnaissance phase, for comment. The questionnaires were finalised and despatched to **116** statutory agencies on 19 September 1994 and to **51** voluntary agencies on 30 September 1994.

During November, reminder letters were sent to those agencies which had not returned the questionnaires. Non-responding agencies then received a second reminder letter or telephone call in December 1994 and January 1995. At this point, it was discovered that some of the questionnaires had been sent to adoption projects that had since closed, reducing the voluntary sample to **44** agencies. This figure was taken into account when calculating the overall response rate, which reached just under **72%** (115 of the 160 adoption agencies returned a completed questionnaire). Figure 24 (below) shows the response rate for each region.

Figure 24

Response rate for agencies in each region returning agency questionnaires

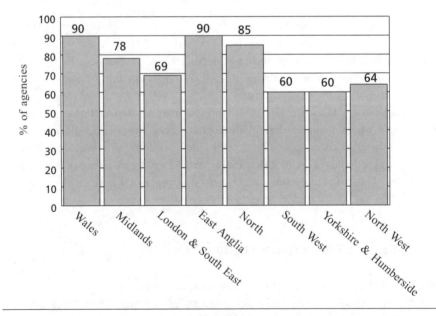

[2] The questionnaire was long (25 pages) consisting of both tick-box questions and open-ended questions where respondents were asked to answer in their own words.

The topics covered in the questionnaire were:
- agency adoption statistics
- agency organisation
- agency policy and practice
- support for older children, birth families, temporary foster carers, and adoptive families
- evaluation of and comments on support services

5.2 Agency interview survey

The purpose of the interviews was to gather information that could not be sought by the postal survey, to amplify some of the points raised in the questionnaires, and to elicit information about support services peculiar to individual agencies from a representative sample of adoption agencies. To obtain a representative sample of agencies, an elaborate sampling frame was devised.

The sampling frame aimed to ensure
- a representative geographical spread of agencies and, thereby, of support service provision in England and Wales (with around one third of agencies to be interviewed in each region);
- various types of agencies (statutory/voluntary; London boroughs/shire counties/ district borough councils; satellite projects of large voluntaries/individual projects);
- agencies with various sizes of child care caseload (no. of children in care per 10,000 pop; no. of children aged 5–9 as percentage of all looked after children);
- agencies in various organisational settings, including the purchaser/provider split, and whether adoption was undertaken by centralised or decentralised social work teams; and
- agencies with various levels of support provision.

This information was gleaned from information gathered in the reconnaissance phase. Using this frame, a total of **48** agencies were selected for the subsample, **32** statutory and **16** voluntary. Figure 25 shows the percentage of agencies interviewed in each region.

The interview schedule comprised a list of topics for discussion. These included
- the preparation for adoption of children, adoptive parents and birth parents
- the role of the agency once the adoption order has been granted
- issues concerning contact
- issues concerning disruption
- the purchaser/provider split and its implications for adoption practice
- the structure of the agency and its effect on its adoption work
- aspects of the agency's support provision it considers to be innovative
- problems arising in the provision of support in older children adoptions

Figure 25

Percentage of agencies in each region which were interviewed

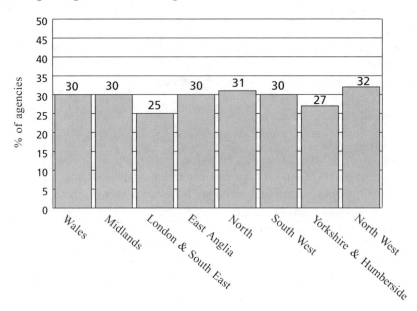

The interviews were conducted fairly informally allowing both interviewer and interviewee to digress from the schedule when other issues of interest to the research were raised.

Between January and the end of June 1995, all agencies in the subsample were interviewed except three (which, despite reminders, had not responded in time for our cut-off date). All **45** interviews were recorded and transcribed in full, and **36** transcripts were coded and analysed using the qualitative analysis program, NUDIST.

6 Stage 3: The family study

The family study comprised two parts:
a) a postal survey of adoptive parents who had adopted (or were in the process of adopting) a child of five years of age or above who had previously been in the care of the local authority; and
b) interviews with a sample of adoptive parents drawn from those who responded to the postal survey.

6.1   Postal survey of adoptive parents

All agencies interviewed in the agency study were asked whether they would be willing to aid the family study by sending out questionnaires, on behalf of the researchers, to those adoptive parents who fell within the criteria for inclusion in the sample. All 45 agreed to be approached. In June 1995, the researchers contacted the agencies again, explaining in more detail what this stage of the research involved, and setting out criteria for the selection of cases. Agencies were asked to identify cases between 1 January 1992 and 31 December 1994 where:

a) a looked after child had been placed for adoption with an adoptive family approved by them, including where they formally sanctioned adoption to existing foster carers *and*

b) the child was five years of age or more when adoption was sanctioned by the local authority looking after her/him.

Agencies were advised that these criteria applied to both pre-order and post-order placements and to those cases where the placement had disrupted.

In response to this request, **3** agencies (2 statutory agencies in the North and 1 voluntary in London and the South East) stated that they would be unable to help with the postal survey due to reorganisation or staff shortage. A further **2** agencies (1 statutory and 1 voluntary agency – both in Wales) could not take part because, having checked their records, they had no cases that met our criteria for sample selection. This meant that fewer families would be reached in these regions, especially in Wales. For this reason we approached another agency (which was not in the agency interview sample) in Wales for help, and it agreed. In total, **41** agencies (**28** statutory and **13** voluntary) agreed to take part in the family study.

The **41** participating agencies were sent questionnaires between July-October 1995, and these agencies forwarded them to **515** adoptive families (see Figure 26 below).

The same agencies also forwarded reminder letters for families which we sent to them for dispatch in November. The agencies completed "record sheets" for all cases which fitted the sampling criteria, and documented their activity in administering questionnaires.[3]

---

[3] For each questionnaire, agencies were asked to list the child's first name or agency file number (they were also asked to insert the child's name on the front cover of the questionnaire or, in the case of a sibling group placement, the name of the oldest child in the group); the date that the adoption was sanctioned by the agency; the date the questionnaire was sent to the family; if the family was not sent a questionnaire, why; and the date the reminder letter was sent.

By the beginning of February 1996 (our cut-off date), **226 (44 per cent)** families had returned questionnaires. This translates to a **40 per cent** response rate for families approved by statutory agencies and a **59 per cent** response rate for families approved by voluntary agencies. Notwithstanding this response rate, the resulting sample is a relatively large one, and might represent a significant proportion of all adoptions of older children in England and Wales in the three-year period of January 1992 to December 1994.

Figure 27 (below) shows the regional response rates and Figure 28 (below) shows the regional makeup of the response sample.

Topics covered in the questionnaire included:[4]

- how families learned/prepared for adoption
- information about the child's background
- contact with the child's birth family
- support (e.g. practical, financial, specialist)
- case / family details ·

The questionnaire also asked whether respondents would be willing to be interviewed. In response to this, **148 (65 per cent)** adoptive parents replied affirmatively (**66 per cent** for families approved by statutory agencies and **64 per cent** for families approved by voluntary agencies).

Figure 26

Number of questionnaires sent to and returned by families

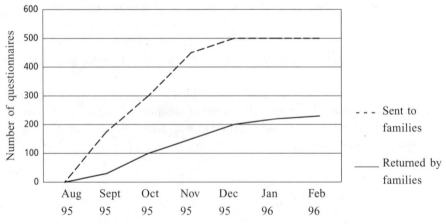

---

[4] Families were asked to answer questions with reference to the adoption of the child whose name was written on the front of the questionnaire (by the agency, see note 3) – this would be the oldest child in the case of a sibling group placement. The questionnaire was long (17 pages) consisting of both tick-box questions and open-ended questions.

Figure 27

Percentage of families returning questionnaires in each region

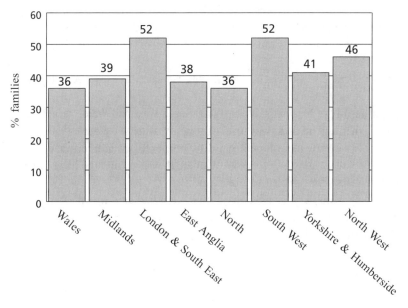

Figure 28

Regional makeup of family postal survey response sample

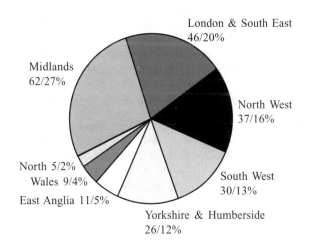

7   Family interview survey

This part of the family study comprised **48** interviews with adoptive families, for the purpose of examining issues which could not be tackled by the postal survey, to amplify adoption "stories" and to explore points of interest arising from the questionnaire.

A sampling frame was devised to obtain a broad sample. These were its principal characteristics:

- All families in the Midlands, North West, South West and Wales[5] which seemed to have either a good or a poor level of support[6] were selected for interview.
- All families where the adopted child or one or both adopters had black or minority ethnic origins, irrespective of where they lived and the level of support they received, were selected for interview.[7]
- All families which experienced disruption were included irrespective of where they lived and the level of support they received (except one which we were unable to arrange).[8]

---

[5] We decided to focus exclusively on half of the regions as categorised by BAAF and serviced by BAAF's regional offices: Wales, Midlands, South West and North West. This was largely a practical decision: to eliminate the extra travel time and expense that would be incurred if we tried to get a national spread of families. Also, since the number of families to be interviewed was such a small proportion of the number of families approved to be prospective adopters, the sample could not be geographically representative anyway. Whereas agency interviews had a national focus, family interviews had a West and South focus.

[6] This was because the focus of the project was on support services. This variable does not relate to a particular question in the questionnaire, but is based on the impression that the questionnaire as a whole gave researchers. We selected cases which indicated a strong sense of "good support" and "poor support", and excluded the cases where families had mixed or indifferent views of the support they received. The rationale behind this was that it would highlight contrasting experiences, and ensure that we had a wide range of stories in terms of support required and received.

[7] While 17 black or minority ethnic families responded to the questionnaire, only seven families responding before the cut-off date for sampling indicated that they were willing to be interviewed – thus it was important that they were all included in the sample. The low number of responses from black families (only accounting for 8% of the response sample in the postal survey) could be due to their being channelled into fostering rather than adoption in the case of older children. Second, it could be because agencies did not realise that they should have included in the sample those children for whom it was decided that adoption was in their best interests, but who remained in foster care. We contacted agencies about this and just under a quarter had excluded such families from their sampling and thus did not send them a questionnaire.

[8] While 13 families responding to the questionnaire no longer had the child living with them due to placement disruption, only three families responding before the cut-off date for sampling indicated that they were willing to be interviewed. Since inadequate support can be a major ingredient in disruptions, it was important to interview all those willing to talk to us. The number of disruptions in the interview sample had risen to five by the time interviews were completed.

- A frequency check was conducted on other variables once the sample had been selected to ensure that the sample was not skewed: These were:
  (a) the stage of the adoption process the case had reached
  (b) whether there was any contact with birth relatives and what type
  (c) whether the adoption was contested or not
  (d) the ethnicity of parents
  (e) whether it was a sibling placement or not
  (f) the sex, ethnicity, and age (both currently and at placement) of child
  (g) inter-agency and same-agency placements
  (h) whether there were other children in the adoptive family
  (i) whether the child had special needs and what type
  (j) the number of adoptive parents
  (k) the type of agency which approved the family (statutory or voluntary)

Under-represented variables were targeted in the final phase of selecting cases. For example, we targeted one-parent families and children with health, behavioural, and emotional special needs.

Figure 29 shows the geographical spread of the final sample of families interviewed using these criteria.

Figure 29

Regional makeup of family interview response sample

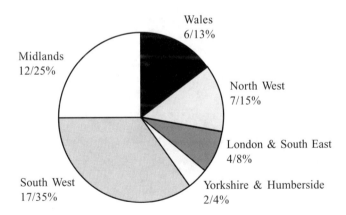

As in the agency interviews, the family interview schedule was semi-structured, largely comprising a list of discussion topics. These included:
- how they came to adopt an older child
- involvement in and support during matching

- the impact of the placement on the family
- critical times in the adoption process
- support before and after the adoption order
- help needed when the placement disrupted or threatened to do so

The accounts told by adoptive parents were very rich, and sometimes lasted up to three hours, thereby producing much data. All **48** interviews (38 with families approved by statutory agencies, and 10 with families approved by voluntary agencies) were transcribed in full and a case summary was written for each family interviewed; **36** transcripts were coded and analysed using the qualitative analysis program, NUDIST.

Appendix B

A note on the family postal survey response rate

1   Introduction

As already noted, the response rate for the family postal survey reached **44 per cent**. It is difficult to know whether this is acceptable or not by looking at the literature because scholars seem reluctant to state what constitutes a "good" or "poor" response rate. A typical statement is: 'Except when done statistically, the desired response rate tends to be entirely subjective and the general rule is "the higher the better"' (Fink and Kosecoff, 1985, p. 18). Where comment has been made, opinion on this topic varies. Some writers, such as Warwick and Lininger, argue that, 'completion rates on many mail questionnaires are notoriously low, with figures of 40 or 50 per cent considered good' (1975, p. 129). Others state that a response rate must be much higher to be considered good, at around 60 per cent (Babbie, 1989, p. 242).

However, these kinds of generalisations about response rates in surveys need to be treated with caution. First, such generalisations distort the fact that surveys are not conducted for the same purpose, and that the response rate does not therefore always have the same significance. This point is made by Hoinville and Jowell when they state that postal surveys 'can also be used effectively for screening purposes to identify a particular minority group of respondents for subsequent interview' (1978, p. 125). Thus the common tendency to judge the strength of a survey by its response rate is a misguided one. The fact that the family postal survey enabled us to select a balanced sample of families for interview is an important achievement and this needs to be acknowledged as such in any discussions of the survey response rate.

Second, views about acceptable response rates often do not reflect important differences in survey designs or sample populations. Thus it is important, while examining our response rate with reference to commentators on research methods, to continually consider how our research design differs from that being discussed. This is especially important in that methods discussions typically refer to large scale market research or attitude polls of general populations, where telephone books are used for selecting the sample. Another problem is that it is not always clear how the survey is conducted, i.e. by telephone, by interview, or by post, and the survey method chosen clearly has implications for the response rate.

Below are some of the obstacles specific to our research design which may help explain the response rate.

2   Implications of the research design

2.1   Knowing the true sample size

In order to calculate a response rate, it is necessary to exclude those respondents who were ineligible or unreachable. Yet, in mail surveys,

> ... we have to assume that a non-response is a refusal unless informed otherwise. This relies on ineligible people contacting the researcher or the post office returning questionnaires of unreachable respondents – neither of which can be relied on. (De Vaus, 1991, pp. 107–8)

A problem with all postal survey response calculations is that researchers cannot know the true number of questionnaires that reach the sample. This problem is compounded in our research because we did not have any control over the family study sample. Although we sent out the criteria for inclusion, we did not select the cases for the sample, nor did we have any information about the cases which were selected apart from that provided by the agency i.e. on the record sheet. In other words, the confidentiality issue in our research resulted in our dependence on intermediaries in selecting the sample.

2.2   Administering the questionnaires

More importantly, we had to rely on intermediaries to administer the questionnaires, to keep accurate records of the number sent out and when, and then send this information to us. Not all agencies did so.

We were also reliant on agencies having up-to-date records of addresses so that questionnaires reached the sample. If a questionnaire was sent to the wrong address, we had no way of knowing that it should be excluded from response rate calculations unless it was sent back to us marked "returned to sender". This issue is particularly salient in our project because adoption agencies may well lose contact with families after the adoption order has been granted or where disruptions have occurred. This cannot be seen simply as a failing of the agencies, for the accuracy of their records in this respect is dependent upon adoptive families informing their agency when they move.

2.3   Administering the reminders

The response rate can have more to do with the persistence of researchers than the quality of the questionnaires themselves (De Vaus, 1993). However, because of the nature of our project, we could not demonstrate "persistence". Normally, a postal questionnaire will be followed by a written reminder and then a telephone reminder (this is what we did in the Agency Postal Survey). But since we could not contact the family sample directly, our persistence was transferred to the adoption agencies, which raised ethical as well as practical considerations. Asking the agencies to send out written reminders proved to be time-consuming enough (for them and for us), but asking them to telephone families as well was just not feasible despite being a general rule in methods textbooks (e.g. Fowler, 1993, p. 46).

While most agencies were obliging in sending out reminders, we know that one did not have time to complete the task (the size of which varied hugely between agencies). Several other agencies did not return their postcard (confirming when reminders were sent out), so we are unsure if the reminders were sent out by those agencies at all. In sum, we know that at least **395** families out of **515** were sent reminders, but this could mean that 120 families in the sample did not receive a reminder.

Textbooks assume that reminders can only be sent to those in the sample who did not respond (e.g. De Vaus, 1991, p. 119). This would make the processes of sending out reminders a much quicker and more straightforward task, but in the family postal survey the process was far more complicated. We could not target non-respondents when sending out reminders without knowing their names and addresses. Equally, we could not allow agencies to carry out this task because we made a commitment to families that the agencies would not be informed about whether or not they had responded. Thus reminders had to be sent to *all* families rather than just non-respondents which made it a much larger task for agencies to complete. And to complete the task twice (if they were to send out a second reminder) would certainly be asking too much from them.

2.4   Conducting the research task in a sensitive manner

One of the reasons why telephone and interview surveys have such high response rates is that personal contact arouses interest and increases respondent motivation (Warwick and Linginger, 1975, p. 129; Fowler 1993, p. 45). Indeed, the more personal the links between the researchers and the researched, the higher the response will be (Fink and Kosecoff, 1985, p. 131). The researchers could not make personal contact because of the confidential nature of the postal survey. Instead, we had to rely upon agencies to contact the sample in an appropriate manner, such as by sending a covering letter from the agency with the questionnaire, or by telephoning/ visiting the respondents before sending it out. However, we know of several instances where neither of these measures had been taken, because a few families telephoned us confused or angry about how they came to receive the questionnaire. Such practices will have had a detrimental effect on the motivation of families to complete and return the questionnaire.

2.5   Timing

Another factor which can significantly influence the response rate is the timing of the survey (Fink and Kosecoff, 1985, p. 18). Due to our reliance on intermediaries, the family study postal survey ran over a six month period. Although it was intended that questionnaires should have been dispatched in July and August, they continued to be sent out by agencies until mid-November due to staff vacations, sickness or changes in personnel, or simply because of the amount of work required to complete the task.

The timing of the survey had two implications. First, the bulk of the questionnaires arrived at the homes of adoptive families in the summer holiday period. Second, the reminder letters arrived just before Christmas. As noted by Hoinville and Jowell, 'December is a disastrous month for postal surveys' (1978, p. 132). Thus the postal survey response rate would have been hindered by two major vacation periods, which would have made the completion of the questionnaire far more difficult for many families. This was not a planning flaw, but rather a consequence of the fact that the survey took longer than expected to complete.

2.6   The topic of investigation

The sensitive nature of the subject might have discouraged some people from responding to the family postal survey, especially if there had been a disruption. Continual reminders/pressure to respond would clearly be inappropriate in this context. Furthermore, people might be hesitant to talk about things that they have tried to forget or rationalise in order to deal with painful or confusing events. As Baddeley (1993, p. 24) has argued, the nature of human memory can be a problem in research that collects retrospective data about sensitive topics or emotive material: 'Memory is essentially a reconstructive process, and subjects will try to make sense of a given incident often recalling their interpretation rather than what they actually observed' (p. 25). Indeed, the fact that the questionnaire asked about the past may have deterred people from responding because they did not feel able to report the events that took place accurately.

2.7   Replacing non-respondents

Other surveys frequently combat low response rates by "oversampling" or replacing non-respondents (Fink and Kosecoff, 1985, p. 63). We could not do this because we wanted to study a very special group of people who met certain criteria. Similarly, surveys often use "proxy respondents" where a questionnaire is filled in by someone on behalf of the sampled person (e.g. another adult living in the same household) (Fowler, 1993, p. 47). Our questionnaire in its content, detail, and the subject of investigation was designed to prevent it from being answered by anyone else. Thus the sampling methods which are commonly used to improve response rates in postal surveys could not be used in this research.

Appendix C

Profile of Disruptions – a sample of five cases

This appendix gives a brief outline of five cases in the family interview sample which had disrupted. They represent only a snapshot of the events which occurred during the placement. In each case, the disruption took place before the adoption order.

1   Case 1

The adoptive family: Mother, father and two birth children, a boy aged 14 and a girl aged nine when child was placed.

The child: a boy, Jason, was 10 when placed. He had been in and out of care all his life. He had lived in at least two children's homes and several foster placements. Contact with his birth mother was terminated two days before he was placed with the adopters when he had a "goodbye party" with his birth mother and two younger brothers. He had not seen his birth mother for two years previous to this.

The placement: The first few months were reasonable, especially Christmas time, which Jason greatly enjoyed. However, Jason's behaviour was challenging from the outset, becoming increasingly so as time went by. His social worker appeared to dismiss the adoptive mother's concerns but, after six months, he received psychiatric help, the whole family attending on some occasions. There was a dispute about who should pay for the psychiatric consultations. Jason appeared to have no fear about hurting himself, deliberately crashing into a fence on his bicycle and cutting himself. He lied, stole, damaged furniture and tried to drive a wedge between the adoptive parents. He also made things difficult for the birth son at the school they both attended.

The disruption: Jason stayed with the family for one year. The decision to move him was made one month before he actually left, the social worker deciding that it would be preferable for him to wait until half term for him to move out. It was a family decision that Jason should leave, although the adoptive father found it particularly difficult to agree. There was no disruption meeting following Jason's departure.

2   Case 2

The adoptive family: a mother and father both of whom had been married once before. The adoptive father had a daughter by his first marriage but she did not live in the adoptive household.

The child: A boy, Graham, was nearly 10 when placed. He had suffered neglect by his birth family. Graham had lived in at least two foster homes, one of which had lasted quite some time. He had wanted to be adopted by these foster carers but they would not agree to do so. He had also experienced an adoption disruption prior to this placement. Two brothers had been adopted elsewhere, but their adoptive parents were not prepared for them to have contact with Graham because it had taken them a long time to settle down and their adopters did not want to risk unsettling them again.

The placement: Graham was placed five weeks after the adopters had been approved to adopt a non-violent child, following introductions over about ten days. The adopters were unable to cope with his behaviour which they considered violent. He tried to throw himself from his bedroom window. He ripped doors off, was up at 3 am. playing with his hamster which he allowed to run loose in the house.

The disruption: Graham left after five days. The adopters could not cope with his wild and violent behaviour. They felt that Graham could ruin their relationship and what they had. The adopters attended two disruption meetings at which they discovered that Graham had a history of what they considered violent behaviour, although the social workers did not describe incidents, such as drawing a knife on a young girl, in those terms.

3   Case 3

The adoptive family: The adoptive mother was herself adopted. She and her husband had an adopted son, Robert, with special needs who was seven at the time of the placement.

The child: A boy, Matthew, was nine when placed. He had been sexually abused by his birth parents who were paedophiles. He had been in care six-and-a-half years during which time he had been in numerous foster homes and in a community home where he thought he would remain. He had been abused at one of these placements. He was separated from his sister because of their sexualised behaviour. She had been sexually abused by the time she was six months old. He had contact with his birth mother and sister in the early part of his placement but this was terminated as it had such a disturbing effect on him and re-sexualised him.

The placement: Matthew had been moved so many times he could not accept that he was going to stay anywhere permanently. Consequently, after four months he would be ready for his next move, but would be heartbroken afterwards. The adopters felt that he pushed them to their limits, seeing how far he could go before being moved on. They also thought he felt let down by them because they did not sexually abuse him themselves. He appeared to enjoy shocking people. He was violent and wild, cruel to animals – he set fire to a cat – he masturbated and urinated in public. He abused Robert and several disabled children at his school. The adopters had not been told that Matthew was an abuser himself before he was placed, only discovering this after he had abused Robert and the children at his school. It was as a result of visits to the Tavistock Clinic some six months into the placement that contact with his birth family was terminated.

The disruption: It became apparent to the adopters that Matthew would have to leave once they realised he had abused Robert, although initially they wanted to keep him but with appropriate support to help them to cope. The decision was taken with the local authority nine months before he actually left. His departure was postponed because the local authority's plans for him kept falling through. Eventually Matthew attempted to re-abuse Robert, the adoptive mother intervened, and Matthew broke her finger. Matthew finally left five days later. At the time of the research interview, the adopters were still in touch with social workers. They had attended a meeting at which the decision to move him to specialist foster carers had been taken, nine months previous to Matthew's departure, but there appeared to have been no disruption meeting after Matthew left.

4   Case 4

The adoptive family: Adoptive mother and father. The mother had one child from an earlier relationship who did not live in the adoptive household.

The children: Sibling brothers, Luke and Ben, were eight and nine when placed with the adopters. Their sister, aged ten, remained in the foster home she had shared with her brothers up to the time of their placement. The children had been abused by their birth family. They had many different foster placements, the two preceding the placement lasting two years. Until their placement with the adopters, the three siblings had always lived together. The adopters had been told they could choose any two of the three children. The brothers had face-to-face contact with their sister who sometimes stayed with them at the adopters. At the time of the placement the children had newly appointed social workers. They had had many changes of social worker over the years.

The placement: The boys were very disturbed and their behaviour challenging.

Four months after being placed, the mother was so concerned about Ben that she called a meeting with the social workers at which she expressed her fears. She was told that he was just testing her and that things would improve. Six months went by during which the deterioration continued. The mother called another meeting with social workers prompted by a discussion with Ben in which he had told her that he would like to leave. She felt that if Ben was going to leave, Luke should do so too, as heart-breaking as that would be, because he had never lived without one or both his siblings. The foster carers who cared for the siblings before the placement would not contemplate having Luke back, although they were very happy to have Ben back. The mother felt she was pressured into keeping Luke against her better judgement. Ben left having been in the placement for a year. The local authority would not permit the brothers to have contact. It was only after the adoptive mother's persistence that a meeting took place six months after Ben's departure. She thought that Luke would have a better chance of settling down if he could satisfy himself that Ben was alright. However, Luke's behaviour became more and more wild, aggressive and violent. He was expelled from school. He attacked the adoptive mother with a hammer and the father with a baseball bat.

The disruption: Following this attack, ten months after Ben's departure, it was decided that Luke should leave. A disruption meeting had been held after Ben left during which the adopters discovered far more about the children than they had been told previously. The adoptive mother was anticipating a disruption meeting following Luke's departure, some time after the interview. Ben had returned to live with his birth father. Luke was to be placed with carers on a farm – something he had always wanted – and their sister had been placed in a long-term foster home.

5   Case 5

The adoptive parents: The adopters had no children of their own after 18 years of marriage. They applied to adopt and were recommended by their social worker for one child under four; but the adoption panel did not ratify the recommendation. They subsequently saw an advertisement for brothers, aged seven and eight and, after making enquiries, were encouraged by the local authority to foster them with a view to adoption.

The children: The boys were two and three when they were taken into care having been grossly neglected by their birth mother. They had already experienced 12 different placements and one adoptive placement which disrupted after three months.

The placement: The boys' behaviour was wild, aggressive and exhausting from day one. They lied, stole, exposed themselves, caused havoc at school. One threatened the adoptive mother with a knife. The parents were totally exhausted trying to look after them but did their best to develop strategies for coping. For example, the boys would not sleep for more than five hours, often taking a long time to go off to sleep. The father would sit in the bedroom for two hours or more at a time to help coax them to sleep. Incident after incident occurred over a period of 18 months culminating in an episode which resulted in the father beating one of the boys.

The disruption: As a result of the beating the boys were removed. The father was charged with GBH. This was reduced to ABH of which he was convicted. It was only in preparing his case, which cost £12,000, that the adopters saw all the files relating to the boys. He was not sent to prison because the judge felt he was so full of remorse. As a result of the proceedings, the father lost his job and, at the time of the interview, had not succeeded in obtaining another.

Appendix D

Regional Consortia

These were the regional consortia subscribed to by agencies completing questionnaires:

Midlands

Midlands Voluntary Agencies
Midlands Family Placement Group
Black Country Consortium
East Midlands Family Placement Group
West Midlands Consortium
West Midlands Regional Family Placement Consortium

London and South East
London Voluntary Agencies Adoption Group
London Regional Fostering and Adoption Group

Eastern Counties

Eastern Counties Adoption and Fostering
East Anglian Adoption Consortium
Eastern Counties Inter-Agency Consortium

North

Northern Regional Consortium
North East Adoption Consortium

North West

North West Consortium
Greater Manchester Consortium of Adoption Agencies
Merseyside Consortium
Cheshire Consortium

Appendix E

Designation of Agency Respondents

This appendix lists the designations of workers completing the agency questionnaire

- Principal Assistant, Children and Families
- Administrator
- Adoption Adviser / Family Placement Adviser
- Adoption Agency Manager
- Assistant Director, Children and Families
- Central Operations Manager
- County Adoption Officer
- County Child Care Manager
- Development Officer, Children and Families
- Direct Service Manager
- Director of Social Services
- Director of Social Work
- Divisional Family Placement Officer
- Divisional Family Placement Manager
- Fieldwork Manager
- Head of Planning and Strategic Development, Children and Families
- Placements Manager
- Planning Officer, Adoption and Fostering
- Policy Development Officer
- Principal Children's Officer
- Principal Officer, Adoption
- Principal Social Worker
- Professional Assistant
- Professional Officer, Fostering and Adoption
- Project Leader
- Provider Manager
- Resource Manager, Family Placement
- Secretary
- Senior Adoption and Fostering Officer
- Senior Care Manager
- Senior Practitioner

- Service Manager, Adoption and Fostering
- Service Manager, Children and Families
- Service Standards Manager
- Staff Officer, Children's Services
- Team Leader, Care Services
- Team Leader, Adoption and Fostering
- Team Manager, Adoption and Fostering

Bibliography

Adoption: A Service for Children, Department of Health and Welsh Office, London, 1966

Adoption Law Review, *Discussion Paper No. 1, The Nature and Effect of Adoption*, Department of Health, London, 1990

Adoption Law Review, *Discussion Paper No. 3, The Adoption Process*, Department of Health, London, 1991

Adoption Law Review, *Consultative Document on Adoption Law*, Department of Health, London, 1992

Adoption: The Future, Cm 2288, HMSO, London, 1992

ADSS and NCH, *Children Still in Need – Refocusing Child Protection in the Context of Children in Need*, NCH Action for Children, London, 1996

Ainsworth M D S, Bell S M and Stayton D J, 'Infant-Mother attachment and Social Development: Socialisation as a product of reciprocal responsiveness to signals', in Richards MPM *The Integration of a Child into a Social World*, Cambridge University Press, 1974

Aldgate J and Hawley D, 'Helping Foster Families Through Disruption', *Adoption & Fostering*, 10:2, 1986

Babbie E, *The Practice of Social Research* (5th edn.), Wadsworth, Belmont, California, USA, 1989

Baddeley A, 'The Limitations of Human Memory: implications for the design of retrospective survey', in Moss L and Goldstein H (eds) *The Recall Method in Social Surveys*, University of London Institute of Education, London, 1979

Barth R and Berry M, *Adoption and Disruption Rates, Risks and Responses*, Aldine De Gruyter, New York, 1988

Berridge D and Cleaver H, *Foster Home Breakdowns*, Basil Blackwell, Oxford, UK, 1987

Bevan H K and Parry M L, *Children Act 1975*, Butterworths, London, 1978

Booth M, *Avoiding Delay in Children Act Cases*, Lord Chancellor's Department, London, 1996

Borland M, O'Hara G and Triseliotis J, 'Permanent Outcomes for Children With Special Needs', *Adoption & Fostering*, 15:2, pp. 18–28, 1991

Borrie G J and Lowe N V, *The Law of Contempt* (3rd edn), Butterworths, London, 1996

Boswell J, *The Kindness of Strangers*, Allen Lane, The Penguin Press, 1988

Bowlby J, *The Making and Breaking of Affectional Bonds*, Tavistock Publications, London, 1979

Bowlby J, *Attachment and Loss, Volume 3: Loss, Sadness and Depression*, Pelican Books, 1985

Bowlby J, *Attachment and Loss, Volume 2: Separation, Anxiety and Anger*, Penguin, London, 1991

Brebner C M, Sharp J D and Stone F H, *The Role of Infertility in Adoption*, BAAF, London, 1985

Brodzinksy D, 'New perspectives on adoption revelation', *Adoption & Fostering*, 8:2, pp. 27–32, 1984

Caplan G, *An Approach to Community Mental Health*, Tavistock, London, 1961

Caplan G, *Principle of Preventive Psychiatry*, Tavistock, London, 1964

Caplan G, *The Theory and Practice of Mental Health Consultation*, Tavistock, London, 1970

Caplan G, *Support Systems and Community Mental Health*, Behaviour Publications, New York, 1974

Caplan G, *Population Oriented Psychiatry*, Human Sciences Press, USA, 1989

Caplan G and Caplan R, *Prevention of Psychological Disorder in Children of Divorce, in Population Oriented Psychiatry*, Human Sciences Press, USA, 1988

Caplan G and Caplan R, *Mental Health Consultation and Collaboration*, 1993

Caudrey K and Fruin D, *Placing Children with Special Needs In Permanent Families*, National Children's Bureau, London, 1986

Clarke, Hall and Morrison, *on Children* (10th edn), Butterworths, London

Clubb E and Knight J, *Fertility, Fertlity Awareness and Natural Family Planning*, David and Charles, 1997

Coombs R and Hundleby M, 'Post Placement Services For Adopted Children: A Multi-disciplinary Approach' in *Post Placement Services in Adoption and Fostering – Report of a Study Day organised jointly by the Department of Health and the Midlands Family Placement Group*, Department of Health, 1997

Cretney S, 'From Status to Contract?' in Rose F P (ed) *Consensus Ad Idem*, Barry Rose, Chichester, 1996

Cretney S and Masson J, *Principles of Family Law* (6th edn), Sweet and Maxwell, London, 1997

Dartington Social Research Unit and Department of Health, *Looking After Children – good parenting and good outcomes*, HMSO, London, 1995

De Vaus D A, *Surveys in Social Research* (3rd edn.), UCL Press, London, 1991

Department of Health, *Social Work Decisions in Childcare: Recent Research Findings and their Implications*, HMSO, London, 1985

Department of Health, *Protecting Children: A Guide for Social Workers Undertaking A Comprehensive Assessment*, HMSO, London, 1988

Department of Health, *The Care of Children: Principles and Practice in Regulations and Guidance*, HMSO, London, 1989

Department of Health, *The Children Act 1989 Guidance and Regulations, Volume 9, Adoption Issues*, HMSO, London, 1991

Department of Health, *Children Looked After By Local Authorities, year ending 31 March 1996*, A/F 96/12, 1997

Department of Health and Welsh Office, *Adoption Bill – Consultative Document attached to Adoption: A service for Children, supra*, 1996

Departmental Committee on Adoption Societies and Agencies (The Horsburgh Report), Cmd 5499, 1937

Departmental Committee on Adoption of Children (The Hurst Report), Cmd 9248, 1954

Departmental Committee on the Adoption of Children (The Houghton Report) Cmnd 5107 and The Houghton Working Paper: Adoption of Children (1970), HMSO, London, 1972

Dominick C, *Early Contact in Adoption: Contact between birth mothers and adoptive parents at the time of and after the adoption*, Department of Social Welfare, Wellington, NZ, 1988

Donley K, 'The Dynamics of Disruption', *Adoption & Fostering*, 91:2 of 1978, pp. 34–39, 1978

Erikson E H, *Identity: Youth and Crisis*, Faber, 1968

Fahlberg V, *Attachment and Separation*, Michigan Press, 1979

Fahlberg V, *A Child's Journey Through Placement*, BAAF, London, 1994

Fein E, Maluccio A N, Hamilton V J and Ward D E, 'After Foster Care – Permanency Planning for Children', *Child Welfare*, Vol. 62, 1983

Festinger T, *Necessary Risk: A Study of Adoptions and Disrupted Adoption Placements*, Child Welfare League of America, Washington DC, 1986

Finch J, *Family Obligations and Social Change*, Polity Press, Cambridge, 1989

Fincham F D and Grych J H, 'Marital conflict and children's adjustment: a cognitive-contextual framework', *Psychological Bulletin*, 108, pp. 267–290, 1990

Fincham F D and Grych J H, 'Interventions for Children of Divorce: towards greater integration of research and action', *Psychological Bulletin*, 111, pp. 434-454, 1991

Fink A and Kosecoff J, *How To Conduct Surveys: a step by step guide*, Sage, London, 1985

Fitzgerald J, *Understanding Disruption,* (2nd edn), BAAF, London, 1990

Fowler J, *Survey Research Methods* (2nd edn.), Sage, London, 1993

Fratter J, *Adoption With Contact: Implications for Policy and Practice*, BAAF, London, 1996

Fratter J, Rowe J, Sapsford D and Thoburn J, *Permanent Family Placement: A decade of experience,* BAAF, London, 1991

Freeman M D A, *Children, Their Families and the Law*, Macmillan, 1992

Freeman P and Hunt J, *Parental Perspectives in Care Proceedings*, Report to the Department of Health, Centre for Socio-Legal Studies, University of Bristol, 1996

George V, *Foster Care: Theory and Practice*, Routledge and Kegan Paul, UK, 1970

Gilbert N, *Researching Social Life*, Sage, London, 1993

Glaser B G and Strauss A C, *Status Passages*, Routledge and Kegan Paul, London, 1971

Goldstein J Freud A and Solnit A, *Beyond the Best Interests of the Child*, Free Press, USA, 1973

Goodacre I, *Adoption Policy and Practice*, Allen and Unwin, London, 1966

Haimes E and Timms N, *Adoption, Identity and Social Policy: The search for distant relatives,* Gower, Aldershot, 1985

Hall T, 'Preface' in Wedge P and Thoburn J (eds), *Finding Families for 'Hard to place' Children – Evidence from research*, BAAF, London, 1986

Hill R, 'Generic Features of Families Under Stress', *Social Casework,* Vol 39, No. 203, 1958

Hoinville G and Jowell R, *Survey Research Practice*, Heinemann Educational Books, London, 1978

Holman R, 'Exclusive and Inclusive Concepts of Fostering' in Triseliotis J (ed), (1980), *New Developments in Foster Care and Adoption*, Routledge and Kegan Paul, London, 1980

Houghton D and Houghton P (1984), *Coping with Childlessness*, Allen and Unwin, London, 1984

Howe D, 'Adopters' Relationships With Their Adopted Children From Adolescence to Early Childhood', *Adoption & Fostering* 20, pp. 35–43, 1996

Howe D, *Patterns of Adoption,* Blackwell Science, Oxford, 1998

Hughes B and Logan J, *Birth Parents: The Hidden Dimension. The Evaluation of A Birth Parent Project*. Research report commissioned by The Mental Health Foundation, University of Manchester, Department of Social Policy and Social Work, 1993

Hunt J, 'Child Protection, The Court and The Children Act 1989', *Children's Services News*, Department of Health, London, 1997

Illich I, W*hat is a life?* Public Lecture, Cardiff Law School, Cardiff University (unpublished), 1995

Jackson S, *The Education of Children in Care*, Policy Press, University of Bristol. Republished in Kahan B (ed) (1989), *Child Care Research, policy and practice*, Hodder and Stoughton in association with the Open University, London, 1987

Jenkins A S, 'The Tie That Bonds' in Maluccio A N and Sinanoglu P A (eds), *The Challenge of Partnership Working With Parents and Children In Care*, Child Welfare League of America, 1981

Jewett C, *Helping Children Cope with Separation and Loss,* Batsford, 1984

Kagan J, 'Perspectives on Infancy' in Osofsky J D (ed), *Handbook of Infant Development*, Wiley, NewYork, 1987

Klaus K M and Kernel J H, *Maternal Infant Bonding*, C V Mosley Co., St Louis, USA, 1976

Kramer S, 'Parenting yesterday, today and tomorrow' in Utting D, *Families and Parenting,* Department of Health, London, 1996

Kubler-Ross E, *On Children and Death,* Macmillan, 1985

Lahti J, 'A Follow-up of Foster Children in Permanent Placement' in *Social Services Review*, 56:4, 1982

Lambert L, 'Adoption Allowances in England: An interim report', *Adoption & Fostering*, 8:3, pp. 12–14, 1984

Lambert L and Seglow J, '*Adoption Allowances in England and Wales: The Early Years: Report to Department of Health and Welsh Office*', National Children's Bureau, HMSO, London, 1988

Lewis H, Follow-Up Studies of Adoption reproduced in (1976) *Child Adoption: A selection of articles on adoption, theory and practice*, BAAF, 1962

Lindemann E, 'Symptomology and Management of Acute Grief', *American Journal of Psychiatry*, Vol. 101, 1944

Logan J, 'Birth Mothers and Their Mental Health: Unchartered Territory', *The British Journal of Social Work*, 26, pp. 609–625, 1996

Lowe N V, 'The changing face of adoption – the gift/donation model versus the contract/services model', *Child and Family Law Quarterly*, 9:4, pp. 371–386, 1997

Lowe N V and Milsom L, *A Study of Court Differential Workloads in Care Proceedings*, Cardiff Law School, University of Wales College of Cardiff, 1993

Lowe N V with Borkowski M, Copner R, Griew K and Murch M, *Report of the Research into the Use and Practice of the Freeing for Adoption Provisions,* HMSO, London, 1993

Lowe N V and Douglas G, *Bromley's Family Law* (9th edn), Butterworths, London, 1998

Macaskill C, 'Post Adoption Support – Is it Essential?' *Adoption & Fostering*, 9:1, p. 45–49, 1985

Macaskill C, 'Post Adoption Support' in Wedge P and Thoburn J (eds), *Finding Families for Hard to Place Children*, BAAF London, 1986

Maidment S, 'Access and Family Adoptions', 40 *MLR* 293, 1977

Maluccio A N, Fein E, Hamilton J, Klier J L and Ward D, 'Beyond Permanency Planning', *Child Welfare*, Vol LIX 9, 1980

Maluccio A N and Fein E , 'Permanency Planning – A Redefinition', *Child Welfare*, Vol LXII 3, 1983

Marsh P and Triseliotis J, *Ready to Practice? Social Work and Probation Officers, their training and first year of work*, Avebury, 1996

Masson J, Harrison C and Pavlovic A, *Working With Children and 'Lost' Parents – Putting Partnership Into Practice*, York Publishing Services, UK, 1998

Maximé J, 'Some Psychological models of black self-concept' in Ahmed S, Cheetham J and Small J (eds), *Social Work With Black Children and Their Families*, Batsford, London, pp. 100–116 , 1986.

McWhinnie A, *Adopted Children: How they grow up: a study of their adjustments as adults*, Routledge and Kegan Paul, London, 1967

McWhinnie A and Smith J, *Current Human Dilemmas in Adoption – The challenge for parents, practitioners and policy-makers*, University of Dundee Press, Dundee, 1994

Menzies-Lythe I, 'The Functioning of Social Systems as a Defence Against Anxiety' in *Constraining Anxiety in Institutions: Selected Essays*, Vol 1, Free Association Books, 1985

Menzies-Lythe L, 'A Psychoanalytic Perspective in Social Institutions' in *The Dynamics of the Social: Selected Essays*, Vol 1, Free Association Books, 1989

Millham S, Bullock R, Hosie K and Haak M, *Lost In Care: The problems of maintaining links between children in care and their families*, Gower, Aldershot, UK, 1986

Millham S, Bullock R, Hosie K and Little M, *Access Disputes in Child Care*, Gower, Aldershot, UK, 1989

Morgan P, *Adoption and the Care of Children*, Institute of Economic Affairs, Health and Welfare Unit, London, 1998

Murch M and Mills L, *The Length of Care Proceedings*, Socio-Legal Centre for Family Studies, University of Bristol, 1987

Murch M, Lowe N, Borkowski M, Copner R and Griew K, *Pathways to Adoption: Research Project*, HMSO, London, 1993

Nelson K A, *On Adoption's Frontier – A Study of Special Needs Adoptive Families*, Child Welfare League of America, New York, 1985

OPCS, *Marriage and Divorce Statistics 1989*, HMSO, 1990

Packman J, *The Child's Generation*, Blackwell, Oxford, 1975

Packman J with Randall J and Jacques N, *Who Needs Care?* Blackwell, Oxford, 1986

Parker R A, *Decisions In Child Care – A study of Predictions in Fostering*, George Allen and Unwin, UK, 1966

Parker R A, *Planning for Deprived Children*, National Children's Home convocation lecture, 1971

Parker R, Ward H, Jackson S, Aldgate J and Wedge P, *Looking After Children: Assessing Outcomes to Child Care – The Report of an Independent Working* Party, HMSO, London, 1991

Parkes C M, *Bereavement in Studies of Grief in Adult Life*, Tavistock, 1972

Quinton D, Rushton A, Dance C and Mayes D, *Establishing Permanent Placements in Middle Childhood*, Wiley, Chichester, UK, 1997a

Quinton D, Rushton A, Dance C and Mayes D, 'Contact Between Children Placed Away From Home and Their Birth Parents: Research Issues and Evidence', *Clinical Child Psychology and Psychiatry*, pp. 393–411, 2:3, Sage Publications, London, 1997b

Reich D and Lewis J, 'Placements by Parents for Children' in Wedge P and Thoburn J (eds), *Finding Families for Hard to Place Children,* BAAF, London, 1986

Richards, M, '"It feels like someone keeps moving the goalposts"' – regulating post-adoption contact: Re T (Adopted Children: Contact)' in *Child and Family Law Quarterly*, 8:2, pp. 175–179, 1996

Roberts P, 'Reconciling work and home life – parental leave', *Journal of Social Welfare Law*, 19:1, pp. 87–92, 1997

Robertson J, *A Two year old Goes to Hospital,* Child Development Research Unit; New York University Film Library, 1952

Robertson J, *Young Children In Hospital,* Tavistock, London, 1958

Robertson J and Robertson J, 'Young Children In Brief Separation: A fresh look', in *Psychoanal. Study, Child*, 26, pp. 264–315, 1971

Robertson J and Robertson J, *Separation and the Very Young*, Free Association Books, London, 1989

Rowe J, 'The Realities of Adoptive Parenthood', *Child Adoption*, 59, 1970

Rowe J and Lambert L, *Children Who Wait*, Association of British Adoption Agencies, London, 1973

Rowe J, 'Fostering Outcomes: Interpreting Breakdown Rates', *Adoption & Fostering*, 11:1, 1987

Rushton A, Treseder J and Quinton D, 'An Eight Year Prospective Study of Older Boys Placed In Permanent Substitute Families: A Research Note', *Journal of Child Psychology and Psychiatry,* 36, pp. 687–696, 1995

Rushton A and Mayes D, 'Research Review: Forming Fresh Attachments in Childhood. A Research Update, *Child and Family Social Work*, Vol 2, pp 121–127, 1997

Rushton A, Quinton D, Dance C and Mayes D, 'Preparation for Permanent Placement: evaluating direct work with older children'. *Adoption & Fostering*, 21:4 pp. 4–48, 1998

Rutter M, 'Resilience in the face of adversity', in *British Journal of Psychiatry,* Vol 147, p. 598, 1985

Ryburn M, 'In whose best interests? – post adoption contact with the birth family', *Child and Family Law Quarterly*, 10:1, pp. 53–70, 1998

Sarrat A and Felsteiner W, *Divorce Lawyers and their Clients,* Open University Press, London, 1995

Schaffer H R, *Making Decisions about Children: Psychological Questions and Answers,* Blackwell, Oxford, 1990

Schaffer H R and Emerson P E, 'The Development of Social Attachment in Infancy', *Monographs of the Society For Research on Child Development*, no 29 , 1964

Shaw M, *Family Placement for Children in Care,* BAAF, London, 1988

Small J, 'Transracial Placements: Conflicts and Contradictions', in Ahmed S, Cheetham J and Small J (eds), *Social Work with Black Children and Their Families*, Batsford, London, pp. 81–99, 1986

Smith S, *Learning from Disruption: making better placements*, BAAF, London, 1994

Social Services Inspectorate, *Adoption: In the child's best interests? Adoption in three London local authorities*, Department of Health, 1991

Social Services Inspectorate, *Inspection of the Adoption Service: North Yorkshire Social Services Department,* Department of Health, Leeds, 1992a

Social Services Inspectorate, *Inspection of the Adoption Service: Kirklees Social Services Department,* Department of Health, Leeds, 1992b

Social Services Inspectorate, *Children in Need: Report of Issues Arising from Regional Workshops, held between January and March 1994*, Department of Health, London, 1995a

Social Services Inspectorate, *Moving Goalposts: A Study of Post Adoption Contact in the North of England*, Department of Health, London, 1995b

Social Services Inspectorate, *For Children's Sake: An SSI Inspection of Local Authority Adoption Services*, Department of Health, London, 1996

Social Services Inspectorate, *For Children's Sake – Part II: An Inspection of Local Authority Post Placement and Post Adoption Services,* Department of Health, London, 1997

Social Services Inspectorate for Wales, *Local Government Reorganisation, Personal Social Services Monitoring Exercise: Overview Report,* 1996

Stafford G (1993), 'Section 51 Counselling, *Adoption & Fostering* 17, (1) 4-5.

Stein T J, Gambrill E D, Wiltse K T, *Children in Foster Homes, achieving continuity of care.* Praeger, NY, 1978

Thoburn J, *Background Paper Number 2: Review of Research Related to Adoption,* Department of Health, London, 1990

Thoburn J, *Child Placement Principles and Practice* (2nd ed), Arena, Aldershot, UK, 1994

Thoburn J, Murdoch A and O'Brien A, *Permanence in Child Care,* Basil Blackwell, Oxford, 1986

Thomas C with Hunt J, *The Workload of the Care Court Under the Children Act 1989,* Socio-Legal Centre for Family Studies, University of Bristol, 1996

Thomas C, Murch M and Hunt J, *The Duration of Care Proceedings Replications Study: The Child in the Civil Courts Project* 1990–1991, HMSO, London, 1993

Thomas C, Beckford V, Murch M and Lowe NV, *Adopted Children Speaking,* BAAF, London, 1999

Titmuss R M, *The Gift Relationship: From Human Blood to Social Policy,* George Allen and Unwin, London, 1970

Tizard B and Rees J, 'A comparison of the effects of adoption or restoration to the natural mother, and continued institutionalisation on the cognitive development of four year old children', in *Child Development,* 45, pp. 92–9, 1974

Tizard B and Rees J, 'The effect of early institutional rearing on the behaviour problems and affectional relationships of four year old children', in *Journal of Child Psychology and Psychiatry,* 16, pp. 61–73, 1975

Trasler G, *In Place Of Parents,* Routledge and Kegan Paul, UK, 1960

Triseliotis J, *Evaluation of Adoption Policy and Practice,* University of Edinburgh, Department of Social Administration, 1970

Triseliotis J, *In Search of Origins: The experience of adopted people,* Routledge and Kegan Paul, London, 1973

Triseliotis J (ed), *New Developments in Foster Care and Adoption,* Routledge and Kegan Paul, 1980

Turnpenny P, 'The Dilemmas of Sharing Genetic Information' in McWhinnie A and Smith J (eds), *Current Human Dilemmas in Adoption,* University of Dundee Press, Dundee, 1994

Utting W, *People Like Us – Report of the Review of the Standards for Children Living Away from Home*, Department of Health and the Welsh Office, 1997

Van Gennep A, *The Rites of Passage,* Routledge Kegan Paul, London, 1960

Van Keppel M, 'Birth parents and negotiated adoption agreements', *Adoption & Fostering*, 15:4, 81–90, 1991

Wadsworth M, 'Parenting Skills and Their Transmission Through Generations', *Adoption & Fostering,* 9:1, 28, 1995

Wadsworth M, 'Evidence from Three Birth Cohort Studies for Long Term and Cross Generational Effects on the Development of Children', in Richards N and Light P (eds) (1986), *Children of Social Worlds*, Polity Press, Cambridge, 1986

Wall N (ed), *Rooted Sorrows,* Family Law, Bristol, 1997

Ward B and Associates, *Good Grief: Exploring Feelings, Loss and Death with Under Elevens,* Jessica Kingsley, 1993

Warwick D P and Linginger C A, *The Sample Survey: Theory and Practice*, McGraw-Hill, London, 1975

Wedge P, 'Lessons from Research into Permanent Family Placement' in Wedge P and Thoburn J (eds), *Finding Families for Hard to Place Children, Evidence from Research*, BAAF, London, 1986

Woolett A, 'Having Children: Accounts of Childless Women and Women with Reproductive Problems' in Phoenix A, Woolett A, and Lloyd E (eds), *Motherhood, Meanings, Practices and Ideologies,* Sage Publications, pp. 47–65, 1991